WRITERS IN
RUSSIA

WRITERS IN RUSSIA: 1917-1978

MAX HAYWARD

EDITED AND WITH AN INTRODUCTION BY PATRICIA BLAKE

Preface by Leonard Schapiro

Bibliography by Valerie Jensen

A HELEN AND KURT WOLFF BOOK

HARCOURT BRACE JOVANOVICH, PUBLISHERS

SAN DIEGO   NEW YORK   LONDON

"The Russian Empire"—Introduction by Max Hayward from *The Russian Empire: A Portrait in Photographs* by Chloe Obolensky. Copyright © 1979 by Chloe Obolensky and The Warden and Fellows of St. Antony's College, Oxford. Reprinted by permission of Random House, Inc. "Russian Literature in the Soviet Period, 1917–1975"—Originally published in *An Introduction to Russian Language and Literature,* edited by Robert Auty and Dimitri Obolensky, Cambridge University Press. "Dissonant Voices in Soviet Literature"—Copyright © 1961 by Partisan Review. Copyright © 1962 by Patricia Blake and Max Hayward. Reprinted from *Dissonant Voices in Soviet Literature,* edited by Patricia Blake and Max Hayward, by permission of Pantheon Books, a Division of Random House, Inc. "Themes and Variations in Soviet Literature, 1917–1967"—Originally published in *Fifty Years of Communism in Russia,* edited by Milorad Drachkovitch, The Pennsylvania State University Press, University Park, Pa. and London, 1968. "The Decline of Socialist Realism"—Originally published in *Survey.* "Meetings with Pasternak"—Reprinted by permission of Harcourt Brace Jovanovich, Inc. from *Meetings with Pasternak* by Alexander Gladkov, edited by Max Hayward, copyright © 1977 by Collins / Harvill and Harcourt Brace Jovanovich, Inc. "Life into Art: Pasternak and Ivinskaya"—Introduction by Max Hayward from *A Captive of Time* by Olga Ivinskaya. Copyright © 1978 by Doubleday & Company, Inc. Reprinted by permission of the publisher. "Anna Akhmatova"—Introduction by Max Hayward to *Poems of Akhmatova,* selected, translated, and introduced by Stanley Kunitz and Max Hayward. Reprinted by permission of Little, Brown and Company in association with the Atlantic Monthly Press. "Sinyavsky's *A Voice from the Chorus*"—Introduction from *A Voice from the Chorus* by Abram Tertz, translation copyright © 1976 by Collins / Harvill. Originally published in Russian copyright © 1973 by Andrei Sinyavsky. Reprinted by permission of Farrar, Straus & Giroux, Inc. "Pushkin, Gogol, and the Devil"—Originally published in *The Times Literary Supplement.* "Solzhenitsyn and the Russian Tradition"—Introduction by Max Hayward to *From under the Rubble* by Alexander Solzhenitsyn et al. Copyright © 1974 by YMCA-Press, Paris. Reprinted by permission of Little, Brown and Company.

Library of Congress Cataloging in Publication Data
Hayward, Max.
Writers in Russia, 1917-1978.
"A Helen and Kurt Wolff book."
"Select bibliography of Max Hayward's work": p.
Includes index.
1. Russian literature—20th century—History and criticism—Addresses, essays, lectures.   2. Soviet Union—History—19th century—Addresses, essays, lectures.
3. Hayward, Max—Addresses, essays, lectures.   4. Translators—Great Britain—Biography—Addresses, essays, lectures.   I. Blake, Patricia.   II. Title.
PG3022.H34   1983   891.7'09'004   82-47671
ISBN 0-15-183278-1

Designed by Mark Likgalter
Printed in the United States of America   First edition   B C D E

CONTENTS

EDITOR'S ACKNOWLEDGMENTS

For the fellowship that assisted me in this work I thank the John Simon Guggenheim Memorial Foundation. I am indebted to the Ossabaw Island Project and to Yaddo for offering me sanctuary for writing.

For initial and crucial support I thank Edward J. Brown, Victor Erlich, Donald Fanger, and Irving Howe.

I owe much to the patience and encouragement of my friend and editor Marjorie Villiers, who, to my great sadness, died before she could see this book in print.

My thanks to Raymond Carr, the present Warden of St. Antony's, and to Richard Kindersley, for giving me full access to Max's papers and for making me welcome at St. Antony's. I am grateful for valuable suggestions made by Harry Willetts upon reading the introduction.

To Valerie Jensen, who prepared the bibliography, my thanks for helping me clarify many points, large and small.

I am grateful to all the people cited in my introduction who shared their recollections of Max with me. In addition, I am indebted for information and help provided to me by Deming Brown, Violet Conolly, Joseph Dobbs, Laurence Kelly, Anthony Kemp-Welch, Ilya Levin, Chloe Obolensky, Daphne Park, Jean and Abraham Steinberg, John Waterfield, and Helen Wolff.

I warmly thank my good friend and attorney Fred Marcus for his expert assistance on several matters concerning literary rights.

My deepest gratitude is reserved for Ronnie Dugger, my husband, who sustained me during the hardest part of this work, offering his always valuable reflections on my introduction, and indispensable support, as I relived Max's death in trying to re-create his life.

PREFACE

by Leonard Schapiro

It is a privilege to be given the opportunity of introducing Patricia Blake's admirable anthology of Max Hayward's widely scattered articles and prefaces. For many readers this volume will offer the first opportunity to become acquainted with the work of this fine scholar, whose early death was so lamentable a loss. He left behind him no major work. His friends, who much regretted the fact that he never embarked on a book, hold various theories to explain this omission, so unusual in an age of graphomania among Sovietologists. My own guess is that in his heart he felt too modest, too diffident to bestride the stage on his own—he saw himself always as the editor, the interpreter, the introducer, the translator. This characteristic modesty also meant that he was a most unassuming and self-effacing collaborator with others. But we are fortunate that Patricia Blake has been able to assemble so much of his work to form this collection. The penetrating light which shines from these short writings demonstrates yet again how often Max could express in a few pages more than some writers can say in a volume.

He was a superb translator from Russian, and that for a simple reason: he was master of both Russian and English, which is rare among our present translators. Turgenev has left a description of Flaubert worrying away at the improvement of a translation from the Russian that Louis Viardot and Turgenev had prepared—polishing here, altering there, changing a word in order to improve the nuance of a sentence or avoid an echo. I was reminded of this on an occasion some years ago when I was concerned with Max in extensive revision of a translation of a Russian text. He showed the same intense search for the right word, the same terrier-like restlessness to get each sentence right. I think also his success as a translator was due to a deep sense of affinity with the author to be rendered into English. As Pasternak wrote in 1944: "A translation must issue from an author who has experienced the effect of the original long before he embarks on his labors. It must be the fruit of the original, and its historical consequence."* But it must also show scrupulous respect for the original, which must speak through the translation. It requires the kind of self-efface-ment of which only the truly modest are capable—and perhaps explains why the art of translation has often been spoken of contemptuously by great creative writers.

These two qualities of Max Hayward as translator were espe-cially evident in 1966 when he collaborated with Patricia Blake to edit a volume of Andrei Voznesensky's poems, *Antiworlds*. The novel feature of this volume was that six American poets, including W. H. Auden (if "American" is the right description for him), cooperated with Max to produce their translations—with Max making available to them in meticulous detail the meaning of the Russian. The result of this experiment was to produce—at any rate in some cases, notably where Auden's translations are concerned—not only accurate versions of the original Russian, but English poems in their own right. The experiment was repeated for the work of five young Leningrad poets, including Joseph Brodsky, in 1972, with Hayward advising the poet-translators, as well as translating some of the poems himself, for an anthology edited by Suzanne Massie.

Voznesensky is one of the half dozen Soviet authors about whom the English-speaking public owes much of its knowledge to Max Hayward. No one could have hated the cant, the pompous insincerity, and the pretentious drabness of so much of modern Soviet literature as Max. But at the same time he was the first to welcome those rare authors who, in the appalling circumstances

---

*Quoted by Sinyavsky in his introduction to the Soviet collection of Pasternak's poems published in 1965.

of Soviet life, tried, within the limits of possibility, to write sincerely and truthfully. As far back as 1963, at a conference attended by a number of distinguished specialists on Soviet literature from the United States, he was almost alone in voicing a note of optimism when he said that "the gains hitherto made by the Soviet writers in their struggle for greater independence, however relative and precarious this independence may be, are great enough to warrant the conclusion that a totalitarian régime can be challenged from within . . . [and] to have demonstrated that a 'monolithic' political structure is more fragile than was once thought." This, it will be recalled, was said before the birth of *samizdat.* It was on this occasion, too, that Max had high praise for Voznesensky: "Rather like Pasternak, whom he regards as his only teacher, he expresses . . . freedom of the spirit through freedom of language." Max was on friendly terms with both Voznesensky and Yevtushenko. Voznesensky paid a warm tribute to Max at a public reading of poems in Washington, D.C. This was in 1979, shortly after Max's death. The tribute was, with Voznesensky's permission, broadcast to Russia by the Voice of America—a mark of the poet's courage and integrity.

Of course, Pasternak was the lodestar of all that brave band of men and women among the Soviet intelligentsia who groped for some dignity, some sincere reality in the sea of what the Russians call *poshlost*—a word which defies translation, and which synthesizes every form of meanness, vulgarity, and cant. Max's first major achievement was his collaboration with the late Manya Harari, which resulted in 1958 in a masterly translation of *Doctor Zhivago.* He continued to collaborate with Manya Harari (and after her death with Marjorie Villiers) on the press which they founded, the Harvill Press, which largely under Max's guidance and advice published many of the Soviet writers in whom traces of sincere talent were discernible. A number of Max's essays were concerned with Pasternak, and the most remarkable of all was his introduction to his translation of Alexander Gladkov's *Meetings with Pasternak,* which is reprinted in this volume. Scarcely over 27 pages long, it tells us more about Pasternak than many a much longer exposition.

Another of Max's major contributions to our knowledge of Pasternak was his meticulous editing and translation of the memoirs of Olga Ivinskaya.

Pasternak apart, it was to Solzhenitsyn and Sinyavsky—the other two giants in true, as distinct from captive and false, Soviet culture—that Max devoted much of his attention. His translation of *One Day in the Life of Ivan Denisovich* was done in collaboration with Ronald Hingley. In the Introduction, written jointly with Leopold Labedz (these frequent collaborations were another sign of Max's diffidence or modesty), he says of this work: "Like all great works of art, it is outside place and time. In showing one man, in one particular time and place, in the most sordid setting imaginable, Solzhenitsyn has succeeded in strengthening our faith in the ultimate victory of civilized values over evil." The whole of Max Hayward's work on Soviet literature may without exaggeration be said to have been one devoted search for signs of this "ultimate victory." If civilization ever returns to Russia, its people will have cause to be grateful to this quiet scholar. The translation of *One Day*, which tried to capture the flavor of the original by rendering it into uneducated Anglo-American speech, was not entirely successful. But it was a good deal better than the version which appeared around the same time in England.

The most significant study of Solzhenitsyn which Max wrote has remained almost entirely unpublished, until now. This is the long introductory essay to the English translation of *From under the Rubble*, of which in the end only a fragment was printed. Much of this essay, which now appears in full in this volume, is devoted to the very salutary warning against identifying Solzhenitsyn as a Slavophile, and against viewing his controversy with Sakharov as a revival of the nineteenth-century dispute between Slavophiles and Westerners. In this context Max draws attention to a much-neglected passage in the third volume of *The Gulag Archipelago* in which Solzhenitsyn, in a manner quite uncharacteristic of the Slavophiles, argues the need for legal principles as the only foundation for society. (This passage was, in fact, published in *The Times* of London years before the third volume of *Gulag* appeared in translation.) At the same time, Hayward pointed to the inappropriateness in present-day conditions of any analogy with the way in which the Westerners in the nineteenth century looked to Western Europeans as an inspiration for radical and revolutionary ideas. This essay, as well as the first item in this volume, the superbly compressed introduction to a book of photographs of pre-revolutionary Russia, demonstrate that Max Hayward's mastery of things Russian was not confined to language and literature.

Max Hayward's interest in Sinyavsky, one of the most significant Russian literary figures of this generation, dates back to the time when his identity with the mysterious Abram Tertz was as yet uncertain. Max translated *The Trial Begins* himself,* and encouraged the publication of the translation of "Tertz's " other works by the Harvill Press, himself collaborating, again with Ronald Hingley, on the translation of a volume of stories. His most important writings on Sinyavsky will be found in this volume.

Mayakovsky, Nadezhda Mandelstam, Akhmatova—on all three and many more, Max had original things to say. His superb translation of the two volumes of Mrs. Mandelstam's memoirs was a labor of love, to which he devoted much time and care. His loss to British post-war scholarship on the Soviet Union—which has not been all that distinguished for its integrity or political balance—is enormous. The loss to the people of the Soviet Union is even greater—whether they acknowledge it or not. For Max Hayward drew attention to spiritual qualities in their midst at a time when most of them lacked either the courage or the perception to acknowledge them, and probably saved these people from a little of the opprobrium which posterity will justly heap upon them.

No account of Max Hayward can omit to mention his work as a teacher, mainly at Columbia University and at St. Antony's College, Oxford. As many of his former students have told me, he was a patient and inspiring guide. He aroused in his students

---

*First published in *Encounter* in January 1960.

the same kind of affection and respect that he evoked from his numerous friends on both sides of the Atlantic, in Greece, and in Israel. Indeed, perhaps his most memorable quality was his gift for friendship, and this too was a matter of character. He did not override his friends with his own vanity. He was reserved about his feelings, as if fearing to obtrude them on others. He had a great talent for observation, and his judgments were always fresh, original, illuminating, and stimulating. Those who were privileged to enjoy his friendship know that the world is a poorer place now that he is gone.

INTRODUCTION

by Patricia Blake

In a tribute to Max Hayward the Slavicist Victor Erlich wrote, "For some 25 years he labored tirelessly and selflessly to bring to the West the good tidings about the resurgence of the free Russian spirit." Only a most unusual sort of scholar would have set out on such a course, as Max did, before the death of Stalin in 1953. The free spirit of Russia had seemingly been extinguished and literature, as Boris Pasternak remarked, had ceased to exist. Exile, suicide, disgrace, or death in the camps had overtaken the country's finest writers and poets. Those who had fortuitously survived, like Pasternak and Anna Akhmatova, worked in silence. Fiction, drama, poetry, and criticism were forums for exhortation. Such material could scarcely be regarded as a fit subject for literary scholarship in the West, though a few sociologically minded academics, mostly Americans, were attempting to study Soviet life "through the prism of Soviet literature," as the phrase went.

But Max was an unorthodox scholar. He had started out with a gift for learning a language, notably Russian, "fully, with perfect pitch, embracing its heartbeat," as his friend and collaborator Vera Dunham put it. Gradually, however, his erudition grew until it spanned several fields—Russian literature, history, politics, linguistics—though he could not be said to belong to any one. Through much of the 1950's he did the slogging work that was needed to uncover the changes that were taking place in Soviet cultural policy. He seemed to be the only person with stamina enough to read *Novy Mir* from cover to cover. No novel or play was too tiresome for him to scrutinize for traces of Aesopian language or for some smidgen of sincerity amidst all the old, familiar cant. As Leonard Schapiro has written in his preface to this volume, Max was forever seeking signs of some "victory of civilized values over evil." In the 1960's, when talented, free-thinking young poets and writers made their appearance in Russia, Max was among the first to recognize their liberating role.

Meanwhile, Max was periodically refreshed by translation. His taste was enlarged and his literary sensibility sharpened by the intimate relationship a great translator achieves with a work of art. He had the good fortune of encountering works that had broken out, wholly intact, from the shambles of Stalinism: Pasternak's *Doctor Zhivago*, Akhmatova's *Requiem* and *Poem without a Hero*, Andrei Sinyavsky's *A Voice from the Chorus*, and Nadezhda Mandelstam's two-volume memoir, *Hope against Hope* and *Hope Abandoned*. The good fortune was also the authors'. "He did more than anyone I could name to make 'dissonant voices in Soviet literature' resound in clear and graceful English," Erlich wrote. For every book Max translated there were a dozen others by Russian writers that appeared as the result of his ministration. And as this volume attests, Max was also a fine writer who brought to his subject strong analytical powers, much erudition, seriousness of purpose, and reserves of saving wit and mischief.

At the stark moment of Max's death I wrote that he had acted as the custodian of Russia's literature until such time as it could be restored to its people. While it is surely true that he carried the burden of that mission, and passed it on to others, my formulation fell short of the forces that animated him. Consulting with many of his colleagues and friends and reflecting now upon his life, I believe that he was moved by a deeper underlay of feeling. His friend Leszek Kolakowski put it most simply: "Max was a profoundly pessimistic man whose sympathies lay with the common people." The Polish philosopher understood that Max deeply mistrusted all utopian ideologies, including Marxism. "He believed that ideologues and politicians should leave people alone. In spite of his Oxford education, he felt he belonged to the street; he was on the side of the poor." It was that strain of compassion for an abused people and their disinherited literature that gave his work its importance and his life its singular poignancy.

Max Hayward's Russian was flawless. He was so fluent that the Russians he met often refused to believe he was not a native speaker. When pressed to admit that he was an émigré, or at least the son of émigrés, he would sometimes sally forth with the information that he was a Cockney. By that he meant to express his class loyalty rather than a fact. Max—his full name was Harry Maxwell Hayward—was born in London on July 28, 1924, in the respectable lower-middle-class neighborhood of Whetstone, N. 20, well beyond the sound of the bells of Bow Church. His father Harry and his mother, the former Emily Schofield, were unmistakably from Yorkshire. They had alighted in London in 1924 when Harry Hayward, then an itinerant mechanic, found work at the Carrimore truck factory.

Max was equally fond of identifying himself as a Yorkshireman. When asked to repair a leaky faucet or a broken typewriter—he was unexpectedly adept at fixing things—he would invariably boast that he came from a long line of Yorkshire mechanics. Yet he actually never lived in Yorkshire. His childhood and youth had been spent in many different places, towns and cities, where his father had sought work. In 1935, when Max was eleven, and his brother Anthony six, the family paused in Dunstable, then moved on in 1938 to Liverpool, where Max's father worked for Rootes Aircraft.

Max's sense of place came to reside in language. As a young man he devised a mode of speech for himself that incorporated elements of the English he had heard spoken in the places he had lived in as a child. Only a natural-born linguist with an ear for the subtle variables of British speech could have succeeded in this without sounding artificial. Max was proud of his system and would readily explain its components, which ranged from Liverpudlian to Welsh. Most distinctively he had preserved the short Northern "a"—a salute to his Yorkshire forebears.

His first efforts at learning foreign languages, French at eleven, Latin at twelve, and German at thirteen, were oddly unpromising.

His report cards from Dunstable School showed progress that scarcely advanced from "satisfactory" to "fair." The study of divinity was definitely not his strong point at that school, either. His "excellents" were earned in drawing—apparently a lapsed talent. Most of his teachers commented on his untidiness—one of his most persistent and, to his friends, most endearing traits, tempering as it did the effect of a formidably analytical mind.

In 1938, when the Haywards moved to Speke, then a rough working-class district of Liverpool, Max's father insisted that he try out for one of the 120 scholarships given by the Liverpool Institute. This was one of the elite state grammar schools that offered promising lower- and middle-class children something like the education that was provided to the upper classes by the English public schools. Max's winning a scholarship at the Institute constituted a decisive turn in his life, breaking him forth from the predestined course of his class and putting him on track for a university education.

In Speke the boys in the street gangs were always on the lookout for the "grammar school pigs," the despised traitors to their class. During the first days of the school term the boys lay in wait for Max as he set out from Speke across town to the posh Institute. The tall, preternaturally skinny adolescent was an easy target, decked out as he was in gray flannel trousers and navy-blue blazer bearing the Institute's Latin motto, mercifully unintelligible in Speke: "Not for ourselves alone but for the whole world." In later years Max often told how he was beaten up on his way to the Institute. "They'd dressed me up as a pig," he would explain, and if his memory had been released by drink he might add, "Since then I've always been a fake and a defector." To his dear friend and mentor, George Katkov, he sometimes insisted, in Russian, "I'm a *muzhichok* [a peasant]—don't forget it and don't let anyone else forget it."

In his Liverpool years Max was known as Harry. But at the Institute they called him Happy; it was a school joke. Misery was writ on him then, and straight through to his mid-forties. Reginald Christian, now Professor of Russian at St. Andrew's University, Scotland, was a schoolmate of his and remembers him as aloof, sardonic, and extremely scruffy. Max made no friends, Christian recalls, nor did he participate in the various activities that were expected of the boys in Liverpool's imitation Eton. Sports were out of the question because of an underdeveloped left arm and hand.

Still, in Max's last year at the Institute he did participate in the school's Literary and Debating Society. Christian has preserved the minutes. Though they are rendered in the schoolboy-jocular mode, Max's distinctive style and sense of humor shine through. On January 27, 1942, the motion before the Society was, "That the time has come for the reannexation of Ireland." Max's contribution to the debate was summarized as follows:

"H. M. Hayward, as usual, thought the motion ridiculous. But he generously disregarded his own feelings and condescended to give the Society the undoubted benefit of his learned opinions. He divided the motion into three parts which he called adverbial implications. He dealt first with the question of time, and insisted that though six months ago we could have invaded Ireland with profit, now our shipping position in the Atlantic was so much improved, there could be no possible advantage in such an attack. Second, the motion implied that the manner of an invasion must necessarily be violent—and violence would antagonize the Irish and bring out all their natural obstinacy. Finally he dealt with the question of place. Why, he asked, should we waste our resources in an attack upon Ireland when there were so many places higher in the invasion list."

At the end of the debate the Chairman called upon Max to sum up his case. Max "declared that no one had been very provocative. He boldly admitted that his political morality was shocking, but the considerations he had put forward were those that would occur to any modern politician. Questions of this sort must be judged on topical and transient principles."

By the standards of the Liverpool Institute, Max suffered from several disabilities. He had been entered, not at eleven, the usual age for starting grammar school, but at fourteen. Moreover, he had not studied Greek, which put him at a disadvantage in a school that offered a classical education. Normally, as soon as the boys entered they were divided into four streams on the basis of competitive examinations. The top thirty students were put in the Classics stream. The second best studied the Sciences and French and Latin, while the third lot was relegated to Modern Languages, usually French and German, plus English literature and history. The fourth stream comprised the boys who had failed to make it into the other three. Because Max arrived Greekless and three years late, he was unqualified for the Classics stream. But his placement in Modern Languages, which may have seemed disgraceful at the time, turned out to be a blessing for Slavic studies in Britain.

He was still at two removes from Russian. What interested him most at the time was Romany. He had often visited encampments of Gypsies during his childhood peregrinations through Britain, and in Liverpool he began to teach himself their language so he could communicate with them at their nearby caravan sites. His sympathy for them was profound. Indeed, nothing so exemplifies Max's lifelong compassion for the insulted and injured of the world as his feelings for Gypsies. In the Soviet Union in the late 1940's he once wept with emotion, he told me, when he glimpsed a tattered caravan of Gypsies on the Georgian Military Highway near Tiflis, a rare tribe that had survived Stalin's genocidal policy against Gypsies. Max had a personal sense of identification with the Gypsies' nomadic life, their alienation, their impoverishment, their outlaw status, and the brutality of their existence.

His first efforts to learn Russian sprang from his interest in them. He had been encouraged by the remarkable Dora Yates, a librarian at the University of Liverpool who was a specialist in Gypsies and the Secretary of the Gypsy Lore Society. What happened was this. One day when he was leafing through some old volumes in a second-hand book stall in Liverpool, he came upon a huge illustrated work on Gypsies, in Russian. He brought it to Miss Yates, who congratulated him on his find. He then started teaching himself Russian so that he could read the book.

In a letter to Mr. M. R. Perkins, the Curator of Special Collections at the Liverpool University Library, on May 8, 1978, Max recalled Miss Yates's kindnesses to him. "Many years ago, in the middle of the war," he wrote, "I was befriended by Dora Yates, whom I often went to see in her room at the University Library. She was very kind to me and encouraged my passionate interest in Gypsies by paying my subscription as a member of the Gypsy Lore Society for several years. She was one of the most extraordinary people I have ever met, and I owe her a great debt of gratitude for helping me at that time. It was actually entirely thanks to her that I took up the study of Russian." Max regretted that he had not been able to visit Miss Yates before her death. "I have been quite out of touch with Gypsy matters for many years," he wrote, "however I do have a nostalgic interest in them, and sincerely hope that the Society still flourishes."

Max carefully preserved Miss Yates's letters to the youngest member ("by far") of the Gypsy Lore Society. To the lonely adolescent they had evidently meant a great deal. In these letters she urged him to continue studying German on the ground that it would prove useful for research in Romany. She also put him in touch with a number of Gypsy families who were living in and around Liverpool. In a letter of September 22, 1939, shortly after the Liverpool Institute boys had been dispatched to the relative safety of Wales, she wrote: "You are very fortunate in being evacuated to Bangor as this is one of the best centers in Wales for Gypsies."

During that cold, grim wartime winter of 1939–40, Max looked up Miss Yates's Gypsy friends (including "an Eisteddfod Prize harpist") and, to the consternation of the Liverpool evacuees, he began to study Welsh. According to Reginald Christian, this was something none of the other schoolboys would have dreamed of doing. He recalls that one of Max's favorite occupations was visiting old cemeteries to decipher the inscriptions on tombstones. Max always retained his interest in Welsh and he made a hobby of Celtic languages in later years. When I first knew him in the late 1950's, he often, at odd times and in unexpected places —such as, for example, during a lengthy police examination of our baggage at Belgrade Airport—fished out of his pocket for study a small Welsh grammar. He also had a store of Welsh songs to drink by. He was particularly fond of the Saucepan Song, whose refrain he would render with tremendous verve—a performance I could never persuade him to repeat after he went off alcohol for good in 1963. *"Sosban fach yn berwi ar y tân,"* it went, *"Sosban fawr yn berwi ar y llawr / A'r gath wedi scramo Joni bach."* ("Little saucepan boiling on the fire / Big saucepan boiling on the floor / And the cat has scratched little Johnny.") This was followed by a series of ear-splitting miaows.

Another of Max's fine performances during his drinking days involved his sudden, emphatic assertion that he was giving up Russian *forever*—in favor of Celtic studies. He would become lyrical at the prospect. "I'll spend the rest of my days sitting on a cliff on the Cornish coast taking notes on the chanteys I'll hear coming from the ships below." Then with a great yip he would ask, "You know what'll happen then?" A pause, and then: "A small boat will come nosing round the cliff, full of MI-5 men trying to find out what the hell I'm really up to."

Max went to Oxford in 1942 with a scholarship at Magdalen to read German. According to Christian and Katkov, Max really wanted to study Chinese. Christian, who had come up a year earlier, recalls that Max, fascinated by Liverpool's large Chinese settlement, had already begun to study the language. Max told Katkov, who heard him spin out his most hyperbolic tales, that he had been thwarted by a lunatic professor of Chinese who was too busy pursuing female students to teach.

In reality, it was Max's career as a German scholar that was cut short during his first term at Oxford. Never one to suffer inaccuracies in any foreign language, he set out to correct his professor of German, a Goethe scholar who was not a master of colloquial speech. The professor took offense. Having got off to a bad start, Max dropped German for good and began Russian. Still, he retained a splendid command of the German. Twenty-five years later, when he and I traveled to Austria to work on verse translations with W. H. Auden, Max was usually taken for a German.

At Oxford there seemed to be little doubt that Max would become a pure linguist. In late 1942 A. J. M. Craig, one of the Liverpool Institute's graduates at Oxford, provided the school paper with a report on Max and other old boys: "Dear Editor, You ask for news. . . . Mr. Hayward is reported to have been heard speaking English on one occasion last term. But most of his time is spent discussing in Tibetan with a Russian friend the use of Armenian labials in the Croatian dialect of Yugoslavian."

Max displayed no interest in literature at Oxford, according to Harry Willetts, a close friend at the university. To Max in those years literature was a source of language and little else. He liked to present himself, then and later, as a low-brow, nonliterary type —a "vulgar factologist," as he characterized himself in 1962 at the Conference on Soviet Literature he helped organize at St. Antony's College. This part of his persona no doubt belonged to Max the *muzhichok*. As long as I knew him it was one of his favorite bits of mischief to declare that he had never read *War and Peace*, a boast that unfailingly, and most satisfactorily, sent Slavicists into shock (and also a claim he often betrayed unawares by allusions drawn from his intimate knowledge of the novel).

The late Professor Sergei Konovalov, who held the Chair of Russian at Oxford, evidently took Max at his word and decided to civilize the self-styled country bumpkin who had blundered into the community of scholars. Konovalov arranged for Max to take tutorials with Lord David Cecil and Isaiah Berlin. Max called them collectively "the Lords." According to one of Max's friends at Oxford, "with the Lords he was meant to learn to write polished waffle on literary subjects."

Nadezhda Gorodetzky, one of Max's teachers at Oxford, with whom he read the Slavophiles, put him on to some out-of-the-way writing. Her reading lists had a slight tinge of decadence, with religious overtones. They included Leonov, Bunin, Andreyev, Remizov, and Rozanov. Leonov was probably the first Soviet writer Max read. At any rate he was deeply impressed by *Vor* (The Thief) and regarded Leonov as a great, though flawed, writer —a view he carried into his forties, though with dwindling assurance about his greatness.

Max became president of Oxford's Russian Club. A program presented by the club in 1943 offered such diverse entertainments as Dr. B. F. Steiner on "The Carpathians" (with lantern slides) and Dr. C. M. Bowra on "The Translation of Russian Poetry." These lectures were followed by an afternoon social at Lady Margaret Hall, which Max almost certainly failed to attend. According to Willetts he was deadly scared of the Oxford girls, most of whom had come from posh schools.

The private miseries which Max took with him to Oxford were scarcely alleviated at Magdalen, one of the snootier colleges. In some ways he felt more alienated than ever. For one thing, he was acutely conscious of the fact that the university's normal complement of undergraduates was then serving in the armed forces. Max had been deemed unfit to serve because of his arm. When he tried to join the Royal Air Force as a Russian interpreter in 1944, he was told that he could not be considered because "our present rule is that all linguists must be fit for overseas."

Max never really felt at home in Oxford, except perhaps at the end, as he lay dying in Churchill Hospital. It was then that he gave me and our mutual friend John Jolliffe an animated account of how Oxford had appeared to him during the war. The place was like an island populated by assorted castaways—oddballs, cripples, refugees. His most powerful memory was the relentless cold. There was simply no way to keep warm—a condition that Max experienced in whatever climate he found himself until, in the last decade of his life, he discovered Greece. He was very taken with Auden's poem "Good-bye to the Mezzogiorno":

> Out of a Gothic North, the pallid children
> Of a potato, beer-or-whiskey
> Guilt culture, we behave like our fathers and come
> Southward into a sunburnt otherwhere

The unusually high proportion of oddballs at Oxford during the war actually suited Max very well, for no one felt odder than he did. He established a small circle of friends, most of them foreigners. One of the circle recalls a strange Indian graduate student who was writing a thesis on Byron and Lermontov, and an American economist who was playing the market. There were some German-speaking refugees: Georg Rapp, who fenced and wrote poetry, and Victor Gugenheim. The latter recalls Max as a "marvelous, quirky, self-educated, moody, brilliant, complex and basically rather unhappy person. One loved him." Max's English friends included Harry Willetts, David Watkins (an extremely talented linguist), and Henry Knorfle, a law student whose puns vastly amused Max.

Willetts, Max's closest friend in those years, had been invalided out of the army in 1944 and had come up to Oxford to read Byzantine and modern Greek studies at Queens. Konovalov, whom Willetts had called on to see about studying Russian, said, "You must meet Hayward." Somebody then pointed Max out to Willetts, who has a clear memory of the occasion: "My first view was of someone who looked to me not a boy, but not quite an adult person. He was wearing a torn scholar's gown tied together with a knotted piece of string and he was wheeling an ancient bicycle out of the Taylorian."

Some members of Max's circle used to meet after lunch in his "set" or rooms on the front quad at Magdalen. Though the view was grand enough, hard upon Magdalen's Deer Park, the room was shabby and dank. Willetts remembers that it had a sofa, two chairs, an utterly inadequate electric fire, and "something dull and dingy on the wall." Even the Magdalen Bursar, to whom Max vainly appealed for a change of rooms, conceded in a letter that he had noticed when he went around "what a miserable set yours was."

Max possessed only the barest minimum in the way of books. Willetts recalls that he indulged in no frivolous or casual reading. "He was a most methodical student, and did everything thoroughly." The austerity of this life was reinforced by the rigid discipline that was then maintained at Oxford. Students were forbidden to frequent the pubs, and there were still rules about when you could go in and out. Max's chief amusement was movies. He would frequently interrupt the intellectual talk in his room with the imperative: "Better go to the pictures." In the summer he would go punting, that is, he would recline in the boat in "a magisterial position," as Willetts puts it, while others punted.

Max graduated with a first in 1945. His marks were communicated to him by one of his examiners, the French scholar

Enid Starkie. Writing on an open postcard, she enjoined him not to tell anyone his marks, because she was supposed to inform him of only the lowest and the highest. His highest was Alpha Plus on prose, translation, and essay, his lowest, Beta Double Minus on "the first period of literature." He got Beta on the "other period of literature," whatever that may have been. Her summary: "You were obviously strongest—indeed exceptionally strong—on the linguistic side."

Max remained in Oxford for two years after his graduation. At first he did some work for Konovalov, who had embarked on a vast scheme to produce Russian readers. Willetts has preserved a letter from Max in which he proposes that they collaborate on a reader, a project that never came to pass. Max was at loose ends. Though the war was over and life in Oxford had returned to normal, he and his friend Harry looked like "a pair of refugees" to Ronald Hingley, who had recently been demobbed and had resumed his undergraduate studies. To the former army officer Max looked, and indeed was, "spectacularly unmilitary." Hingley remembers him as a "vague graduate student" who went around with a copy of the Igor Tale in his pocket.

It was during this time in Oxford that Max's life first touched upon Boris Pasternak, who was to become his personal and literary hero and the object of his unremitting devotion for twenty years. Apparently by the sheerest accident Max rented a room in the huge old house at 20 Park Town that belonged to Pasternak's sister, Mrs. Lydia Slater. During the two years he lived there he was a favorite of Pasternak's four nieces and nephews. It may have been then that Max was first introduced to Pasternak's work. It is more likely, however, that he was treated to the paintings and drawings of Boris's and Lydia's father, the late Leonid Pasternak, who was the principal idol of the Slater household.

Though by 1946 Max had become a Bachelor of Letters candidate under Konovalov and the recipient of a £150 scholarship, he was casting about for something else to do. He tried out for a job as a U.N. interpreter, but was told that he had applied too late to take the qualifying examination.

The first person to make the fateful proposal that put Max on the road to Russia was the President of Magdalen, H. T. Tizard, the scientist who had been responsible for Britain's crucial radar defenses during the war. In a letter written in 1946 congratulating Max on his first, Tizard wrote, "I think it is important for your future career that you should spend some time in Russia, preferably at one of the universities." The Soviet government was scarcely prepared to accept foreign students. An inquiry to the Soviet Embassy in London by the Oxford University Registry elicited the reply that Max had no chance of going to a Russian university "in view of the great lack of facilities, including living quarters, transport, and so forth owing to the aftermath of war."

At this point Isaiah Berlin, then a Fellow of New College, had the idea that Max should work in the British Embassy in Moscow. In May 1946 Max received a letter from the Foreign Office which said, "We have heard from Mr. Isaiah Berlin that you have expressed an interest in doing some work for our Embassy in Moscow." The prospect promptly brought forth an objection from Tizard, who wrote to Max, "My opinion is that it would not be a good thing just at the moment to get a temporary appointment at the British Embassy in Moscow." The assumption he made was a reasonable one during the Stalin era: "I doubt whether you would really get to know Russians that way."

Tizard much preferred another idea that Max had proposed, to study in Prague, and enlisted a Magdalen Fellow, the historian A. J. P. Taylor, to help arrange it. Taylor, who had recently returned from a stay in Czechoslovakia, came forward with practical advice and a letter of recommendation to the British Council, which then awarded Max a scholarship to study at Charles University in Prague. Taylor wrote to Max that the British Council "will be so unused to receiving an application from any candidate of real merit that their organization will be quite upset. Still, even the British Council with its unfailing gift for sending the wrong person and doing the wrong thing can hardly turn you down."

Max spent the academic year of 1946–47 in Prague. One could never get much out of him about this period in his life, perhaps because the seeming normality of Czechoslovakia, during the lull before the Communist takeover, did not much kindle his interest.

He and William Barker, who had been teaching Russian at Liverpool University, were the only English students at Charles University. Together with twelve students from the United States, they founded an Anglo-American Club. But Max kept mostly to himself, concentrating on learning Czech. He had discovered Karel Čapek and set out to translate a chapter from his *Fables and Tales,* which had only recently been published in Prague. Max submitted this, his first effort at literary translation, to Čapek's British publishers, Allen and Unwin, but they were not interested.

Čapek's darkly comic visions of robots and salamanders gone amok appealed to Max. Certainly, *R.U.R.* and *War with the Newts* were better preparations for his forthcoming stay in Moscow than any current piece of political writing about the Soviet Union. Probably, Čapek provided the young English linguist with his first experience of the language of symbol and fantasy that has alone proved capable of encompassing the monstrousness of modern totalitarian societies. When Max first returned from Russia he could scarcely talk about the country without quoting Čapek. In the late 1950's when I first began collaborating with Max, references to newts and robots served as our shorthand for a variety of features of Soviet society.

The Foreign Office, which had been taking its time considering Max for a temporary post in Moscow, informed him in July 1947 that he had been appointed a Third Secretary there. On September 10, 1947, Max arrived in Moscow, where he was to serve for exactly two years. Bill Barker, his friend from Prague, had also been sent to the Soviet capital, where he was Max's chief. Max was one of a group of able university graduates in Russian, mostly from Oxford, who had been dispatched to Moscow as the result of an enlightened post-war Foreign Office scheme.

According to Barker, the F.O. had acted out of concern over the fact that the majority of people who received visas to visit the Soviet Union were communists and fellow travelers. Indeed, most writing and reporting about Russia published in Britain (as elsewhere in the West) displayed an uncritical pro-Soviet bias. It was hoped that the young English scholars in Moscow, who would later occupy influential positions in journalism, teaching, and other professions, might become a nucleus of informed opinion about Russia in Britain. Barker headed the group of seven young men in the so-called Russian Secretariat whose task it was to analyze the Soviet press.

Max arrived in Russia a complete political innocent. Though at home, out of class loyalty, he declared himself pro-Labour, he had hardly any interest in politics, domestic or foreign. His governing passion was language, and his main purpose in going to the Soviet Union was to perfect his knowledge of Russian, especially colloquial Russian. Nothing had prepared him for the series of historical disasters that befell the Soviet people during his stay in Russia.

During his first winter in Russia, a campaign was launched against foreigners and the Soviet citizens who had associated with them during the wartime Allied collaboration and its afterglow. In the latter part of 1947 a decree was passed making it a crime for any Soviet citizen to give foreigners any sort of information. Travel within the country became increasingly difficult for foreigners. Soviet women who went out with foreigners were rounded up and dispatched to the Gulag under Article 7-35 ("Socially Dangerous Elements") of the Criminal Code. The outburst of xenophobia was especially virulent where the British were concerned. In *Pravda* a few weeks after Max's arrival the British military attaché was accused of spying. During the winter two junior members of the embassy were threatened with arrest and trial, one for alleged blackmarketeering, the other for supposedly infecting a Russian girl with syphilis.

In early 1948, on one of his first official missions for the embassy, Max attended a poetry reading (on the theme "Down with the Warmongers!") where he witnessed a deeply affecting public demonstration on behalf of the beleaguered Pasternak. The experience, of which Max gives an account on pp. 204–07 of this book, was a shattering one; it brought home to him in the most graphic way the damage that had been done to Russian culture by the 1946 purges of the artistic intelligentsia.

In 1948 there erupted a ferocious campaign against Soviet music, the only branch of the arts that had been spared during the 1946 purges. For months Max's days were spent reading the articles and letters from supposedly indignant readers that flooded the Soviet press with denunciations of Shostakovich, Prokofiev, and other composers. Max, who had no ear for music and could not be lured to concerts, developed a fondness for Shostakovich at the high tide of his execration. Years later Max presented me with a record of Shostakovich's ultrapatriotic Seventh Symphony. He gave me this surprising gift with a knowing smile I found faintly irritating. But reading Shostakovich's posthumous memoirs after Max's death, it occurred to me that Max might indeed have sensed something I hadn't. He was just the person to have been attuned to the fact that Shostakovich had been trying to evoke in his symphony, not the German attack on Russia, but Stalin's war against his own people.

In the summer of 1948 Max was witness to the destruction of the biological sciences in the Soviet Union. In August Stalin's charlatan agronomist, Lysenko, triumphed over opposition in the Soviet Academy of Agricultural Sciences. There followed a purge of the country's biologists who had resisted the absurd doctrine that heritable changes can be brought about by the environment. At the same time Stalin embarked on an anti-Semitic campaign that characterized Jews as "rootless cosmopolitans," and that resulted in the mass arrest of Jewish writers, the closing of the Jewish State Theater, and the suppression of virtually all Jewish newspapers, periodicals, and publishing houses.

Among the diplomats and foreign correspondents in Moscow at that time, only those who had earlier established relations with Soviet citizens seemed to appreciate the human tragedies unfolding outside their sealed-off compounds. Life within the diplomatic community could be quite agreeable. After the war the usual round of dinners, receptions, and tennis parties at the diplomatic dachas had resumed. There was even an Anglo-American dance band, the Kremlin Crows, run by the AP correspondent Eddy Gilmore.

Max, however, was in no way suited for these entertainments. Barker recalls that "Max was the only person I have ever seen arrive at his first diplomatic post with all his effects in a knapsack." Dressed in a cheap English suit, complete with baggy trousers, he looked more like a Russian in those austere times than a British diplomat. The junior members of the embassy ragged him by asking him for the name of his tailor.

He found a congenial roommate in Hugh Lunghi, who, like himself, was not a career diplomat. Lunghi had served as a staff officer and interpreter in the British Military Mission to the Soviet Union during the war, when Russians met with Allied personnel with relative impunity. Lunghi had close ties with the country; his mother was Russian-born and he had spoken Russian since childhood. After the war he had stayed on as Third Secretary to work in the Russian Secretariat. He and Max shared a three-room Embassy apartment near the Krasnyye Vorota metro station with Sharik, a mean-tempered stray dog Lunghi had acquired on a trip to the Caucasus. Sharik, who tended to bite strangers, followed Max about slavishly.

Lunghi had a Russian fiancée, a voice student at the Moscow Conservatory, and he was pulling every string he could think of to obtain permission from the Soviet authorities to marry her and leave for England. Since Soviet law forbade marriage to foreigners, permission could be granted only as a result of high-level intervention. Max became friends with the young musician, who often visited the Hayward-Lunghi flat. The two men sometimes spent weekends at her parents' dacha.

In 1947 Lunghi's fiancée was arrested for consorting with a foreigner. That struck at Max's heart. In the months that followed, he accompanied the distraught Lunghi on visits to NKVD headquarters in the Lubyanka Prison, where Lunghi attempted to deliver food parcels for his fiancée. Thus within a year of Max's arrival in the Soviet Union he was participating in the quintessential Stalin-era experience, standing in line outside a prison in the hope of delivering a parcel or getting some scrap of news about a friend or relative in the Gulag. Twenty-five years later he was to translate, in collaboration with Stanley Kunitz, Akhmatova's great poem *Requiem,* which bears witness to the agony of all the children, husbands, wives, and friends who were victims of the terror:

"In the terrible years of the Yezhov terror I spent seventeen months waiting in line outside the prison in Leningrad. One day somebody in the crowd identified me. Standing behind me was a woman, with lips blue from the cold, who had, of course, never heard me called by name before. Now she started out of the torpor common to us all and asked me in a whisper (everyone whispered there):

" 'Can you describe this?' And I said: 'I can.' Then something like a smile passed fleetingly over what had once been her face."

Max was very good at interpreting the Soviet press. Barker recalls that he quickly developed the knack of reading the newspapers as Soviet citizens did, grasping the message that was usually buried in the dense verbiage of a *Pravda* editorial. He was also able to get around Moscow and talk to ordinary Soviet citizens, when the occasion arose, as no career diplomat in the embassy dared to do. Members of the Russian Secretariat had in fact been given some license to mingle with the population. The F.O. reckoned that the scholars who had been pulled in from the outside were "expendable," as Barker puts it. Diplomats were required to exercise extreme caution so as not to lose their visas, but the temporary employees might be expelled from the country without causing much embarrassment in London.

According to some of his contemporaries in Moscow, Max was not always taken for a Russian when he mingled with the *narod* (the people) at least not on that first trip. Though he spoke the language perfectly and was attuned to the colloquial vocabulary, the little turns of speech and intonations that are characteristic of a specific walk of life naturally eluded him. Mostly, he was taken for a Soviet Jew or a Balt. The usual question Soviet citizens put to him was "What Republic do you come from?" His ability to communicate with people was, of course, not just a matter of his linguistic gifts. "He had a remarkable rapport for things exotic and alien," says Barker, who had quickly grasped one of his outstanding characteristics. "He had an uncanny knack of getting on to the same net with very alien people."

Max's accounts of his forays outside the embassy amazed and

sometimes alarmed his superiors. Scarcely in the orthodox mold, his official reports were full of sympathy for Russians, bursting with comic detail and profoundly serious. One example that has survived is the account of a twelve-day trip to the North Caucasus that Max and a junior member of the embassy made in May 1949. Though coauthored (the other man prefers to remain unidentified), this astonishing document bears Max's distinctive stamp. Who else but Max could have extracted the full flavor of the following experience in Pyatigorsk:

"We left our rucksacks in the hotel and found what was obviously the chief restaurant in the town. It was clean enough but, like all the restaurants we saw, almost empty. There was a band playing old American and German tunes in bouncing Russian style and a blowsy looking female 'vocalist.' When we had almost finished our meal, two waiters, whom we discovered were Armenians, came up and said they had a bet with the violinist about our nationality. They believed we were from the Baltic States or Czechoslovakia, while the violinist thought we were Americans.

"We told the Armenians we were English, whereupon we were immediately joined at the table by a drunken young Soviet Army officer (his badges of rank were missing) who had overheard us. The Armenian waiters immediately asked the officer to leave our table. This request provoked the officer to a fit of temper. Disregarding the Soviet law which forbids manifestations of racial hostility, he turned on the waiters and called them 'Armenian dogs,' 'prostitutes' and even 'Turks.' After some useless pleading the Armenians retreated. The officer thereupon explained that his outburst of fury was directed not against Armenians in general but against those 'sly Armenian dogs' who serve as waiters in North Caucasian restaurants and 'get above themselves.' He then inquired what sort of people we were. To this question, the first of many similar ones, we gave what was to become our standard answer, namely that we were members of the British Embassy spending ten days' leave on an excursion around the Caucasus. At this the officer said, 'I would willingly help you and show you around Pyatigorsk but I am suspicious of you.' 'Why?' we asked. 'Because,' he replied, 'we have suffered too much from foreigners.

We have been invaded by Tartars, Germans, Frenchmen, Poles, Swedes and Englishmen.' This was the frankest expression of suspicion we encountered on our journey, but we have little doubt that it represents a widespread mood."

Clearly, many Soviet citizens in the provinces were unaware of the prohibition against talking with foreigners. As usual Max's natural affinity with exotic and alien people brought them forth in large numbers. For example: "At Beslan, a large Ossetian village of no great character, we were accosted by an Ossetian. Speaking bad Russian, he gave us a rather incoherent lecture on Byron and boasted of his own great abilities as a poet and painter. Only lack of money, he said, and his shabby clothes (they were, indeed, shabby) prevented him from studying at an Institute and making a name for himself." In Tiflis, "as we walked up the street this old Georgian, after asking if we were Germans, and on learning we were English suddenly burst out with a surprising vehemence into a condemnation of the Soviet regime. 'They,' he said, 'have spoiled everything in Tiflis—they are a bunch of Fascists.' He told us he had been in America in 1910 and wished he had never returned to Russia. 'They' had taken everything away from him and reduced him to beggary."

When the two Englishmen got into what purported to be a taxi in Tiflis, the young driver of the "broken-down old machine" turned to them and said urgently that "if we were stopped by an 'Inspector' we were to say that a Major of the M.V.D. had just put us in the car! It turned out that he was driving *nalevo* (literally, on the left, or on the side). He was actually chauffeur to the M.V.D. Major who was head of the local forced labor camp. . . . He asked for his exorbitant fee before we got to the station and when we arrived, jumped out and made a great show of wringing our hands as if he were seeing off some old friends."

Everywhere they saw signs of the Gulag. "Near one station, when we were already in Georgia, we saw a group of wretched barefooted women repairing the permanent way. They were guarded by an M.V.D. man armed with a rifle. This group was typical of many similar ones we saw, especially in Kutaisi. In Georgia we frequently caught sight of small forced labor camps, often adjacent to building sites or factories and distinguished by barbed wire fences and raised sentry boxes at each corner."

Two German P.O.W.'s they met in a hilltop park in Tiflis at first thought the Englishmen were M.V.D. spies because they were too "ill-dressed" to be foreigners. When apprised that they were English, the P.O.W.'s gave them a full account of the number of prisoners in the area and how they were being treated. A young girl they met in a restaurant told them she thought "all the trouble between England and Russia was due to the governments of the two countries. We do not know how our government represents us abroad. We have suffered much from our government and will probably suffer from it in the future." She then told them "quietly and in a matter of fact way" that her father, an engineer, had been arrested in 1938 for "counterrevolutionary activities" and that he had died in a camp.

During their entire trip they were followed by the secret police, at first discreetly. During the last six days, however, after Max and his friend went for a walk in the countryside near Tiflis, the team of police assigned to them came out into the open. "We soon became aware of our followers, three young Georgians, who behaved like children playing Red Indians in their attempts to keep themselves concealed in the bushes behind us. We sat down in the sun amid low scrub on the hillside and the followers sat down nearby, peeping at us from time to time. They had by that time got hold of two young women whose presence, they apparently believed, gave them the appearance of idle picnickers."

In their hotel on their last day, the travelers met a woman from Siberia who had been a pilot during the war and was on her way to a holiday camp. She told them she knew it was "inconvenient" to have contact with foreigners. Some of her girlfriends had been persecuted for associating with British and American sailors in Odessa. Still, and in spite of a warning from the floor matron, she persisted in wanting to talk to the two men. When she later met the Englishmen in a park, she was accompanied by her two nieces. "As we sat talking in full public view a militiaman came up. Ignoring us he said sharply to the woman, 'Get up.' She obeyed and walked off with the militiaman out of the park with the two little girls running beside her. We were profoundly shocked and went back to the hotel feeling depressed and guilty. We can only hope that the girl got off lightly with a warning."

In early 1949, soon after David Kelly arrived in Moscow to take up the post of British Ambassador, Max was called upon to act as Kelly's interpreter in an interview with Stalin. Obtaining the interview had been quite a coup for Kelly; since the war only the French Ambassador had succeeded in meeting with the dictator. Though the ambassador had a staff interpreter, Kelly had decided to take Max to the Kremlin on the advice of Barker, who had said Max would do a superior job.

The British were given only a day's notice of the interview, which was scheduled for ten o'clock at night. The Ambassador, the minister Geoffrey Harrison, and Max were driven to the main gate of the Kremlin, where a group of officers examined their passes. They were then admitted to the fortress and escorted by a pilot car through the grounds. Bells were rung at intervals to announce their passage. They stopped at a building on the other side of the Kremlin, alongside Red Square. The group entered a small door, climbed a flight of stairs, and passed through two rooms where secretaries were working. Finally they were ushered into a large room with a table. The walls were decorated with portraits of Russian generals. Stalin then entered, accompanied by Foreign Minister Andrei Vyshinsky and Vladimir Pavlov, the head of the department of the Soviet Foreign Ministry that dealt with the British Commonwealth. As Kelly noted in his memoir of the meeting, Pavlov was also "a brilliant interpreter."

The dictator, who was in his uniform as Generalissimo, held out his hand and said, "Stalin." Once the group was seated at the table Kelly made a five-minute presentation. He said that both Britain and the Soviet Union were engaged in postwar reconstruction, that there was no possibility of aggression on Britain's side, and that he hoped there would be opportunities for discussion to help remove existing suspicions. Kelly then turned to Max for interpretation into Russian. But Max was silent, visibly awestruck. Pavlov then said quietly that he had been taking notes and would interpret for both Kelly and Stalin, which he proceeded to do, as

Max remained frozen speechless during the entire twenty-five-minute interview.

The discussion between Kelly and Stalin was scarcely earth-shaking. Stalin said that coexistence was possible, but that suspicion had grown stronger since the signing of the "meaningless" North Atlantic Pact. Kelly assured him that the United States was no more capable of aggression than Britain. The rest of the discussion centered around the problems of British personnel in the embassy who had become involved with Russian women. Kelly touched upon the case of the wretched English clerk who had been accused in the Soviet press of infecting a Russian girl with syphilis, indeed, of having brought his infected blood to the Soviet Union in order to spread disgusting diseases there. For their part, the British maintained that the clerk had caught the disease from the Russian girl. The clerk, who did not enjoy diplomatic immunity, had been ordered by the ambassador to remain sequestered in the embassy to avoid trial. (He was obliged to stay there until the Khrushchev era.) The mention of this case made Stalin laugh. "Such problems arose from boredom," he said. Upon that note the group departed the Kremlin.

The paralyzing effect of Stalin's presence on Max scarcely needs explanation. Yet to one of his colleagues Max confided that he had gone blank when he caught sight of Stalin's disability, which he had known nothing about. The dictator's withered arm and smallish hand, so like Max's own, lay still upon the table. By the time Kelly began to speak and Stalin started doodling on a sheet of notepaper with his good hand, Max's attention had hopelessly wandered, never to be recovered on that something less than historic night.*

In 1949, when Max returned to England from Russia, he took up the post of University Lecturer in Russian at Oxford. In all his years at Oxford this was the only time he would ever be called

---

*For this reconstruction I am indebted to Sir Geoffrey Harrison, Sir William Barker, and Joseph Dobbs. I have also drawn upon Sir David Kelly's account of his meeting with Stalin in *The Ruling Few* (London: Hollis & Carter, 1952), wherein Max's presence is not mentioned.

upon to teach at the university. His hold on the job was precarious. By all accounts, Konovalov, who had appointed him, soon lost patience with his eccentricities and with his original way of teaching traditional subjects.

In the postwar period, when Oxford's Russian School was small, Max was required to teach a wide variety of subjects ranging from Russian history to linguistics. Michael Glenny, who was an undergraduate at the time, remembers Max's course in Russian phonetics as first-class entertainment. "He made fascinating what had been a dull, pedantic exercise," says Glenny, who has since become a well-known translator from the Russian. "He had the marvelous ability to be rigorously analytic while at the same time introducing elements of absurdity and humor. For example, he would break down a word into its smallest phonetic components, then suddenly compare it with another word that was similar in sound but completely incongruous in meaning. The class would just break up in laughter."

Outside of classes, Max was a regular at the Russian Club, where he amused students with some of his store of *chastushki,* the satirical, industrial-age Russian jingles which he collected for the fun of it. He also had a good deal to tell students that was drawn from first-hand experience of mass police terror in the Soviet Union. "That was invaluable," says Glenny, "for in those years it was virtually impossible to learn Russian without getting a strong dose of Stalinist propaganda from both teachers and students."

It was during this period in Oxford that Max began to drink heavily for the first time. He was often hung over at his morning classes, though he did turn up to teach, which was not always the case after he went to Leeds University in 1952. In some respects the next four years, which he spent at Leeds as Head of the Department of Russian, were Max's lost years. John Fennell, who was then teaching at Nottingham University, remembers visiting him at his tiny flat, which to Max's delight was situated on Cemetery Place. "It was immensely depressing: a dismal room filled with Russian newspapers and journals. Max reveled in the gloom of it all." Willetts, who was teaching at Manchester University, recalls that he led a "picaresque life" in Leeds. "He got mixed up with immigrant Ukrainian textile workers and joined the local Ukrainian Club." Max, who was usually reticent about his years at Leeds, did like to regale his friends with accounts of his pub crawls through the slums with a certain Balashov, who had a checkered past in the Soviet Union. At least some of these excursions might pass for research for the dictionary of Soviet underworld slang that Max was proposing to put together at the time.

While at Leeds, in 1953, Max produced the three articles that are his first published writings. A piece that appeared in the *Universities Quarterly* on "The Curriculum in Russian Studies" opened with a statement that seemed bound to give offense to teachers in Russian departments throughout Britain: "I do not propose to discuss in detail the arrangements at present existing in the universities at which Russian is taught, since it would be difficult to do so without being invidious." The tone in which he proceeded to make eminently practical suggestions for changes in the curriculum was hardly more ingratiating. Arguing that more language instruction and fewer compulsory courses were needed, he wrote: "The average student has scarcely had time to get a somewhat precarious grasp on the modern language before he finds himself floundering in a morass of historical grammar"; "students of Russian are compelled to swallow large and repugnant doses of philology"; "some students undoubtedly regret the time they are obliged to spend deciphering the incomparably turgid language of Russian medieval texts."

Writing in the Leeds University journal *The Gryphon* on the eve of Stalin's death, Max showed how much he had learned in Russia and how deeply he had been affected by the experience of Soviet totalitarianism. His article, "The Russian and His Regime," is astonishingly informed and sophisticated for the time. It stands up on every point of fact and nuance thirty years later, when incomparably more is known about the Soviet Union. Part historical summary and part report on his stay in Russia, Max's article focused on the human cost of "socialist construction" and on popular resistance to it. "Almost every major measure of the

Soviet Government has been carried through in the teeth of massive though unorganized opposition from wide sections of the people," he wrote, ticking off the Kronstadt Rebellion, the Antonov Uprising, enforced collectivization, and industrialization, which he compared (citing Ilya Ehrenburg) with the building of the pyramids by slave labor. Fully understanding the immensity of the Gulag Archipelago, he wrote of a "vast forced labor camp empire" and of the postwar "mass deportations."

Max was angry. "In some quarters it is regarded as almost indecent to mention such facts as these . . . but they are essential background to any study of 'Soviet Man' unless one is content to accept uncritically the myth created by Soviet propaganda and apparently accepted by many people in the West, irrespective of their political views, that the Russian people are an undifferentiated mass of docile devotees of 'communism.'" Max was at pains to point out "a diversity of outlook" among Russians, drawing on his own experience. "Anyone who lives in Russia for any length of time, provided he knows the language and has opportunities of meeting people unofficially and without witnesses (which is by no means easy in present conditions), soon becomes aware that the vaunted 'moral-political unity' is to a considerable extent fictitious." He reported that most of the intellectuals he had been able to talk to "expressed great resentment at the restrictions on their freedom of expression." And he noted powerful though necessarily unexpressed ill-feeling among industrial workers about the draconian labor laws. Finally, he wrote that economic progress had been achieved at the expense of reverting to, and in many cases intensifying, some of the most obnoxious features of czarist Russia.

His main point was this: "It is often argued that this was inevitable owing to the anarchic, undisciplined nature of the Russians, and that in any case the Russians have always had (and therefore deserve) a tyrannical form of government. This view seems to me highly questionable and uncharitable."

This article offers a glimpse of Max's intense and unremitting dislike of Western apologists for the Soviet Union. Nothing made him angrier than the suggestion that Russians were at one with their rulers or that they were deserving of or insensitive to oppression because they had never known anything else. He regarded such notions not only as misguided or wrongheaded, but as an insult to the peoples of the Soviet Union. Few outsiders had a more deeply felt awareness of their suffering than Max. He knew it in his bones. Until the end of his days he would remain as unforgiving of whitewash by fellow travelers in the West as he was tolerant of the subterfuges and deceptions of Soviet citizens seeking to survive.

Ronald Hingley has recalled one of Max's responses to whitewash: "For Western citizens sympathetic to the Soviet Union in the wrong way, as he saw it—whether they were categorizable as fellow travelers, parlor socialists or radical chic-ists—he felt blistering contempt, and would occasionally depart from his usual courtesy to maul them with awesome brutality. . . . Hayward once coined an elaborate conceit whereby he imaginatively transferred the conventional fellow-traveling approach from its traditional Soviet pabulum to an imaginary Hitlerite setting. When Western sympathizers would attempt, in his presence, to justify the horrors of Stalin's concentration camps as an economic necessity, he was apt to murmur, in what he thought were the appropriate simpering tones, a mock exculpation of atrocities no less vile as perpetrated in Auschwitz, Buchenwald, and Dachau. 'What you must realize,' he would make his imaginary Hitlerizing fellow traveler explain, 'is that Germany had, at that time, *a perfectly genuine shortage of soap.*'"

Max's first article on Soviet literature offers a good example of his sympathy for the survival strategies of Russian writers. The piece, entitled "The Eternal Triangle in Soviet Literature," published by *Twentieth Century* in 1953, is essentially an exercise in abstracting the plots of approved Soviet fiction and drama. In a subtle reading of a Stalin Prize play by Alexander Korneichuk, *Hazel Grove,* Max demonstrated the dynamic of the "eternal triangle," a plot device involving an "autocratic" figure, a "liberal," and a party comrade who reconciles the two according to the "law of the dialectic." Max's observations on that "law" and other aspects of the ideology that govern the Soviet people remain relevant: "Probably no regime in history has succeeded to such an extent as the Soviet regime in isolating itself from the people by such an impenetrable fog of claptrap." As Max pointed out, the vaunted power of the "dialectic" to metamorphose human beings was not based on the ineluctable force of the idea, but on coercion. "Bitter experience has taught Soviet people that resistance to the Stalinist 'dialectic' is not only futile, but suicidal. Hence the extraordinary spectacle of scholars and writers denouncing their life's work, with praise to Stalin on their lips. To regard such sudden conversions as sincere would be to do a grave injustice to the majority of those concerned."

In the summer of 1955 Max returned to Moscow. He had accepted a second, temporary appointment to work in the British embassy's Russian Secretariat, where he had served so successfully in the late 1940's. This time, however, his stay was to end in disaster, for he was already in the grip of alcoholism. To his friends he sometimes told stories of his vodka-induced devilry that summer. Hingley, his pal and drinking buddy in later years, recorded some of them in *The American Scholar*:

"One wonders whether, during the entire history of the Soviet Union, there has ever been any foreign visitor more categorically 'un-visa-worthy.' What capitalist hyena but he would have contrived to spend a night in Moscow carousing with a uniformed colonel of Stalin's secret police? . . . His impishness in wandering around central Tiflis, asking to be directed to 'Beria Square,' gains its piquancy from Beria's status at the time; once Stalin's chief henchman, he had been liquidated and converted into an 'unperson'—as his square had of course been hastily converted into someone else's square—shortly before these bland inquiries were directed in impeccable Russian at a succession of disconcerted Georgian men-in-the-street. Then again, who but Hayward would have immortalized a visit to Astrakhan by striking up an acquaintance with the organizer of that otherwise dreary city's chief call-girl circuit? This arch-pimp of the Caspian was glad to explain his pricing policy, itemizing a tariff that ranged from the odd 'succulent morsel' *(baba s bagazhom)* at the top to the 'clapped-out junk' (as I bowdlerize *vyyebannoye barakhlo*) at the foot of the scale."

My own favorite is Max's spirited account of what took place when he was sent on an official mission to look after a high-level diplomat's wife who wished to go to Leningrad to sight-see. Fed up with the usual Intourist foul-ups, he began drinking as soon as the pair reached the Astoria Hotel in Leningrad. By late evening he had worked himself up to a transport of fury that was compounded of all the griefs he had accumulated during his earlier, two-year stay in the Soviet Union. Anyone who has lived in that country for any length of time can hardly fail to appreciate what he did next. He picked up the phone in his room and demanded that the hotel operator connect him with NKVD headquarters. Evidently frightened, the operator did so. When Max verified that he was talking to the NKVD he yelled, *"Svolochi! Svolochi!"* (Swine! Swine!)

Surprisingly, the Soviet authorities failed to lodge a complaint about Max's behavior to the British embassy, which remained more or less unaware of it. His downfall came after a trip to the Caucasus, which he had undertaken with a young British diplomat who was also a fluent Russian speaker. Accounts vary about what Max actually did on that trip, but he appears to have caused some sort of *skandal,* as the Russians say, in a Tiflis restaurant. According to one report, he climbed on top of a table and denounced Stalin in Russian, using a wide range of the "four-letter" words he knew so well. Some Georgian diners objected violently to Max's insults; though Stalin was dead, de-Stalinization had not yet taken place and, besides, many Georgians never gave up viewing their late countryman as a national hero. The police were said to have had to intervene in the ensuing melee. Still, the Soviet authorities in Moscow persisted in ignoring Max's shenanigans and his embassy was not notified. It was his traveling companion who insisted that the two men return at once to Moscow.

A diplomat at the embassy, who was a friend of Max's, recalls what followed: "At the time, Max was unorthodox, undisciplined, and intractable, while his companion on the trip was orthodox and ambitious. He immediately squealed on Max to Cecil Parrott, the minister who was in charge of the embassy in the absence of Ambassador William Hayter." A stickler for decorum, Parrott ordered Max to leave the country immediately. That ended Max's chances of returning to the Soviet Union in any official capacity.

In retrospect, it seems clear that he could not have been kept on at the embassy; his alcoholism made him a target for various kinds of exploitation by the Soviets, including blackmail. Still, Parrott's summary dismissal seemed brutal. When Max's diplomat friend went to his hotel room to try to console him on his last night in Moscow, Max was "very upset, very bitter, and very drunk." He felt strongly that he had been unjustly treated. At one point he reached for his British passport and had to be restrained from tearing it up. "It was the nearest symbol of bureaucracy he could lay his hands on," his friend explains.

Max returned to Moscow for two weeks the following summer, this time on assignment for the *Daily Telegraph*. He was determined to drink less—he could still, in fact, stop drinking for weeks at a time—and did not get into any scrapes. It was just as well; the NKVD was waiting for him. The close attention he was given by the secret police was striking at that time, four months after the Twentieth Party Congress, when surveillance of foreigners had become less systematic and more discreet. From the outset, Max was constantly shadowed by two men on foot. Surveillance was soon reinforced by eight more plainclothesmen traveling in two cars. In intelligence parlance, such an operation is known as "intimidation surveillance." Obviously, the authorities were convinced that Max was much too knowledgeable and were determined to isolate him from Soviet citizens. This was to be his last trip to Russia.

Max's encounters with the NKVD and with Soviet bureaucracy in general were the subject of an article he wrote that was headlined "How Not to Make Friends"—one of two short pieces published by the *Telegraph* on July 20 and 21, 1956. Though he offered an impressive account of how he had been shadowed and prevented from traveling outside Moscow, he was, as always, fair-minded. "Yet it is clear," he wrote, "that a great deal has changed and that the authorities are in a sense genuinely anxious to extend contacts with the outside world."

Judging from his other *Telegraph* piece, Max's shadows had not succeeded in completely intimidating Russians who wanted to talk with him. He gained a powerful impression of the public mood in Russia in the wake of the Twentieth Congress. All the Russians he met were aware of the contents of Khrushchev's "secret" de-Stalinization speech at the Congress, which, he wrote, "had the effect of liberating people from fear with one blow." He heard people attack Stalin in public places "in the choicest Russian Billingsgate." A man shouted, "How was it that this Georgian tangerine-seller managed to rule the Russian people for so long?" A worker Max encountered in a "restaurant" (actually, it was a proletarian dive on Gorky Street frequented by visiting Georgian black-marketeers) gave vent to anarchist sentiments. " 'What prevents real friendship between the peoples?' he demanded. He answered his own question: 'The State.' "

Returning to Leeds after his trips to Russia, Max felt defeated and depressed. Drinking heavily again, he had trouble keeping up with his university duties. His affliction had already damaged his health. Toward the end of his stay in Leeds, after he had been hospitalized following a bad bout, he seemed to be living on the chocolate bars he bought when he went out for the cigarettes he chain-smoked.

Rescue was at hand. In 1956, at this very low point in Max's life, he was invited to become a Research Fellow of the Russian and East European Center that was being established at St. Antony's College, Oxford. David Footman, who was in charge of setting up the new center, remembers that Max was "in appalling health and very unhappy; we hoped that he would be happier when he joined us." And he was. For the next twelve years or so, Max's association with St. Antony's was his life-line. He had acquired a solid base which was as much a home as it was an academic setting. And he had gained two friends, F. W. Deakin, the Warden, and George Katkov, a College Fellow, who recognized his great human qualities and the contribution he might make to Russian studies, if only he could be let alone.

Let alone he was. "It was obvious that he didn't like administration and routine," Footman recalls. He was given few chores to perform and those he had, he liked: buying books and periodicals for the Center and setting up a reading room. At first he could scarcely participate in the weekly college seminars; his first attempt to talk on Soviet literature ended in mid-lecture, when "he dried up from sheer nerves," according to Footman. The following term, however, he got through some seminars and even began teaching Russian to four or five St. Antony graduate students. This class, which was "more like a family party," says Footman, had to be kept secret from the university's Faculty of Medieval and Modern Languages, which is in charge of teaching Russian literature and language at Oxford. Later, Max was to take on a number of students for tutorials, and to supervise theses, with the encouragement of the Faculty.

He cheered up and drank a bit less. He took to accompanying Footman, who was a racing enthusiast, to the half-dozen tracks outside Oxford. Max was not interested in horses. He would head straight for the cheapest enclosure and begin talking to the working-class fans, while stuffing himself with whelks, winkles, and jellied eels.

That Max should have found a haven in the heart of Oxford was a miracle wrought by Bill Deakin. St. Antony's was Deakin's creation. He had become its first warden in 1950 at the request of the then University Vice Chancellor, Maurice Bowra, when it was established as the first graduate college in Oxford. Deakin, who had recently visited graduate schools in the United States, wanted to establish regional studies centers on the American model at a single Oxford college. The university had raised money from private French sources for St. Antony's, which was full of foreigners of every description. In short, it was a thoroughly untraditional and unsnobbish place.

Max was more open with foreigners than with his English colleagues about his attitude toward Oxford. Kolakowski, who first met him there on a visit from Poland in 1958, recalls: "He would occasionally burst out with his intense dislike for Oxford—the aristocratic, arrogant, self-confident, self-satisfied Oxonian university milieu. Though he had good friends at Oxford he felt, as a working-class man, that he didn't belong there. St. Antony's was different."

Max held Bill Deakin exempt from his class prejudice, so much so that when, after Max's death, I mentioned this trait of Max's to him, he reacted with astonishment and disbelief. Max had enormous respect for Deakin, an historian eleven years his senior who had led the first British Military Mission to Tito in 1943, during the partisan fighting, and who later served as First Secretary at the British Embassy in Belgrade. Max was warmed by Deakin's evident affection for him and by his unswerving support during the years when Max was often incapacitated by drink. Max's unreliability and unruliness meant nothing to Deakin, who delighted in his original mind, his idiosyncrasies, and his spirit of devilry. Seeing the two friends together, as I sometimes did, one had the impression that though they had traveled a very long distance to meet, they were amazingly alike in temperament. With Deakin's support Max was elected to an "Official Fellowship" at St. Antony's in 1960, which gave him membership in the college's governing body and, in effect, life tenure, without imposing teaching obligations beyond those he voluntarily assumed.

Max was extremely fond of Pussy Deakin, Bill's Rumanian wife. "I was a foreigner and hence, to him, classless," she says. Exotic, beautiful, intelligent, Pussy was, I believe, Max's first ideal of a woman. She made frequent efforts to straighten him out, scolding when he arrived, tight, for dinner or with buttons missing from his jacket and shirt. She also badgered him to get married. Max told her: "With my background—just listen to the way I talk—and my intellect, who could I find? And I like sophisticated, good-looking women." For his part, Bill urged him to patch things up with his mother and father, with whom he had virtually broken relations. He would dutifully go off to Sheffield, where his parents then lived, but the excursions would end in a row. Though Max would continue to return to his parents' home from time to time, he remained estranged from his father.

It is not glib psychologizing, I think, to suggest that in George Katkov, Max found a Russian father. This was, simply, the best thing that ever happened to Max. The two men had extraordinary rapport. Both were originals, the one a tall, mustachioed, hugely impressive *ancien régime* Russian *intelligent,* the other a prodigious offshoot of the British working classes. They talked constantly, excitedly, and at breathtaking speed, their conversation a puzzlement to the outsider seeking to follow the permutations of their interest in Russia. Max was always testing his Russian against Katkov's superb command of his native language, Max correcting his elder (by twenty-one years) and being corrected in a game that never seemed to tire either one.

A grand-nephew of Mikhail Katkov, the nineteenth-century conservative publisher, Georgi Mikhailich (as Max always called him) had emigrated to England in 1939, settling in Oxford after the war. A philosopher and historian, G.M. had worked for the BBC before becoming a University Lecturer in Soviet Institutions and a Fellow of St. Antony's. He had come to know Max in the early 1950's, and it was he who first helped haul Max out of what Pussy Deakin called "his dark hole" at Leeds by recommending him to St. Antony's. A man of immense kindness and generosity of feeling, G.M. drew Max into the light and warmth of his family circle in Oxford.

These generalities hardly do justice to the singular charm of evenings spent at the Katkovs on Chalfont Road. For well over a decade Max had dinner there virtually every night he was at Oxford. I too came to know the pleasures of those evenings, when Max proudly extended the hospitality of the Katkovs to include a visiting American friend. Out of a hopelessly poky back kitchen would come a plenitude of Russian dishes, concocted and laid out on the long dining table by Elisabeth, G.M.'s wife. Dinner could go on for hours in the Russian fashion, the two men taking up their discourse where they left off, against a background of teasing and jokes played on Max by the four Katkov daughters, Tanya, Nina, Madeleine, and Helen, nicknamed Chepupakha (Vladimir Nabokov's rendering of the Mock Turtle in his translation of *Alice in Wonderland*). Max was manifestly a member of the family. Yet he never came to dinner unbidden; he waited every day for G.M. to phone and invite him. Otherwise, he would not come.

In 1956 Max made one of his periodic plunges into a new language.* This time he chose one of the most daunting, Hungarian. He had an immersion system which he had devised: he holed up in his rooms at the college and with a Hungarian grammar and dictionary in hand he taught himself the language in six weeks—a remarkable feat. As it happened, he was soon to be able to put his passive knowledge to active use.

It is characteristic of Deakin that after the Soviet invasion of Hungary in 1956, he was the first to conceive and act upon the idea of bringing refugee Hungarian university students to Britain to continue their studies. Having obtained backing from London University and established an Inter-university Committee, Bill left for Vienna with guarantees of places in all British universities for Hungarian students. Upon arrival he received a cable from Max: "Please let me come and join you." Max did go, and stayed for the two weeks it took to select the students and get them aboard planes to England. It was an impressive military-style operation, accomplished with a minimum of red tape. Max, who had stopped drinking for the duration of the operation, helped Bill interview the candidates. "Within a fortnight he was speaking reasonable Hungarian," Bill recalls. Max kept up with some of the students he helped bring to England. Among these, the poet George Gömörri established a Hungarian and Polish library at St. Antony's and under Max's guidance translated the poems from *Doctor Zhivago* into Hungarian.

It was G. M. Katkov who brought *Doctor Zhivago* to Max. The background was this. On a short trip to Moscow in 1956, G.M. had met with Pasternak; the poet told him that he had given the

*Before he died, Max had mastered fifteen modern languages and two classical ones, Latin and Greek. His greatest achievement was of course his perfect command of Russian, but he knew the other major Slavic languages in this descending order of proficiency: Czech, Serbo-Croat, Bulgarian, Polish. Of the Romance languages he knew French well and had a working knowledge of Italian, Spanish, Portuguese, and Rumanian that could be activated after a few days' contact with native speakers. His German was excellent. So was his modern Greek. He had a passive knowledge of Hungarian, Hebrew, and Welsh. (I am not counting his early speaking acquaintance with Romany and brief flurries with Ladino and Lallans.)

manuscript of a novel to the agent of the Italian publisher Feltrinelli. (Pasternak's farewell remark to the agent was: "You are as of now invited to my execution.") Pasternak was now concerned that Feltrinelli would not publish the book, especially since Pasternak expected to be forced by the Soviet authorities to instruct Feltrinelli to halt publication (eventually Pasternak sent such a cable, but Feltrinelli ignored it, publishing *Doctor Zhivago* in Italian in November 1957). He gave another copy of the manuscript to G.M., asking him to get it out of Russia in some secure way and to see to its translation and publication in England as quickly as possible.

Possible translators were discussed. Pasternak suggested Isaiah Berlin, who had translated Turgenev's short novel *First Love*. G.M. said he thought the Zhivago poems would present a special translation problem. The poet was not worried. "It's quite easy," he said. "Just look at my translations of Rilke." "Easy for you," said G.M.

G.M. then suggested "someone quite special" to translate the poetry. "There's one man, a poet, who is completely bilingual: Vladimir Nabokov." Pasternak said, "That won't work; he's too jealous of my wretched position in this country to do it properly."*

G.M. recalls: "I gave Pasternak my promise that *Doctor Zhivago* would be well translated and I kissed him on it." The manuscript duly arrived in Oxford and G.M. had a chance to read it through. "I saw that it would shake the literary world," he says. He went to Isaiah Berlin and told him that Pasternak wanted the

---

*He was right. Nabokov was to publicly ridicule *Doctor Zhivago* and mock Pasternak's suffering at the hands of his Soviet persecutors by producing a parody of Pasternak's famous poem "The Nobel Prize" (1959). A stanza of Pasternak's poem reads: "But what wicked thing have I done, / I, the 'murderer' and 'villain'? / I, who force the whole world to cry / Over my beautiful land." In his parody Nabokov referred to some of the critical reaction to his own *Lolita*: "But what wicked thing have I done? / I, the seducer and villain? / I, who force the whole world to dream / Of my poor girl child." Nabokov, in a final stanza, suggests that though he is out of synchronization with the Soviet era, it is ultimately to him that Russia will erect a monument (*Vozdushnyye Puti*, II, New York, 1961, and *Newsweek*, June 25, 1962).

book translated and published quickly. "That's all nonsense," Berlin said. "It's an interesting novel, but whether it's published now, or fifteen years from now, doesn't matter."

G.M. says: "I decided to give the manuscript to Max, who had never done any translations, to test his reaction. I didn't tell him that I was thinking of him as a possible translator. The novel was an enormous shock to him; he was simply electrified. The Zhivago poems meant much less to him. He had no inkling of poetry at the time, but it would gradually grow on him." In fact, Max was to produce plain prose versions of the poems that are, in my view, the best translations that have been made so far in English. (They appeared only in the British edition of *Doctor Zhivago*.)

To test his own potential as a translator, Max studied three pages of the book. He then went for a walk during which he told to himself what he had read in English, as if recounting it to friends. After that, he came to G.M. and wrote it out without referring to the Russian text. The test was a success.

At this time, several other copies of the manuscript were circulating in Europe, some mysteriously, causing no end of confusion and leading to the publication in 1958 of an unauthorized edition in Russian. According to Max's friend, Leopold Labedz, at least two British publishers turned the book down when it was submitted to them by Feltrinelli. Meanwhile G.M. had brought Manya Harari into the picture. Manya immediately understood the book's importance and obtained publication rights for Harvill, the small house which she had founded with Marjorie Villiers and which had become a subsidiary of the giant Collins firm. Labedz recalls that at this time "Collins had no idea what they had in *Doctor Zhivago*."

Since speed had been requested by Pasternak, it was decided that the book needed two translators. G.M. brought Max and Manya together for a collaboration and a friendship that was to endure until Manya's death in 1969. To translate *Doctor Zhivago*, they decided to do alternate chapters, then revise each other's work. G.M. was the ultimate arbiter, going over everything for accuracy and nuance.

Max repaired for a time to a room in his parents' house near

Sheffield, while Manya worked on her chapters at her beautiful town house on Catherine Place in London. There were difficulties, G.M. recalls. Max was very slow and careful, while Manya went forward boldly and confidently, making a great many mistakes. The two met over each other's versions in Manya's top-floor eyrie, a low-ceilinged, immensely untidy little room that the two chain-smoking translators kept filled with smoke. An open box of chocolate creams and one of Manya's poodles, breathlessly yapping on the ash-strewn floor, completed the picture of the work place where for fifteen years Manya edited for the Harvill Press some of the most important works of contemporary Russian letters, including Konstantin Paustovsky's memoirs, Mikhail Bulgakov's *The Master and Margarita,* and several books by Andrei Sinyavsky.

Manya was a small-boned, frail-looking woman of great distinction and beauty; she was also one of the most strong-willed and principled people I have ever known. She had been born Manya Benenson into a wealthy St. Petersburg Jewish family that emigrated to England during the First World War. A Roman Catholic convert, she was married to Ralph Harari, a member of the Sephardic banking family. I had an unforgettable early glimpse of her in November 1955 in Moscow, where I was on my first journalistic assignment in the Soviet Union and where Manya was making her first return visit to her native land. I found her looking very small, helpless, and cold in the drafty lobby of the National Hotel. She had somehow lost her fur coat, she told me. Actually, I believe, she had given it away. On a later visit her generosity got her into trouble and she was twice arrested. On a trip to Yalta, she had been cut to the heart by the plight of some beggar women huddling outside a church. She was determined to help them. She gave them money and clothing, even managing to set them up in a hotel as she wandered through the town vainly seeking to buy a blanket for the infant of one of the beggars. In the Soviet Union, such an unheard-of act of charity by a foreigner could only serve to rouse the ire of the authorities. Manya's effort was as foolhardy as it was painfully touching. Though Max was a vastly more contained person than Manya, they must have encountered each other on the same deep level of excruciated concern.

Manya and Max finished the translation of *Doctor Zhivago* in a year. In January 1959, after a visitor to Russia brought Pasternak a copy of the British edition of his novel, he wrote to Billy Collins, the publisher, that he was "eternally" the "enthralled debtor" of his English translators. Pasternak was a judge of translation; he had produced the classic Russian translations of seven Shakespeare plays. I myself can testify to Pasternak's enthusiasm. In May 1959, when I visited him in Peredelkino, bringing messages from Manya and Max, he held out his arms to me with extraordinary fervor, saying: "I embrace my translators." At the height of the Soviet attack on him for having published *Doctor Zhivago* abroad, he took the quite risky step of instructing Feltrinelli to send Manya and Max each a gift of £4000 out of his royalties. The sum was a fortune to Max, who like Manya had received a minimal fee for the translation, but he gave £2000 to G.M., who was in the hospital at the time.

The Harari-Hayward translation of *Doctor Zhivago* was published by Harvill in England in September 1958 and in an "Americanized" version by Pantheon Books in the United States in October. The same month Pasternak was awarded the Nobel Prize for Literature. Early reviews were ecstatic. In London the *Times* asked, "A new *War and Peace?*" while the *Daily Express* declared that "no novel of this century has drawn such worldwide acclaim immediately upon publication." Meanwhile the mounting attack on Pasternak in the Soviet Union served in the West to sharpen both support for the author and interest in his book.

It was in the light of all this publicity that Max prepared to leave for the United States, to take up a research fellowship at the Harvard Russian Research Center which was to run from mid-September to the end of June. Though he had sought the appointment, he was balking at the last moment. He was sure his plane would crash. His friends Dan and Winnie Davin suggested that he hold an American Wake before leaving. They explained that this was an Irish custom that had been established during the potato famine, when the Irish had been forced to flee to America in large numbers; an American Wake was traditionally held each time a member of a family departed. The wake duly took place in Max's rooms at St. Antony's. During the party he asked Davin, who was head of the Clarendon Press, to witness a hastily scrawled will that left his books, and what possessions he had, to the college. For the rest of his life, Max would write a similar makeshift will every time he left Oxford. When his Ukrainian scout cleaned his rooms he would find the wills under various objects or squirreled away in cabinets. At the end Max made a proper will, in which, after a legacy to his mother, he carried out his original intention.

The morning after the American Wake, Pussy Deakin had someone rouse Max and bring him to the Warden's house so she could sober him up. As she had cautioned him earlier to buy some new clothes for America, he arrived in a Marks & Spencer suit that still had white tailor's stitching on the pockets. It was the only set of clothes he brought with him for the hard New England winter. He left, as he usually did, with only a flight bag that held a few books and papers.

Shortly after Max's arrival at Harvard, *The New Yorker* of November 15, 1958, published a review of *Doctor Zhivago* by Edmund Wilson, America's foremost literary critic. Wilson wrote: "*Doctor Zhivago* will, I believe, come to stand as one of the great events in man's literary and moral history . . . a great act of faith in art and the human spirit." But readers of the translation, he cautioned, would scarcely be able to come to the same conclusion as Wilson, who had read the book in Russian.

"The reader of the Pantheon translation," Wilson wrote, "should be told that *Doctor Zhivago* is a richer, a solider, a subtler, and more intense work than he will be able to find out from this version of it. So much of the detail has been scrapped, so many of the descriptions have been dismantled, and so many of the conversations have been telescoped that there are moments when one could almost imagine the translators have been doing a job for the *Reader's Digest.*"

To substantiate his charge, Wilson offered a number of examples of mistranslation. One was a howler for which Manya and Max were responsible. A reference in the book to Arzamas, a literary society to which Pushkin belonged, had been identified only as a place name. Wilson also picked up a few other errors, the worst being that Lara's hair had been called "dark" (a confusion that had been prompted by Pasternak's description of her hair as scattered on a pillow: "the smoke of its beauty . . .") and that gold bells on fire towers had been identified as "the golden tops of belfries." Six other translation errors noted by Wilson had not been made by the British translators. They had been introduced in the course of "Americanizing" the Harari-Hayward version for Pantheon. The mistakes do not appear in the British edition.

Most of Wilson's objections came down to questions of interpretation. In a typical quibble, he wrote: "The intent observation of Pasternak is constantly sacrificed. The rich soil 'which shows brown in the sun with varying shades of chocolate and coffee' is turned into 'the black soil . . . shimmered with rich golden browns.'" But Wilson's translation of Pasternak's *"smuglela na solntse shokoladno-kofeinym otlivom"* is too flat and mechanical. The American edition's "shimmering" is not quite right either, though hardly worth all the fuss. The original Harari-Hayward version as it appeared in England is closer to the Russian: "the black soil . . . was sun-burnt to a coffee-chocolate brown." ("Sun-burnt" is quite ingenious.)

The worst howler was committed by Wilson himself in his review. Following a long passage in which he attempted to extrapolate Pasternak's religious views from the novel, he wrote: "The translators made Zhivago say to his love when they part for the last time, 'Farewell . . . until we meet in the next world,' but this is not in the text and would be contrary to Zhivago's cosmology. What Pasternak makes him say is that he will never see her again 'in life'; he merely bids her 'farewell in this world,' which does not imply meeting in Heaven."

The "next world" is indisputably in the Russian text: *"Proshchai . . . do svidaniya na tom svete."* The phrase is simple and straightforward; it would be clearly understood by a first-year Russian student. Wilson's mistake does not seem to have resulted from a hasty reading. He had apparently pondered the line, which seemed to him to confound his notion of Pasternak's "cosmology."

So gross a mistake raised the question—later to be pursued with a vengeance by Vladimir Nabokov—of Wilson's proficiency in Russian. It would seem that this most erudite man's great weakness was that he loved to display linguistic expertise he scarcely possessed. A favorite pastime of his late years was fiddling about with exotic languages—notably Russian, Hungarian, and Hebrew. Where Russian was concerned he sometimes relied on people who had little to offer by way of linguistic or literary competence but the fact that they were native Russian speakers. Many of Wilson's attempts to wring significance out of Pasternak's use of the number five ("the five barless windows of the house in Siberia are the five wounds of Jesus") and his choice of Christian names and surnames ("It is obvious that Pasternak wants to suggest *zhivoy*, 'alive, living' by the name Zhivago") appear to have been inspired by Evgenia Lehovich, a ballet teacher who later collaborated with Wilson on a piece called "Legend and Symbol in *Doctor Zhivago*" (*Encounter*, June 1959). (Decoding of this kind is best left until the author is dead. Max showed me a letter written by Pasternak that contained a laconic comment on the "Legend and Symbol" article. "Whoever has seen such symbols in *Doctor Zhivago*," Pasternak wrote, "has not read my novel.")

The most damaging part of Wilson's review of *Doctor Zhivago* was of course not his catalogue of translation errors, but his charge that the Harari-Hayward version had debased Pasternak's book. This was nonsense. Though the original translation as modified by its Americanizers lost some of its elegance and sharpness and was coarsened by some banality of language, both the British and the American versions are remarkably true to the original.

I have looked at the files kept by Max and the Harvill Press in the wake of the Wilson review. Manya was outraged; she shot off a letter to Wilson, commenting in detail on each of his charges of mistranslation, politely calling attention to his own mistake and pointing out that six of the errors had been made in New York, without consultation with the original translators. The reply from the irrepressible Wilson is not in the files, but Marjorie Villiers,

Manya's partner at Harvill, commented on it in a letter to Helen
Wolff. She and her husband Kurt were Pasternak's editors at
Pantheon. "Manya has had a letter from Edmund Wilson," Villiers wrote. "He doesn't seem to know Russian thoroughly as he
makes nine mistakes which one would think he could avoid in
criticizing a specific sentence. . . . He also refers to a sentence not
in our edition which is plainly wrong." Meanwhile, Kurt Wolff
had written to Wilson, thanking him for his rave review in *The
New Yorker*. He told Wilson that some of the errors he had
mentioned had been corrected in the British version at the last
minute, but that the translators had neglected to inform Pantheon of the changes.*

No defense of the Harari-Hayward translation was ever made
in public. In her letter to Helen Wolff, Villiers wrote: "We
understood from Max that you did not want *The New Yorker* to
get a reply to Wilson's article so Manya has shouldered the six
inaccurate 'improvements' you made to our text, and Wilson's
own piece of nonsense about heaven. [Edward] Crankshaw who
has seen both texts has been boiling to reply to it; but as he is
going to Russia I daresay he will forget to do so and we will not
remind him."

Wilson's review loomed large in Max's life. He was devastated
by the sweeping nature of the criticism. He felt that literary
people in America were under the impression that he had somehow spoiled *Doctor Zhivago*. One immediate result was that he
went on a bender in Cambridge that landed him in the hospital.
It was typical of him that a few months later he cheerfully agreed
to meet with Wilson over cocktails in Boston. They never discussed the *Doctor Zhivago* translation and soon became drinking
buddies. When Max came to visit me on Cape Cod in the early
1960's, Wilson would sometimes invite Max to his house in
Wellfleet, where the two met in the friendliest way.

In 1965, it was to Max that Wilson turned for help when

---

*Taking into account the handful of actual errors detected by Wilson, Max later some-
what revised both the British and the American editions.

Nabokov exultantly nailed Wilson for the mistakes in Russian he had made in his critique of Nabokov's translation of *Eugene Onegin*. Though Wilson was beyond rescue for his out-and-out errors, Max formulated for him some ingenious ripostes on disputed questions of pronunciation (including the comical rejoinder that Nabokov favored the Minsk accent over that of St. Petersburg), for which Wilson, without naming Max, credited "a professional English linguist who specializes in Russian" (*New York Review of Books*, August 26, 1965).

My first meeting with Max came about two weeks after he had been hit by the Wilson review. Marshall Shulman, then Associate Director of the Russian Research Center at Harvard, had had the wonderful idea of sending him to see me in New York. Max arrived one November morning at my door dressed in a U.S. Navy surplus pea jacket that had been given to him in Cambridge by a pitying Walter Laqueur, a very much smaller man than Max. The jacket had been bleached pinkish by age and, possibly, washing. All but one button was missing. The most striking thing to me about his appearance were the long streaks of ash, like snail trails, that covered the entire front of his dark suit. His fine and, yes, aristocratic face was ashen as well. His malaise was frightful. He never looked me in the eye. He asked if I had any Guinness in the apartment; he settled for Bourbon. Once installed in the darkest corner of the living room he drawled out, "Well, I suppose you're one of the American admirers of Pasternak." I was not yet accustomed to the British ironic mode. Taken aback, I said, "I am, and so what?"

Like most of his women friends, I was touched by his obvious helplessness in all the practical matters of everyday life. I bought him at Macy's a green duffel coat with a hood, which cheered him up. And I put him to work on a collection of Mayakovsky's lyrical verse that I had undertaken in 1958. A novice, and with little knowledge of Russian at the time, I had commissioned the Irish poet and translator George Reavey to translate the poems I had selected. He had already produced some versions, which looked very odd to me. Roman Jakobson confirmed my suspicions: they were full of frightful mistakes. It remained for me to persuade

Reavey to make vast numbers of corrections without hurting his feelings. Max stood by while I softened George up with whiskey and compliments on his more felicitous renderings. Then Max moved in for the extraction; a little Russian patter, a reassuring smile, and the whole offending passage had been painlessly removed. Reavey was a jolly fellow who enjoyed these sessions, which lasted through much of the winter, as much as we did. At the same time, Max had begun translating some of the poetry and the play *The Bedbug,* which we had decided to include in the book. One day as I was finishing my introduction, Max electrified me by arriving at my apartment with a Hebrew grammar and with language records, which he proceeded to play on my hi-fi. It was his first immersion in that language.

Besides the Mayakovsky book, *The Bedbug and Selected Poetry,* Max and I were to work together on two anthologies of contemporary Russian literature in translation and a volume of Andrei Voznesensky's poetry—a translation project involving six American poets who knew no Russian. We were a good team, I believe. By the end of our collaboration we were so attuned to each other's ideas that we could write a perfectly seamless essay together. Max was a solitary man who, in those years, had to have company in order to work. "He needed a setting," Deakin remembers. I provided some serious company and a setting in which he felt comfortable.

Max loved New York. For the next decade he managed to come back nearly every year for lectures, scholarly conferences, and short-term research or teaching appointments at Columbia University. He had quite soon become a popular figure in literary circles. In Oxford he had kept to himself and a few friends; he never went to London if he could avoid it. In New York I had introduced him to some literary friends who liked him and who invited him to dinners and parties.

In general, Max felt comfortable in America, which he perceived as a classless society. It was a relief to him that no one cared or was even aware of his proletarian background, or associated his way of speaking with class. How important accent was to him was brought home to me when I took him to a party at the house of an American girlfriend of mine who had attended an English public school. After chatting a bit with our hostess, Max whispered to me with a look of panic: "She talks like the Queen!"

British friends were impressed with how quickly he had become a New Yorker. Here is how it looked to Hingley: "Manhattan was his favorite village, and he was established there when I first arrived on American soil. I put up at the same hotel, the Chelsea, while he introduced me to the natives and purveyed instructions in the language. Without his help I would never have known how to interpret the amiably ferocious query 'On?' as uttered by the proprietor of a Twenty-third Street delicatessen in reply to my order for a pastrami sandwich. Instructed by Max, I at once knew that my answer should be 'rye' or 'pumpernickel.' I quickly discovered that I only had to mention his name for all doors to be opened. 'He cuts a wide swath here,' someone told me. It was no overstatement."

Dan Davin, who came to New York frequently on business for the Clarendon Press, used to take long instructive walks with Max, who would feed him such information as, "New York is like a boiling kettle whose lid is tightly fastened down by Irish policemen." One of Max's favorite New York stories was associated with a night he once spent with Davin in the city's Irish bars. As Davin retells it, Max woke up in his room at the Chelsea with a shocking headache, shrouded with guilt. Someone was knocking on the door. He tried to ignore the noise, burying his head in his pillow. The pounding continued. Finally he got up and opened the door a crack. "Who's there?" he asked. A deep voice was heard replying, "The exterminator." Max knew he had come for him.*

Still, he was lonesome for St. Antony's. To Bill Barker he complained that people were being too nice to him. "I'm nostalgic for the discomforts of England," he wrote. He missed G.M., with whom he exchanged letters several times a week. He often

---

*British readers may wish to know that in the United States the exterminator comes for rats and cockroaches.

reminisced about the Horse and Jockey and the Gardener's Arms in North Parade, pubs which functioned, when Max was in Oxford, as seminar rooms for students of Russian. His first winter in America was the only time he ever talked with me about the misery and trauma of his childhood, his personal life, and his attachment to G.M. and Bill Deakin. America had been an opening-up and Max was at his most vulnerable. He was alive with pain.

Max was in Oxford in mid-August of 1960 when Olga Ivinskaya (Pasternak's "Lara") and her daughter Irina were arrested on trumped-up charges of currency speculation two months after the poet's death. Fear for Ivinskaya's safety had been an obsession in the final years of Pasternak's life. "If, God forbid, they should arrest Olga," he wrote to a friend in the West, "all tocsins should ring, for an attack on her is in fact a blow at me."

Max took Pasternak's injunction to heart. His energy was astonishing. He traveled around Britain persuading prominent people like Bertrand Russell to appeal to Khrushchev on the two women's behalf. When he learned that Eleanor Roosevelt was passing through Paris, he flew to France. Her assistant, Diana Michaelis, recalled how Mrs. Roosevelt had been impressed with Max's meticulous presentation of the facts. In spite of her concern for civil rights, she had never before attempted to intervene with the Soviets on behalf of a prisoner of the regime. But she readily agreed to write a letter to Khrushchev along the lines he suggested. Meanwhile, the Western press was full of stories of the martyrdom of Ivinskaya, who had already served four years in the camps for her association with Pasternak. All this pressure and publicity did not prevent the Soviet authorities from sentencing Ivinskaya to eight years and her daughter to three. It may, however, have contributed to the decision to release them early, Irina in 1962 and her mother in 1964.

Max's authority and conviction made him extraordinarily effective at arousing public opinion on behalf of imprisoned Soviet intellectuals. He was to engage in this kind of political action one more time, when Andrei Sinyavsky and Yuli Daniel were arrested in 1965. Max and Leo Labedz put everything aside in order to gather signatures to appeals and protests. Max, who was a frequent contributor to Leo's journal, *Survey,* collaborated with his friend on a book about the notorious 1966 trial of the two writers.

Max's interest in Sinyavsky and Daniel dated back to the death of Pasternak. I recall studying with Max some shattering pictures of the procession to the grave site; he identified for me two men who had helped carry the coffin: Sinyavsky and Daniel. We were soon to become involved with them, without knowing it. I obtained and published in our anthology, *Dissonant Voices in Soviet Literature,* a powerful *samizdat* story, "This Is Moscow Speaking," by Daniel, who was known to us only by the pseudonym Nikolai Arzhak. *The Trial Begins* and stories by Abram Tertz, which Max had translated for Harvill, were revealed at the trial to have been written by Sinyavsky.

After Sinyavsky's release from the camps and departure from Russia for France, he became "Max's émigré," says Edward Kline. Max felt such a kinship with Sinyavsky that he was moved to collaborate on a translation of the exceptionally difficult *A Voice from the Chorus.* Kline, who worked most closely with Max in the last decade of his life, recalls that Max wanted to come to Sinyavsky's aid when the writer was attacked in émigré circles for his book on Pushkin. Though Max hardly ever agreed to review books, he came forward with his essay on Sinyavsky, "Pushkin, Gogol, and the Devil" (reproduced in this volume), which is one of his finest pieces of literary criticism.

Max needed to bring his work round full circle in this way. At the center, always, was the figure of Pasternak. In the mid-1970's he persuaded Helen Wolff, now at Harcourt Brace Jovanovich, and Marjorie Villiers, at Harvill, to publish Alexander Gladkov's *Meetings with Pasternak.* Max felt that the book had been undeservedly slighted—it would surely never have been published in English without his intervention—and although he was exhausted after completing his translation of 1,300 pages of Nadezhda Mandelstam's memoirs, he consented to translate Gladkov. He then vowed never to do another translation. Shortly thereafter, the manuscript of Olga Ivinskaya's memoir *A Captive of Time* was brought to him. He felt obliged to do it. He told Villiers, "It's unfinished business." He reminded her that Pasternak had said one must behave to Ivinskaya as one would to him.

In 1962 I returned from a short trip to Russia full of enthusiasm about the work of the young writers and poets who were breaking down all the conventions of orthodox Soviet literature. On my way home I met with Max in Geneva and persuaded him to edit with me an anthology of the exciting new Russian writing which we ultimately entitled *Halfway to the Moon,* after a story by Vasili Aksyonov. I also wanted to lure Max into a scheme to translate the work of the young Russian poet Andrei Voznesensky in collaboration with some American poets. Max would have to act as the linguistic interpreter since the Americans I had in mind at the time, W. H. Auden, Richard Wilbur, and Stanley Kunitz, knew no Russian. Max thought it couldn't be done. I had brought Voznesensky's poetry from Moscow and he pronounced it too difficult, too allusive, and too full of linguistic play to cross the cultural divide. Still, he was willing to try. In New York the following winter, just as Khrushchev had undertaken a vast campaign against the unorthodox new writers, Max met with the three American poets. Together they produced some splendid Voznesensky translations which we included in our anthology. Meanwhile, I raised some foundation money so that we could pay our original poets, and a few more, including Jean Garrigue and William Jay Smith, to translate a whole book of the Russian's verse.

Voznesensky, who arrived in England on a short visit in the spring of 1963, had another idea altogether. At the time, his English was rudimentary and he knew little about poetry in English. But he had heard that Robert Lowell had refused Lyndon Johnson's invitation to a White House party. When I joined him and Max in London to talk about the projected book, he declared that he wanted to be translated by Lowell. This, Max and I were determined to avoid, having seen some of Lowell's "imitations" of Osip Mandelstam. I explained to a resistant Russian that if Voznesensky had written "horse" Lowell would render it as "raspberry"—a prospect that Andrei professed to relish.

Max came to London from Oxford only two or three times during Andrei's visit. Max seemed frail, but I had no idea how sick he was. On one occasion he took Andrei and me on a tour of Westminster Abbey. I had never been inside before. Neither had Voznesensky, who was in England for the first time. We walked through it in silence, all of us plainly overwhelmed. When we emerged, Max asked Andrei, "Well, what do you think?" He gave a curious answer. "It reminds me of Pasternak," he said, unknowingly touching Max's heart.

Max nearly died of drink that spring. He moved into the Katkov house, where G.M. nursed him. The doctor told Max that if he didn't swear off alcohol at once he had no time at all to live. When he felt better he called on Pussy Deakin and told her what the doctor had said. When she asked what he planned to do, he replied that he would take a little walk and think it over. After a time he returned and told Pussy he had made up his mind. "If God gave me this brain," he said, "I'm not going to spoil it with drink." He stopped drinking—and smoking—then and there. It was a heroic achievement.

In July, by way of distraction, I proposed to Max that we go to Austria, where Auden had a house, in order to work with him on the Voznesensky translations. Max liked the idea. He had been vastly impressed with Auden in New York when they had worked on a version of Andrei's "Parabolic Ballad."

The theme was set for our whole stay when we were greeted along the highway out of Vienna airport by a series of billboards flashing one word, the brand name of an Austrian ice cream that is strikingly similar to the four-letter Russian word for ass. There was no end to the laughter provoked by that sign, which pursued us nearly all the way to Wystan Auden's house near Kirchstetten.

He was waiting for us, standing on a hillock with a spade in his hand, a magnificent edifice. I now know he looked just as Voznesensky later described him, like a burnt-out cathedral. I wondered what Max would make of him *in situ*. I had known Wystan for years and had visited him when he and Chester Kallman lived in Forio d'Ischia, so his domestic arrangements could scarcely hold any surprises for me. But for Max? I had no idea how much of Wystan's work he had read or indeed whether he was aware that he was a homosexual. And I had absolutely no intention of preparing Max for anything; he was always irritated at me when I volunteered any information about our friends' love affairs or breakups, let alone sexual preferences—he regarded all such talk as low gossip.

Wystan brought us round to the house, where he introduced us to a twenty-year-old boy in a bikini who was seated on the ground with his back to a wall. Wystan identified him as the boyfriend of Chester Kallman, Wystan's own long-time lover (as he helpfully explained to Max), who was currently living in Greece. Chester had dispatched the boy, who was Greek and spoke no English, to Kirchstetten so that he might recover from tuberculosis. The boy, we learned, was an *evzone*, on military sick leave. Now without his skirt, his tasseled hat, pompoms on his shoes, and other accoutrements of the Greek military honor guard, he looked disarmed and depressed.

Max took this in with perfect composure. Soon Wystan was all business. He and Max got down to work in the middle of a field where Wystan had plunked down some new garden furniture he was proud of. Max and I had already established a system for working with the poets who were contributing to our book. We prepared some literal versions; when the poet had selected what he or she liked, Max would do the crucial work of explaining the associations, the exotic references, the slang, the jargon, and also the obscenities sometimes concealed in Voznesensky's rhymes. Wystan was exceptionally demanding. He wanted what he called prosodic models. These were transliterations of the Russian text into the English alphabet, with an interlinear English translation in the same word order as the Russian original.

Every day of our stay Wystan sat out in the field studying the Russian rhyme scheme on the prosodic model we had prepared overnight, while Max read the poem to him in Russian. Then they would sort out the sense. It was a joy to hear the two men work together, both so quick to penetrate the living heart of a line in brisk, commonsensical tones, both so English, after all.

Wystan again tried to shock Max. After the translation sessions the poet would sometimes read bits of his new work to us, mostly from *Around the House,* which he was putting together then. Fixing Max in the eye he read "The Geography of the House": "Lifted off the potty, / Infants from their mothers / Hear their first impartial / Words of worldly praise: / Hence, to start the morning / With a satisfactory / Dump is a good omen / All our adult days."

Max was politely appreciative. Nothing Wystan said could disconcert him. Wystan tried a similar tactic with Voznesensky when I accompanied him to their first meeting, which took place in Auden's apartment on St. Mark's Place in New York. Wystan had immediately launched into a monologue on the problems of translation, while the Russian watched him silently, plainly awestruck. Suddenly Wystan asked Andrei, "Now what would you do in Russian with the saying 'he doesn't know his ass from a hole in the ground'?" Though by now Andrei understood English quite well, he turned to me for elucidation. I fumbled for words, gripped by hysterical laughter as the emergent image grew starker as I translated it. Andrei joined me in laughter that may have seemed excessive to our host. Andrei asked for a sheet of paper, wrote out his rendering of the saying, signed it, and presented it to Wystan. When I reproduced the translation for Max he pronounced it to be a true gem of Russian obscenity.

I often was not present when Max met with the poets who contributed to *Antiworlds,* our Voznesensky volume. Richard Wilbur, who provided some of our most beautiful versions, gave William Jay Smith an account of his collaboration with Max: "With all the precision that his expert counseling demanded, Max was incredibly leisurely in his approach. Each time he came into the living room, he went like a dog to his favorite spot at the end of the sofa, sat down, and launched immediately into a relaxed conversation on a wide variety of subjects. The two men circled around the poems for a good while, but when they finally came to examine them in detail, the information that Max provided was thorough and exact. Max operated like a tuning fork, giving the proper pitch of each word and assisting the poet in not straying from it."

Bill Smith, who contributed the most verse to *Antiworlds* and who later worked with Max and Vera Dunham on a second volume of Voznesensky's poetry, *Nostalgia for the Present,* has written a tribute to Max entitled "A Prince among Translators." "During our sessions Max never once consulted a Russian-English dictionary," Smith wrote. "He was himself a walking dictionary, able to give the equivalent of a word not only in English but in French, Spanish, Italian, German. . . . He served not only as a dictionary but as an encyclopedia, giving complete information on each poem's place in the work of Voznesensky, its place alongside the work of other contemporary poets and poets of the past, its historical, political, sociological and scientific allusions. . . . His romantic nature had in it something of the wide-eyed openness of the child, which made for his unrestrained humor and his constantly fresh approach to poetry."

The poet Stanley Kunitz worked with Max, first on Voznesensky translations and later on the volume they produced entitled *Poems of Akhmatova.* "Max's poetic insights were greater when he came to Akhmatova," says Kunitz, "perhaps because the interpretative difficulties were more severe. Voznesensky was somewhere in the background and could be consulted and his language was closer to the contemporary idiom. Though Max had always been just and precise in his readings of Voznesensky, he had not felt the need to make a creative leap. With Akhmatova he was capable of working within the poet's imagination." Kunitz asked Max to indicate in his literal versions any word that had interior ambiguities. "Max was very excited about doing that. In his literals he gave every possible connotation of a word, rooting out the sense. His approach was that of a scholar studying a text; he could have been working with Etruscan."

Like so many people who knew Max, Kunitz was impressed by his modesty. "He was very sure of himself as a linguist and felt that he was accurately rendering the sense of a line. But I never felt he was competitive. He never asserted himself and I had to insist that his name appear on the title page of the Akhmatova volume."

Max frequently helped other translators. He was especially pleased to offer his assistance to beginners. "He had a way of making you feel that you were not importuning him—that the work itself was all-important," says Ellen de Kadt, who had turned to him for help in translating Roy Medvedev's *On Socialist Democracy*. Max, who had a powerful didactic streak, asked her to read what she had done out loud. "That way I could hear every word or expression that jarred in English; I got some withering glances from Max during these readings. But when I finished the work he turned to me with such a look of gladness and gave me all the credit. 'You can really feel you've done it,' he said."

Harry Shukman's debut as a translator was a collaboration with Max on Yevgeni Shvarts's play *The Dragon*. "Working with him was like taking a holiday," Shukman recalls. "We would throw dialogue back and forth until we came up with a nice-sounding phrase. There was never any competitiveness. Some other master of the craft could have made you feel like dirt, but never once in our relationship did I feel overpowered by Max. He was the same with students, treating them with extreme gentleness; he was never cruel, even with the worst."

As I had with other friends of Max, I talked with Harry about the extraordinary charm Max exercised over people. After all, he had been a quiet, diffident, and, at times, markedly unsociable man. Yet he possessed a luminous charm that defied definition. It was Harry who put his finger on it. "For a long time I thought that Jews in the Soviet Union were Max's major interest in life," said Harry, who has made a specialty of that subject at Oxford. "Max talked with you about what mattered most to you as if nothing in the world interested him more."

By the late 1960's Max and I had completed our last collaborative effort, an expanded edition of our Voznesensky book, and I gradually began to lose the thread of Max's life. It started in Greece where I spent several months in 1968. In Athens one morning I had breakfast in an outdoor café with Max's friend

Dimitri Obolensky, who holds the Chair of Russian and Balkan History at Oxford. I told him I was overwhelmed by the beauty of Greece. "You ought to persuade Max to come here," he said. "Greece is the only substitute for Russia." I thought: it is for Dimitri perhaps—he's a Byzantinist—but for Max and me, never.

Still, there was something to the observation made by Dimitri, who is a Russian exile. I remembered it a few months later when Max and I escaped for a week from the New York winter to St. Martin, an island in the West Indies that made me yearn for the Cyclades. I talked then to Max about Greece, urged him to take a trip there, and told him about Dimitri's remark.

Before I knew it, he was gone. In my mind I could never really follow him to Greece. The whole of my life had taken its shape from Russia. Since I was barred from returning there—like Max, because of my writings—the pain of losing contact with the living country had never relented. Greece was light, beauty, and ancient history, but Russia was my *place,* here and now. Max had found another place. Some one of his friends who knew his life there will, I hope, pick up the narrative. I can only sketch in a few details.

He went for the first time in 1969 for a Russian cause. Suzanne Massie had invited him to join her in Greece so they might work together on an anthology of unofficial Leningrad poets. He also visited John Campbell, another St. Antony's Fellow, and an expert on Greece. During a trip through the mountain region around Epirus, Campbell told him: "If you live in Greece and look behind the pleasant surface, you will see that little has changed for the past two and a half thousand years." That is strong stuff. How could Max resist? When he learned Greek, first modern, then classical, he was mesmerized by the continuity of language. Soon he read Homer in Greek, and like so many travelers before him, he constantly compared past and present. Often, in the mornings when he lived in Spetsai, he would walk along the shore with his friend Jane Joyce and tell her stories out of the *Iliad.* He had committed pages of Homer to memory, much as he had learned Pasternak years before, and he could reproduce conversations between Zeus and Hera, and describe every detail of the armor of warriors in battle. He was critical of existing translations of Homer; during the last year of his life he wrote an elaborate proposal for a new translation of the *Iliad* which he wished to undertake, together with an introduction and commentaries on each book of the poem. He wrote to St. Antony's inquiring about how he might sever his relation to the college and he told friends he was considering giving up his British nationality and becoming a Greek citizen.

He set about building a little house on the Aegean island of Spetsai, fifty yards from the home of Jane Joyce and her husband Robert, a retired American diplomat. It was they who created the setting for Max's last years. They found the contractor to build his house and watched over every detail when he went away. Jane helped him pick the furniture and found a servant who would tidy up. When the house was finished and he had them over for dinner for the first and last time—it was their pleasure to tell the story —he served them an omelet and four different kinds of sardines, in cans.

Max was the island's intellectual and the resident foreigners vied to invite him to parties, though he mostly dined at the Joyces'. Bob Joyce has shared with me a memoir of Max which gives a good idea of social life on Spetsai. "Our contribution to the last decade of Max's life was to help introduce him to our world of comparatively superficial *mondanités*," Joyce writes. "Max and I were not enthusiastic party-goers, especially dinner entertainments. In Spetsai during the summer season dinner starts about nine o'clock. By eleven the free-flowing booze has pretty well taken over and loosed tongues which have little regard for accurate information on the current international political scene and less for established historical fact. Ladies always outnumber the men present by three or four to one; and the female approach to political issues is often inclined to be emotional and frequently based on hastily read copies of *Time, Newsweek* or the pronouncements of political pundits in the *International Herald Tribune, The Daily Telegraph.* . . . Passionate arguments at times developed. . . . Max never interjected himself into these arguments. But occasionally when his opinion was asked, he spoke quietly. . . . His few words were listened to with great respect."

Social life on Spetsai became so frenetic in July and August that the Joyces and Max often rented a house on the quieter and less fashionable island of Kythira. But even out of season Max met a wide range of celebrities at the dinners in Spetsai, among them Truman Capote, Baron Keith of Castleacre, Mary Martin, Winston Churchill, the prime minister's grandson, and Swifty Lazar.

Still, it seemed that Max had not abandoned Russia altogether. Anne Kindersley, who visited Spetsai with her husband Richard, a St. Antony's Fellow, recalls this scene: "As I sat lazily on board a Greek caique moored for a day's picnic off Spetsai and watched Max and Richard swimming side by side, there floated across the water the words, '*samizdat . . . Novy Mir . . .* Tvardovsky.'" Russians and specialists in Russian began to come to Spetsai in increasing number. Max had a separate apartment built onto his house and invited the Katkovs to visit whenever they pleased. He loaned the house to Leonard and Roma Schapiro and to the Kolakowskis.

Max began spending at least half of every year in Greece, sometimes much more. For a brief time, however, Israel was to compete for his attention. I had long been aware of his particular liking for Jews and his interest in things Jewish. When he visited Israel in 1975 and 1977 I received ecstatic letters and postcards. "This is quite the most interesting country I've been to," he declared. "I'm having a glorious time. . . . Jerusalem is unbelievably fascinating," he wrote on the illustrated stationery of Mishkenot Sha'ananim, the cultural center and retreat for writers and artists in Jerusalem, where he spent three months in 1977.

Max's old friend Baruch Knei-Paz, a political scientist at the Hebrew University who had been a St. Antony's student, says: "Max flourished in Jerusalem. People were attracted to him instantly and felt the need to take care of him. Academics sought recommendations from him for jobs or promotions. Soviet émigrés pressed manuscripts on him. He could never say no." Max traveled to the Golan Heights and the Sinai, where he was taken by the brutal power of the desert scenery. "I now realize why the Jewish God is wrathful," he said. He was despondent about Israeli politics and worried about the country's future. Says

Knei-Paz: "He had somehow caught the national spirit. He saw values of importance in Israel. Once he told me: 'If Israel disappears we are all done for.' "

Still, Max was established in Greece. His periods of residence at St. Antony's grew increasingly brief and perfunctory; since Bill Deakin had retired from the college in 1968 and moved with Pussy to the south of France, Max felt less and less connected to Oxford and, indeed, to England. To his old friends Max rarely spoke about his life in Spetsai, but grossly exaggerated stories went around that he was moving in fashionable society, or at least café society. These tales of high life in Spetsai were received with astonishment and, apparently, some resentment. Hingley's reaction was by no means unusual: "He was now making new friends who—from my point of view—could hardly be said to have known the real Max at all; but they, no doubt, might feel that they had the right to say the same of me and other associates of his middle years."

Hingley had seen, as I and others had, that Max had lost some of the gusto and mischievousness that were so much part of his nature before he stopped drinking. Hingley perceived "a profound personality change" in Max, which he summed up by saying that he became "strikingly less self-indulgent." "The change included giving up nicotine, alcohol, the provocation of improprieties, and the frequent company of some old friends, such as myself, who had previously been far more ascetic than he in their habits but now found themselves markedly less so. We still met, without restraint, and always on the most affable terms. But he was somehow just not there."

In retrospect, it seems to me that Max had gone to Greece as much for plain survival as for love of Homer. He had grown frailer than any of us realized, except for G.M., who still watched over him and worried. Max had so abused his health in his earlier years that now, in cold climates, he was subject to frightful bouts of bronchitis and flu. In Greece the sun warmed him, and he was loved and cosseted by friends. I believe he was never happier. His island, like Odysseus', was "a rugged place, but a good nurse of men." There, as it turned out, he did some of his best work—for Russia.

During his Greek decade, Max translated the memoirs of Nadezhda Mandelstam and the books on Pasternak by Gladkov and Ivinskaya. He collaborated on a translation of Sinyavsky's *A Voice from the Chorus* that is an English-language classic. He wrote his best literary essays, on Pasternak, Sinyavsky, Akhmatova, and Solzhenitsyn. He was a regular advisor on Russian books to his friends Helen Wolff at Harcourt and Marjorie Villiers at Harvill, and he was editing a vast anthology of twentieth-century Russian poetry for Doubleday. With Ed Kline he revived the long-defunct Russian-language publishing house, Chekhov Press, in New York. Under Max's editorship, the press published a number of writers who could find no home for their books at the time, either in the Soviet Union or abroad—among them Nadezhda Mandelstam, Joseph Brodsky, and Lydia Chukovskaya.

In December 1978 Max flew from Greece to New York to consult with Ed Kline on some Chekhov Press business. Within a few days Max experienced sudden, excruciating pain. A medical examination showed that he had widespread cancer: there was very little time left. I am not sure how much he was told in New York. When I went to see him at the apartment of Ed and his wife, Jill, who were caring for him, he behaved quite naturally, in spite of pain. We talked for hours as we always had of what we called "the onion"—short for the Soviet Onion. But he did not generally feel up to seeing people or to talking on the phone. The only call he made, as I recall, was to Kyril Katkov, G.M.'s brother, who lives in New York. Max did, however, want to see Voznesensky, who was in town for readings. I brought Andrei around and the two men chatted easily for a little while. After the meeting, in the taxi, Andrei wept uncontrollably.

After Christmas Max flew to London—on the Concorde, to shorten his flight time because of the pain. He was as proud as a child to have flown on the Concorde; in the hospital he brought out a parchment-like document attesting to his flight on the superplane and displayed it to me. Marjorie Villiers met him at Heathrow—he was in a wheelchair—and drove him into London, where he complained testily that there were so few people in the streets—not like New York!

Anne and Richard Kindersley took charge of Max then with immense tact, kindness, and love. Anne says: "He was able for a time to remain in his own rooms and to attend the hospital as an outpatient, due to the devoted care of Bohdan Ryhajlo, his college scout for seventeen years. Max knew, though he didn't choose to admit it, that his days were almost certainly numbered. He met illness by treating everything connected with it as a new experience: 'I'm learning to be the Compleat Invalid.' He was given one painkiller that had been in use among the ancient Greeks and rediscovered by modern medicine; a dip into Liddell and Scott and the *Odyssey* revealed, to Max's satisfaction, that Helen of Troy had slipped the same drug into her guests' wine glasses at a dinner party, 'to drive away grief and sorrow.'

"When, after three weeks, he went into hospital, he found there a new and absorbing world, where the old man in the next bed provided an opportunity for studying the Oxfordshire dialect, a nurse turned out to have started life as a Byzantine scholar. He shared with his immediate neighbors the kind of casual goodfellowship found among regular pub companions.

"During the last few weeks of his life, Max lived very intensely. But he was also facing his own death, slowly, reflectively, and at times, it was evident, with great difficulty. He seemed to be thinking things through: he recalled in detail Socrates' speech in the *Apology* as being, for him, the finest way to face death. In the end, he achieved a serenity which was to reassure visitors who dreaded going to see him in hospital. His pain was controlled and he was able to keep his prized independence because of the imaginative and highly skilled medical care he received in the hospice unit, Michael Sobell House, at the Churchill Hospital."

Max called the hospice that Anne describes "Chez Sobell." So many people came to have lunch, tea, and dinner with him there that he tied an engagement book around his neck with string so it would not get lost in the bedclothes. Visitors kept the refrigerator in the ward filled with champagne, caviar, pâté, and other delicacies which they consumed with Max, who had regained some of his appetite and was drinking wine. Presents arrived. The Schapiros came with smoked salmon and Ellen de Kadt with chocolate truffles; Isaiah Berlin brought a bottle of Bull's Blood wine from Hungary; Kolakowski presented his three-volume history of Marxism to Max, who kept it on display beside him.

I believe Max had had no idea of how much he was loved in England. It was a homecoming and a reconciliation. His mother and brother came to visit with him. Former students, Fellows past and present, old friends and drinking buddies he had not seen in years arrived. Friendships that had ended were resumed; the intervening years seemed to have been canceled out. One afternoon as I was sitting with him he spotted through the window a man with a halo of white hair making his way with difficulty on the path to the hospice. "It's the old Bursar," Max told me, very moved. They had not known each other well, but he had come. As always, Max found his way to his interlocutor's main interest, which in this case was India. He got the old Bursar, Peter Hailey, talking about the years he had spent as a British civil servant in that country. "I always wanted to go there," Max said. "But I suppose I've left it a bit late."

Max's recent inquiry about resigning from the college was never mentioned. Neither, directly, was the nature and gravity of his illness; that was plainly his desire. Those who flew in from abroad professed to be on some other business as well. The Deakins came from France, Jane Joyce from Los Angeles, and Katkov from Spetsai, where he had been staying in Max's house. Max told me he wanted to make sure that G.M. would have the house for as long as G.M. lived; the best plan, he thought, would be to leave it to the college.

I stayed in Oxford for a week, visiting Max for two or three hours every day. The Kindersleys were brilliant behind-the-scenes traffic managers, so I was assured of times alone with him. They were among our very best. We talked nonstop about "the onion" and toasted each other in wine. A little later on, after I had gone back to New York, he grew weaker and he had more trouble concentrating. Still, he and Harry Shukman spent nearly a whole afternoon working together on an article Harry was writing about Soviet Jews. The day before Max's death on March 18, 1979, as he drifted off into a coma, he asked Richard Kindersley to read him the summary of a novel by Aksyonov, which had come by the morning post.

New York City
August 1982

PART 1

1

Among Max Hayward's gifts as a scholar, writer, and teacher was an exceptional ability to encapsulate entire historical periods in a single, substantive essay. "The Russian Empire," which covers some sixty years of cultural history, is just such a miracle of compression. It is his last major piece of writing; it is also one of his rare excursions out of the Soviet period into the nineteenth century, evidently made under the spell of the prerevolutionary photographs discovered and assembled by the scenic designer Chloe Obolensky. Written with grace, wit, and obvious pleasure in the material at hand, his essay served as the preface for Mrs. Obolensky's book The Russian Empire: A Portrait in Photographs *(New York: Random House, 1979; London: Cape, 1980). It also provides the historical background to the somber times ahead for Russia and her literature: the Soviet era that engaged Max Hayward's unbounded interest and that is the subject of the present volume.*—ED.

The Russian Empire

A Western traveler journeying through Russia, Baedeker in hand, at any time from the mid-nineteenth century to the Revolution would have encountered a vast empire caught up in the many changes that were bringing it into the "modern world" and would usher in its doom. It would have been an incurious traveler who would not have wished to arm himself with some preliminary information on the main historical, social, and regional features which have always combined to produce in the outsider an impression of a country so unaccountable in its mixture of the familiar and the totally strange that it has often seemed a puzzle, a bundle of contradictions not to be fathomed by the Western mind. For their part, while sometimes sharing—and even encouraging—this view of themselves, the Russians have traditionally been amused by such lack of comprehension and the corresponding tendency to invent quaint myths about them. There is a well known, though perhaps apocryphal, Russian story about a French traveler in the last century who, on returning to Paris, wrote a book in which he related, among other details, that on one occasion he had sat drinking tea under the shady boughs of a majestic *klyukva* tree. This exotic-sounding word, introduced for the sake of local color by the Frenchman, refers to the humble cranberry, which grows on small bushes, and is now used in Russian to describe the kind of egregious errors to which foreigners are thought to be prone. The visitor may be excused his "cranberries," and the Russian his amusement at them, but it must be admitted in all seriousness that there is a good deal even in the external aspect of the country to prompt bewildered questions. How, first of all, did the Russian Empire come to cover such an unimaginably vast stretch of the earth's surface and embrace such an extraordinary variety of different people? Why did it have two capitals, and why—as one may fancy at the outset from the contrast between these cities—does it seem to present now a "European" and now an "Asiatic" face? Does Russia belong to the West or to the East, to both or to neither? The last question is one that has frequently exercised the Russians themselves and provoked controversy among them.

In its origins Russia was distinctly European. Its heartland lies in the area along several great rivers—the Western Dvina, the

Dnieper, and the Volga—which, between them, link the Baltic coast with the Black Sea and the Caspian. The population was Slav and, apart from minor tribal differences, identical in language and race with other peoples to the west and southwest— the ancestors of today's Poles, Czechs, Slovaks, Croats, and Serbs. Vikings trading with Byzantium and the Arab world along the river routes organized the eastern Slavs into some kind of loose political entity, of which Kiev, a trading depot on the Dnieper, became the center.

The Vikings were eventually assimilated by the Slavs, leaving behind only the world *Rus* (later turned into *Rossiya*), by which they were known, and a few personal names such as Olga, Igor, and Vladimir, which in these Slavicized forms now conceal their Germanic origin. It was the connection with Byzantium which proved decisive for Russia's future when, toward the end of the tenth century, the Eastern form of Christianity was adopted by the ruler of Kiev. According to a picturesque but perhaps fanciful account in the old Russian chronicles, this step was taken as a matter of free choice, after a comparison had been made between the various alternatives to paganism. Islam was rejected because the faithful are not allowed to drink alcohol. It was supposedly the splendor of the great cathedral of St. Sophia in Constantinople which swayed the Russians in favor of Greek Orthodoxy. In becoming part of Eastern Christendom, Kiev entered the sphere of the Greek-Byzantine culture that went with it. The Russian language was written in a modified form of the Greek alphabet and developed a capacity to express abstract ideas and form new words after the Greek pattern, as Byzantine works of theology, history, and geography were translated into it. By the middle of the eleventh century, Kiev—now with its own cathedral of St. Sophia—was a city of some consequence in the eyes of the world, and its ruler became linked by dynastic marriages with Poland, France, and other Western countries. The title of the ruler of Kiev was a Scandinavian word related to the English *king* and generally translated as prince or duke. There were other Russian towns, such as Chernigov, Smolensk, and Novgorod, far to the north, which also had their princes, but the one in Kiev was recognized as the senior among them and called great prince (or, more usually in English, grand duke).

But loyalties among the rulers of the various towns—at first little more than fortified trading posts—as well as loyalties to the Great Prince were fragile, and owing to constant internal strife Kievan Russia was denied the political coherence needed to ward off external enemies. Kiev itself was extremely vulnerable to hostile incursions from the east, and in the middle of the thirteenth century, when it was in any case already in decline, it was sacked by the Tatars (sometimes referred to as Mongols—the name of the Tatar Horde's ruling elite). After the conversion to Christianity, this was the second most decisive event in Russian history. The center of gravity of Russian life now shifted from the relatively fertile south to the much more inhospitable northeast, where agriculture was hampered by long winters and poor soil. Its only advantage was the shelter afforded by dense forests. From this precarious fastness, the princes of a number of towns—over which Moscow became predominant by the second half of the fourteenth century, when its ruler assumed the title of Great Prince—were gradually able to restore Russia's fortunes during a long period of contention among themselves and of diplomatic dealings and intermittent warfare with the Tatars, who themselves in the course of time became enfeebled through internal disunity. It should be emphasized that during the two and a half centuries or so of her submission to the Tatars, Russia was not occupied by them, but only paid tribute. It was the prime duty of the princes to collect it, and they had to make humiliating journeys to the capital of their Tatar overlords on the Volga, but apart from occasional punitive raids there was little direct interference with Russia's internal affairs, and none with the Church— which indeed flourished at this time, playing a crucial part in preserving and reaffirming a sense of national identity after the shock of conquest. The Russians' allegiance to their Byzantine-Christian culture was thus in no way threatened. A number of Tatar words—such as, significantly, the one for money—entered the Russian language, but otherwise Tatar influence was mainly

6

visible only in dress and manners, such as the kaftan and the habit of prostrating oneself before those in authority. (These things naturally did much to persuade later Western travelers of the basically "Oriental," or "Asiatic," nature of the Russians, as did degrading punishments such as flogging with the knout, visited on high and low alike.) But the psychological consequences of the "Tatar Yoke" were far-reaching. It resulted in a certain remoteness from the rest of Christendom, so that Muscovy—as the successor to Kievan Russia became generally known to its neighbors—turned in on itself and took on the conservative, ingrown aspect of a beleaguered culture deprived of easy communion with its sources and driven, as a matter of self-preservation, to cling to the outer forms of ritual and observance. The need for flexibility in dealing with the Tatars made for a kind of behavior in relations with foreigners that came to appear in Western eyes as crafty or insidious, in "Eastern" fashion.

Just as serious, perhaps, from Russia's point of view, as the Tatar Yoke—and more enduring—were the conflicts which also began to develop in the thirteenth century with the expanding powers to the West—first with the German Order of the Teutonic Knights and Lithuania, and later with Poland and Sweden. As the new Russian state was gradually consolidated by Moscow during the fifteenth and early sixteenth centuries by a process of absorbing all the other principalities—and of simultaneously loosening the Tatar hold—it was natural that the need for territorial security should come to seem paramount. This could, of course, only be obtained by continually pushing back Russia's frontiers over the immense, largely flat, and featureless expanses stretching out to seeming infinity on all sides. One has only to look at the map to see that this was the logic imposed by geography on Russian history. It would be oversimplifying, however, to say that Russia was inevitably driven by this logic to adopt a centralized, autocratic form of rule more in the spirit of its waning Asiatic overlords than in that of the rising powers of the West, with whom the contest for territory, much of it inhabited by Russians, would be fiercer and lengthier than anywhere else. There were certainly other potentialities, inherent from Kievan times, in the development of Russian statehood. This was shown by the example of the principality of Novgorod, which in the twelfth century took on the aspect of an oligarchic city-state, not unlike Florence or Venice, and governed itself in accordance with an elaborate rule of law.

But Novgorod was subdued by Moscow in the fifteenth century. Its destruction was completed in the next century by Ivan the Terrible, who ruthlessly subdued his own Muscovite aristocracy (the boyars) in a way which established the principle of absolute rule once and for all. This was another crucial turning point in Russian history, radically marking it off from that of the rest of Europe, where in the feudal period a precedent had been set for the rise of social groups or classes able to curb the sovereign's power.

The reign of Ivan the Terrible saw the beginning of Russia's expansion. In the east there was little resistance, since the Tatar Golden Horde had by now broken up into the three separate khanates of Kazan, Astrakhan, and the Crimea. The first two were conquered by Ivan in the middle of the sixteenth century, giving Russia control of the length of the Volga down to its delta on the Caspian Sea, and opening the way for a rapid and more or less unimpeded Russian advance across the Urals into Siberia. Shortly afterward Ivan began the much more difficult confrontation with Poland and Sweden, which finally ended, in Russia's favor, only in the eighteenth century. Muscovy's emergence as a serious rival to its neighbors was accompanied by a significant change in the ruler's title: Ivan the Terrible had himself crowned not as great prince but as czar. The word *czar* (derived from Caesar) was used by the Russians and other Orthodox Slav nations as the equivalent of *basileus*, the Byzantine term for emperor. Its assumption by the rulers of Muscovy suggested that they saw themselves as the heirs of Rome and Byzantium—with all that that implied in terms of an eventual claim to dominion over the whole of Christendom. The idea of Moscow as the "Third Rome" ("and a Fourth there shall not be") was indeed formulated by a Russian churchman at the beginning of the sixteenth century and seemed reasonable by the lights of the time: Byzantium had fallen to the

Turks in 1453, and Muscovy, by now confident of completing its liberation from the Tatars, could well feel entitled to inherit the imperial mantle as the only remaining defender of Orthodoxy. The Byzantine double-headed eagle was adopted as the Russian emblem of state, and various documents were put about purporting to show that the Russian czar was actually descended from the Roman and Byzantine emperors.

Yet it is a matter of dispute as to how far the advancement of this claim meant that successive Russian czars seriously embraced the universalist pretension of their supposed Byzantine predecessors by way of what we should nowadays call an ideology. Perhaps not to the extent sometimes maintained in a latter-day search for the roots of "Russian imperialism." In their actual dealings with other nation-states the czars, on the whole, displayed a cautious realism not usually found in persons swayed only by some visionary belief. The beguiling thought that they were natural successors to former ecumenical rulers no doubt constantly lurked in their minds as they proceeded, in the course of the next two centuries, to build the largest empire the world has known, but they are just as likely to have been guided mainly by the pragmatic considerations—and in the later stages also by sheer force of inertia—which had made continuous territorial expansion so irresistible to other nations as well. As with other empires, "ideology," for the most part, simply followed the flag.

After a brief period of internal political turmoil ("the Time of Troubles") at the end of the sixteenth and beginning of the seventeenth centuries—during which the Poles succeeded for a short time in putting their own man on the throne of Russia— a new dynasty, that of the Romanovs, resumed under strong absolutist rule the course charted by Ivan the Terrible and his predecessors. The main external preoccupation was henceforth with the Poles and the Swedes, but Russia's decisive thrust to the west came only in the next century, under Peter the Great, and the seventeenth century was more notable, during the reign of Peter's father, for several internal developments. The most important single event was a schism in the Russian Orthodox Church, which toward the end of the preceding century had established its own patriarchate, thus marking its formal independence from the now subjugated Constantinople. The Russian schism was not provoked by the kind of doctrinal problem that had played an important part in the beginning of the breach between the Eastern and Western churches in the ninth century a few years before Russia's conversion to Christianity, but arose from causes that seemed trivial at first sight. The patriarch, with the approval of the czar, had invited Greeks to revise the Russian liturgical books and correct errors which had crept in during centuries of recopying. One such error was the misspelling of the name of Jesus. There were also minor divergencies in ritual—the Russians, for instance, made the sign of the cross with two fingers instead of with three, as in current Byzantine practice. The motive for correcting these faults was to enhance the credentials of Moscow as the new center of Orthodoxy, but such "interference" by the Greeks in the affairs of their church was bitterly resented by many Russians. It was argued that while Byzantium, for its sins, had fallen to the Turks, Russia had survived and grown strong—which must mean that the faith had been preserved in pristine form. And there was also a suspicion that the Greeks—many of whom had taken refuge in Italy after the fall of Constantinople—might be trying to smuggle in "Latin heresy" under the guise of the ostensibly formal modifications they proposed.

The leader of the opposition was an intransigent priest called Avvakum, who, in his stubborn single-mindedness, was the precursor of many Russian dissenters to come. The example of him and his numerous followers (called Old Believers) belies the notion that all Russians have always been slavishly submissive to authority. Avvakum was probably the first person of note to be sent to Siberia for his beliefs. He described his experiences in a moving account of his life, which can still be read as a work of literature. The persecution of the Old Believers gave rise in time to the formation of several religious sects which were distinguished by their total rejection of ecclesiastical and secular authority. Some of them were very extreme and bizarre—the one, for example, which practiced self-castration—and they were clearly the product of a profound and lasting disarray provoked by the schism in the Russian religious consciousness.

Another, less dramatic but nonetheless significant, development during the reign of Peter the Great's father in the late seventeenth century was the beginning of a slow percolation into Russia of Western cultural influences and manners. This was the inevitable effect of contact—albeit antagonistic—with Poland. The smoking of tobacco, though still mentioned in scandalized tones, was one example. More serious was the idea of a secular art and literature. The written word, when not used for official or commercial purposes, had hitherto been the almost exclusive preserve of the church, but now there were examples of its use in verse and in plays for the theater, a new source of entertainment in a few private houses and also at the czar's court. The techniques of icon painting began to be applied occasionally to secular portraits. Much of all this was imitative of Polish or other foreign models, but it was the start of what might have been a slow, organic, and relatively painless assimilation by Russia of what it wanted or needed from the West. In the upshot, however, this happened in a very different way.

The story of Peter the Great's brutally rapid and abrupt "Europeanization" of Russia at the beginning of the eighteenth century is too familiar to need recounting in any detail. It was as shattering and fateful in its consequences as anything in previous Russian history, and it created traumas and cultural ambiguities which could not easily be absorbed or resolved by following generations.

Peter's idea was a simple one, and he carried it out with a ruthless, overbearing energy never perhaps equaled by any other reforming autocrat. It had been borne in on him during his visit as a young man to Holland and England that to continue the expansion of her frontiers Russia would have to borrow all the necessary arts of war and peace from Western Europe. The first priority was the building of a navy to defeat the Swedes and secure Russia's hold on the Baltic—and also on the Black Sea, which was controlled by the residual Tatar domain in the Crimea (now under Ottoman suzerainty). He laid the foundations of Russian

heavy industry by creating ordnance factories, manned by con-
scripted serfs, in the Urals. Knowing it would be precarious in the
long run to rely on the borrowed achievements of Western science and technology, he established institutions of higher learning, at first with a practical emphasis on subjects such as
navigation, medicine, and mathematics. But his grander vision of
an academy of sciences was realized after his death, and just after
the middle of the eighteenth century the first Russian university
was founded in Moscow. Young Russians were sent abroad to
study, and foreign teachers were invited to Russia. In a very few
years a country that for centuries had been culturally self-contained, admitting outside influence only in very controlled fashion, suddenly began to take on an alarmingly cosmopolitan
appearance—at least in Moscow and the new capital of St. Petersburg, where the upper classes adopted Western-style dress and
were compelled by imperial fiat to shave off their beards. The
Russian language was flooded with barbarous-sounding and ill-
digested foreign words, and the resulting jargon was only gradually
domesticated and turned into a more or less harmonious amalgam
by Russia's first great writers, such as Pushkin, at the beginning
of the nineteenth century. As though to symbolize this portentous
change in Russia's aspect, Peter began to style himself in a manner more immediately recognizable to the West by including the
Latin word *imperator* in his title.

The greatest and most conspicuous outward token of the new,
Europeanized, Russia was of course St. Petersburg. The old capital of Moscow kept its status for ceremonial occasions, such as the
coronation of a new czar, but after some hesitation on the part
of Peter's immediate successors, St. Petersburg was henceforth to
be the seat of the court, and the administrative center of the vast
and still expanding empire. Peter mobilized all necessary men and
materials to build the city at great speed—and at a high cost in
human life—on land wrested from the Swedes and inhabited by
a sparse population of Finnish fishermen. Nothing could have
been more unsuitable as the site of a new city than this marshy
delta of the Neva River—as would be attested by generations of
pallid government clerks, students, and other downtrodden in-

habitants of the kind so frequently portrayed in nineteenth-century Russian literature. It was intended not only, in the famous phrase, as a "window on Europe," but also as the clear expression of a challenge: "From here we shall threaten the Swedes," in Pushkin's words.

The city served notice that henceforth Russia would fight its western neighbors, if necessary, in the panoply of their own most advanced technical skills. But it took the rest of the century to absorb more than just the cruder externals of what the West had to offer. Andrei Sinyavsky has put it brilliantly: "In the eighteenth century Russia was ruled mainly by women. It was not of course mere chance or the whim of fate that placed almost only representatives of the weaker sex on the autocrat's throne in such a cruel and, on the whole, virile century. A certain design is discernible here—something which allowed the century's profile to assume a softer, blander outline. . . . Peter's edifice had to be made habitable and needed all those finishing touches that could best be added by women with their understanding of service at table, cuisine, fashion, and other such domestic matters. Thanks to the rule of these barbarian women with a weakness for entertainments, dresses, masquerades, and courtly manners, Russian civilization assimilated Western ways and tastes with such natural ease that a hundred years after Peter it was able to rear a Pushkin in its lively and fragrantly hothouse atmosphere. . . . Without women on the throne . . . neither Russian classicism nor Russian baroque could have brought forth their golden fruit on the swamp turned by Peter into a building site."

The "golden fruits of Russian classicism and baroque" (many of them the work of Italian architects such as Rastrelli) are manifest in the public buildings, palaces, and magnificent interiors in St. Petersburg, but it is also evident that in parts of Moscow and in small towns in the provinces—even in parts of St. Petersburg itself—that Peter's "Europeanization" of Russia, so splendidly manifested in architecture, affected only the upper crust of society and became less apparent the further it radiated from the new capital and the lower it descended in the social scale. Moscow, a homely, sprawling city, often fondly likened by its inhabitants to a large village, inevitably began to pride itself on being the "more Russian" of the two capitals. The difference between them was reflected in a number of everyday ways—in the dress of the bearded Moscow merchants, for example, with their leather boots and double-breasted kaftans (as opposed to the European-attired shopkeepers of St. Petersburg), and even in speech: that of St. Petersburg was a little clipped, and members of the upper classes sometimes affected a French pronunciation of their *r*'s, while Muscovite speech was pleasantly rounded and drawling and less prone to the use of foreign words.

Yet, though it was often disdainfully described as such even by Russians, Moscow was never "Asiatic" in any meaningful sense. Much in the city's general appearance, as in the case of other older Russian cities, is due to more archaic influences no less European than those which went into the making of St. Petersburg, but assimilated more slowly and modified over the ages in ways that lend them a peculiarly "Russian" flavor. Moscow's main glory, the Kremlin (the word means citadel, and other Russian cities also have kremlins), is partly the work of Italian architects who were invited in the fifteenth century, by Ivan the Terrible's grandfather, to reconstruct and add to it, with results that justify a Russian poet's description of it as Florence in Moscow. The numerous churches that are the most striking feature of any older Russian city—Moscow, with pardonable hyperbole, traditionally claimed to have "forty forties" of them—ultimately derive from a Byzantine model, but transformed to such an extent (notably by the addition of a larger number of cupolas) that they came to be the most distinguishing mark of the Russian scene.

Even more important, perhaps, than the material impact of Western Europe on Russia during the eighteenth century was the borrowing of its artistic forms—literature, theater, music, ballet, and painting. The first products of this apprenticeship were often imitative and sterile—rarely, at least in literature, rising above a gauche "neoclassicism"—but they prepared the way for the uniquely rich and original achievements of the following century. If a millennium of slow, tortuous, constantly menaced cultural developments thus at last came to brilliant fruition, it cannot be denied that Peter's precipitate "opening to the West" was mainly responsible. This positive side of what he did makes it difficult, even now, for many Russians to draw up a final balance sheet of his reign. He was cruel and arbitrary in the way he imposed his reforms, trampling on and flouting age-old habits. Forcing his subjects to ape the ways of Europe, he violated Europe's very spirit. Having been impressed, for instance, by the salons in the Western capitals he had visited during his youthful grand tour, he *ordered* the nobility of St. Petersburg to attend social gatherings together with their wives, who had until then been segregated in almost Oriental fashion. This comic episode was typical of his entire approach.

The wholesale importation of the material and cultural benefits of the Renaissance—in which Russia had not partaken—was carried out in such a way as to make a mockery of the humanism at the basis of them. Instead of blending naturally with the country's own established traditions, all these sudden innovations had a dislocating effect, which probably underlies much of what to foreigners seems overwrought about the "Russian soul." They created a feeling of unreality which came to haunt the Europeanized elite—particularly the intellectuals, who, feeling neither entirely European nor entirely Russian, found themselves more and more painfully concerned during the nineteenth century with the enormous cultural gulf between themselves and the ordinary people. The famous controversy between the Slavophiles and the Westernizers raised the question of Peter's responsibility for this situation, and both sides were agreed that a way must be found to make the nation whole again.

Yet the profound disturbance in the national psyche caused by Peter's reforms was perhaps not unfruitful: it certainly contributed to the peculiar moral climate in which the hypersensitive mind of a Gogol or a Dostoyevsky constantly received the kind of impressions that make their work so alive to the dilemmas and paradoxes of human existence in general. Fittingly, the main hero of some of their most significant works is St. Petersburg itself, the epitome of everything that both troubled and nourished their imaginations. The elegant "Northern Palmyra," with its rows of

Italianate palaces, its magnificent granite-clad embankments, its bridges over the Neva and finely wrought iron grilles along its canals, seemed like the phantom emanation of some stupendous sorcery. As the seat of the world's most omnipotent officialdom, it weighed heavily on its citizens, often inducing black melancholia or persecution mania; a frequent theme in St. Petersburg literature is appropriately that of the split personality, or the "double." The most balanced view of what Peter and his city meant to Russia is given by Pushkin in his poem *The Bronze Horseman* (the title refers to St. Petersburg's most striking monument, the equestrian statue of Peter by the French sculptor Falconet), in which admiration for the czar's work is tempered by compassion for the victims it would always continue to claim.

By the end of the eighteenth century, thanks particularly to a great deal of building under Catherine the Great, St. Petersburg had more or less assumed its final shape. At the same time the Russian empire had reached almost to its final extent—apart, that is, from the conquests made in Central Asia in the second half of the nineteenth century and the acquisition of several smaller areas. Crushing defeats inflicted on Sweden and Poland in the west and on the Ottoman-controlled Crimean Tatars in the south —as well as the beginnings of Russian penetration into the Caucasus—led not only to a huge accretion of territory, but also to the incorporation of various whole nations and ethnic groups, some of which contributed importantly to Russian life and culture. The retrieval from Poland, already beginning at the end of the seventeenth century, of extensive regions in the west and southwest populated mainly by Russians, had the effect of practically doubling the country's Slavic stock.

But these were "Russians" with a difference. A consequence of the destruction of Kievan Russia in the thirteenth century and of the subsequent occupation of much of its territory, first by the Lithuanians and then by the Poles, was that, during the long period of the formation of a new Russian state centered on Moscow, some perceptible divergencies inevitably appeared between the "Great" Russians—as those of Muscovy were called—and the "White" and "Little" Russians in the Polish-dominated lands to the west and southwest. The Great Russians were certainly affected by centuries of intermarriage with non-Slavic peoples—hence the broad faces with high cheekbones often thought "typically Russian"—and, by the time they had regained all the areas lost after the sack of Kiev in 1240, other pronounced differences in language and general outlook had come to mark them off from the population there, despite common origins. A vital, continuing bond, on the other hand, was that most of the White Russians and Little Russians, despite pressures to convert to Roman Catholicism, had remained Orthodox; but, all the same, their long contact with the Poles had exposed them to Western influences and permeated their speech with Polish words.

All this was further emphasized by a contrast in the physical environment. In Little Russia (or, as it is now called, the Ukraine—literally, "Borderland") the rather bleak, heavily forested, and inclement Russia of the north gradually yields to rich, open steppe land (famous for its black earth) which, despite the oceanlike monotony of its horizons and severe winters, has an altogether more "southern" aspect. The image evoked by the Ukraine in the minds of Great Russians is of a land more abundant than their own, and of a people more vivacious, who speak with a pleasing lilt and live in whitewashed, straw-thatched adobe houses—very unlike the gray wooden *izby* of the north—with gardens of sunflowers, watermelons, and hollyhocks. In the nineteenth century a great poet, Taras Shevchenko, gave shape to a separate Ukrainian consciousness, which in turn led to a movement for autonomy or independence from the "Muscovites," as the Great Russians, somewhat pejoratively, were often called. The same tendency developed later among the much less numerous White Russians (also known as Byelorussians), who live to the northwest of the Ukrainians in an undulating wooded landscape with abundant streams, lakes, and marshes and for whom fishing is a major occupation. Because of the peculiarities of their speech, as well as the preservation of ancient folk customs, many White Russians began to feel entitled to the distinct identity already conferred by long separation from their coreligionists further east.

Another important result of the reacquisition of these ancient territories was that Russia inherited from her defeated and dismembered rival the largest Jewish community in the world. In the fourteenth century, because of intolerable persecution, there was a large exodus of Jews from Germany to Poland during the reign of a king who encouraged their immigration at a time when other settlers with urban skills (including Germans and Scots) were being imported to help populate the towns in his entirely feudal country. Many of the Jews settled in villages or small towns in the eastern part of the country, where the landlords were Polish and the local peasantry White Russian or Ukrainian. In some of these places they formed the majority of the population. First under Polish and then under Russian rule —as almost everywhere else in Europe—while due advantage was taken of their services as traders or craftsmen, they were subjected to a formidable array of restrictions, and the threat of violence always hung over them, particularly when difficult times called for scapegoats.

Nevertheless, in precarious coexistence with their neighbors, the Jews of this region struck such deep roots in the local way of life over five centuries that they seemed inseparable from it: Jewish artisans, innkeepers, or musicians (who could well be invited to entertain at a Christian wedding) became a familiar part of the scene—though always standing out from it because of their religion, dress, and the use of Yiddish, a medieval German dialect with Hebrew and Slavic elements in the vocabulary. Under Russian rule they were confined by law to the areas (the Pale of Settlement) already inhabited by them in Polish times, but there were various loopholes, and during the nineteenth century small Jewish communities with their synagogues arose in St. Petersburg, Moscow, and other cities outside the Pale, even in Siberia. A series of pogroms which began toward the end of the nineteenth century—and which were connived at, if not fomented, by the secret police as the traditional means of canalizing popular discontent in areas heavily populated by Jews—provoked large-scale emigration from the Pale of Settlement to the West, particularly to America. On the other hand, by the twentieth century many Jews outside the Pale had assimilated or adapted to Russian society—not always at the price of abandoning their religion—and were playing an increasingly important part in the country's cultural life (music, the arts, literature, and scholarship), as well as in spheres such as commerce and law. (Other small Jewish communities were later incorporated into the Russian Empire: e.g., those of Bukhara in Central Asia, and the "Mountain Jews" of the Caucasus, both speaking Iranian languages, and the Tatar-speaking Jewish sect known as the Karaim, who lived mainly in the Crimea.)

The crushing of Poland and Sweden in the eighteenth century also brought into the empire the small but highly prized countries now known as the Baltic states: Estonia, Latvia, and Lithuania (the last of which had independently ruled over White Russia and a large part of the Ukraine before concluding a union with Poland in the sixteenth century). Their capitals—Tallin, Riga, and Vilnius—were medieval cities of a Western kind, with narrow streets and fine Gothic and Romanesque architecture. From the early Middle Ages the indigenous peoples of Latvia and Estonia had been under the rule of a German land-owning class, many of whose members soon began to distinguish themselves in the service of Russian autocracy—mostly in the higher reaches of the administration, the police, and the army. Though they retained their German titles of nobility, these "Baltic barons" often became Russified in time and were noted for their devotion to duty. In Lithuania there was a native aristocracy which, however, became completely Polonized after the union with Poland—only the peasantry continued to speak Lithuanian, an Indo-European language which is of major interest because of its preservation of features elsewhere extinct. Like the German landowners and the German merchants who dominated the trade in the cities, the Latvian and Estonian peasants—close in language to the Lithuanians and Finns, respectively—were mostly Lutherans, while the Lithuanians had become Catholics as a result of their long association with Poland. (During the Lithuanian-Polish domination over White Russia and the Ukraine, there were some attempts to "win back" the local population from Orthodoxy, and some success was achieved at the end of the sixteenth century by the creation of the so-called Uniate Church, which allowed the use of the Eastern rite in return for allegiance to Rome.)

If the Baltic area, with a social structure and general aspect of an essentially Western European type, formed a rather incongruous appendage to Russia, the same was even more true of Poland. By the three partitions with Prussia and Austria at the end of the eighteenth century, Russia obtained all the territory to which she had a legitimate historical claim, but early in the next century she also seized most of Poland proper, including the capital, Warsaw, and the great textile city of Łódź. Until they eventually regained their independence after the First World War, the fervently Catholic Poles remained the most recalcitrant of the subject people in the Russian Empire and, as visitors to Warsaw could see at a glance, Poland was the measure by which Russia's distinctiveness from the West could most easily be gauged.

The early nineteenth century also saw the annexation of two further countries at Russia's western extremities: in the north, Finland—which was, however, allowed to retain considerable internal autonomy; and in the south, Bessarabia, whose incorporation brought Russia to the threshold of the Balkans and gave her a Rumanian-speaking population, together with such local minorities as Sephardic Jews (whose language was the slightly Hebraicized Spanish called Ladino), Bulgarians, and Gypsies. The last stirred the imagination of Pushkin, who after a visit to Bessarabia wrote one of his most famous poems about them. By way of Poland and Central Europe other groups of Gypsies also entered Russia, which, with its wide-open spaces and traditional tolerance of vagrants, was naturally congenial to them. They followed the same occupations as elsewhere—tinkering, horse trading, fortune telling. As musicians and singers in fashionable places of entertainment, they came to have a place in the upper-class life of St. Petersburg and Moscow, where marriages between Russian noblemen and Gypsy women were not unknown.

The Russian conquest in the late eighteenth century of the north shore of the Black Sea, with its fertile and sparsely settled hinterland (known as New Russia), resulted in the incorporation into the empire of the defeated Crimean Tatars, who had once been part of the Golden Horde and had come under Ottoman rule in the late fifteenth century. Many of them preferred to emigrate to Turkey rather than accept Russian domination, but enough remained to count as a substantial part of the Crimea's population, and to achieve renown for the excellent wines they produced, until the end of the Second World War, when they were all deported to Central Asia.

As elsewhere in the Ottoman Empire, in whose commerce and administration they played a prominent part, there were many Greeks in the Crimea, and from the end of the eighteenth century they formed a large colony—chiefly merchants, but later also professional people such as doctors and teachers—which gradually extended to all the towns along the Black Sea coast: Mariupol, Taganrog, and particularly Odessa, the great port founded by Catherine the Great, in which Greeks and Jews became the most notable elements of a very heterogeneous population. (The Greeks who settled along the Black Sea coast after the Russian defeat of the Crimean Tatars were following in the footsteps of their distant ancestors, who had established colonies in the region in ancient times.)

Of all the areas to fall under Russian control at the end of the eighteenth and the beginning of the nineteenth centuries, the most exotic in terms of its physical and human geography was the immense Caucasian mountain range, which stretches over six hundred miles from the northeast corner of the Black Sea to the Caspian. This formidable barrier between Asia and Europe, inhabited by dozens of different peoples speaking difficult and mutually incomprehensible languages, made a deep impression on the Russian imagination, and no other part of the empire occupies such an important place in Russian literature. The heart of the Caucasus, both geographically and culturally, is Georgia, whose last king, at the very beginning of the nineteenth century, voluntarily put his country under Russian suzerainty in order to save it from the Persians. For similar reasons, but at a slightly later date, the Christian Armenians to the south also accepted Russian rule as a lesser evil than conquest by the neighboring Muslim powers. Both Armenia and Georgia—once on the easternmost marches of the Byzantine Empire—had been converted to Christianity some six centuries before the Russians and boasted ancient literatures written in their own distinctive alphabets. With such an irrefutable claim to represent a far older civilization, the Georgians and Armenians are inclined to think of themselves as more advanced than the Russians and often chafed under their rule, but the overwhelming need for the Orthodox czar's protection gave them little alternative but to acquiesce to it. Until the coming of the Russians, the Christian kingdoms in the Caucasus were extremely vulnerable to Muslim incursions—all the more so in that many of the small tribes in the mountains of the north Caucasus, such as the Circassians, the Chechens, and the Lesghians, had at various times been converted to Islam during successive invasions by the Arabs in the seventh century and later, and then by the Persians and the Turks. The most numerous Muslim people in the Caucasus was the one living in the southeast region now called Azerbaijan. In the nineteenth century its inhabitants were always referred to as Tatars, and since their language—closely related to Ottoman Turkish—generally served as the lingua franca among the mountain tribes, the name was sometimes confusingly applied to other Muslims as well. The area around Baku, the capital of the "Tatars" on the Caspian, was known already to the ancient Persians for the flammable liquid that gushed from its soil and not surprisingly became the center of a fire-worshiping cult. The Russian oil industry was established there in the late nineteenth century.

Russian contact with the Caucasus was prolonged and intimate, because of the presence of large military garrisons needed in the sporadic warfare waged for well over half a century with the mountain tribes that stubbornly and bravely resisted Russian domination. The most outstanding of the Muslim leaders was Shamyl, who led a holy war against the Russians and was subdued only in 1858. In the eyes of many Russian officers who served there over the years, it was a uniquely romantic setting, and through them this view of it became well established in the salons of St. Petersburg. Georgia, with its mountains higher than the Alps, its ancient monasteries and churches, and its rich, well-watered lowlands (where the vineyards, said to be the world's most ancient, produce splendid wines such as Tsinandali) had a particular appeal. The Georgians—a race apart, who speak a language unrelated to Indo-European—are a strikingly handsome people justly renowned for their expansiveness, hospitality, independence, and pride, and generations of educated Russians tended to idealize them as exhilaratingly different from themselves.

In the work of the two greatest Russian poets, Pushkin and Lermontov, and of later writers, the Caucasus—and Georgia in particular—came to stand for the kind of freedom of the spirit hardly favored by the crushing hierarchies of their own society as it had developed in response to the needs of autocratic rule. It is rare that an imperial relationship has been reflected in the literature of the dominant power in such a fruitful and creditable manner.

The same cannot be said of the later Russian thrust into Central Asia, on the other side of the Caspian. This was completed in the second half of the nineteenth century and was a nakedly colonial venture (not unconnected with the need for cotton to supply Russian textile factories) which brought under uncongenial Russian rule a number of mainly Turkic-speaking Muslim peoples, ranging from nomads such as the Kirghiz and Turkomans to the ancient urban communities of Samarkand and Bukhara. In the late nineteenth century there was a good deal of Russian settlement in these areas, and a number of new towns were built in Russian colonial style.

This rapid sketch of the growth and ethnic composition of the Russian Empire is necessarily incomplete—it would take pages merely to list all the peoples and tribes scooped up by it during its progress over one-sixth of the earth's land surface, and attention has been focused here mainly on those which had an impact on Russian life in general. But there were many others—hunting peoples of Siberia, such as the Samoyeds, the Tungus, the Ostyaks, and the Yakuts; the Georgian-speaking Khevsurs of the Caucasus, who wore costumes resembling medieval coats of mail; the Kalmucks, a Buddhist Mongol people noted for their skill with horses, who emigrated from China in the mid-sixteenth century and occupied the arid, salty lowlands north of the Caspian; the oddly Nordic-looking Ainu of Sakhalin, with their animistic religion, centered on the cult of the bear. As though this ethnographic wealth were not enough, colonists from neighboring countries came to live in Russia at various times. Orthodox Serbs from the Austro-Hungarian and Ottoman empires were invited to occupy lands in "New Russia" after its conquest under Catherine the Great, who also settled Germans on the Volga near Saratov, in the justified belief that they would set an example of good husbandry. In the late nineteenth century many Chinese and Koreans came into the country via the newly acquired Far Eastern regions; there was a Chinese quarter in Vladivostok, and Chinese tea merchants were a familiar sight in Nizhni Novgorod.

But unlike America, Russia was not a "melting pot." By and large, each of the many peoples inhabiting the empire kept to its own territory, and there was little internal migration—except, of course, for such natural wanderers as the Gypsies and, to a limited extent, Jews, Armenians, and some others. In the late nineteenth and early twentieth centuries there was considerable officially encouraged movement by Russian and Ukrainian peasants to Siberia (particularly after the building of the Trans-Siberian railroad), but otherwise relatively few left European Russia for these remote areas except as fur traders, miners (of copper, lead, and silver as early as the eighteenth century, and later of gold), soldiers, administrators, and of course convicts and exiles. Many non-Russians, however, were attracted to St. Petersburg and Moscow, and certain ethnic groups sometimes became associated with particular trades or professions there—Tatars from Kazan, for instance, worked as janitors or rag-and-bone merchants, and there were mosques in both cities for these and other Muslims. Despite a notable lack of racial—as distinct from religious—prejudice, there also seems to have been little intermixture through marriage, except in some areas of early colonization (Finns and Great Russians, for example, as already mentioned) or unstabilized borderlands and, sometimes, in a statistically insignificant way, at the top of the social scale. There were unions, for example, between

Russian and Caucasian aristocratic families, as well as some min-
gling of Tatar and Russian blue blood, particularly after the fall
of Kazan in the sixteenth century, when a number of the Golden
Horde's nobles converted to Orthodoxy and became Russified,
leaving only their names as witness to the partially Tatar origin
of several of Russia's first families. (Otherwise, however, there is
scarcely any literal substance to Napoleon's famous dictum that
"if you scratch a Russian you will find a Tatar.")

Although they are not, strictly speaking, a separate race, special
mention must be made of the Cossacks. They were a product of
the vague nature of Russia's frontiers during the early days of her
expansion toward the east and the south, when fluctuating fortunes of war with the Tatars created a no-man's-land in which
adventurous spirits and fugitives could lead a free life, combining
agriculture with border warfare. Many were runaway serfs from
the central Russian areas or from the Polish-dominated southwest, but through intermarriage in the ethnically confused borderlands they developed into a fairly distinct type, though always
remaining Russian or Ukrainian in language. By the very nature
of their origins they were excellent fighters, but also rebellious
ones who could be fickle in their allegiance to one side or the
other. In the final analysis, however, their Orthodoxy tended to
make them loyal to Moscow, and they eventually lost their independence as a result. They played a vital part in the gradual
extension of Russia's frontiers; it was a Cossack force, acting on
its own initiative, which in the time of Ivan the Terrible broke
residual Tatar resistance to the complete Russian conquest of
Siberia. The best known and largest Cossack settlements arose in
the southern borderlands, along the lower reaches of the rivers
Dnieper and Don—a location of considerable strategic advantage
during the long-drawn-out triangular conflict between Poland,
Muscovy, and the Crimean Tatar vassals of Turkey. Until the late
seventeenth century the Ukrainian-speaking Cossacks on the
Dnieper (called Zaporozhians, from the name of their headquarters "beyond the rapids") constituted a kind of independent republic which, although nominally under Polish suzerainty,
effectively controlled the Ukraine for a while; only at this time did

its people briefly enjoy something resembling national autonomy. During the eighteenth century both the Zaporozhians and the Don Cossacks were brought under firm Russian control, soon losing both their freedom and the rough democracy (under elected atamans, or hetmans) which went with it. Though the higher-ranking ones tended in the course of time to become assimilated into the Russian land-owning officer class, the Cossacks as a whole, in their prosperous villages on the Don and the Dnieper, remained a special community of yeoman farmers always ready to serve as cavalrymen in wartime. There were other Cossack settlements in the Caucasus on the rivers Kuban and Terek, and also in Siberia along the frontiers with China. In the late nineteenth and early twentieth centuries Cossack units were often used for the suppression of internal unrest, with the result that their earlier renown as dashing freebooters gave way to the unflattering image, in the public eye, of a brutal gendarmerie.

It remains to attempt a brief description of the state of Russian society as it had become by the middle of the last century, and of the main developments in the ensuing period, until the First World War. There were only four officially recognized classes (or estates, as they were known): the gentry, the peasants, the clergy, and the "townspeople." The last, ill-defined, category included artisans, merchants, cabdrivers, and the like, and as the towns grew in the latter half of the nineteenth century it became, needless to say, the principal avenue of upward mobility. Otherwise it was difficult to ascend the social scale, and there were also some specific prohibitions against transferring from one estate to another. Yet it is possible to exaggerate the rigidity of the system —"townspeople" were sometimes rewarded by ennoblement for services to the state, and by the end of the nineteenth century many peasants had joined their ranks as artisans, shopkeepers, and factory workers—or factory owners. The distinguishing feature of the Russian system was not the existence of barriers between the classes, which were probably not much more impassable than elsewhere, but the fact that, for the historical reasons already noted, all were equally subordinate to the autocracy. It was only by virtue of service to the czar that the gentry owned land and commanded the labor of the serfs who tilled it. It is true that Peter III, the ill-starred husband of Catherine the Great, in 1762 freed the gentry of the obligation to serve, but by this time it could make little difference: acceptance of autocratic rule had become ingrained, and though in many respects, as the mainstay of the civil administration and the army, the landed gentry in Russia seemed much the same as in the West, it had never aspired, as a class, to assert itself against the power of the sovereign. Court camarillas on occasion attempted to promote one candidate to the throne against another—one unpopular czar, Paul I, was even assassinated—but members of the nobility never collectively challenged the autocracy as such, except in 1825, when a group of conspirators (the "Decembrists") made a confused attempt to upset the existing order in radical fashion. Their tragic rising was doomed to failure because it enjoyed neither the sympathy of the gentry as a whole nor the effective support of the peasant soldiers vital to its success. Thereafter individual noblemen who displayed reforming zeal in an undesirable direction were more than ever unceremoniously reminded of their basic lack of rights and, if sent to Siberia, would discover—as Dostoyevsky did—that their only remaining privilege was to be confined in better conditions than lower-class convicts. In terms of social and economic standing, members of the Russian gentry, as in other countries, differed very widely. In the higher range there were grand families, like the Sheremetevs, who owned palaces in St. Petersburg and vast country estates with thousands of "souls," as serfs were officially styled for fiscal purposes. On their estate near Moscow—and they were not alone in this—the Sheremetevs even maintained their own theaters, for which serfs were selected and trained as actors and singers. (A standard Russian word for "good-for-nothing" is *shantrapa,* derived from *chantera pas*—the comment uttered in the presence of a serf who failed his audition.)

But Russian country gentlemen were much more typically impoverished, living in anything but luxury on run-down, often heavily mortgaged, estates, and were certainly in no position to provide for their own entertainment in such a lavish manner. As is clear enough from nineteenth-century literature, staving off *taedium vitae* was a major problem for landowners, sparsely dotted about as they were in a countryside notorious for its poor roads. Many, but not all, found distraction in some form of civil or military service which took them away from home, at least in their more active years. But others retired early to what they may have hoped would be a life of contented sloth—which more commonly turned into one of frantic boredom. The Scottish traveler Mackenzie Wallace tells of a Russian country gentleman who *in extremis* used to have his servants waylay passersby on the nearest road and then forcibly subject them to his drunken company for several days before allowing them to proceed. Yet though there were enough Squire Westons among the Russian gentry to inspire some anecdotes, as well as the lampoons of satirists (themselves mostly of the gentry, too), it must be said that this gentry also abundantly displayed the compensating virtues of a leisured class anywhere. Apart from the fact that many of its members served their own country selflessly and with distinction, the world at large is likewise indebted to it for almost all of Russia's great writers and composers, and also for many of her scientists and scholars. Nor should it be forgotten that despite a general record of submission to the autocracy, the gentry produced numerous individual rebels—the army officers who staged the abortive insurrection mentioned earlier were landed aristocrats—and some outstanding apostles of political radicalism, among whom Bakunin and Kropotkin became internationally known and influential.

The mention of the word *serf* brings us to the social class which formed the broad base of the pyramid at whose apex stood the czar. Serfdom was not universal in the Russian empire; it scarcely existed in Siberia, because by the time there was large-scale peasant settlement there it had been abolished. Neither was it an absolutely inescapable condition, since serfs could, and occasionally did, buy their freedom or were sometimes manumitted. But it was the lot of the great majority on both private and state lands in the central Russian regions and most of the Ukraine. The peasants were not enserfed until the sixteenth century; before then they had been free to leave their masters every year, by tradition on St. George's Day in November. The introduction of serfdom meant that the peasants were bound to the land in the same way and for the same reasons that their masters were bound to the czar's service. During the eighteenth century, however, just as the privileges of the landowners were made absolute, so were the rights of their serfs whittled away until they became virtually slaves who could be—and, notoriously, often were—bought and sold, even if it meant separating them from their families. Perhaps the very worst aspect of a serf's life was that, from the time of Peter the Great, he could be sent into the army for twenty-five years. For the young serfs of military age this was a gruesome lottery, since a fixed quota had to be provided by every village, and the selection was often arbitrary and could be vindictive. Of all the foreign words borrowed in Peter's time, perhaps the most feared and hated was *rekrut*.

One of the crucial events of the nineteenth century was the emancipation of the serfs in 1861. It may well be that it was motivated mainly by economic and political self-interest—awareness of the inefficiency of serf labor and fear of increasing peasant turbulence if nothing was changed—but conscience also played its part: Russian literature is witness to the shame and embarrassment felt by some landowners at their almost unlimited powers over the peasants. If the gross abuse of these powers was the exception rather than the rule, so no doubt was the ideally patriarchal treatment of the peasants sometimes claimed in nostalgic retrospect—a sentimental memory occasionally shared even by ex-serfs, like the old family retainer in Chekhov's *Cherry Orchard*, who believes the rot set in with freedom. In most cases, however, relations between masters and serfs were unhappy, morally and economically debilitating to both. After decades of inconclusive discussion about the need for emancipation, Russia's defeat in the Crimean War finally made it inevitable. Yet the conservatives (many of them lesser landowners with few assets other than the serfs and their labor) were right in foreseeing that it would eventually lead to further changes of a more uncontrollable kind.

While retaining its full powers, the autocracy was henceforth increasingly unable to prevent or inhibit the growth of autonomous social forces and found itself confronted by a dilemma resolved only by its own downfall in 1917. Its political decline was inevitable, whether it acquiesced in or opposed the new trends. Like the subject of a well-known Russian ballad, the czar would perish if he turned to the right at the crossroads, and also if he turned to the left. (The czar who went furthest to the left, Alexander II—known as the Liberator because of his emancipation of the serfs—did perish at the hand of assassins, and the reaction of the two succeeding reigns must be seen in this light.) Attempts to achieve a constitutional compromise with irresistible forces of opposition in the early twentieth century only underlined the fact that emancipation, by gradually blurring the lines of division in society through the creation of a relatively free market in labor, had unleashed new economic interests which could not easily be harnessed to the autocratic will in the name of expansion of national frontiers—a process which in any case had by now almost attained its natural limits. In other words, important elements in society for the first time began to assert themselves vis-à-vis the state and thus implicitly to challenge the prevailing logic of Russian history, which had always previously seemed justifiable as the condition of sheer national survival, if in no other terms. It is true that the country had been no stranger to violent outbreaks of social unrest: there had been urban riots over economic grievances in the mid-seventeenth century, and savage mutinies on the turbulent outskirts of the empire, such as the cossack Pugachev's rising during the reign of Catherine the Great.

None of these, however, was directed against the autocracy as such; the aim of Pugachev's rebellion was actually to put himself, as the "legitimate" czar, on the throne "usurped" by Catherine. The Decembrists of 1825 enjoyed no significant support from their own, or any other, class in society. Just as the beginnings of this basic change in the relations between Russian society and the state were precipitated by defeat in the Crimean War, so the first major political price for it was exacted about fifty years later by defeat in another war, this time with Japan, as the inevitable result of further reckless territorial expansion in the Far East.

Widespread unrest and a naval mutiny in 1905 forced Nicholas II to grant a halfhearted constitution and call an elective assembly, the Duma. This was an admirable body of its kind—representative, in its original form, of all social classes and of the major national minorities—but it was bedeviled from the start by conflict with the autocracy as to the degree of its powers in legislation and over government.

Both before and after their emancipation the peasants, of course, constituted the overwhelming majority of the population, and once he left St. Petersburg the foreign traveler would rightly have felt that no country was more quintessentially rural. The poverty-stricken appearance of the countryside and the villages was often commented on by both foreign and Russian writers, and a common impression was that the peasants were sunk in squalor and ignorance. To many a passing visitor they seemed feckless, shifty, drunken, and altogether besotted. In view of the extremely unfavorable climate—not to mention the effect of several centuries of serfdom—they could hardly have been expected to resemble the seemly and industrious cottagers of Western Europe (or at least of Western Europe's fond imagination!), but only a superficial observer would have failed to see that they were nevertheless the ultimate source—or at any rate the custodians— of many of the distinctive or original aspects of Russia's life and culture.

This was acknowledged during the nineteenth century by educated, Europeanized Russians in a way that had no real parallel in the West. Their almost worshipful attitude toward the peasantry may have been largely determined by the agonized sense of cultural isolation already mentioned—and was liable to degenerate into mere silliness—but it was based on a recognition, moving even in its occasional excessiveness, of qualities that were justly felt to be possessed by no other people in quite the same degree. The testimony of Russian literature certainly suggests that the Russian peasants not only displayed the Christian virtues of charity, compassion, and forbearance in unusual measure, but also that they were endowed with a natural sense of equality and justice (though not, alas, with the need to enforce it by law). This peasant

egalitarianism may have been one of the few positive consequences of servitude, and it was embodied in a peculiar institution, the village commune *(mir)*, which every few years redis-
tributed among all peasant households the land available for their
personal tillage, thus ensuring fair and equal treatment and foster-
ing a sense of co-ownership. The meetings of the *mir*, under an
elected elder, also instilled a feeling of collective responsibility for
village affairs, and although it did not make for good farming, the
existence of the commune encouraged a widespread belief in the
late nineteenth century that there was a ready-made basis here for
a form of popular socialism. At one time even Karl Marx was
persuaded that Russia could thus achieve the millennium without
going through a capitalist phase.

In their very appearance, the peasants preserved a style that was
unadulterated, at least until late in the nineteenth century, by
European influences. The men were invariably bearded (though
they cut their hair in a rough fashion) and wore homespun gar-
ments, of which the most characteristic was the red-dyed shirt or
long smock. In winter they kept warm in sheepskin coats or
kaftans of thick cloth. The women had colorful *sarafans*, and on
special occasions sometimes replaced their simple kerchiefs with
a high, embroidered headdress called a *kokoshnik*. Shoe leather
was scarce and expensive, so footwear was generally plaited from
strips of bark or other materials, including even horsehair, and
boots were also rolled from felt. There was an ingenious self-
sufficiency in everything—utensils, and even plowshares, were
made of wood. Many everyday products of peasant skill demonstrated an affecting sense of beauty, or at least a need to relieve
the drabness of life with color and decoration—as seen from
astonishingly intricate fretwork carving on the outside of houses,
embroidery, painted spoons, and other wooden household objects.
Among the many cottage industries in which whole villages sometimes specialized was icon-painting—that of Palekh being particularly remarkable. Russian folklore—fairy tales, songs, and in
some areas epic poems about a legendary pre-Muscovite past—
was outstandingly rich and expressive, as one would expect from

a people who had to while away long, monotonous winter months in virtual idleness.

The most impressive testimony to the collective genius of the peasantry is the Russian language itself. None other—not even the closely related Slavic languages—can match it in its breathtaking resourcefulness. Its quality shows particularly in a wealth of pithy proverbs and sayings unrivaled throughout Europe. As Turgenev said in a famous hymn of praise to it, "Such a language can only have been given to a great people." The peasantry preserved it from the disastrous invasion by foreign words in the eighteenth century, and Russia's leading writers could count themselves fortunate in being able to draw on the bounties of unadultered popular speech. The contribution of folk elements to the work of some nineteenth-century composers, such as Glinka, also testified to the debt which the national culture owed to the peasants.

As was of course foreseeable, emancipation created as many problems as it solved, if not more. The peasants were given the freedom that the majority had undoubtedly yearned for ever since it had been taken away in the sixteenth century. It was, however, a very conditional freedom. To an important extent the peasants were now their own masters as regarded the disposal of their labor, but they still had to have the permission of the communes before leaving their native villages and—most grievous—were required to pay compensation to the gentry for the land they had always, as serfs, tilled on their own account. A peasant who went to work in the towns, as many now did, would still have to pay this through his commune, which, as before, had responsibility in such matters for all its members, even if they were absent. (When by the early twentieth century this huge peasant debt got hopelessly in arrears, it was simply canceled by government decree.)

There were many new causes of antagonism, too numerous and complex to be detailed here, between the ex-serf and his former master, and emancipation did anything but initiate an era of harmony in the countryside. One particularly sore point was that woodland on the estates was no longer easily accessible to the peasants. The landowners, whose own economic decline continued apace, naturally wished to capitalize on this valuable asset, and the peasants were always trying to steal it from them; the need of the northern Russian peasant for wood to heat the large brick stove on which he and his family slept during the long, cold winter was insatiable. (In the southern steppe regions, where there was little timber, dry dung called *kizyak* was commonly used as domestic fuel.) These difficulties were compounded during the second half of the nineteenth century by a rapid growth in the rural population and a consequent shortage of good land, which was not relieved by the extensive opening up of Siberia for peasant settlement until it was too late to avert the social and political disasters to come. Agriculture stagnated, and in many northern and central regions there was visible impoverishment. Individual landowners and peasants tried to modernize and diversify farming on their land by introducing machinery, but a general shortage of capital for agricultural investment restricted the scope of such ventures. Only in the "black earth" south did more efficient large-scale farming produce a surplus of wheat for export, which accounted for much of the trade that passed through such flourishing Black Sea ports as Odessa and Novorossiisk. The poor, perennially underfertilized soil of the north, on the other hand, continued to yield little more than subsistence crops, such as the rye from which the peasant baked his staple black bread, oats for his horse, and the flax from which his clothes were made. It also supported the cultivation of such vitamin-providers as cucumber and cabbage, the pickling of which was essential to the maintenance of life during the winter—hence the great importance in the peasant economy of salt (which, like the other great sustainer, vodka, was a state monopoly).

Side by side with agricultural decline in some areas went another inevitable consequence of emancipation: economic differentiation among the peasants. In a single commune it was possible for a minority to grow richer by acquiring additional land and hiring the labor of their poorer fellow villagers. In theory this could—and did, in individual cases—make for better agriculture, the less efficient being overtaken by the more enterprising. But the moral loss to the peasantry as a whole soon became depress-

ingly apparent—to judge in particular by the less flattering portrayal of peasants to be found in the literature of the late nineteenth and early twentieth centuries (in some stories and plays of
Chekhov, for example). Even without this literary evidence it
could be assumed that, with expanding opportunities for individual advancement or self-enrichment—whether still on the land or
through migration to the towns—the all too human qualities of
rapacity, greed, and envy were bound to make their inroads. The
commune, once the locus of a peculiar kind of rural democracy,
tended now to be restricted more to the function of a tax-collect-
ing mechanism—the aspect that had always chiefly recom-
mended it to the authorities.

Emancipation was followed shortly by other reforms which also
contributed importantly to the modernization of Russian society.
The first of these was a new legal system. Justice had always been
administered in rough-and-ready fashion by landowners or officials, and the dominant factors which in Russian history had
militated against any effective challenge to autocratic power had
also been highly unpropitious not only to the emergence of proper
legal institutions, but also to the cultivation of a sense of law.
When, on a visit to the Inns of Court in London, Peter the Great
was informed that the bewigged gentlemen who met his aston-
ished gaze were lawyers, he is supposed to have said, "I have only
one such scoundrel in the whole of my empire—and him I mean
to hang when I return!" (He was better pleased by Woolwich
Arsenal, where, in the words of a contemporary English account,
"he did himself in the throwing of bombs assay.") Whether true
or false, this story well illustrates the kind of tradition that has led
students of Russia to doubt that rule of law could ever take root
there.

But the new legal institutions introduced in the 1860's functioned well enough, by all accounts. They were a workable compromise between the French and the English systems, and
provided for trial by jury. It is true that the independence of the
Russian judiciary could be overridden in political cases—and serious interference began just fifteen years after the reform, though
not without severe provocation, when a would-be terrorist assas-

sin, whose guilt was beyond doubt, was acquitted by a jury. The main criticism of the postreform legal system was, in fact, that the juries tended to be far too lenient, and that it was therefore difficult to obtain convictions in criminal cases, whether or not they had a political aspect. This was probably indicative as much of traditional Russian sympathy for the unfortunate as of automatic opposition to the authorities or of indifference to law as such. Even so, service on juries undoubtedly gave many Russians of all classes (including peasants) a taste for due process, which in time was bound to lead to a more widespread understanding that legal formality is not incompatible with justice and mercy. By the twentieth century it was possible to obtain an excellent legal training at Russian universities, and the bar was a respected calling which attracted people of outstanding ability. (Alexander Kerensky, who became head of the Provisional Government in July 1917, after the fall of the monarchy in February of that year, began his career as a defense lawyer, sometimes handling the cases of members of the party which later, in October 1917, ousted him from power and then proceeded to demolish the fragile foundation of both law and democracy in Russia.)

The creation of a new legal system only underlined the fact that Russia was still basically—though henceforth much less arbitrarily —ruled by an officialdom almost entirely drawn, except at its lower levels, from the gentry. While England was moved to reform her civil service after the Crimean War, no such thing happened in Russia, where an elaborate hierarchy of fourteen grades, with exact equivalencies between civil and military ranks, retained overriding powers as the instrument of the czar's will. Like so much else in post-Muscovite Russia, it had been established by Peter the Great, and was decked out with grandiloquent titles and imposing uniforms, both largely inspired by German models. With their reputation for venality, particularly in the provinces, Russian officials were not well loved, and they were the favorite butt of satirists; yet some were cultivated and humane, and they perhaps hardly deserved to be reduced to the lowest common denominator of the bribe-takers and martinets in their midst. ("There's only one decent man," remarks a character of

Gogol, "in this town—the public prosecutor—and he's a swine!")

However, even if they had all been paragons of virtue, the trouble was that they were neither numerous nor competent enough to manage the affairs of such a vast territory, and after emancipation the practical need for ways of improving the administration became glaringly obvious. It was met to some extent by shifting a good deal of responsibility for local affairs in the countryside—road and bridge-building, health, schools, etc.—to newly created elective assemblies called zemstvos (similar bodies —in effect, municipal councils—were set up in the towns a little later). Despite their admitted limitations and chronic lack of funds, these not only made tangible improvements in rural life, but also gave invaluable lessons in the theory and practice of self-government; little wonder that in the upheaval of 1905 they emerged as a considerable force on the side of parliamentarianism. The franchise for zemstvo elections was weighted in favor of the gentry, but there were also peasant members—which meant that, for the first time in Russian history, there was a forum for open debate on matters of common concern between representatives of the two classes always socially most divided from each other.

The last but not least important—and perhaps most overdue —of the reforms was that of the army, introduced eighteen years after the end of the Crimean War. The cruel selective levy of peasant youths was abolished and replaced by universal conscription. The term of service was reduced from twenty-five years to six at the most. It was altogether more equitable and just, providing for exemptions on an eminently rational basis. University students were not called up, though they could volunteer as privates, nor were the only sons of peasants.

Thanks to the spontaneous and eventually fateful movements it set in train, the most significant development in the postemancipation era was the rapid expansion of industry, henceforth nourished by an influx of "free" labor from the villages. The overall direction of economic policy remained in the hands of the state, but even though its interests often coincided with those of the private entrepreneurs (increased production of textiles and steel, for instance, was obviously of mutual benefit), the government became increasingly concerned with the difficulty of controlling or regulating the thrusting new energies released by this inevitable and essential process. The dilemma was reflected in a conflict during the late nineteenth century between the czar's ministry of finance, which put the emphasis on encouragement for industrialization, and his ministry of the interior, which was justifiably alarmed at the social consequences. Ironically, the emancipated peasantry not only supplied the labor force required by industrial growth, but also made a significant contribution to the entrepreneurial drive behind it.

In itself this was not something entirely new. It had always been possible for a trickle of peasants to better themselves by becoming artisans or merchants. Long before emancipation some managed to buy or were granted their freedom and went off to seek their fortune in the towns, or else stayed at home to engage in a lucrative trade or craft; others, while remaining serfs, could work as artisans on condition that they paid a regular quit fee to their masters—a welcome source of cash for those whose land was unproductive. Since this often occurred in central and northern areas, Moscow and St. Petersburg in the early nineteenth century had a ready source of manpower for their incipient industries. Serf labor could also simply be switched from agriculture to industry: as already noted, the first Russian ordnance factories under Peter the Great were manned by serfs, and later on it was not unknown for private owners of factories or mines to *buy* the serfs needed to operate them. After emancipation the trickle of peasant recruitment to industry developed, if not into a flood, then at least into a steadily broadening stream, and with the beginnings of investment banking—and also thanks to an influx of foreign capital and managerial skill—rapid growth was guaranteed. For French, British, Belgian, Swedish, and other investors, Russia was an attractive proposition. Apart from relatively cheap (if not always very experienced) labor, there were infinite natural resources to be exploited: ubiquitous timber, oil in Baku (from which Alfred Nobel made part of his fortune), gold and other minerals in Siberia, coal and iron in the Donets basin—here the main town was founded in 1870 by a Welshman, John Hughes, and named Yuzovka in his honor. By the end of the century the heavy dependence on river transport, with its seasonal stoppages, had been much reduced by a boom in railroad construction.

All of this enhanced the country's potential for economic takeoff. Despite such limitations as the continuing primacy of the autocracy's strategic and political considerations over mere commercial ones, and the relative timidity of native capital, Russia could anticipate giant industrial expansion. Indeed, in the twentieth century, before the First World War, she compared favorably with the advanced Western countries in her rate of economic growth (though not, of course, in actual volume of output). It is possible, judging by her advance toward truly constitutional government in the aftermath of the war with Japan, that she would also have found an appropriate means of mitigating the social cost of this progress, in much the same way as Western industrial nations did. But with the further disastrous war, which began in 1914, time suddenly ran out, and the blandishments of revolution understandably proved seductive to an army consisting largely of peasants whose loyalty and age-old capacity to endure had been strained beyond any reasonable measure.

It was at first sight a peculiar feature of the Russian road to capitalism that not only the new working class but also many of the entrepreneurs (themselves, as already mentioned, often of serf origin) should have been a source of disaffection in the last decades of imperial rule. Despite a certain amount of protective factory legislation, the uprooted peasants living in squalid, overcrowded slums or bleak industrial barracks on the outskirts of St. Petersburg, Moscow, and other cities had obvious reasons for discontent, having lost even the rudimentary social security offered by the commune or extended family in the villages. Although by the turn of the century they were still a small proportion—under three million—of the total population, their concentrated proximity to the seats of power justified the Marxist view of them as the social force with the highest revolutionary potential, and working-class unrest in the two capitals indubitably played a part, even if not a crucial one, in bringing down the monarchy. For their part, the emergent Russian capitalists—who were particularly active in the old, established textile industry and in the manufacture of sugar from beet—showed growing impatience with a bureaucratic, *dirigiste* regime which inhibited the full application of their bursting energies. It was natural that many of them should have hankered after a political remedy, and in the elections to the Duma after the Constitution of 1905 they mostly supported the liberal Cadet (Constitutional Democrat) Party, whose eventual contribution to ending the autocratic rule was certainly more decisive than that of either of the two rival revolutionary movements (the Social Democrats, split after 1903 into Mensheviks and Bolsheviks, who put their faith in the proletariat, and the Social Revolutionaries, who looked rather to the peasantry). Some leading Russian industrialists expressed their discontent or relieved their consciences in other ways: the textile magnate Savva Morozov, for instance, gave handsome subsidies to the Bolsheviks, and there are well vouched-for stories of Russian capitalists fomenting strikes in their own factories (a good portrait of a "progressive" Russian tycoon is that of Kologrivov in Boris Pasternak's *Doctor Zhivago*). Yet others distinguished themselves by enlightened welfare policies in the treatment of their workers. There were no doubt many more who were mean, narrow-minded, and grasping, in the tradition of the ingrown merchant world from which part of the new capitalist class derived, but on the whole the nouveaux riches of St. Petersburg and Moscow enjoyed a reputation for generosity, and also for exhibiting the kind of wild impulsiveness, flamboyance, and spontaneity which, Russians had good reason to feel, distinguished them from the straitlaced Western European bourgeois.

Illustrative anecdotes abound: one memoirist, for example, related how a certain Moscow tycoon issued a standing invitation to all his friends and associates to join him every morning for "elevenses"—at which the champagne ceased to be served only when his top hat, placed upside down on a table, could hold no more corks from the bottles emptied in rapid succession. At a more exalted level, such openhandedness was beginning to manifest itself by the end of the nineteenth century in patronage and art collecting on a scale and in a manner which compared favorably with those of any Western country. Most notable perhaps was Sergei Shchukin, who in the early twentieth century attended salons in Paris where he personally selected and bought many paintings by Picasso and Matisse (all now in a Moscow art gallery).

Finally, a little must be said about two other groups in Russian society: the clergy and the intelligentsia (the latter was not officially recognized as a separate class). It may seem incongruous to bracket these together—though not, perhaps, if one considers that both, in their different ways, contended for the soul of the nation, and that some outstanding members of the intelligentsia were actually sons of priests. The Russian church has often been criticized for its submissiveness to secular authority. It should be remembered, however, that of all the social groups or institutions which at one time or another might have withstood the overriding claims of the autocracy, the church was the least well placed to do so—partly, indeed, because of the very nature of its teaching (with a particular emphasis in Orthodoxy, furthermore, on the supreme importance of meekness and humility). Even so, its total subordination to the temporal power came comparatively late: only in the eighteenth century, when Peter the Great—not for nothing widely regarded as Antichrist incarnate—abolished the patriarchate and put the church under the control of a body called the Holy Synod which, though composed of clergy, was always in effect controlled by a lay official. Catherine the Great completed its humiliation by confiscating the extensive landholdings of the monasteries, which had supported the church as a whole, and virtually making the priests into salaried servants of the state.

But despite this double blow, the church continued to exercise its ministry as an inseparable part of the daily life of the great majority of the population. It may be that the learning of the average village priest scarcely extended beyond mere literacy, and that the deeper spiritual needs of many simple souls were more readily satisfied by the sects that arose out of the Schism (and later by some Protestant movements of foreign inspiration); the church nonetheless remained the chief visible repository and guardian of the country's millennial traditions and, for most people, the only source of mystery and ritual in an existence which would otherwise have been intolerably cheerless. The very beauty of Russian churches (with their gilded or brightly painted cupolas and whitewashed walls, they were generally the only brick or stone buildings and often stood on higher ground, overlooking the gray, straggling wooden villages), the magnificence of the choral singing, the rich vestments of the priests, the solemn processions with banners on the many feast days, the icons, lamps, and lighted candles—all this could scarcely fail to inspire awe, if not piety. As in the Greek church, priests were allowed to marry—which meant that the clergy was largely a self-perpetuating hereditary calling—and in general led a life similar to that of their parishioners, even working on the land allotted them. The church hierarchy, on the other hand, was celibate and drawn from among the so-called black clergy—that is, the monks.

By comparison with Western churches, the Russian one was not very active in proselytism or education. There were some missions to pagan tribes in Siberia and Alaska, and attempts were made to counter Catholic and Protestant influence in the western areas, where it was particularly strong; some Latvian and Estonian peasants, for example, were converted to Orthodoxy, and Ukrainian Uniates reconverted to it. Otherwise the Russian church was fairly tolerant of other denominations, and there was at least one case in which it allowed non-Orthodox missionary work among Muslims in the empire: by Scottish Presbyterians in the Caucasus. The church attended to its own education more than is sometimes appreciated—there were four major "spiritual academies," which carried on theological studies at a higher level, and some youths were trained for the priesthood at seminaries—particularly in the southwest, where, owing to the long Polish domination, a somewhat incongruous emphasis was put on the study of Latin.

Although it arose in part outside the church, an impressive corpus of speculative religious thought in the works of some writers (including Dostoyevsky) in the late nineteenth and early twentieth centuries demonstrated that Russian Orthodoxy was capable of an intellectual vigor certainly no less than that of the secular systems of belief which competed with it.

An important aspect of Russian religious life were the virtually professional pilgrims, or "wanderers," who roamed the country in large numbers, supporting themselves by the alms always forth-coming among an exceptionally charitable population. They were an embodiment of one of the outstanding features of the Russian spirit—a restlessness which often drove people of all social classes to set off in search of the ever-elusive combination of truth and justice summed up in the untranslatable word *pravda* (and now, alas, appropriated as its title by the world's most mendacious newspaper).

This spiritual restlessness was also well exemplified by the intel-ligentsia. It is, of course, significant that the term *intelligentsia* itself has been borrowed from Russian by English, being rightly felt to have a sense not easily conveyed by any Western equiva-lent. Needless to say, until emancipation, higher education at the eighteenth-century University of Moscow and at others (such as those of St. Petersburg, Kazan, and Kiev) founded in the nine-teenth century was largely, but not exclusively, restricted to mem-bers of the gentry, and it was certainly only they who had the means and the leisure to devote themselves to cultural pursuits— though often concurrently with some form of civil or military service.

Not surprisingly, too, the first expressions of intellectual discon-tent with the status quo arose in the same milieu. But in a country where only the limitless expanse of its territory could match the enormity of the social problems bequeathed by its history, it was understandable that the contemplation of those problems by an educated elite, culturally isolated from the great mass of the nation and deprived of any say in its government, should fre-quently have induced anguish or even despair. Hard put to con-ceive of a way out for which they might personally work with any expectation of success, many felt both guiltily frustrated and hopelessly out of place. The figure of the so-called superfluous man, followed after emancipation by that of the "penitent noble-man," occupied a central place in the nineteenth-century literature. With the ruthless candor typical of it, this literature also shows how easily undirected concern for the fate of Russia—and then, since there was nothing to be done about it, for the whole of mankind—could spend itself in fatuous talk, heroic posturing, or sheer humbug. An inevitable result was that the intelligentsia engaged in a constant search for all-embracing formulas or systems of ideas which might seem to provide not only a complete view of the world but also a total solution to all its problems.

This is the reason for the almost incredible ferment produced in Russia by German philosophy. The excogitations of Schelling, Hegel, Fichte, and later Marx were received as intoxicating revelations and stirred debate with a passion which might well have startled their authors. (Eager translations of such writings also had a disastrous effect on the style of Russian abstract prose.) The idea of trial and error, of piecemeal progress, had little appeal. Alexander Herzen, one of the most judicious nineteenth-century Russian thinkers, poked kindly fun at the intelligentsia's hunger for maximalist panaceas in a novel with the symptomatic title *Who Is to Blame?* His hero, a young nobleman who goes to study medicine in Germany, dazzles everyone with his brilliance and wit, but when it comes to the humdrum business of anatomy classes he lets it be known that he is not interested in finding a cure for the common cold—only in discovering a way of making men immortal.

But this undeniably quixotic streak in the Russian intelligentsia was, on the whole, a function of an altruistic devotion to ideas and to visions of social betterment scarcely equaled in intensity anywhere in Western Europe—and frequently accompanied, moreover, by a disarming capacity for merciless self-examination. In the few years before emancipation, and particularly afterward, with the gradual broadening of educational opportunities to include greater numbers of commoners, a tougher, more assertive generation came to put its imprint on the intelligentsia. As we see from Turgenev's novel *Fathers and Sons,* the cultivated, well-bred scions of land-owning families found themselves challenged by the sons of clerks, minor officials, priests, country doctors (still a very lowly calling), and others whose only social advantage over the peasantry was an ability to read and write. These newcomers put their faith in the natural sciences and in the promise of quick salvation held out by the positivist view of life. Having no time for art, poetry, or the amenities of life, they were proud to be called nihilists by their critics, and they joined the intelligentsia in sufficient numbers to bring about a distinct coarsening of its grain in the 1860's and 1870's, a period which also saw the beginnings of a revolutionary terrorism destined to become endemic. At their worst, individual members of the intelligentsia could certainly be as boorish and nasty as those portrayed in Dostoyevsky's *The Possessed*, but they were hardly representative of the majority. At the beginning of the twentieth century a significant group of intellectuals (among them Nikolai Berdyayev) revolted against the philosophical utilitarianism of the previous generation and severely criticized the intelligentsia as a whole for its immoderacy and self-willed isolation from society at large.

The attention attracted by the intelligentsia in the specific sense of a caste or corporation alienated from, yet bent on changing, society, should not obscure the fact that by the beginning of this century the greatly expanded educational system was turning out a good number of doctors, engineers, lawyers, schoolteachers, and other professional people. These, while they might individually, if only by virtue of radical inclinations, have felt they belonged to the intelligentsia, were nonetheless mainly concerned with getting on with their jobs, and in the course of busy careers could easily drift away. Members of the gentry impoverished by emancipation and forced to sell their land were an important source of recruits to the new professional class. (Educated persons or intellectuals of "reactionary" or even moderate or neutral political views scarcely qualified as members of the intelligentsia in its proper sense.) Not everybody had the time or stamina to sit up half the night in earnest debate, to the accompaniment of endless cigarettes and glasses of tea—not to mention that at certain periods, particularly after the assassination of Alexander II, any resulting activities could bring trouble with the police, or arrest and exile to Siberia. It seems likely that in time the intelligentsia, in the special sense of the word, would have dwindled proportionally to form, as in the West, a relatively small minority of the educated or professional community. In the end, however, it was destroyed by the Revolution it had so ardently desired and worked for—but which turned out, tragically, to be of stuff very different from that of the intelligentsia's generous dreams.

By the end of the nineteenth century, academic standards at universities in Russia were probably as high as anywhere in Europe, and Russians had already made fundamental contributions to science and learning (Lobachevsky in mathematics and Mendeleyev in chemistry, to name only two), but schooling was still woefully inadequate. Census figures show that at the turn of the century less than a quarter of the population was able to read —though this figure disguised enormous regional variations, ranging from almost universal literacy in the Baltic states to an almost equal absence of it in Central Asia. Ever since Peter the Great had founded institutions of higher learning without bothering to create at the same time elementary and secondary schools, Russian education had been notably top-heavy. It was only after emancipation that obsessive official fears of the consequences of educating the peasantry were to some extent abated, with the result that the number of schools in the villages began to increase rapidly. This process was aided by the newly created zemstvos and by the church, which was encouraged to open more parish schools in the hope that the harmful proclivities thought inseparable from book learning might thus be held in check. However, even if a peasant now had a better chance of learning the three R's, it was still very hard for him—partly for understandable economic reasons, and partly owing to less excusable official policy—to climb the educational ladder any higher. He would be lucky to get into a trade school and thence graduate more smoothly into the rising urban class of artisans and skilled workers.

By and large, access to secondary education, including some excellent private schools, continued to be weighted in favor of the gentry. However, persons of humbler origin, particularly in the towns, were not ipso facto excluded; in view of the uncommon talents, persistence, or luck needed to cross the hurdles, there tended to be a natural selection of persons of exceptional quality from the lower classes. By the twentieth century it was not un-known for university professors to be of peasant stock. (Secondary schools were modeled on German lines, with an emphasis on Greek and Latin—which, as elsewhere, was as stultifying to some as it was enriching to others—but in the second half of the nineteenth century it became easier to opt for modern languages and science in nonclassical and commercial schools.)

Education for women was at first slow in developing at any level, but here too, in the late nineteenth century, there was surprisingly rapid progress—particularly after the establishment in the 1870's of the Higher Courses for Women at Moscow and St. Petersburg universities. In this way, and also through study abroad, a growing number of Russian women were able to qualify for the medical, legal, and teaching professions. There were no specific restrictions on the entry of non-Russians into secondary schools and universities, except in the case of Jews—but even this was far from being a total ban; though they were officially limited to a very small percentage of the student body by the so-called *numerus clausus*, a significant number nevertheless received higher education during the latter half of the nineteenth century, and some went on to occupy high academic posts—such as, for instance, the father of Boris Pasternak. (Official discrimination against Jews was, incidentally, on religious, not racial, grounds, and a Jew could escape his legal disabilities by converting to Russian Orthodoxy.)

A good reason for dwelling on education at the end of this outline of prerevolutionary Russian history and society is that the old regime is often judged to have been particularly negligent in its provision of opportunities in this area, and hence to have been doomed to stagnation, or at least to have been incapable of social progress as understood in the West. A backward glance at mid-Victorian England might, however, suffice to suggest that, at least in the light of such a comparison, the Russia of the czars was not as hopelessly benighted or resistant to change as is often thought.

2

This essay is the most comprehensive of Max Hayward's periodic overviews of the Russian literary scene. Occupying the foreground are the political events that have governed both the form and the substance of published writing during much of the Soviet era. Still, the literary achievement of the beleaguered writers, however faint at times, remains at the center of his concerns. The essay was his contribution to An Introduction to Russian Language and Literature *(Robert Auty and Dimitri Obolensky, eds., Cambridge: Cambridge University Press, 1977).* —ED.

Russian Literature in the Soviet Period, 1917–1975

Soviet literature is essentially an extension into the postrevolutionary period of the Russian tradition, and one should more properly speak of Soviet *Russian* literature. The term *multinational Soviet literature,* insofar as it might imply that various strands from the non-Russian cultures of the Caucasus, Central Asia, and other areas have been brought together in some process of mutual enrichment, is only of rhetorical significance. The fact is that, so far, Russian culture has remained predominant throughout the Soviet period, and Stalin's famous slogan "national in form and socialist in content" was in practice an assimilationist one. Campaigns against "bourgeois nationalism" in the 1930's destroyed whatever promise of free development might have been held out to non-Russian cultures in the 1920's.

In formal, aesthetic terms, Soviet Russian literature of the 1920's largely grew out of trends—at first allowed to compete more or less freely with each other—which had arisen before the Revolution. No new style developed that was not rooted in symbolism, futurism, or in run-of-the-mill realism in the nineteenth-century manner. Most of the leading Soviet poets of the early 1920's were living representatives of these prerevolutionary trends. Thus, for example, Alexander Blok, Andrei Bely, and Valeri Bryusov were associated with symbolism; Vladimir Mayakovsky and Boris Pasternak with futurism. In prose, Maxim Gorky, Alexander Serafimovich, and Vikenti Veresayev carried on the realist tradition. This is not to say that some postrevolutionary movements could not claim originality by virtue of setting themselves up in opposition to trends that were dominant in the old era. There were attempted new beginnings which have left their mark on the modern history of Russian literature. Noteworthy in this respect was the group founded in Petrograd in 1921 and called the Serapion Brothers (from the hermit Serapion in a tale by E. T. A. Hoffmann). Its avowed aim was to free Russian prose from ideological trammels and to break away from traditional psychological realism by putting more emphasis on structure and plot. Their manifesto was written by a literary scholar and playwright, Lev Lunts, who died prematurely in 1924. Some major Soviet prose writers, such as Mikhail Zoshchenko, Konstantin Fedin, Yevgeni Zamyatin, and Veniamin Kaverin, were closely connected with this movement (which had ceased to exist as such by the mid-1920's), but in later years the original program of the Serapion Brothers was fiercely denounced by party critics because of its "apolitical" premises, and its members went very different ways in the second decade after the Revolution.

Another significant movement in the 1920's which is sometimes thought of as special to the Soviet period (though it started in 1916 as the Society for the Study of Poetic Language [Opoyaz]) was the school of literary criticism usually referred to by its enemies as "formalist." Its exponents, who included some leading literary scholars and writers such as Viktor Shklovsky and Yuri Tynyanov, preferred to speak of the "formal method." By the end of the 1920's it had proved to be ideologically unacceptable, and in later decades the word *formalist* came to be applied indiscriminately as a term of abuse to any kind of stylistic experiment or supposed originality of form. Shklovsky was a founding member of the Serapion Brothers and gave them theoretical support by emphasizing that literary criticism should concern itself first of all with formal or artistic quality, treating content or the message of a work of art as secondary or incidental. Such a challenge to the Russian tradition was bound to provoke a fierce reaction—particularly as the message was so important to the new rulers. But until it began to disintegrate in 1927, the formalist movement was a fertile source of new critical ideas and a stimulus to many writers (whatever group they may have been associated with) whose main allegiance was to literature as such, rather than to any particular set of social and political values.

For the most part, however, the various groupings and "isms" which arose in the 1920's were short-lived or unproductive, failing to attract major talents or provide a new point of departure for them. Some were little more than echoes of foreign trends, while others were attempts to revive or refurbish prerevolutionary ones. Such endeavors were less an indication of new creative vigor than of a frenetic desire to exploit (or adapt to) a postrevolutionary situation which, as time was soon to show, became increasingly uncongenial to any form of intellectual or artistic avant-garde— such things can flourish only under the patronage of an affluent, ideologically tolerant bourgeoisie. All the early Soviet movements with pretensions to aesthetic innovation thus died of inanition or were suppressed, but since they contributed to the comparatively heterogeneous flavor and vocabulary of the 1920's, the main ones must be briefly described.

Imaginism, which borrowed its name from the English *imag-*

ists, was launched in 1919 and petered out in 1927. Its adherents believed in the primacy of images in poetry, and their major theme—an obvious one at a time of rapid urbanization—was the doom of the lonely individual in the modern city. Sergei Yesenin, the only major poet to be associated with them, no doubt joined the imaginists largely because their manifesto stressed important elements that already existed in his own poetry; in the hands of lesser poets (A. Mariengof, V. Shershenevich), imaginism degenerated into the piling on of images, often outrageous or vulgar, for their own sake. The result was like a cheapened version of Mayakovsky. An extreme, even more sterile, form of imaginism was the group calling themselves *Nichevoki,* who proclaimed their affinity with the Western dadaists and rejected any kind of social purpose or content: art was to be in the name of "nothing" *(nichevo).*

Constructivism, a popular catchword throughout Europe in the 1920's, was applied to a wide range of modernist tendencies in all the arts (notably the Russian followers of Le Corbusier in architecture, and Naum Gabo—who emigrated from the Soviet Union in 1922—in painting and sculpture). In literature it appeared as a further development of some trends in part of the futurist movement: worship of modern technology and the belief that a poem is a "construction," to be designed and put together like a product of the engineer's drawing board. As an organized movement (the so-called Literary Center of the Constructivists, founded in 1924), it attracted several poets such as Eduard Bagritsky and Ilya Selvinsky. The constructivists were unable to compete seriously as a left-wing avant-garde with the heirs of futurism grouped around the journal *LEF* (Left Front of the Arts, 1923–25, later renamed *Novy LEF,* 1927–28). Under the editorship of Mayakovsky, *LEF* inevitably became the main focus for those who combined the avant-garde temperament with militant commitment to the cause of the Revolution and the new regime, and it could boast more talented young recruits (Aseyev and Kirsanov, among others) than any other left-wing movement in literature. Apart from the dominating presence of Mayakovsky, *LEF*'s great asset was the support of the formalists (which perpetuated an old alliance with the futurists). Being in some ways politically more royalist than the king, the *LEF* group was bound to run into trouble at the end of the decade and to come under attack as an assembly of "petit bourgeois" intellects from even more militant claimants to be the true representatives of the proletariat in literature.

In retrospect one can see that the 1920's were distinguished from the prerevolutionary period less by the emergence of any new concepts than by certain overriding factors extraneous to literature and the arts, which were now on the way to losing whatever autonomy they had once possessed. What decisively marks off Soviet literature from Russian literature is a radically altered relationship between writers, society, and the state, and the fact that the choice of subject matter was inevitably dictated by the great historical and social changes wrought by the October Revolution. In this sense, there was not much essential difference between those who passionately believed in "commitment" (such as the members of *LEF*) and those who balked at it (such as the Serapions): the overwhelming preoccupation of Russian writers after 1917, whatever literary grouping they might previously have belonged to or now joined, was with the sense of the historical cataclysm through which they had lived, with their attitude to the new society, and with its attitude to them. The stuff of literature was hence furnished by the revolutionary events themselves, by their aftermath in the Civil War, and then by the gradual emergence of a new society with a vastly changed fabric and texture.

From 1918 to 1929 the literary life of the country was not yet subject to the harsh and direct political interventions of later years. Censorship was formally reestablished by a decree of the Council of People's Commissars in 1922 under the name Glavlit (Chief Directorate for Literary Affairs), but like its czarist predecessor it was preventive in character, and for most of the 1920's nobody was *required* to give public assent to beliefs not sincerely held. In July 1925 the party central committee issued a judicious-sounding resolution not to arbitrate—at least for the time being —between the various warring literary groups. With the tolerant and sophisticated Anatoli Lunacharsky in charge of cultural affairs, and with a high proportion of the Bolshevik leaders

(Lenin, Trotsky, Bukharin, etc.) being intellectuals—even though expressing contempt for their own kind—it was taken for granted that the creative process was not amenable to crude administrative control. It was also understood that in the arts, as well as in science and technology, the new society would have to lean on prerevolutionary tradition and achievement.

Workers from the factory bench and peasants from the plow could not be magically converted into engineers, writers, and painters. An attempt to create a specifically proletarian culture by the so-called Proletkult, through which workers and peasants were to be rapidly trained as poets and novelists, was discountenanced by the party and abandoned as early as 1923; the whole idea was politically obnoxious to Lenin, since it presupposed autonomous or spontaneous "proletarian" activity not subject to party control. In literary terms, as is evident from the products of Kuznitsa ("the Smithy," founded as a splinter group of Proletkult in 1920), the proletarian poets were derivative in their techniques, freely borrowing from the idiom of the futurists and the symbolists in their hymns of praise to the Revolution and the machine; their calls for the depersonalization of man in the collective and for a radical break with the old culture seemed like a parody of Mayakovsky and were probably not very appealing to the flesh-and-blood proletariat. (Some members of the group, such as Mikhail Gerasimov, Vladimir Kirillov, and Vasili Kazin, could claim to be genuine proletarians or peasants by birth, but their most militant theoretician, Alexei Gastev, was the son of a schoolteacher.)

Just as in science, technology, and industrial management the party had to rely in the early years of the Revolution on "bourgeois specialists," so in the field of literature and the arts it invited the collaboration of "uncommitted" writers, some of them inherited from the old regime, and known as fellow travelers *(poputchiki)*, putting up for the time being with their vacillating unreliability in ideological matters and their tendency to put artistic integrity above mere political considerations. The party's basic policy in the first decade after the Revolution, until the last years of the 1920's when Stalin triumphed completely over his rivals, was to work for the adherence of writers to the revolutionary cause, to lead them to a social and political commitment which, it was hoped, would make them real allies (and not just ineffectual, false conformists) in the attainment of the party's distant goals, as well as in its day-to-day struggle to achieve moral authority over the population. In these conditions of relative latitude, Soviet literature of the 1920's seems rich and varied by comparison with what it was to become. Some of it even helped to create an atmosphere, conveyed in artistically effective terms, of genuine revolutionary fervor, which, however, faded as the years went by.

The October Revolution itself was greeted at the time in ecstatic, even religious, terms by several poets who even before the Revolution had tended to view the universe and human history as mere reflections of the transcendental. The symbolists Blok and Bely, for instance, interpreted the Revolution as a millennial event, equaled only by the coming of Christ. Sergei Yesenin mistook the grand designs of the Bolsheviks for a plan to build a rural utopia in which there would be universal reconciliation and brotherly love. Only Mayakovsky was able to combine a beatific vision of the future promised by October with some political grasp of the Revolution's true nature. As early as in April 1917 he had written, "Today, the great heresy of the socialists is coming true as an unheard-of reality." He was contemptuous of the mysticism which saw the hand of God in the great historical events, and he accepted with enthusiasm the crucial idea of class warfare *à outrance*. It is interesting to contrast Blok's "Twelve," with its glimpse of Christ invisibly leading the revolutionaries, with the cheerful blasphemy of Mayakovsky's *Mystery Bouffe*, staged by Meyerhold in 1918 in honor of the first anniversary of the Revolution. In this boisterous mock mystery play, entry into the proletarian kingdom on earth is forbidden "to the poor in spirit" and granted only to him "who has calmly planted a knife into the enemy's body and walked away with a song." During its whole existence, the Soviet regime has never found a better literary ally than Mayakovsky—though his flamboyant identification with it was a mask for personal unhappiness. As Andrei Sinyavsky has pointed out in his essay *On Socialist Realism*, Mayakovsky was the only Soviet poet to create a style fully in tune with, and expressive of, the new epoch. Stalin had good reason to proclaim him the greatest poet of the Soviet era.

In many ways, this earliest period in Soviet literature was its finest. Certainly there were never again to be such poetic tributes to the Revolution as then rang out in unmistakably genuine accents. It was, however, only a small minority of Russian writers who wholeheartedly accepted October. The Bolshevik seizure of power was seen by many Russian intellectuals as a usurpation. When Lunacharsky, shortly after his appointment as People's Commissar of Enlightenment, invited more than 120 writers and artists to a conference in December 1917, only five appeared (they included Blok, Mayakovsky, and Meyerhold). Some of Russia's greatest writers were cool or hostile. Even Maxim Gorky, one of the future sponsors of "socialist realism," denounced Lenin in his newspaper *Novaya Zhizn* during 1917–18. Nikolai Gumilev, the leader of the acmeists (who favored clarity of diction and concreteness of image as opposed to the diffuseness of the symbolists), was shot as a counterrevolutionary, and his wife, Anna Akhmatova, saw the Revolution as the beginning of a time of troubles in which poetry would be "like a hungry beggar, knocking at the door of strangers who will not open up." Osip Mandelstam (who had been associated with Gumilev and Akhmatova in the acmeist Poets' Guild formed in 1912) also soon found himself hopelessly at odds with the new regime. Boris Pasternak by 1917 had the reservations about man's ability to transform his own nature, or to direct the course of history, which he was to articulate in *Doctor Zhivago* four decades later. A number of Russian writers (Ivan Bunin, Alexei Remizov, Dmitri Merezhkovsky) emigrated for good; others (Alexander Kuprin, Marina Tsvetayeva) emigrated only to return much later, in the 1930's. Yet others (Alexei Tolstoy, Ilya Ehrenburg) emigrated briefly and returned in the early 1920's, when it seemed that Russia was safe for the progressive literary intelligentsia and indeed more congenial in some ways than before. In his satirical novel *Julio Jurenito* (1922) Ehrenburg had remarked sardonically that Bolshevik prisons would not differ greatly from bourgeois ones. It was perhaps in this spirit that the majority of the fellow travelers settled down in the years of the

New Economic Policy (NEP) to a relatively detached consideration of recent history and of the new social realities. The apocalyptic days had gone by. Blok died in 1921, already deaf to the
"music of the Revolution"; Yesenin committed suicide in 1925;
and only Mayakovsky seemed able to sustain the epic charge
which the Revolution had given his poetry (*Vladimir Ilyich
Lenin,* 1924, and "All Right," 1927).

The prose of the 1920's is for the most part lacking in clear-cut
commitment to the revolutionary cause. The outstanding early
prose work on the theme of the Revolution and Civil War, Isaac
Babel's *Red Cavalry,* was even at the time of publication (1926)
attacked for the author's apparent detachment from the grandiose events he had witnessed. But Babel's purposes were literary,
not political or didactic. He wanted to lift Russian prose out of
the rut of psychological realism, and to introduce "southern"
color and flamboyance into the traditional Russian "grayness."
He believed that his native Odessa might become a new literary
capital which would be in conscious opposition to the coldness
and drabness of the north. As he said in his programmatic literary
essay "Odessa" (1917), "Doesn't it seem that in Russian literature
there has so far been no real . . . description of the sun?" Although
Babel himself soon fell silent and was arrested in the late 1930's,
his idea did bear some fruit in the Soviet period. If there is any
Soviet prose with a specific flavor not entirely derivative of the
prerevolutionary styles, it is to be found in this southern Russian
"school of Odessa," with its colorful, romantic flavor. Valentin
Katayev and Konstantin Paustovsky, for example, managed to
carry some of its quality even into the 1930's and 1940's (e.g.,
Katayev's *Lone White Sail,* 1936). Another writer associated with
this group—although he was not born in Odessa and stood somewhat apart from the others—was Alexander Grin, who in his
rejection of Russian realism went so far as to invent his own
romantic country of "Grinland."

Apart from this exotic element, soon to wither in the cold
climate of Stalinism, the most memorable prose of the 1920's is
perhaps that which exploited the rich social incongruities of postrevolutionary society. The satire of Ilf and Petrov (also "Odes-

sans"), Bulgakov and Zoshchenko triumphantly revived the spirit of Gogol—to whom some of them were explicitly indebted for their literary manner and devices. The Russia of Lenin could vie with that of Nicholas I in its comic potentialities.

At a more solemn level, the prose literature of the 1920's was preoccupied with recent history and the changed status of the individual (particularly the intellectual) in society. In the novels of Boris Pilnyak, Leonid Leonov, Alexander Fadeyev, Mikhail Sholokhov, Vsevolod Ivanov, and Yuri Olesha, to mention the best of the chroniclers of the Civil War and postrevolutionary life, there is a search for self-definition which provides a certain thematic continuity with the prerevolutionary Russian prose tradition, where the problem of national and individual identity was always a paramount concern. There are often also conspicuous formal influences of the past (Dostoyevsky in the case of Leonov; Tolstoy in that of Sholokhov and Fadeyev). Pilnyak, Ivanov, and some others strove to elaborate an original style, but their so-called ornamental manner, with its elaborate ringing of the changes on verbal motifs, also had antecedents in prerevolutionary writing (notably that of Bely and Remizov).

Common to most of this fellow-traveler prose of the 1920's was the implication that the Revolution, however disagreeable or even squalid it may have been, was nevertheless something that flowed naturally from Russian history. Pilnyak, in what was chronologically the first Soviet novel, *The Naked Year* (1922), established the cliché of the Revolution as an unleashing of elemental cleansing forces which were sweeping away the past like a raging blizzard. He also coined the phrase "men in leather jackets" to denote the Bolsheviks—who were at first depicted by him and other fellow travelers as an emanation of revolutionary anarchy. Soon, however, as in Pilnyak's later novel *Machines and Wolves* (1923–24), the commissars are shown more realistically as representatives of a powerful organizing will essentially in conflict with revolutionary turmoil. By the mid-1920's the clash between old and new, town and country, man and machine, anarchy and discipline, is the predominant theme of Soviet prose. The attitude of the individual writer to the new regime, which began to look less

ruthless as the unheroic years of NEP went by, could be benevolently neutral (Leonov), fervently pro-Bolshevik (Fadeyev), or
skeptical to the point of hostility (Pilnyak). But almost all the
leading novelists of the time shared a feeling that they were
witnesses of a process beyond good and evil—a contest between
implacable historical forces which individual human beings could
scarcely influence. Society was seen as an arena for the interplay
of impersonal forces against whose background individual self-
assertion was a futile gesture.

The fellow travelers thus helped to create a public mood in
which dissent, even the clinging to one's personal idiosyncrasies,
was at the best quixotic and comic and at the worst the reprehensible posturing of doomed solipsists. The puny eccentrics who
resisted were bound, in the phrase of the time, to be thrown onto
"the rubbish heap of history." Even where the author sympa-
thizes with such characters, as Olesha does in his *Envy* (1927),
the lone, romantic rebel is made to wallow hopelessly in his own
debasement. Olesha's antihero says: "We envy the coming epoch.
It is the envy of old age." Such last-ditch individualism was
frequently identified with *meshchanstvo*—a petty concern with
one's own private life and feelings, a longing to hide in what
Mayakovsky called the "musty matresses of time." As opposed to
this we soon see the "positive hero," the brash "new man,"
portrayed sympathetically, if rarely convincingly. He may be an
iron-willed Civil War leader, as in Fadeyev's *The Rout* (1927), or
an industrial manager, as in Olesha's *Envy*. The inevitable doom
of those individuals or social groups who fail to march "in step
with history" is a major theme of Sholokhov's *Quiet Don* (vols.
1–3, 1928–33; vol. 4, only 1940), though there is an underlying
assumption running through the novel that ultimately the doings
of men are subordinated to the higher judgments of nature.

Yet with all this there was generally a strong element of doubt
and ambiguity in the literature of the NEP period. Throughout
the 1920's there was no certainty that the "new" would really
triumph. The Bolsheviks may have held the commanding political heights, but in social terms the daunting question of "who—
whom?"—as Lenin had put it—was still conspicuously un-

resolved. In Leonov's *Badgers* (1924), for instance, the victory of the leather-jacketed Bolsheviks from the town looked by no means assured, and there seemed to be much foolhardiness about their challenge to peasant Russia. Leonov was typical in his ambivalence; the reader can never be sure whether the author was more impressed by the superhuman doggedness of the commissars or by the seemingly invincible inertia of the masses.

The 1920's—particularly the second half—were an unhappy and, at least in terms of publication, a rather barren time for poetry. The center of the stage was held by Mayakovsky and some of his admirers and imitators (notably Semyon Kirsanov and Nikolai Aseyev), but their bravura was in sharp contrast to the mutedness or silence of most of Russia's lyric voices. It is now known that, despite the relative mildness of censorship during the 1920's, some poets, in particular Mandelstam, were virtually banned from publishing in the Moscow literary periodicals, though they were sometimes able to appear in print in the less "vigilant" provinces. Such proscription could sometimes be overcome by appeals to powerful patrons (Mandelstam was able to publish a volume of verse in 1928, thanks to the help of Bukharin), or concessions of an ideological nature, but an even graver problem was that the general atmosphere caused a kind of "dumbness" which affected Akhmatova, Pasternak, and Mandelstam in varying degrees. Mandelstam was able to write no new verse, only some prose, between 1924 and 1930. Akhmatova published nothing between 1924 and 1940. Pasternak deliberately turned from lyric poetry to an epic style which he felt was more in keeping with the era. His two long poems *1905* (1925–26) and *Lieutenant Schmidt* (1926–27) were attempts to come to grips with the theme of revolution and were, as such, a concession to the spirit of the times. It is perhaps significant that the most affecting lyric poetry was Yesenin's—his agonized but submissive disillusionment was powerfully conveyed in such poems as "Return to My Native Place" and "Soviet Russia," written a year before his suicide in 1925. The romantic prose of such writers as Babel and Ivanov was paralleled in the poetry of Eduard Bagritsky and Nikolai Tikhonov, both of whom wrote epics on heroic themes in exotic settings which showed some influence of the "counterrevolutionary" Gumilev. A highly original poet of the 1920's was Nikolai Zabolotsky, whose work is, on the surface, a kind of bizarre verbal genre painting, but embodies a pessimistic philosophy that brought him into official disfavor in later years.

At the turn of the decade, Stalin's "revolution from above," the first Five-Year Plan, and the beginning of collectivization temporarily resolved the doubts of several of the leading fellow travelers. There was even a resurgence of the millennial fervor which had been felt by some at the time of the October Revolution. Maxim Gorky's decision around this time (1929) to return to Russia and lend his authority to the Soviet regime was combined with evident approval of Stalin's measures to push Russia toward a future which, it was confidently expected, would see real social justice and an end to the cultural schism between people and intelligentsia. The more skeptical some writers had been, the more enthusiastic they now appeared to be. Leonov in his *Soviet River* (1929), Katayev in *Time Forward!* (1932), and Pilnyak in *The Volga Flows to the Caspian Sea* (1930) seemed to proclaim the imminence of victory over the physical environment and human nature itself. One of the most remarkable novels of this period was Ehrenburg's *The Second Day* (*Out of Chaos*, 1933–34), in which the author argued that the intellectual who still gave priority to the claims of conscience and independent moral judgment was, in effect, betraying the higher cause of socialism. In a debased and vulgarized form, the theme was typical of much "socialist realist" literature in the 1930's. Those who would not submit or see the light—so the message ran—would be unmasked and destroyed.

The actual doctrine of socialist realism was launched only in 1932. The idea, and the term itself, were introduced to the literary community, without any previous public debate, in a leading article in *Literaturnaya Gazeta* in May of that year. In the previous month the party had suddenly announced the liquidation of all the existing literary organizations and groups. By this time, because of the worsening political atmosphere, the existence of some of them was already largely nominal, but they had all once reflected important and genuine differences. Mention has been made of movements which in one way or another claimed to be innovative. But there were also voices, representing perhaps the majority of the leading Soviet writers, which spoke out strongly in favor of a more conventional view of the nature and function of literature. Chief among these was the Marxist literary critic and editor Alexander Voronsky, the guiding spirit of a group calling itself Pereval (The Pass), which arose at the end of 1923 and was associated with the literary journal *Krasnaya Nov* (Red Virgin Soil). A declaration published there in 1927 spoke of the need to preserve continuity with Russian and world classical literature. In his theoretical writings, Voronsky developed the view that art could not be seen as a mere social instrument or reduced to the sum of the techniques employed in its production (as both the constructivists and *LEF*—with support from the formalists— maintained), but sprang from intuitive or subconscious impulses beyond rational control or explanation. This implied that art was above the class struggle, and Voronsky was accused by the militant left of deviating from Marxism in favor of Bergson's intuitivism. (More seriously, he was later denounced—perhaps for reasons unconnected with his literary views—as a Trotskyist, and he disappeared during the purges.) Although Voronsky came to grief because of his theoretical arguments, his spirit of compromise as editor of *Krasnaya Nov* (from 1921 until his dismissal in 1927) accorded well with the actual party line almost to the end of the 1920's.

Apart from the neutrality implied in the party's resolution of 1925, the "conservative" literary tastes of Lenin and other Soviet leaders tended to favor middle-of-the-road resistance to both "bourgeois-intellectual" and "proletarian" intransigence of the left. After the collapse of Proletkult, the cause of proletarian militancy in literature had been taken up by the Russian Association of Proletarian Writers (RAPP), formed at a conference of proletarian writers in January 1925. Bowing to the party's resolution of July of that year, RAPP modified its aggressive attitude to the fellow travelers, but it never lost sight of its aim of "proletarianizing" Soviet literature. (Few of its members were actual proletarians by origin—least of all Leopold Averbakh, its general secretary from 1926 until its dissolution, or Fadeyev, the most notable writer connected with it.) RAPP prepared the way for socialist realism by insisting that Soviet writers abandon the "wait and see" attitude of the fellow travelers and make a positive commitment to communist ideology. They also elaborated what was to be the main aesthetic requirement of socialist realism, namely that writers "learn from the classics," putting the literary techniques of nineteenth-century Russian realism at the service of the proletariat and the party.

Although, typically, he was to liquidate its authors, Stalin found this formula well suited to both his political aims and his personal tastes. In 1929, after the final breaking of his opponents in the party, Stalin allowed RAPP to start a campaign of intimidation against uncommitted writers. Two leading fellow travelers, Boris Pilnyak and Yevgeni Zamyatin, both of them officials of the largest literary organization, the Union of Writers (little more than an ordinary professional association and not to be confused with the Union of Soviet Writers after 1934), were hounded on account of work which had been published abroad. Zamyatin's antiutopian novel *We* had been written in 1920 and was published abroad in 1924. Pilnyak's *Mahogany* appeared in Berlin in 1929. There was no law against Soviet writers publishing abroad, but these two particular cases were used as a pretext for impugning the political reliability of the two authors in question and of the fellow travelers in general. This was the first such concerted campaign against intellectuals designed to cow them and force their allegiance. Pilnyak recanted, in a manner that was to become familiar, but Zamyatin refused to yield and was allowed to emigrate (in 1931).[1]

Although it took some time for the lesson to sink in, this was the point of no return for Soviet intellectuals. Paradoxically, however, the party resolution of 1932, which condemned the "excesses" of RAPP and ordered its liquidation, looked at first like a gesture of reconciliation. It was announced that writers were

---

[1]See the following chapter.—ED.

now to belong to a "unified" organization which would be open to all, irrespective of their class antecedents (i.e., whether they had been proletarians or fellow travelers), as long as they were prepared to give their general assent to party policy and to the literary doctrine of socialist realism. At first it looked as though the party was simply providing a relatively loose organizational and doctrinal framework which, almost in the spirit of Pereval, would give scope to a wide range of individual talent—from, say, Fadeyev to Pasternak. The first Writers' Congress, in 1934, which was held to inaugurate the new Union of Soviet Writers, seemed to confirm this impression. Furthermore, the rise of Hitler and the beginnings of the "popular front" policy appeared to dictate ideological tolerance in an antifascist camp which had to embrace liberal opinion on an international scale.

But things soon took a very different turn. The progressive deterioration of the political situation in Russia after the murder of Kirov (1934) destroyed the conditions for independent creative activity of any kind, and by 1939 the best that any Soviet writer who wished to keep his integrity could hope for was to be allowed to fall silent. Babel, Pilnyak, and many other Soviet writers were arrested and died in camps. Akhmatova chose silence, Pasternak took refuge in translation, and Mandelstam, who in 1934 had written and read to some friends a poem condemning Stalin, spent three years in exile before being finally sent to his death in a concentration camp at the end of 1938. After Stalin walked out of the first performance of Shostakovich's opera *Lady Macbeth of Mtsensk* in 1936, it was made plain that socialist realism had to be interpreted as a crass and eclectic style which reminded some Russians of the folksy vulgarity associated with the reign of Alexander III. "Formalism" (widened to mean any kind of stylistic originality) was now treated as a political crime, and when Meyerhold, in a final gesture of despair, publicly refused to accept socialist realism in a speech in 1939, he was arrested and disappeared.

When it was first launched, socialist realism was supposedly meant to denote a literary manner which had arisen spontaneously, as a natural development of nineteenth-century "critical" realism, differing from it only in the vital respect that it was optimistic or affirmative in its view of the progress of mankind toward socialism. It was held to have been exemplified in Gorky's *Mother* (1906) and later in some of the fellow-traveler writing of the 1920's—Fedin, Leonov, Sholokhov, and others were regarded as having written socialist realist novels well before the term had become a standard one. In fact, the doctrine has always been definable less in literary terms than in terms of the political demands made of writers and artists at various periods. Anybody who in the 1920's had supported the Soviet regime or given an optimistic appraisal of its prospects was later described as a socialist realist (unless he was swept away in one of the recurrent purges). In the 1930's, to qualify as a good socialist realist it was safest to write historical chronicles, such as those of Alexei Tolstoy on Ivan the Terrible and Peter the Great, which contained thinly disguised flattery of Stalin. The most widely acclaimed product of socialist realism on a contemporary theme was the pedestrian but uplifting novel by Nikolai Ostrovsky, *How the Steel Was Tempered* (1932–34).

As has often been pointed out, the war brought relief to writers in the sense that nothing more was required of them than to play a minor part in a clear-cut struggle for national survival which overrode or made irrelevant the question of artistic integrity. Some of the semidocumentary fiction of the war period has at least a certain graphic immediacy which ensures its survival: Konstantin Simonov's *Days and Nights* (1943–44), Vasili Grossman's *The People Immortal* (1942), and particularly Petr Vershigora's *Men with a Clear Conscience* (1946), an uncompleted novel about the partisans, are refreshingly superior to some of the blatantly falsified accounts of the war which appeared later. Although, by the nature of things, only rhetorical or epic poetry was called for (Alexander Tvardovsky's long ballad about the ordinary Soviet soldier Vasili Tyorkin was immensely popular), there was also a revival of true lyric poetry; this was the heyday of the middle generation of poets, such as Alexei Surkov, Margarita Aliger, and Konstantin Simonov, who wrote poems with a personal ring, less encumbered by the obligatory official stereotyped sentiment which disfigured most of the poetry published after the war until Stalin's death. In these conditions of comparative relaxation, Akhmatova and Pasternak (his collection *On Early Trains* [1943] contains poems on topical wartime themes) were able to publish again after years of silence; this gave rise to a widespread feeling among the intelligentsia that peace might bring with it a change for the better.

But all hopes were dashed by the Central Committee decrees (1946–48) on art and literature associated with the name of Andrei Zhdanov, the member of the Politburo who dealt with cultural matters. Akhmatova was denounced by Zhdanov as "half nun, half whore," and the journal that had published her verse was liquidated. For the remaining years of Stalin's life the Soviet creative intelligentsia lived in a constant state of fear, and the political demands made on writers were so excessive as to destroy even the propaganda value of literature. Socialist realists were now required to ignore the grim realities of Soviet postwar life and present instead fanciful pictures of material abundance and social harmony.

In the years since Stalin's death in 1953, Soviet literature has benefited from a gradual abatement of the paralyzing terror which had been the chief instrument of rule since the early 1930's. In theory the party has continued to maintain that literature must be regulated by ideological and administrative controls, but in the absence of total terror these controls became progressively less effective, particularly after Khrushchev's selective denunciation of Stalin's "mistakes" at the Twentieth Party Congress in 1956 —this was a fatal blow to the myth of the party's infallibility. There have been three major attempts to set the clock back: in 1954 as a reaction to the first cautious challenges after Stalin's death to official doctrine (Vladimir Pomerantsev's essay "On Sincerity in Literature" in *Novy Mir*, No. 12, December 1953, and Ehrenburg's novel *The Thaw* in *Znamya*, May 1954); then, in 1957, in panic at the Hungarian revolution and the literary response to the Twentieth Congress (e.g., Vladimir Dudintsev's *Not by Bread Alone* and Alexander Yashin's short story "The Levers"); and finally, in 1962–63, when Khrushchev, provoked by an exhibition of what he took to be modern painting, for a brief while set about checking the "liberal" trend set in motion by his own impetuous initiatives.

The capacity of the Soviet leadership to exploit literature for its own ends continued to decline after Khrushchev's fall in 1964, despite clumsy efforts by his successors to restore a measure of ideological discipline. The party still disposes of a formidable apparatus of cultural control and repression, but its will to use it has weakened in the face of a greater independence of spirit at home and the need to achieve at least an appearance of respectability abroad. In the mid-1970's the conflict with China and the concurrent policy of détente with the United States clearly imposed certain restraints in the handling of the consequences of "destalinization" and of some of Khrushchev's specific interventions in literary matters, particularly his speech to the Third Writers' Congress in 1959. On this occasion he said that the writers should not come running "to the government" for the settlement of all their disputes, thus implicitly (and perhaps unwittingly) suggesting that literature and the arts were an area of Soviet life which could not, or should not, be an object of absolute party control.

Whatever his reasons for this concession, the immediate result was a certain tolerance—apart from the interlude of a few months in 1962–63—for the public airing in circumspect language of differences of opinion in literary matters. An open fissure was thus allowed to develop in the "monolith" of ideological unity which Stalin had maintained by repeated waves of terror. In this unprecedented situation, the party began to pursue a policy of holding a balance between the so-called conservatives (or "dogmatists," as they are often styled by their opponents in the Soviet Union) and the liberals who sometimes refer to themselves as progressives. The former are joined together by a vested interest in maintaining the rule of mediocrity and are clearly nostalgic for the straightforward situation of Stalin's time; they militantly uphold the doctrine of socialist realism, put loyalty to party discipline above artistic independence, and are identified with a scarcely veiled nationalist, even chauvinist (and anti-Semitic) mood. There were signs in the second half of the 1960's that some of the dogmatists were as disenchanted with the post-Stalin leadership as the liberals, and that the Politburo of Brezhnev and Kosygin, trying to steer a "centrist" course, was at times as disturbed by opposition from the right as by opposition from the left. Some novels by right-wingers, such as Vsevolod Kochetov (*What Is It You Want?*, 1969) and Ivan Shevtsov (*Love and Hatred*, 1970), called unambiguously for the restoration of strong rule and ideological order. Both novels provoked controversy in the Soviet press, some critics attacking and others defending them. This in itself was a good example of how radical divisions in literary (and, by implication, political) opinion could now be revealed in public.

Apart from Mikhail Sholokhov, there are few writers of genuine literary achievement among the conservatives. Not surprisingly, their ranks contain a high proportion of provincials who tend to be resentful of the more sophisticated metropolitan writers. Officeholders in the various writers' organizations are also, needless to say, predominantly conservative. They are especially strong and militant in the Writers' Union of the RSFSR, which was set up in 1958 as a counterweight to the Writers' Union of the USSR, where the liberals (particularly in its Moscow branch) were occasionally able to exert influence and even get themselves elected to the board. But by and large the liberals have been excluded from positions of authority in the cultural establishment and, like their counterparts in the last century, they have made their voices heard mainly through certain literary periodicals, especially *Novy Mir*.

During the editorship of the poet Alexander Tvardovsky (who resigned under pressure in 1970), the monthly *Novy Mir* became a latter-day equivalent of *Otechestvennyye Zapiski (Fatherland Notes)* in the period (1868–77) when it was edited by N. A. Nekrasov. By its choice of authors (Solzhenitsyn, among others) and the skillful use in articles on current affairs of the kind of veiled language which in Russia is traditionally called Aesopian, *Novy Mir* gave expression to the liberal position during the 1960's. Its principal demand, sometimes defined editorially in so many words by Tvardovsky himself, was quite simply for truth and sincerity.

In the liberal view, a writer's loyalty can only be to his own conscience. Believing that there is nothing incompatible between patriotism and an openness to outside influences, the liberals have also been in favor of breaking down cultural barriers between Russia and the West. Unlike the Westernizers of the last century, probably few of them are naive enough to think that the West can offer some ready-made solution to Russia's political and social problems. They appear to believe, however, that literature and the arts, by gradually changing the general climate of opinion, can contribute to a slow process of reform.

The moral commitment of the post-Stalin liberal writers, and the consequent need to relate their work to the general political background, make it difficult to assess their achievement in purely literary terms. There has been little writing in prose to compare with the best work of the 1920's. Novels and stories that created a stir in the immediate post-Stalin years represent at best a kind of inverted socialist realism. Ehrenburg's *Thaw* (1954), which gave its name to this period, can be interpreted as a polemic with his own earlier *Second Day*; its implicit conclusion is that in times of conformism imposed by terror the only honorable course for the individual is to try to maintain, at least privately, some kind of personal integrity of intellectual and moral judgment. The next important work of the thaw period, Dudintsev's *Not by Bread Alone*, appeared in the auspicious climate created by Khrushchev's revelations about Stalin at the Twentieth Party Congress in 1956. Flat and ill constructed, with a schematic conflict between "good" and "bad," it is distinguished from a standard socialist realist novel only by its reversal of the values that had hitherto been obligatory. Instead of being vested abstractly in the party, "good" now resides, according to Dudintsev's reappraisal, in the conscience of individuals who are prepared to fight for the truth as they see it. The characters in Ehrenburg's *Thaw* had been passive in their resistance to "collective" pressure, but Dudintsev's hero fights actively and heroically for what he believes to be right. The highlight of the first phase of post-Stalin "liberalization"—and a contributing factor in its abrupt suspension—was the publication in the second half of 1956 of two volumes of a

literary anthology entitled *Literaturnaya Moskva.* Edited by Veniamin Kaverin, Konstantin Paustovsky, and others, it was something in the nature of a collective gesture on the part of a whole
group of Soviet writers. A novel by Emmanuil Kazakevich in the
first volume, *The House on the Square,* gave a revealing description of the atmosphere in the Soviet army of occupation in Germany. The second volume contained what was perhaps the most
explosive work to appear by the end of 1956: Alexander Yashin's
short story "The Levers," a study in the falsity of public attitudes
engendered by Stalinism.

In the following years the "new wave" prose gradually shifted
the focus of its interest from public values (roughly speaking, the
question of how individuals should behave as members of society
or of the party) to the exploration of more private aspects of life.
The typical genre was now the long short story or short novel
(povest). This was partly a reaction against the long-windedness
of Stalinist literature, but it also reflected a lessening concern with
the broad social background against which small private dramas
may be acted out. At first this low-key fiction, of which some of
the most successful practitioners are Vladimir Tendryakov, Yuri
Kazakov, Vasili Aksyonov, I. Grekova (Yelena Ventzel), Vitali
Semin, Yuri Nagibin, Yuri Trifonov, Andrei Bitov, Nikolai
Dubov, Georgi Vladimov, Anatoli Gladilin, Viktor Nekrasov, and
Vladimir Voinovich, met with great hostility, and it is still
frowned on by the conservative critics, who complain about its
"abstract humanism" and concern with the trivia of human existence, rather than with the grand perspectives of the "building
of communism." What is most offensive to its enemies about this
new prose is the absence of "positive heroes" who, in classical
socialist realism, were supposed to serve as inspirational models to
Soviet readers. This is not to say that the new fiction does not
raise, if only by implication, some of the broader issues of Soviet
society. There are of course specific problems which arise from
the havoc caused by the years of Stalinism. The extent, for example, to which the Russian countryside was pillaged in order to pay
for industrialization has been demonstrated in an impressive body
of writing, mainly in the form of sketches *(ocherki)* and short

stories. Reminiscent of the populist prose of the last century in their frank documentation of the country's major social problem, the writings of Valentin Ovechkin, Yefim Dorosh, Sergei Zalygin, Fedor Abramov, Boris Mozhayev, and others came close to saying outright that the party's agricultural policy has been a disastrous failure from beginning to end.

Some of the writers in this group (often referred to collectively as the *derevenshchiki*, "village writers") have tended to emphasize a more positive aspect of the countryside as a repository of traditional values which are disappearing in the towns. This is a remarkable feature of some of Tendryakov's stories. Sometimes there are distinctly religious or Slavophile undertones, as in the sketches and stories of Vladimir Soloukhin. Other interesting "village" prose has been written by Vasili Belov, Valentin Rasputin, and Vasili Shukshin.

Little of literary worth has been published by way of humorous or satirical prose writing on contemporary themes—in this, as in other respects, the post-Stalin years have not been able to match the 1920's. All that springs to mind are some of the stories by Fazil Iskander (who in less constraining circumstances might have blossomed into a writer of major satirical talent), and one story by Vasili Aksyonov. A humorous prose epic by Vladimir Voinovich remains unpublished in the Soviet Union.

An important branch of prose in the last decade or so have been retrospective and relatively unvarnished accounts, in the form of semi-memoirs or fiction, of the wartime experience. Some of the assiduously fostered myths of the Stalin period have been disposed of by Konstantin Simonov and—most effectively of all from a literary standpoint—by Vasili Bykov.

Some of the older fellow-traveler writers have also made noteworthy contributions to post-Stalin prose. Like Ehrenburg, both Leonov and Katayev have published novels in which they seem to take issue with their earlier attitudes and rationalizations. From the literary point of view the most rewarding of these works is Katayev's *The Holy Well* (1966), a dream journey into the author's own past with a curious (and avowed) indebtedness to Fellini's film technique. There is a devastating portrait of a literary timeserver who may well embody some of the features of his own past that Katayev now most regrets. The story also contains a gruesome image for the Soviet writer obedient to Stalin's whims: a cat which had been trained to speak by its Georgian owner and dies while trying to mouth the latest polysyllabic catchword. Leonov's *Yevgeniya Ivanovna* (1963) is a similar study in fellow-traveler "revisionism," though the implications are deeply buried beneath layers of characteristic ambivalence. The heroine is a Russian woman taken into emigration at the end of the Civil War by her husband and then abandoned by him. After marrying a distinguished English archaeologist (she presumes her Russian husband is dead), Yevgeniya Ivanovna goes with him to Soviet Georgia, where she meets her ex-husband, who has now become an exponent of the crass "national Bolshevism" which was the author's own credo in the late 1920's and 1930's. Not all surviving novelists of the older generation have gone so far in rebutting their own earlier beliefs; some who no doubt had fewer illusions, such as Kaverin and Paustovsky, have made telling contributions to the liberal reappraisal of the Stalinist past. Sholokhov, on the other hand, in speeches at Writers' and Party Congresses, has adopted an outspokenly right-wing line (in 1966, for instance, at the Twenty-third Party Congress, he called for stern measures against dissident intellectuals).

The greatest and most original achievement of post-Stalin prose to be published in the Soviet Union is undeniably Alexander Solzhenitsyn's short novel on Stalin's concentration camps, *One Day in the Life of Ivan Denisovich* (No. 11, 1962). It is ironic that this work, which must be judged primarily for its lasting worth as a work of literature in the grand Russian tradition, should have appeared as the result of a squalid political intrigue. There seems no doubt that Khrushchev personally sanctioned its publication by *Novy Mir* because he thought that a frank account of Stalin's concentration camps would help mobilize public opinion behind him at a moment when his position was threatened by his rivals in the presidium. Once again, in order to gain a tactical advantage —as in his revelations about Stalin in 1956—Khrushchev failed to take into account the long-term effect of his actions. By exploding the limits of what, thematically speaking, had hitherto been possible for Soviet writers, and by giving the stamp of quasi-official approval to a work which implicitly questioned the legitimacy of all the Soviet regime's basic claims, Khrushchev prepared the ground for the opposition to the party's control of literature which spread among the Soviet literary intelligentsia during the following years. Solzhenitsyn himself, in an open letter to delegates at the Writers' Congress in May 1967 and in a subsequent letter to the Board of the Writers' Union in December 1967, denounced the censorship of Soviet literature and the failure of the Writers' Union to protect the interests of its members.

But the literary significance of *One Day in the Life of Ivan Denisovich* is far greater than its political impact. As in any true work of art, the aesthetic quality transcends the content, i.e., the documentary, ideological, or political aspects of the raw material. Even the best of other post-Stalin prose writing tends to rely in considerable degree for its literary effect on the reader's awareness of the peculiar social and political context in which it is written. If such awareness of the context were to be taken away, much of this writing would seem far less significant. Without the knowledge that it is written in defiance of certain previously imposed standards, and that a challenge to them still involves difficulties or hazards for the author, one would lose the odd sense of tension which Soviet literature derives from its nonliterary context: it is the difference between watching a man walking on a tightrope and watching a man walking on the ground. The remarkable feature of this first published work of Solzhenitsyn is that, though his subject is peculiarly Soviet, it is at the same time independent of the geographical and historical context. In other words the political implications of his novel, as well as the time and place in which the action is set, are incidental to the author's achievement of having fashioned a statement of universal application out of the squalid material of life in a concentration camp. One day in the life of Ivan Denisovich seems uncannily symbolic of one day in *anybody*'s life. Like Kafka's *The Trial*, Solzhenitsyn's novel shows the human condition as a captive state from which there is no escape and for which there is no rational explanation.

The feeling of being trapped and doomed is considerably heightened by making the reader see the concentration camp through the eyes of an illiterate peasant who is unable to rationalize his predicament as an intellectual would. To achieve this effect, Solzhenitsyn resorted to the device known as *skaz,* in which the language of the narrative is the same—in a slightly stylized form —as that of the main characters and of the particular milieu in which they live (in this case the speech of a peasant from central Russia intermixed with concentration camp slang). This in itself raises the novel to a higher literary level than any other prose published in the post-Stalin period. It was the first challenge in many years to the drab, emasculated idiom of socialist realism from which few of the younger prose writers referred to above have succeeded completely in emancipating themselves.

After 1966, when his short story "Zakhar the Pouch" appeared in *Novy Mir,* Solzhenitsyn was unable to have any further work published in the Soviet Union. His two long novels *The Cancer Ward* and *The First Circle* circulated in manuscript, as a result of which copies found their way abroad, where they were published in Russian and other languages (1968 and 1969). Both these novels are more directly autobiographical than *One Day in the Life of Ivan Denisovich.* Nerzhin, the main character in *The First Circle* (which was written over a period of ten years, 1955–66), to some extent represents the author himself, as does Kostoglotov in *The Cancer Ward.* After his arrest at the front in 1945, Solzhenitsyn was sentenced to eight years' imprisonment, the first four of which he spent mainly in the peculiar institution described in *The First Circle*—a prison on the outskirts of Moscow in which scientists and technologists were confined in comparatively mild conditions, as long as they agreed to work on special projects— such as new spying gadgets—commissioned by Stalin and Abakumov, the head of the secret police. Solzhenitsyn was sent there on the strength of his knowledge of physics and mathematics. Disobedience meant being consigned to a forced labor camp of the type described in *One Day,* and this is what happened to Solzhenitsyn at the end of 1949. On his release in 1953 he was required to live in exile in Kazakhstan. After falling ill with some form of cancer, he was allowed to go to a hospital in Tashkent, the scene of *The Cancer Ward* (written in 1963–66), which thus forms the third part of a trilogy.

The First Circle and *The Cancer Ward* are much longer, more ambitious, and consequently less sharply focused than *One Day*, but they give a revealing panorama of Soviet life during the late Stalin years and the first two or three years after his death. Missing is the peculiar effect of distance that *One Day* achieves by interposing a semiliterate narrator between the author and his experiences. Owing a good deal in language and technique to Tolstoy, Solzhenitsyn's long novels bear a closer relation to the tradition of nineteenth-century Russian prose. In the summer of 1971, Solzhenitsyn authorized the publication in Paris of a new novel, *August 1914*, the first part of a series of volumes whose purpose is to explore the roots of the Russian Revolution and to call into question the official version of Soviet history. At the end of 1973, Solzhenitsyn further released for publication in Paris the first part of *The Gulag Archipelago*, a vast study of the Soviet prison and penal system from the Revolution to the present day, written between 1958 and 1967. The publication of this impassioned work, which contains passages of remarkable descriptive power, was the last straw for the Soviet government. Evidently not daring to apply harsher measures for fear of the effect on world opinion, the authorities stripped him of Soviet citizenship and forcibly exiled him to West Germany in February 1974.

It is to the poets rather than to the prose writers (with the exception of Solzhenitsyn) that one must look for new departures in language and style in the post-Stalin era. The revival of Russian poetry in the last fifteen years or so can perhaps be explained in part as a spontaneous revolt against the stultification and debasement of the Russian language under Stalin. It was the poets who had been most sensitive to the destruction or mutilation of the sort of private values which are the natural realm of poetry. Poetic language had become hopelessly bombastic and public. From the prosodic point of view it was required to be so conventional that even imitation of Mayakovsky was viewed as dangerous "formalism." Most authentic poetic voices—those of Pasternak and Akhmatova, for instance—had again been silenced after the brief interlude of wartime, and such poets as continued to publish were virtually indistinguishable from each other. It was not until after 1956 that this torpor gradually came to an end and new voices were heard. At first, as in prose, the new wave of post-Stalin poetry was remarkable more for what it said than for its style— which remained, on the whole, unadventurous. Yevgeni Yevtushenko made his debut as a "civic" poet concerned above all to expose the evils of Stalinism, voicing the moral revulsion of his generation in a somewhat eclectic manner but with skill and courage. He was one of the first to speak frankly of many important issues, such as anti-Semitism ("Babi Yar," 1961) and the danger of a reversion to Stalinism ("Stalin's Heirs," 1962). Yevtushenko's early achievements may seem less remarkable with the passage of time, and he has been criticized for his supposed triteness and failure to find a distinctive accent of his own. But he is a genuine lyric poet, sometimes resembling Yesenin in his candor about himself, who has felt forced to speak out urgently in a manner that did not always do justice to his best qualities. These have found expression in his more intimate, lyrical poems, which attracted less attention than the "civic" ones. In his work of later years he shows himself to be master of a firm and fluent poetic manner unmistakably his own.

Andrei Voznesensky, who burst onto the scene a little later than Yevtushenko, immediately created an impression of considerable originality. If Yevtushenko had been concerned with the moral enlightenment of his audience, Voznesensky aimed rather at reinvigorating the idiom and accents of poetry. In his early verse he caught the attention by his virtuosity in handling the Russian language, his ability to exploit the connotative associations of words in such a way as to achieve unusual effects of irony and ambiguity.

It is impossible to give here any idea of the range and quality of Russian poetry at the present day. Yevtushenko and Voznesensky created an atmosphere in which poets sometimes achieved the status of popular idols. In the early 1960's public hunger for verse was such that the sports stadium of Luzhniki in Moscow could be packed by almost 15,000 people for a poetry recital (although in the post-Khrushchev era the authorities have discouraged appearances by "controversial" poets at large public gatherings and on television).

Among the younger poets who have made a name for themselves in recent years one may mention Bella Akhmadulina, Viktor Sosnora, Yunna Morits, Yevgeni Vinokurov, Alexander Kushner, Vladimir Kornilov, David Samoilov, and Naum Korzhavin (who emigrated to the West in 1974). Joseph Brodsky, perhaps the most accomplished and original of the post-Stalin generation, has never been published in the Soviet Union, apart from several short items which appeared in anthologies in 1966 and 1967. In 1964 he was tried as a "parasite" and banished to the Arkhangelsk region, where he worked on a collective farm before being released the following year in the wake of a worldwide outcry. From the two collections of his work that have appeared in the West it is evident that his talent is in a different mold from that of Voznesensky, Yevtushenko, and his other contemporaries. This may in part be due to its having been nurtured not in Moscow but in Leningrad, where the finer reverberations of Russia's "Silver Age" of poetry never entirely died away through decades of terror, war, and famine. Mandelstam once defined acmeism as "nostalgia for world culture," and although Brodsky cannot be described as an acmeist in any meaningful sense, he does appear consciously to have adopted the acmeist concern for Russia's links with Europe and with "Judeo-Christian culture" (Mandelstam's phrase). The futurists and some of the symbolists (including Blok) were more inclined to stress Russia's cultural separateness. Like Mandelstam and Akhmatova (to whom he was very close in the last years of her life), Brodsky is a true European, as can be clearly sensed in the very texture of his poetry. It has a "classical" intonation, as opposed to the frenetic "romantic" quality of Voznesensky, Akhmadulina, and others. In 1972 Brodsky emigrated from the Soviet Union and went to live in the United States.

Although they are not perhaps poets in the strict sense of the word, there are several writers and performers of songs who in recent years have achieved great popularity—for the most part unofficially—with the Soviet public. Resembling French *chansonniers*, they comment on many aspects of Soviet life in sharply satirical fashion. The most lyrical of them is Bulat Okudzhava. Alexander Galich is noteworthy for his effective use of a racy Moscow vernacular.

Several poets of the "middle generation" who survived the Stalin era deserve mention together with the younger poets whom they sometimes encouraged and defended. Such are Boris Slutsky, Olga Berggolts, Leonid Martynov, Arseni Tarkovsky, and Alexander Tvardovsky. The last is best known for his editorship of *Novy Mir*, but his two epic poems *Into the Far Distance* and the satirical *Vasili Terkin in the Other World* are major landmarks of post-Stalin literature. Tvardovsky was not an innovator, but his handling of conventional verse forms in such a way as to achieve an easy colloquial effect is masterly.

No survey of the Soviet period of Russian literature would be complete without a consideration of two features which are perhaps the most striking result of the relaxation of Stalinist controls. The first is the "discovery" of works which were written many years ago, by authors long since dead, and which have been published in the Soviet Union after their "rehabilitation"; the second is the process by which works circulate in manuscript, later finding their way abroad to be published there.

In prose, the most significant of the belatedly published works is Mikhail Bulgakov's *The Master and Margarita* (1966–67). It was finished not long before the author's death in 1940 and is a comic masterpiece unsurpassed in Soviet literature. Outwardly it is a picaresque novel about the adventures of the devil and his companions in Moscow at some indeterminate time in the late 1920's or early 1930's. As the title implies, it is also a retelling of the Faust legend in a Soviet setting, but the most extraordinary feature, interwoven as a subplot, is a brilliantly imaginative version of the condemnation and execution of Christ. If Bulgakov had been known only by his earlier works he would rate as no more than a gifted satirist, a Soviet imitator of Gogol, but the publication of *The Master and Margarita* revealed him as a great Russian writer who at first sight seems out of place in the shallows of Soviet prose. No Soviet writer has ever dared approach the problem of evil—a central preoccupation of nineteenth-century Russian literature—in such a direct and challenging fashion. A lesser, unfinished novel by Bulgakov, *Theatrical Novel (Black Snow)*, was published in 1965, a quarter of a century after it was written. Apart from being very funny, it is interesting for its satirical portraits of Stanislavsky and Nemirovich-Danchenko. It is only in recent years that any word of criticism has been voiced about the stultifying effect their apotheosis under Stalin had on the Soviet theater, and the belated appearance of Bulgakov's novel has contributed to the slow emancipation of the Soviet stage from "the Method."

Another prose writer who has to some extent been "revealed" by posthumous (but still very selective) editions of his work is Andrei Platonov. He published a certain amount in the 1920's and early 1930's, but later found it more and more difficult to get into print. Platonov has the rare distinction for a Soviet writer of having been a true proletarian. His father was a mechanic in a railway workshop, and he himself went to work at the age of fifteen. The heroes of his stories and novels are also often skilled workers and mechanics, and it is immediately apparent that he writes from a sense of personal identification with them. Like many real workers, he was dismayed by the bureaucratization of the "workers' and peasants'" state and gave vent to his feelings in a mordant satire, *The City of Gradov* (1929), which is modeled, as one sees from the title, on Saltykov-Shchedrin's famous mock chronicle of Russian despotism, *The Story of a City* (1869–70). Like the poet Nikolai Zabolotsky, Platonov has a philosophical concern with the interplay of *homo faber* and nature: the mechanic, or any creative person, is seen as an organizing, harmonizing element in the apparent chaos of the world. The eerie quality of the situations and environments he describes, matched by a deliberate quaintness of language reminiscent of some *skaz* writers (such as Leskov in the nineteenth century and Zoshchenko in the Soviet period), creates an effect of conspicuous originality against the general background of socialist realist prose. Although never imprisoned, he was publicly denounced several times for "slander," and in the postwar years his name, like that of Babel, Zamyatin, Pilnyak, Bulgakov, and others, was expunged from the record. The republication of his earlier writings and posthumous publication of some later work have made him into an exciting "discovery" for a younger generation of readers in the Soviet Union. But at least two important long works have still to appear there: *Chevengur,* a novel about the early years of the Revolution, and *The Foundation Pit (Kotlovan).*

Several other outstanding works of Russian literature have so far been published only in the West—though in a few cases Western publication has been followed by full or partial publication in the Soviet Union. The most famous example is Pasternak's *Doctor Zhivago.* Having failed to get it published in the Soviet Union shortly after Stalin's death, Pasternak deliberately arranged for its appearance abroad. It was the first time in many years that anyone had dared to do this: ever since the persecution of Zamyatin and Pilnyak in the late 1920's there had been no greater sin for a Soviet writer than to send a work out of the country. It required uncommon courage on Pasternak's part to come forth as a witness—thereby easing the way for others—after all the silent years of terror. His anguished decision to "break the spell of the dead letter" is described in "Hamlet," the first of the cycle of Zhivago's poems at the end of the novel. Some of these poems have been published over the years in the Soviet Union. "Hamlet" was even quoted in full in an article by Voznesensky on Pasternak as a translator—in this context the censor evidently thought it was a translation from Shakespeare! But the novel itself remains under a ban, though it is probably no more anti-Soviet than *The Master and Margarita* or *One Day in the Life of Ivan Denisovich,* the only two novels published in the Soviet Union which stand comparison with it. Like all great works, it has several levels of meaning, some of them too deep, perhaps, to be appreciated by the present generation of readers. At the first and most superficial level, it is a *roman à thèse.* This aspect need not be thought unworthy of discussion, since it was Pasternak's conscious intention to condemn not only Marxism (dismissed by

79

Zhivago in a few contemptuous phrases), but also what might be called the *Russian* ideology which in the nineteenth century made possible the uncritical adoption of ready-made doctrines in general. The unspeakable tragedies of the Soviet period were seen by Pasternak as to some extent a consequence of the maximalist temperament of the Russian intelligentsia, of its belief in the possibility of all-embracing solutions. He makes it quite clear that in his view there has been only one revolution in human history —namely, the coming of Christ with the simple assertion of the freedom of the individual personality. From this larger view, the seizure of power by the Bolsheviks in 1917 was, he implies, an attempt at counterevolution, throwing us back to Roman times when there were leaders ("pockmarked Caligulas"—Pasternak's only reference to Stalin) and herdlike peoples. At deeper levels, Pasternak tries to reach beyond the perspective of mere history, in which the Soviet episode appears only as a single day, to the even broader context of eternity and nature—this is the real background against which Zhivago's temporal ordeal is to be seen. *Doctor Zhivago* must be considered a *Soviet* novel because its starting point is the author's own experience of the Soviet era, but by making his readers view it in the light of poetic infinity he achieves a singular effect of transcendence.

For a similar reason two long poems by Akhmatova, also published in full only abroad, are essentially Soviet. *Requiem* (written between 1935 and 1940) is a lament for her second husband, her son, and all her compatriots who disappeared into concentration camps in the 1930's (her son survived a second imprisonment after the war). It is a work of simple dignity which, as befits a memorial, needs no comment or explanation. The same cannot be said of *Poem without a Hero,* written between 1940 and 1942 but published for the first time in New York in 1961 (the first part, under the title *A Petersburg Tale,* was published in the Soviet Union in 1965). This is a cryptic work which is not easy to understand without some knowledge of the St. Petersburg social scene in 1913. As has been pointed out by Kornei Chukovsky and others, Akhmatova, even in her intimate lyric poetry, has a keen sense of history and likes to record events and exact dates in the manner of a chronicler. The events may seem personal or trivial, but she has a way of making them significant in relation to the wider context of the era. In *Poem without a Hero*, a series of narrative episodes interspersed with lyrical digressions, she allows herself the scope of an epic poet in order to try to make sense of the era; the result is a remarkable work in which personal and national destiny are intertwined. In the tradition of Pushkin's *Bronze Horseman* and Blok's *Retribution,* she sets out to illuminate the present and future in the light of the past. The poem was written at a particularly terrible time for Akhmatova, personally and for her country. At a precise moment in 1940—it happened, as she tells us, while she was looking through some old papers—she thought back beyond the years of Revolution, famine, and mass arrests to 1913, the last peacetime year after which "the real, not the calendar, twentieth century" was to begin. She remembered, in particular, the suicide of a young poet which shocked the glittering, morally corroded intellectual world to which she belonged. She appears to suggest that everybody was guilty, that the young poet was sacrificed on the altar of his contemporaries' vanity and wickedness. The idea that the catastrophes to come were a collective punishment on a society that scarcely deserved to survive gains from being conveyed with Akhmatova's usual restraint and matter-of-factness. Though her view is less Olympian than Pasternak's in *Doctor Zhivago* (perhaps because her personal ordeal was greater), she too transcends the Soviet experience, making it bearable to herself in religious terms as one link in a chain of sin, retribution, and possible redemption.

The widespread circulation in typescript of many other works not published in the Soviet Union has resulted in the appearance of an extensive literature parallel to the officially sanctioned one, and sometimes misleadingly referred to abroad as "underground." In Russia it is known as *samizdat* ("self-publishing," by analogy with *gosizdat*—"state publishing"). Many of these works are not, in any real sense, politically subversive and have in some cases been submitted for publication to literary journals or state publishing houses; but having been rejected by censorship, they circulate, with or without the knowledge of their authors, in the manner of chain letters—that is, they are typed out in several copies, passed on to others, and then typed out again. Though there are penalties for the circulation and harboring of material judged to be "anti-Soviet," there is nothing in Soviet law that forbids the copying out and passing on of manuscripts as such. Inevitably, however, the growth of *samizdat* has led in recent years to several trials of writers accused of slander against the Soviet system. The first was that of Andrei Sinyavsky and Yuli Daniel in February 1966. Then, at the beginning of 1968, several young writers were tried and sentenced because they had edited a *samizdat* literary journal and organized protests against the harsh sentences passed on Sinyavsky and Daniel.

It is impossible to give here a comprehensive account of *samizdat*. Perhaps its most successful literary products, apart from those already mentioned, have been the stories of Sinyavsky and Daniel, first published abroad under their pseudonyms, Abram Tertz and Nikolai Arzhak. Stylistically, Daniel's stories have much in common with the "new wave" prose of his contemporaries, such as Tendryakov, Nagibin, and others. In "This Is Moscow Speaking" (1962) and "Atonement" (1964), he deals in a vivid manner with the moral damage inflicted by Stalinism. Sinyavsky, as he emphasized at his trial, writes in a consciously experimental fashion, seeking to revive an element of fantasy which had been largely lost in the later Soviet period. In his essay *On Socialist Realism* (1960), he wrote that he put his hope in a "phantasmagoric art . . . in which the grotesque will replace realistic descriptions of ordinary life." Most of Sinyavsky's work (*Fantastic Stories, Lyubimov,* "Pkhentz") illustrates this proposition and reveals him as a writer of unusual imaginative gifts and deep literary culture. The articles published under his own name before his arrest, and his book on *The Poetry of the Revolutionary Era* (written with A. Menshutin, 1964), show him also to be a critic and scholar of rare quality. In 1972 he was released from imprisonment after serving six years in a concentration camp, and in the following year he was allowed to leave the Soviet Union for France.

The exile of Solzhenitsyn and the emigration of other Soviet writers—indeed, the whole chain of events begun by the imprisonment of Sinyavsky and Daniel in 1966—are symptomatic of total estrangement between an important section of the Soviet literary community and the authorities. On the surface, order has been restored: *Novy Mir* has ceased to play the role it played under Tvardovsky as the focus of "liberal" opinion; editorial and censorship controls have been progressively tightened up; and a number of active dissidents have been expelled from the Union of Soviet Writers (e.g., Lydia Chukovskaya) or forced into emigration. By the standards of Stalin's times these are mild sanctions, but they have had their effect: the threat to deprive a writer of his status and livelihood can sometimes be used to extract statements condemning colleagues or renouncing work published abroad. But this has become much harder; few writers of consequence (with the exception of Katayev) joined in the campaign mounted against Solzhenitsyn before his exile, and some—including Yevtushenko—spoke up in his support. There is now a wholly new and unprecedented situation in which the party can impose its will on writers only in a quite negative and self-defeating way. By rigorously controlling publication through its monopoly of the press, it stimulates the further growth of *samizdat*—a process it seems powerless to stop without the reintroduction of full-scale police terror. By victimizing writers who have become too openly defiant, it provokes further discontent and resistance. Though it is unlikely that there can be any resumption of the "liberal" trend in literature without a general political change, there seems to be even less chance that the party can reassert its authority over the writers or force them to give up all of the considerable gains of the last twenty years: they are still very much better off than they were in 1953. The present party leadership is no doubt mainly concerned to limit the political consequences of literary dissent, and it must be sadly aware of the futility of trying to do more.

3

This essay was written to introduce the anthology of contemporary Russian literature of the same title which first appeared as a special issue of Partisan Review *(No. 3–4, 1961) and later in book form* (Dissonant Voices in Soviet Literature, *Patricia Blake and Max Hayward, eds., New York: Pantheon Books, 1962; London: Allen and Unwin, 1964). It is another of Hayward's evocative surveys of Russian literature since the Revolution, in this instance keyed to the works contained in the anthology. Bleak as his portrait of the Soviet period may be, he is as always quick to celebrate the "courage, patience, intelligence, and fortitude" of Russian writers. The last lines of his essay go far to explain his own commitment: "One day it will perhaps be shown that not only Russia, but the whole world, is indebted to Soviet literature for keeping alive, in unimaginable conditions, that indefinable sense of freedom which is common to all men."*

The appearance of Partisan Review *occasioned some comments in the English-language Soviet journal* Soviet Literature *(December 1961), which were later republished, together with Hayward's reply in* Partisan Review *(No. 2, Spring 1962). The editors of* Soviet Literature *had dispatched an interviewer to Leonid Leonov in the hope of eliciting a negative response. But Leonov seemed to agree with the analysis of his writings given by Hayward, who held him in unusually high regard. Leonov was evidently flattered by his remark that the novelist may have regarded his attempts to accommodate his work to socialist realism "as a kind of podvig (spiritual feat) in the Russian Orthodox tradition."*

It was left to the conservative critic Alexander Dementyev to supply the mandatory rebuke. The special issue of Partisan Review *was characterized as "nothing but falsehood" and its editors as*

"slanderers and falsifiers." Referring to the anthology's most important inclusions, Dementyev spoke of Zamyatin's "malicious article," Pilnyak's "notorious story," and "the poorest book Mikhail Zoshchenko ever wrote." In his reply, Hayward said that Dementyev's article had been reproduced in Partisan Review *"primarily as an interesting specimen of a certain style of Soviet polemics, which is now happily rarer than it used to be. The victims of such attacks in the Soviet Union itself now fortunately have less to fear than was the case some ten years ago when Mr. Dementyev and his like would rely on full support from the 'secular arm.'"*
—ED.

Dissonant Voices in Soviet Literature

This miscellany of Soviet writing covers a period of forty-four years, beginning with an early prose fragment by Boris Pasternak written in 1918 and ending with Yevgeni Yevtushenko's "Babi Yar" and a short story not so far published in the Soviet Union, "This Is Moscow Speaking," written by a Russian author under the pseudonym Nikolai Arzhak.[1]

Most of the voices represented here are dissonant, not in any political sense, but in that they do not speak in that trite and monotonous accent which, owing to the long and bitter years of Stalin's dictatorship, is still regarded by many people in the West as the sole voice of Soviet literature. The editors have given pride of place to writers who were murdered, hounded into silence, or

---

[1] Yuli Daniel.—ED.

otherwise persecuted (e.g., Isaac Babel, Boris Pilnyak, and Boris Pasternak), and to some others (e.g., Ilya Ehrenburg and Konstantin Paustovsky) who despite their overtly "conformist" past have attempted, in the years since Stalin, to restore the literary and human values all but destroyed by him. The physical limits imposed on an anthology of this sort and, in some cases, the difficulty of finding hitherto untranslated pieces of suitable length, made it impossible to include specimens of the work of many writers such as Yuri Olesha, Leonid Leonov, and Alexander Tvardovsky, so that the picture which emerges is inevitably very incomplete, but the editors hope they may have succeeded in their principal aim of showing that the Soviet period has been by no means as barren in literary achievement as is often supposed. Apart from years of utter sterility—notably the years 1947 to 1953—there has been a fairly steady output of work, some of which is not unworthy of the great tradition from which it ultimately springs.

Needless to say, much Soviet writing can only be appreciated against the background in which it was produced, and the purpose of this introduction is to sketch the changing climate in which Soviet writers have lived and worked.

The Russian intelligentsia, not least the writers, were divided in their attitude to the Bolshevik Revolution of October 1917. Many, like Ivan Bunin, Leonid Andreyev, Alexander Kuprin, Boris Zaitsev, Dmitri Merezhkovsky, and others, could not reconcile themselves to Lenin's usurpation of power and emigrated at the earliest possible opportunity. Others like Ilya Ehrenburg, Alexei Tolstoy, and Maxim Gorky were more ambivalent in their attitude. At first skeptical of the new regime, they made their peace with it—for different reasons—and loyally served it, once they had convinced themselves that it was there to stay. It is interesting to note that it was the very few *Marxist* writers, such as Yevgeni Zamyatin and Maxim Gorky, who were at the time the most implacably hostile to Lenin's coup d'état. Like Rosa Luxemburg, Gorky prophesied that the Bolshevik seizure of power would inevitably lead to the dictatorship of one man, and he violently denounced Lenin for his arrogance and "seigneurial" contempt for the Russian people. Zamyatin, in his article on

"Literature, Revolution, and Entropy," clearly foresaw all the dangers the Bolshevik monopoly of power posed for the free development of literature and the arts. Unlike Gorky, who had a fatal weakness for successful strongmen, Zamyatin remained irreconcilably hostile and managed to emigrate from the Soviet Union in 1931—not long after Gorky finally returned to Moscow to become Stalin's confidant and advisor in literary matters. In the latter capacity Gorky was responsible for the formulation of the doctrine of "socialist realism."

There was a third category of writers, notably Alexander Blok, Andrei Bely, and Sergei Yesenin, who greeted the October Revolution with unbridled enthusiasm as the secular consummation of a mystic vision. Politically naive, they saw in the *grand chambardement* of October the beginning of a millennial "revolution of the spirit" which would somehow, out of the chaos, the squalor, and the bloodshed, produce a spiritual transfiguration of mankind ("Transfiguration" is the title of one of Yesenin's poems in 1917) and the realization of ancient dreams. By a strange irony, therefore, Soviet literature had its beginnings in the religious ecstasy of a small group of poets who were the very antithesis of the cold-blooded engineers of October. An even greater paradox is that Blok, the ethereal, otherworldly symbolist, and Bely, the even more otherworldly esotericist (he was the leading Russian disciple of Rudolf Steiner), greeted the Revolution with poems steeped in Christian imagery. In Blok's "Twelve" (1918), Jesus Christ "in a white crown" leads the triumphal march of the Red Guards, and in Bely's "Christ Is Risen" (1918) Russia's ordeal by revolution is compared to Calvary: the martyrdom of the Cross will be followed by the Resurrection. Yesenin, too, used religious symbols to convey his vision of the Revolution as the dawn of a golden age for the Russian peasants. In his poem "Inonia" (1918), dedicated to the prophet Jeremiah, he violently rejected Christ, in the grand tradition of Russian atheism, in favor of Man, the omnipotent Demiurge: "I shall fear neither death / Nor javelins, nor hail of darts, / Thus speaks according to the Bible, the prophet Yesenin, Sergei. / My hour is at hand, I fear not the scourge. / I spit out of my mouth the Host, the body of Christ. / I will not accept salvation through his torment and the Cross: / I know another teaching which pierces the eternal stars. / I behold another Coming / In which death doesn't dance on truth. . . ."

This kind of inverted religious language was also characteristic of Mayakovsky's work. Even before the Revolution, in "Cloud in Trousers" (1915), he had proclaimed himself the John the Baptist of the Revolution: "at the head of hungry hordes, / the year 1916 cometh / in the thorny crown of revolutions. / In your midst, his precursor, I am where pain is—everywhere; / on each drop of the tear-flow / I have nailed myself on the cross. . . ." His first major work in honor of the Revolution was a mock mystery play, *Mystery Bouffe* (1918), a brilliant farcical reenactment of the story of the Flood, with God, Methuselah, Beelzebub, and Lloyd George playing minor roles. Mayakovsky's transposition of the revolutionary drama into biblical language was, of course, utterly lighthearted and frivolous compared with Yesenin's anguished blasphemy, but his approach was just as eschatological; communist critics regarded him as a utopian visionary rather than as a "proletarian" poet. As late as 1934 he could be described by one such critic, N. Plisko, as "a peculiar kind of utopian socialist, a spokesman of that petty-bourgeois humanistic intelligentsia whose ideological development eventually led to their acceptance of the October Revolution.". Of *Mystery Bouffe* the same writer said that it still contains "strong echoes of the problems which exercised Mayakovsky in the prerevolutionary period: abstract man and the socialist paradise."

Despite all his flamboyant self-identification with the cause, it was only Stalin's offhanded canonization of him in 1935 which led to the creation of "proletarian" credentials for him and his enthronement as the great tribune and drumbeater of the Revolution. This he certainly was in his own estimation, but he understood the true nature of the Revolution scarcely better than Blok or Yesenin. The result was tragedy for all three of them and their last days, in the words of Pushkin's poem, were "without divinity, without inspiration, without tears, without life, and without love." Blok was the first to realize his mistake. When he died in 1921 he was already deaf to the "music of the Revolution" which only three years earlier had inspired him to write the first and greatest poem of the Soviet era. The unspeakable agony of his disillusionment is conveyed by Zoshchenko's portrait of him in "Before Sunrise."

For Yesenin, who committed suicide in 1925, the years of disabusement were more productive. Unlike Blok, he was able to rescue something from the wreck of his dreams and transmute his disenchantment into poetry, which perhaps better than anything else expresses the tragic alienation of the Russian intelligentsia in the 1920's. Quickly understanding that October would not, as he fondly imagined, usher in a peasant paradise of which he would be the prophet, he reconciled himself with gentle submissiveness to the role of a stranger in his own land. He was not against the new way of things, but he could not be a part of it. In a poem written in 1920, he drew a picture of a poor little foal pathetically trying to race a steam engine; the image well expressed his belated recognition that October meant the advent of a harsh and ruthless machine age which would have no use for his "gentle songs." In "Soviet Russia," written shortly before his death, he accepts, in a mood of trusting patriotism, all that has happened in the country and offers up his soul to October and May. He could no more compete with the crude "proletarian" versifier Demyan Bedny than the poor foal could catch up with the locomotive, but in a pitiful gesture of defiance he refused to abandon his "beloved lyre" to the Revolution. He did not live to see the day when it would inevitably have been wrenched from his grasp.

The case of Mayakovsky is the most intriguing of all. The self-appointed poet laureate of the Revolution, only too anxious to abandon not only himself but his lyre to the service of the party ("I want the Gosplan to sweat / in debate, / assigning me / goals a year ahead. / I want / a commissar / with a decree / to lean over the thought of the age"), he seemed, on the surface, to be more in tune with the new age than any of his contemporaries.

In fact, however, he was one of those hypersensitive and introspective intellectuals for whom only total involvement in the turmoil and chaos of universal upheaval can offer any solution to hopeless inner agony. The Revolution, or rather his image of it, supplied a personal need which had nothing to do with his overt political convictions. When the image began to fade and when he could no longer hide the fact from himself, he put a bullet through his heart.

Boris Pasternak, the fourth great poet of the Soviet era and the only one to survive its worst rigors, was not spellbound by the Revolution. Judging from the evidence of *Doctor Zhivago*, he may have felt a momentary thrill of admiration at its "splendid surgery," but we may surmise that it was as short-lived as with the hero of his novel. Yet perhaps he understood the revolutionary temperament better than most of his contemporaries. The portrait of Antipov-Strelnikov in *Doctor Zhivago* is full of sympathetic insight into the character of a man who sacrifices life and love to an impersonal cause. The fragment "Without Love" shows that Pasternak was preoccupied with this problem as early as 1918. The title, which in Russian is an invented word (*bez-lyubye*, meaning roughly "lovelessness"), evidently refers to the suppression of all personal feeling in the name of the Revolution, about which the young social-revolutionary conspirator Kovalevsky is thinking as he travels with his easygoing friend Goltsev to some industrial town in the Urals.

The contrast between Goltsev and Kovalevsky foreshadows the relationship between Yuri Zhivago and Antipov-Strelnikov in the novel written some forty years later. While Goltsev is thinking of the woman he loves (who, like Lara in the novel, goes to the front as a nurse), Kovalevsky is entirely absorbed in his thoughts about the Revolution—thoughts which "meant more to him than his fur coat and his belongings, more than his wife and child, more than his own life and more than other people's lives. . . ." There is an obvious symbolism in the fact that, while dreaming his dreams of revolution, Kovalevsky imagines that this companion is asleep and that he himself is awake. In reality it is the other way round: it is Goltsev, with his more down-to-earth thoughts, who is awake. "Without Love" hence already contains in embryo one of the central themes of *Doctor Zhivago*, namely the problem of men such as Kovalevsky and Antipov, who attempt to apply "final" solutions to all the problems of humanity and who eventually wake up to the illusoriness of their efforts.

In the first decade after the Revolution it was possible for such moods as these to be expressed with more or less freedom. True, there was a fairly tight censorship, known as Glavlit, but its functions were mainly negative, i.e., to prevent the appearance in print of openly "counterrevolutionary" work. The Soviet prose of the period was, on the whole, remarkably objective in portraying the realities of the Revolution, the Civil War, and the period of NEP. The brutal naturalism of Isaac Babel was accepted almost without criticism; Leonid Leonov was able to show, in *Badgers* (1924), the hostility of the peasant masses to marauding Bolshevik requisitioners from the towns, and in *The Thief* (1927), the demoralization during NEP of an idealistic communist who had fought in the Civil War; Mikhail Sholokhov described in the first two volumes of *Quiet Don* (1928), with an impartiality quite impermissible by later standards, the complicated clash of loyalties—by no means explicable only in terms of class warfare—which the Revolution produced among simple people.

Almost all the human problems which arose in the aftermath of the great upheaval—the conflict between town and country, the collapse of utopian illusions, the inner doubts of the intellectuals, the material hardships of the population as a whole—all these and many other problems were presented truthfully, if not always sympathetically, in early Soviet literature. Most of the best writers of the period belonged to the category dubbed by Trotsky as the "fellow travelers." For the most part intellectuals by origin, they varied considerably in the degree of their loyalty to the new regime, but like "bourgeois specialists" in other fields, they were endowed with special skills which made them indispensable to it and they were, therefore, at first protected from excessive interference by the so-called "proletarian" writers. The latter were as vociferous as they were untalented, but their attempts to force the fellow travelers into absolute conformity were given little official encouragement until 1929. Until this year general party supervision of literary and artistic affairs had been the responsibility of

Anatoli Lunacharsky, one of the most cultivated of the Old Bolsheviks and himself a writer of standing, who exercised great tact
in his handling of cultural problems. Under his aegis there was an
uneasy coexistence between the fellow travelers, grouped mainly
in the All-Russian Union of Writers, and the proletarians of the
Association of Proletarian Writers (RAPP). In his memoirs *People, Years, and Life*, Ilya Ehrenburg writes of Lunacharsky:

> In their reminiscences of him people have spoken about his
> "enormous erudition" and his "many-sided culture." I was
> struck by something different: he was not a poet, he was ab-
> sorbed in his political activities, but he had an extraordinary
> love for art and he always seemed to be tuned in to those elusive
> waves to which many others are deaf. On the rare occasions
> when we met we would argue. His views were alien to me. But
> he was very far from any desire to impose them on other
> people. The October Revolution put him in command of the
> People's Commissariat of Enlightenment and there is no deny-
> ing that he was a good shepherd. "I have said dozens of times
> [wrote Lunacharsky] that the Commissariat of Enlightenment
> must be impartial in its attitude toward the various trends of
> artistic life. As regards questions of artistic form, the tastes of
> the People's Commissar and other persons in authority should
> not be taken into account. All individual artists and all groups
> of artists should be allowed to develop freely. No one trend, by
> virtue of its traditional renown or its fashionable success,
> should be allowed to oust another." It is a pity that various
> people who have been in charge of art, or who have been
> interested in it, have rarely remembered these wise words.[2]

The end of Lunacharsky's relatively mild stewardship spelled
the end of freedom for literature in Russia and the beginning of
an enforced state of "entropy" which went on for the next
twenty-two years. The year 1929 was in general the "year of the
great turning point," as Stalin aptly described it, and with the

---

[2]*Novy Mir*, September 1960.

final defeat of all political opposition, whose fate was sealed by the capitulation of Bukharin at the Sixteenth Party Conference, the stage was set for the "revolution from above" which meant the violent transformation of all social and cultural life. In retrospect the NEP period now seemed a golden age of liberalism and laissez faire. Side by side with the collectivization of the peasants went the so-called "bolshevization" of literature and the arts. This was done by encouraging RAPP to assert the hegemony of the "proletariat" in literature, that is, to allow them to do what Lunacharsky had so far managed to prevent. The leadership of RAPP, under its chairman, Leopold Averbakh, consisted of genuine fanatics who no doubt sincerely believed that only the proletariat could create an art that was in harmony with the new way of life, and that hence "class warfare" must be fostered in cultural life just as was now being done in the countryside: the fellow-traveling goats must be separated from the proletarian sheep. To be a proletarian writer did not mean that one was necessarily a worker or a peasant by origin—indeed many of the proletarian writers were intellectuals—but one had to identify oneself body and soul with their supposed cause, and submit unquestioningly to their self-appointed and self-perpetuating "avant-garde," the party. There was at this period a genuine mystique of communion with the proletariat, and some intellectuals were indeed attracted by this possibility of a quasi-religious sublimation of personality. Like all religious processes it seems to offer a way of shedding the awful burden of individual responsibility, and RAPP was successfully able to exploit this appeal in a number of cases. But, like all fanatical proselytizers, they were too impatient to rest content with persuasion and in August 1929 they forced a showdown with the fellow-traveling writers.

This was the first application to Soviet cultural life of the technique of the campaign against certain chosen scapegoats with the object of terrorizing a whole group into submission. The victims of this occasion were Boris Pilnyak, who was chairman of the All-Russian Union of Writers, and Yevgeni Zamyatin, who headed the Leningrad branch of the Union. When both authors were able to show that they were not guilty of deliberately evading

Soviet censorship controls, as charged, the RAPP instigators of the campaign against them changed their tack, and concentrated on the alleged anti-Soviet nature of the works in question. They were said to be symptomatic of the work of many fellow travelers, who were now bluntly told that they must either make manifest their solidarity with the proletariat and their complete loyalty to the party, or forfeit the right to call themselves *Soviet* writers.

The word *Soviet* in this context was henceforth to be interpreted not as a mere territorial designation, but as a definition of the writer's political allegiance. After a series of rigged meetings in the various writers' organizations, resolutions were adopted in accordance with which Pilnyak and Zamyatin, together with the whole of the old leadership of the All-Russian Union of Writers, were removed. At the same time the rank-and-file membership was "reregistered" and as many as one half were "purged." To mark the radical change in the literary situation, the All-Russian Union of Writers now renamed itself the "All-Russian Union of *Soviet* Writers." All this happened in a society that was not yet entirely cowed—the Stalinist terror was only just beginning—and there were individual protests against the way in which the back of the fellow-traveler writers' organization had been broken. The most powerful came from Gorky, who wrote the following in *Izvestiya:*

> The punishment meted out to Pilnyak is far too severe. . . . All my life I have waged a struggle for care in dealing with people and I think that in our present conditions this struggle should be carried on even more intensely. . . . We have gotten into the stupid habit of raising people up into high positions, only to throw them down into the mud and the dust. I need not quote examples of this absurd and cruel practice, because such examples are known to everybody. I am reminded of the way in which thieves were lynched in 1917–1918. These dramas were generally the work of petty bourgeois elements, and one is reminded of them every time one sees with what delight people throw themselves on a man who has made a mistake in order to take his place.

This was perhaps the last publicly voiced protest in the Soviet Union against a literary frame-up. Later victims enjoyed neither the benefit of such support, however muted, from their colleagues, nor the luxury of being able to reply to their accusers. One cannot help wondering whether history might not have taken a somewhat different turn if more had been as courageous and uncompromising as Yevgeni Zamyatin, who wrote in a letter to *Literaturnaya Gazeta* on October 7, 1929:

When I returned to Moscow after a summer journey the whole affair of my book *We* was already over. It had been established that the appearance of fragments from *We* in *Volya Rossii* in Prague was a deliberate act on my part, and in regard to this "act" all the necessary resolutions had been adopted. But facts are stubborn. They are more stubborn than resolutions. Every one of them may be confirmed by documents or by people and I wish to make them known to my readers. [He goes on to give conclusive proof that the publication of parts of *We* in the émigré *Volya Rossii* was none of his doing.] Thus first there was a condemnation and only then an investigation. I imagine that no court in the world has ever heard of such a procedure. . . . A meeting of the Moscow branch of the All-Russian Union of Writers, without waiting for my explanations, or even expressing a desire to hear them, adopted a resolution condemning my "act." The general meeting of the Leningrad branch was called on September 22nd and I know of its results only through the newspapers. . . . From these it is evident that in Leningrad my explanations had been read and that here the opinion of those present was divided. A number of the writers, after hearing my explanations, considered the whole incident closed. But the majority found it more prudent to condemn my "act." Such was the act of the All-Russian Union of Writers and from this act I draw my conclusions: to belong to a literary organization which, even indirectly, takes part in the persecution of a co-member, is impossible for me, and I hereby announce my withdrawal from the All-Russian Union of Writers.

In 1931, after being subjected to all kinds of petty humiliation and virtually having been excluded from the literary life of Russia (his stage version of Leskov's famous *conte* "The Steel Flea," scheduled for production in a Leningrad theater, was withdrawn solely because of the "notoriety" of its author), Zamyatin wrote an astonishing letter to Stalin[3] in which he requested that his "condemnation to death" as a writer be commuted to exile from the Soviet Union, as provided for under the Soviet penal code, and even more astonishingly—owing perhaps to the intercession of Gorky—Stalin granted his request. Pilnyak, on the other hand, made a groveling submission (in private—public recantations were not yet *de rigueur* in cases such as these) and he perished a few years later during the Yezhov terror.

The 1930's were not the worst years for Soviet literature (these were to come after 1946), but they saw the establishment of those features which distinguish it from all other literatures in the world. What makes it unique is that these features were imposed from without. It is obvious that literature need not necessarily suffer from purely negative limitations on the right of publication (nineteenth-century Russian literature and early Soviet literature flourished under censorship), or from the *voluntary* acceptance of a particular set of doctrinal terms of reference (as in the case of Catholic writers), but when matters of form and content are strictly regulated in accordance with such extraliterary criteria as socialist realism, the result is very serious for creative effort.

In April 1932 the Central Committee of the CPSU unexpectedly issued a decree ordering the disbandment of RAPP, the now cowed and emasculated All-Russian Union of Soviet Writers and other residual groups, and setting up in their place the Union of Soviet Writers which exists in the same form today. It was made clear that membership in this new unitary organization would be essential for anyone who wished to make writing his livelihood.

---

[3]The full text is reproduced in Yevgeni Zamyatin, *Litsa* (New York: Chekhov Press, 1955).

One of Stalin's reasons for discarding the proletarians of RAPP (many of whom, including Averbakh, were later denounced and liquidated as "Trotskyists") was no doubt that, once they had performed their task of bringing to heel the fellow travelers, their excessive zeal, which had been an advantage for this purpose, was now only an embarrassment to him. Stalin much preferred compliant fellow travelers to fanatical Marxist idealists, many of whom, like Akim and his uncle in Pilnyak's tale, were indeed temperamentally more in tune with the fervent intellectualism of Trotsky than with with the humdrum empiricism of Stalin. In general the 1930's are remarkable for the fact that genuine Marxists were gradually replaced in many fields by people with a "bourgeois" and even "counterrevolutionary" past who were willing to pay lip service to anything as the price of survival. Thus the bourgeois historians Tarle and Wipper were called in to glorify Kutuzov and Ivan the Terrible while the veteran Marxist, Pokrovsky, was denounced for "vulgar sociologism," i.e., for writing history as Marx and Engels had written it. In literature—with consummate skill, it must be admitted—the former count Alexei Tolstoy showed that his master had a not unworthy forerunner in Peter the Great.

To be a writer one now not only had to be a member of the Union of Soviet Writers but also had to subscribe to the "method" of socialist realism. This method—the question as to whether it is a "method" or a "theory" has never satisfactorily been resolved by the pundits—was elaborated in open debate during the two years between the party decree of 1932 and the First Congress of Soviet writers in 1934, when the doctrine was promulgated by Zhdanov, who made his debut on this occasion as Stalin's great panjandrum in cultural matters. The theory appears to have been devised by Gorky in consultation with Stalin. For Gorky the principal intention was no doubt to keep Soviet literature in the mainstream of the classical realist tradition of which he himself was the last great representative, but for Stalin, as well as being in keeping with his own pedestrian tastes, it must have seemed an attractive way of subordinating literature and the arts to his purpose. Essentially an attempt to combine incompatible elements, it was from the first riddled with contradictions and was hence rarely satisfactorily applied from the official point of view.

What it amounted to was that the Soviet writers were to model themselves on the nineteenth-century Russian classics (Gorky himself launched the slogan "Learn from the classics!") and adopt a kind of composite style based on the language of Turgenev, Tolstoy, and Chekhov (Dostoyevsky was less favored as time went on). All the modernist movements of the beginning of the century and the early Soviet period (symbolism, imagism, futurism—of which Mayakovsky was a product—and the rich "ornamental" style which Pilnyak and others derived from Andrei Bely and Alexei Remizov) were declared to have been an aberration in the development of Russian literature and were henceforth denounced as "formalism." Strictly speaking, formalism had been nothing more than the name of a highly interesting and original method of literary criticism (its protagonists, such as Viktor Shklovsky and Roman Jakobson, referred to it as "the formal method in literature," and its enemies called it formalism) which had concentrated on the analysis of form in art and literature. It arose in the early 1920's among a group of young critics and linguists who set themselves the task of restoring the balance in Russian literary criticism, which had always been almost exclusively concerned with matters of content. In the era of socialist realism the word formalism was misappropriated, like many other terms, and came to cover a multitude of sins. It became a blanket term of abuse for the slightest deviation from the run-of-the-mill "realist" style and was freely applied to anyone, whatever the nature of his offense, who seemed to the now ubiquitous watchdogs to be in any way "offbeat."

But the greatest difficulty for the writers was that, in accordance with the formula laid down by Zhdanov, they were expected to employ the realist style of the nineteenth-century classics in a spirit which was quite alien to its creators. An essential feature of the new doctrine was the sharp distinction to be drawn between "socialist" realism and the "critical" realism of the classics. The latter, it was said, had used the realist method to *negate* the society in which they lived, whereas the Soviet writer was required by the same method to *affirm* the new socialist order, which was *ex hypothesi* the most benevolent and the most nearly perfect ever established on earth. It was therefore incumbent on the writers not only to describe it "realistically in its revolutionary development" (Zhdanov's phrase), but also to assist the party in its task of completing the social transformation now in progress, of consolidating the gains already made, and of educating people in the ways of virtue. Since, in Marxist theory, consciousness always lags behind economic and social change, there were still admittedly many wayward citizens who were slow to realize the benefits of the new order, their minds being infected by "survivals of capitalism." One of the writers' principal duties was to expose and hold up to scorn these "survivals," and thus hasten the day when all would model themselves on the New Man. In the words of Stalin's famous *obiter dictum,* writers were to be "engineers of human souls."[4]

A sanction for this total subjection of literature to the will of the party was found in an essay of Lenin's, "The Party Organization and Party Literature," written in 1905. In it Lenin insisted that anybody who wrote for social-democrat journals should express the general line of the party. At that time, when journals of different political complexions could be published more or less freely in Russia, this was a perfectly reasonable and legitimate demand to make, being designed to exclude interlopers from rival parties. It should be noted, furthermore, that in talking of "literature" in this connection, Lenin was not primarily referring to belles-lettres. After the first Congress of Soviet Writers in 1934, however, this article was given the authority for making *partiinost* (roughly: complete submission to the party line and acceptance of its guidance in all things) the cornerstone of socialist realism. Whether Lenin would have been displeased or not at this chicanery is open to question.

In these conditions, coupled with increasing terror which cul-

---

[4]When and where he said this has never been revealed.

minated in the *Yezhovshchina* of 1937, most Soviet writers were faced with an agonizing choice: either to collaborate or to cease writing altogether. Some, like Pasternak and Babel, virtually ceased to publish. Some sought refuge in translation and in writing for children. The majority, however, collaborated to some degree or another. For the collaborators, willing or unwilling, various inner accommodations were necessary. It was no longer possible, as it had been during the 1920's, to think of oneself as being in some kind of communion with the "proletariat." The alienation of man from man was more complete, in the name of collectivism, than it had ever been, possibly, in the whole of human history.

Leonid Leonov, easily the most distinguished and subtle of the surviving Soviet novelists, and an avowed disciple of Dostoyevsky, continued to write all through the worst period without unduly compromising his artistic integrity. But this was an isolated case. Leonov's rationalization of his position was based on the same sort of mystic nationalism, and probably combined with the same religious messianism, as one finds in Dostoyevsky's *Diary of a Writer*. For Leonov Bolshevism is only one episode in the eternal destinies of Russia. He may even have been intrigued by the special problems of writing within the cramped confines of socialist realism and he may well have regarded his work in these conditions as a kind of *podvig* (spiritual feat) in the Russian Orthodox tradition. His was the noblest type of collaboration and it was undoubtedly motivated by a feeling of duty toward his generation. Not everybody could enjoy the relative luxury of silence and he felt it necessary to convey to his readers—through all the almost insuperable barriers—something of the truth about man and Russia. In this, for all those capable of interpreting his subtle ambiguities, he succeeded well. His most impressive feat was the novel *Russian Forest*, written in the most difficult years preceding Stalin's death and published in 1953. Impeccably socialist realist in tone and structure, this novel yet manages to suggest by devious symbolism that human affairs and the fate of Russia are much more complex than the crude oversimplifications of official thought would ever allow.

Ilya Ehrenburg adapted himself to circumstances, but with far less success from a literary point of view, and for very different reasons from those of Leonid Leonov. Essentially an internationalist in outlook, he adopted the "lesser evil" fallacy that since fascism, of the two competing totalitarian systems which threatened to dominate the world, was palpably the more evil, an intellectual who wished to work for its defeat could not logically refuse support to Soviet communism, even in its rapidly degenerating Stalinist form. After Stalin's death he considerably modified his previous attitude; he became a strong champion of greater independence for Soviet writers.

Leonov and Ehrenburg are the best examples of the two main types of adaptation to the exigencies of socialist realism and stringent party control over literary life. There were, of course, other categories. A small minority, including Alexander Fadeyev who committed suicide in 1956, fanatically believed in socialist realism, and by virtue of their sincerity they were able to use the method with somewhat greater effect than those, like Alexei Surkov (a former RAPPist and Fadeyev's successor as secretary of the Union of Soviet Writers), in whom one may suspect a considerable element of cynical opportunism. Sholokhov stood apart, apparently not caring, writing scarcely anything and basking complacently in his officially sponsored and quite incongruous reputation as the greatest socialist realist of them all. This judgment, together with Stalin's canonization of Mayakovsky, made the work of the literary theorists even more difficult. *Quiet Don,* written well before the promulgation of the new doctrine, offends many of the canons of socialist realism, not least by the comparative objectivity of its treatment of history, its naturalistic language in scenes involving violence or sex, and the moral ambiguity of its hero. In the late 1950's, addressing a group of Czechoslovak writers in Prague, Sholokhov said that he had not the faintest idea of what was meant by socialist realism.

What it meant in practice, particularly in the postwar years, was an extreme schematism in the presentation of character which would scarcely be tolerated in a fourth-rate cowboy film, a falsification, blatant beyond belief, of native and foreign realities, both past and present, and a drab, emasculated language reminiscent of Tolstoy and Gorky at their worst. The latter conducted a campaign in the mid-1930's for the "purity" of the Russian language, and Soviet writers, in their anxiety to avoid being charged with "naturalism" (a cardinal offense against "realism"), began to use a sterilized language carefully shorn of all the expressive slang and dialect which had been characteristic of Russian writing in the 1920's. Plots became more and more simple and their outcome more and more predictable. Optimism reigned supreme and all endings were happy—except, of course, in capitalist countries.

The outbreak of war in 1941 made an immense difference. In a memorable passage at the end of *Doctor Zhivago*, Pasternak has described how the war "broke the spell of the dead letter." The almost universal sense of liberation from the unbearable terrors and shams of peacetime is also conveyed in the poem "1941" by Julia Neiman.[5] The Stalinist terror—and this may well have been one of its principal aims—had so atomized society, mistrust among people (even among members of the same family) was so intense, and the public obligation, again in Pasternak's words, "to praise what you hate most and to grovel before what makes you unhappy" had become so intolerable, that the ordeal of the war came as a blissful release.

In that year of "camouflage," as Julia Neiman says in her poem, people saw each other without masks. Human bonds were restored in the face of death and suffering, and in the camaraderie of war people began to trust each other again. Most Soviet writers served at the front as war correspondents and many were killed. Freed of the enforced hypocrisies of peacetime, they wrote about people and things with relative truth and sincerity. Apart from excellent war reportage there were a number of novels and poems of quality which will survive. Konstantin Simonov's *Days and Nights* and *Russian People*, Alexander Korneichuk's *Front*, Vasili Grossman's *The People Immortal*, Alexander Fadeyev's *The*

---

[5]*Literaturnaya Moskva*, no. 2, November 1956.

Young Guard (before he rewrote it on the instructions of the party) and particularly Petr Vershigora's unfinished *Men with a Clear Conscience*, a remarkable account of partisan warfare in the Ukraine, are real works of literature. Surkov and Simonov will be remembered for their wartime lyrics. The new-found feeling of solidarity and relative freedom from fear made it possible for editors to publish works which could scarcely have appeared in print before the war. Perhaps the most extraordinary example is Mikhail Zoshchenko's "Before Sunrise." Poets who had long been silent, such as Boris Pasternak and Anna Akhmatova, were published again.

The wartime solidarity which had sprung up among Russians was intolerable to Stalin. He regarded mutual trust among people as tantamount to a conspiracy against himself and he hastened to bring it to an end. The greater freedoms which the writers had enjoyed during the war were abruptly destroyed in August 1946. The technique was very much the same as in the case of Pilnyak and Zamyatin eighteen years before. This time the chosen scapegoats were Zoshchenko, Akhmatova, and Pasternak. In a denunciatory speech of unparalleled scurrility Andrei Zhdanov, the secretary of the Central Committee in charge of ideological affairs, accused Zoshchenko and Akhmatova (whom he described as "half nun and half whore") of disarming the Soviet people in their struggle to build communism, of disorienting and demoralizing Soviet youth, and of undermining the principles of socialist realism by writing in a subjective and pessimistic way without regard for the political ideas from which the people supposedly drew its inspiration.

Zhdanov's speech was followed by a decree of the Central Committee which demanded strict observance of socialist realism and announced certain practical measures to insure that there would be no backsliding from it in the future. *Leningrad,* one of the journals which had published offending work, was abolished altogether. Another, *Zvezda,* was put under the charge of a member of the Central Committee. The easygoing Nikolai Tikhonov, whose fellow-traveling past had been anything but orthodox, was replaced as secretary of the Union of Soviet Writers by the fanatical Fadeyev. The orgy of denunciations in the press after this decree was as bad as anything before the war. The atmosphere of terror was reestablished and all the gains made during the war were wiped out.

The years that followed were unimaginable. Literature and the arts ceased to exist in any recognizable form. The cinema was almost completely destroyed. After the Central Committee's decree denouncing, among other films, the second part of Eisenstein's *Ivan the Terrible,* [6] most of the studios were closed down and there was consequently such a shortage of material for the movie houses that several captured Nazi films, dubbed in Russian and billed as "new foreign films," were shown to Soviet audiences. One was the anti-British *School of Hatred,* which had its première in Berlin in 1941. It shows the revolt of some Irish schoolboys against their sadistic English master; it ends with the burning of the Union Jack. Another such film, *The Last Round,* is anti-American and concerns the fixing of boxing matches in New York; the hero is a blond member of the master race. The showing of these films occurred at a time when the West was frequently accused in the Soviet press of borrowing its propaganda techniques "from the kitchen of the late Dr. Goebbels." The whole atmosphere of the period is suggested in Lev Kassil's allegory "The Tale of the Three Master Craftsmen." Its reference to the terrorization of creative artists by Stalin ("King Vainglorious") is so obvious that one may ask how it ever got into print. It seems likely that the censor who dealt with it was not overanxious to admit that he saw any resemblance between the unhappy kingdom of Sinegoriya and postwar Russia. It is probably unique as an anti-Stalinist satire published while Stalin was still alive.

The death of "King Vainglorious" in March 1953 had a liberating effect far greater even than that of the war. In the last eight years, though sudden advances have often been succeeded by alarming setbacks, there has been a constant and cumulative

---

[6]Eisenstein was accused of having depicted the "progressive" praetorian guard *(oprichnina)* of Ivan the Terrible as a band of fascist hooligans like the Ku Klux Klan.

improvement in nearly all spheres. Though ultimate party control of literature and the arts has never been abandoned (and could of course at any moment be restored in all its vigor), it has nevertheless been exercised, on the whole, with restraint and intelligence and has even, for brief periods, been relaxed to a degree which would have been quite inconceivable in Stalin's day. The paraphernalia of socialist realism and particularly the basic concept of *partiinost* have been firmly maintained in theory, but in practice there has often been considerable latitude in the interpretation of them. Outright questioning of the party's right to control literature has always provoked a strong reaction, but that its wisdom may sometimes be doubted by implication is shown by the passage from Ehrenburg's memoirs quoted above. Altogether one has the impression that censorship controls have gradually been relaxed to some extent, much more being left to the discretion of editors. Since "mistakes" are no longer automatically denounced as crimes, editors have become increasingly ready to take risks. This new confidence is well expressed by the editor of *Novy Mir*, Alexander Tvardovsky, who wrote in one of his poems a few years ago: "In future, too, things may be hard, but we shall never again be afraid." The course of events since Stalin's death may be summarized as follows:

At the end of 1953 two articles published in *Novy Mir* cast doubt on socialist realism and the party's guidance of literature. In his article "On Sincerity in Literature," Vladimir Pomerantsev suggested that the only criterion for a writer should be his own inner convictions. Mark Shcheglov, in a review of Leonov's *Russian Forest*, said that the novel's only major defect was that the "negative hero" was not clearly shown to be a product of the Soviet system. Leonov had of course covered himself (or "reinsured," in the writers' argot of those days) by tracing the villains' original sin to the prerevolutionary conditions in which he grew up. This was all the more extraordinary because of one particularly constricting demand of socialist realism: that there could never be the slightest implication that Soviet society might generate its own specific defects. It always had to be made plain that such shortcomings as exist are untypical "survivals of capitalism."

Early in 1954 there was a crop of stories and plays which for the first time dealt with certain ugly phenomena in Soviet life. Ehrenburg's *The Thaw* hinted at the true nature of the prewar purges and openly referred to the officially inspired anti-Semitism of the last years of Stalin's life. Leonid Zorin in his play *The Guests* described a police frame-up, on the lines of the "doctors' plot," and the degeneration of the cynical Soviet bureaucrat responsible for it. Korneichuk's *Wings* was similarly concerned with a deliberate perversion of justice, this time involving the wife of a high party functionary who had been left behind in enemy-occupied territory during the war and who was consequently, like so many others in this category, regarded as a traitor. The play is remarkable for the first use in print of the term "concentration camp" instead of the usual euphemistic "corrective labor camp," and for a highly artificial "optimistic" ending (strikingly different from the denouement of Zorin's play). In *Wings* the victim of the outrage renders impassioned thanks to the Central Committee (at this time headed by Malenkov, who, in the pursuance of power after Stalin's death, was vying with his colleagues for the popular support which would accrue to the one who would first reveal the scope and nature of their late master's misdeeds) for its timely intercession and its determination never to permit such things to happen again. Significantly, this play was never attacked during the "freeze-up" of 1954, and it was the first in a genre which should be approached with caution.

In the first few years after Stalin's death the party undoubtedly indulged in what might be called "literary Zubatovism"[7] as one of its more intelligent efforts to combat opposition without recourse to brutal repression. By allowing certain writers to outbid genuine protest (it is noteworthy that their "revelations" were always more "sensational" than those of genuine oppositionists,

---

[7]Zubatov was a czarist police official in the early years of the century. With the connivance of his superiors he set up trade unions which attempted, with some success, to canalize the workers' revolutionary energies into the comparatively innocuous struggle for economic improvement. It was difficult to tell, in the case of many people associated with this unprecedented experiment in "police socialism," who was genuine and who was not.

who were naturally more cautious), it was evidently hoped that the true writers of the "thaw" might be thereby disarmed and their effects on Soviet readers neutralized. In addition to *Wings,* another patently "Zubatovist" work was Galina Nikolayeva's *Battle on the Way* with its interesting description of Stalin's funeral. This policy was probably associated with such members of the "antiparty group" as Malenkov, and appears to have been abandoned since their disgrace.

The reaction against the first phase of "thaw" literature came during 1954. Simonov attacked Ehrenburg's novel. Pomerantsev's article and Zorin's play were officially condemned in a statement from the Ministry of Culture, and Tvardovsky (as well as Fedor Panferov, the editor of another literary monthly, *Oktyabr*) was dismissed from his post following a public denunciation by Surkov. On the face of it, it looked like a total reversal to Stalinist methods, but in fact it was not. There was no general campaign of intimidation and no gross interference by the party, which was now already committed to the creation of a somewhat better public image for itself in the eyes of both Russia and the West. There was much to live down and a repetition of the Zhdanov scandal of 1946 would have been inconvenient. At the Second Congress of the Union of Soviet Writers in December 1954 there were some notable, albeit cautiously worded, pleas—particularly from Alexander Yashin, Veniamin Kaverin, and Ehrenburg—for a more reasonable approach to the problems of literature.

It was clear, however, that the diehards were still overwhelmingly strong and could count on decisive political support, even though they were not allowed to destroy their opponents as they would have done in former days. In the next two years an uneasy truce existed between both camps, neither side going out of its way to be unduly provocative. After Khrushchev's "secret speech" at the Twentieth Party Congress in 1956, there was a renewed outburst of "oppositional" writing, similar to the one after Stalin's death. In fact 1956 was the *annus mirabilis* of postwar Soviet literature. Apart from Dudintsev's *Not by Bread Alone,* with its indictment of the Soviet bureaucracy and, even more important, its emphasis on the need for intellectual independence, there was the second volume of the anthology *Literaturnaya Moskva*.[8] The feeling of liberation described in Neiman's poem "1941," contained in the collection, applied with even greater force to 1956. The feeling did not last; *Literaturnaya Moskva* was published only a few weeks before the outbreak of the Hungarian Revolution.

Now the party's fear of "revisionism" and the neo-Stalinist exploitation of this fear—they could say in triumph, "We told you so!"—led to a setback which at first looked even worse than in 1954. Khrushchev himself, at a famous meeting in a country villa near Moscow, gathered the writers together and admonished them to adhere more strictly to the principles of socialist realism and never to forget that they were the servants of the party. A hitherto little-known writer from Leningrad, Vsevolod Kochetov, published an "antirevisionist" novel, *The Brothers Yershov*, which was in effect a denunciation of those Soviet writers responsible for the thaw. It has an undercurrent of hostility to the intelligentsia as a whole and contrasts it with the right-minded and loyal "proletariat." There are ugly insinuations about Ilya Ehrenburg, the journal *Novy Mir* (which has consistently in the last few years been the main forum of the more independent-minded intellectuals), and the second volume of *Literaturnaya Moskva*.

That volume had been produced by a group of Moscow writers who evidently tried, some time in 1956, to set up a semiautonomous writers' organization outside the rigidly controlled Union of Soviet Writers. This could easily have led to the creation of a center of intellectual disaffection on the lines of the Petőfi Circle in Budapest. Although it would hardly have been allowed to develop this far, and would certainly not have made the explosive contact with the workers which was so remarkable in Hungary, it is nevertheless fair to say that anything seemed possible in the

---

[8]The best and most revealing story in this collection, "The Levers," by Yashin, was published in the Summer 1958 issue of *Partisan Review*.

hectic atmosphere after Khrushchev's revelations about Stalin. Kochetov had made the ominous point in his novel that there could indeed have been a Hungarian crisis in Russia itself—and that Soviet intellectuals (he sometimes put the word in a pejorative diminutive form, *intelligentiki*) like Ehrenburg (who though not mentioned by name was clearly alluded to) would have been morally responsible. The lesson of the book was that "revisionism" is potential treachery. The intellectuals must therefore be kept firmly under the control of the "proletariat," i.e., the party leadership.

For several months after Hungary there was a violent campaign against "revisionism"; for a short time in 1957 Kochetov was editor of the strategic and hitherto largely liberal *Literaturnaya Gazeta* and there was scarcely any interesting new literature. In general, things looked black. But as in the reaction of 1954, the situation looked more serious than it really was. The party got over its panic about Hungary and, its confidence restored—probably not least owing to the Soviet triumph in outer space—it decided not to use Kochetov, Surkov, and the other neo-Stalinists (by now a thoroughly discredited and very small group utterly despised by the majority of Soviet intellectuals) as an instrument against the opposition. Early in 1958 Kochetov was removed from the editorship of *Literaturnaya Gazeta* and replaced by S. S. Smirnov, the author of a "decent" (i.e., "non-Zubatovist") novel, *The Brest Fortress*, which described without the usual embellishments the military debacle of the beginning of the war.

The Third Congress of the Union of Soviet Writers, which took place in May 1959, marked a very important stage of development in Soviet literary affairs. In a good-humored and conciliatory speech Khrushchev called upon the writers to settle their squabbles among themselves and not come running to the government for the solution of their problems, and to show more tolerance for writers who had "erred" (there was a specific reference to Vladimir Dudintsev). Despite the usual ritualistic mention of the dangers of "revisionism" and the cardinal importance of *partiinost,* the effect of this speech was remarkably beneficial and developments following the Third Congress were on the whole encouraging.[9] By failing to give the neo-Stalinists the decisive support for which they evidently hoped, Khrushchev in fact disarmed them. As a consequence, they have clearly been on the defensive ever since. After the Congress the writers immediately took advantage of Khrushchev's invitation to set their own house in order, ousted Surkov as secretary of the Union of Soviet Writers, and appointed the more moderate Konstantin Fedin in his place. Furthermore, two former victims of Surkov, Tvardovsky and Panferov, were adopted onto the board of the Union.

In the improved atmosphere following the Congress a considerable amount of interesting work has appeared in the literary journals. What is striking about much of this writing is its unorthodoxy, in formal as well as in political terms, by the traditional standards of socialist realism. "Three, Seven, Ace" by the gifted young writer Vladimir Tendryakov is a case in point. It would have been unthinkable a few years ago to suggest, however obliquely, that it would be possible for a whole collective of honest Soviet working men to be corrupted by one evil man. Even more striking is the ending, which leaves the reader in doubt as to whether justice—even socialist justice—will be done or not. Yuri Kazakov's "Outsider" is equally impressive for its sympathetic approach to the frailties of human nature. Yevtushenko's poem "Babi Yar" speaks for itself as an example of the extent to which

---

[9]An interesting sidelight at this Congress was the speech of Boris Polevoy in which he settled accounts with his old friend Howard Fast. One of Fast's reasons for breaking with the Communist Party was that Polevoy, on a visit to America, had lied to him about the fate of Leib Kvitko, one of the twenty or so Soviet Yiddish writers who were shot in 1952—a fact which was revealed in the Warsaw *Folkshtimme* in 1956, but which has still not publicly been admitted in the Soviet Union, where Itzik Feffer, David Bergelson, and some of the other dead Yiddish writers are occasionally referred to as having "died tragically." Polevoy said in his speech that the defection of Fast from the ranks of "progressive" literature was more than compensated for by the acquisition of Curzio Malaparte who, according to Polevoy, had applied for membership in the Italian Communist Party on his deathbed. Malaparte, a former fascist and a correspondent with the Italian division fighting the Russians during the war, is the author of *The Skin*, a novel in which it is suggested, among other things, that all communists are homosexuals.

Soviet writers may now express their commitment to radical change.

There is a new style in prose of almost Chekhovian objectivity, and the once obligatory distortion of Soviet reality, with the presentation of shortcomings in human nature as transitory "survivals of capitalism" untypical of Soviet society, is much less common than it was. The extent to which some Soviet writers would certainly go in dismantling the literary and political orthodoxies of the past, if all barriers to free publication were removed, is indicated by the unpublished story "This Is Moscow Speaking" by the writer who calls himself Nikolai Arzhak.[10] A striking characteristic of this underground fiction is the extent to which it relies on macabre fantasy and eroticism. Like Abram Tertz,[11] Arzhak revolts against the humdrum realism and the sexual prudery so characteristic of the last three decades.

In 1960 there were ominous signs of a comeback on the part of the neo-Stalinists. In July Kochetov, writing in the popular illustrated weekly *Ogonyok,* described *Novy Mir* as "that paltry little journal which spreads its nihilistic poison among our intelligentsia," and his friend in Leningrad, V. Arkhipov, writing in the neo-Stalinist *Neva,* attacked Ehrenburg for undermining the principle of *partiinost* and denounced *Literaturnaya Gazeta* for publishing an article by Norman Cousins described as "cosmopolitan balderdash." At the end of the year, though probably not as a result of this attack, Smirnov was dismissed as the editor of *Literaturnaya Gazeta* and replaced by his deputy, V. A. Kosolapov. Worst of all, Kochetov was appointed at the beginning of 1961 as the editor of one of the leading literary monthlies, *Oktyabr,* succeeding Panferov, who died in 1960.[12]

It is unlikely that the reemergence of Kochetov, which could

---

[10]Yuli Daniel.—ED.

[11]Andrei Sinyavsky.—ED.

[12]Just before his death, Panferov completed a novel, *In the Name of the Young,* which was attacked for its near-pornographic elements. The writer of these lines, who was Panferov's host during his month's visit to England in 1958, is introduced at one stage, under the thinly disguised name of "Mister Wood," in the role of an unsuccessful pimp.

scarcely have happened without strong official support, is a sign of some impending regression in Soviet literature. The most likely explanation is that the party wishes to restore some balance between the two camps which now, for the first time since the 1920's, almost openly exist among Soviet writers. There is even a clear identification of certain journals with both sides: the monthlies *Novy Mir* and *Yunost* and the biweekly *Literaturnaya Gazeta* are on the whole "progressive," while *Neva* (and now *Oktyabr*) and the biweekly *Literatura i Zhizn* are "reactionary." The progressives, now overwhelmingly strong in numbers, are, it is no doubt considered, best kept in check by having the threat of total reaction always hanging over them. This is at least a more intelligent way of imposing restraint on them than by gross administrative interference.

If anybody should doubt that there are indeed "two camps" among Soviet writers (and this is insistently denied by Soviet publicists), he has only to read the speeches of Alexander Tvardovsky and Vsevolod Kochetov at the Twenty-second Party Congress.[13] Kochetov, needless to say, was the spokesman for the reactionaries,[14] and his nostalgia for the clear-cut situation of Stalin's day was only too apparent. He spoke on the last day of the Congress, evidently having requested permission to reply to Tvardovsky's eloquent appeal on behalf of the liberals. It is significant that Kochetov was the only speaker on this last day who did not welcome in the prescribed ritualistic fashion the decision, announced the previous day, to remove Stalin's body from the Lenin mausoleum. Although he never mentions him by name, his speech is almost a point-by-point reply to Tvardovsky.

Tvardovsky had begun by welcoming what he called the

---

[13]Both speeches appeared in *Pravda*, Tvardovsky's on October 25 and Kochetov's on October 31, 1961.

[14]It is interesting that a current term among Soviet intellectuals for the reactionaries is *chernosotentsy*, intended to indicate their spiritual kinship with the extreme right-wing, anti-intellectual, and anti-Semitic groups ("Black Hundreds") under Nicholas II. Their main appeal, as it was then, is to working-class chauvinism. Concomitantly, more progressive trends in art and literature are often colloquially described as "left-wing."

"spiritual regeneration and liberation from certain constraints" which had taken place in "the period after the Twentieth Congress." As a token of this liberation he mentioned the rehabilitation and restoration to Soviet literature of those many writers whose names had been erased from the record as a result of the "cult of personality." But, he said, none of this was achieved without a struggle, and not everybody had understood the "serious and highly complicated ideological changes" which resulted from the Twentieth Congress. In a clear reference to such people as Kochetov, he warned his listeners that "we still encounter certain residual forms of . . . former habits of thought and of literary practice in the way in which our realities are depicted." Despite all improvements since the Twentieth Congress, literature had not yet been able to take full advantage of the favorable conditions created by it, and had often not followed the party in being bold and truthful. There was still too much "reticence" and a lack of "living depth and truth."

Here he reminded his audience of Tolstoy's words: "The hero of my tale, whom I love with all my soul, . . . is *truth.*" This continuing lack of truth, according to Tvardovsky, implied lack of trust in the reader, and went back to that period of universal suspiciousness which was so "fatal to art." Tvardovsky then cleverly suggested that, since one of the functions of literature was to assist the party in educating the New Man, those writers who persisted in trying to deceive their readers about the facts of life in the Soviet Union were in effect cheating the party as well. Suvorov had said that a soldier is proud not only of his exploits but also of his hardships, and it was therefore incumbent on Soviet literature to describe such hardships "without varnishing reality" *(bez lakirovki).* In literature and "in our press in general" there was still too much immoderate boastfulness in the spirit of the cult of personality, too much concentration on red-letter days, and a corresponding neglect of everyday life with all its work, cares, and needs. There were still some writers who believed that reality should be "embellished," and who never went further than the latest party decree in their treatment of shortcomings. Writers who just took their materials from the newspapers and from party documents, he said, were to be compared only with *kolkhoz-niki* who met their compulsory state deliveries of meat by buying it in the shops. It is noteworthy that not once in his speech did Tvardovsky use the terms socialist realism or *partiinost.*

In his reply to Tvardovsky, Kochetov, employing a device which is now characteristic of the literary diehards, quoted some of those remarks in Khrushchev's ambiguous speech to the 1959 Third Writers' Congress which appeared to be favorable to the Zhdanovist treatment of literary problems. He quoted, for instance, Khrushchev's remark that the writers should educate people "primarily by *positive* examples in life." He noted with satisfaction that there had indeed been some books in recent years which laid the main emphasis on "positive heroes," and he picked out for special mention only such writers as Mikhail Bubennov, Anna Karavayeva, and Oles Gonchar, who were notorious under Stalin for their abject conformity, and whom Tvardovsky certainly had in mind in speaking of those who have failed to draw any consequences from the Twentieth Congress. Later on, Kochetov gave a list of approved poets, such as Mikola Bazhan and Maxim Rylsky, who are also distinguished only by their resistance to the wind of change.

Having noted these "successes," Kochetov went on to denounce those who had attempted in recent years to introduce into Soviet literature the "truth" for which Tvardovsky appealed in his address to the Congress. Although he mentioned no names, he was clearly referring to Ehrenburg, one of the main spokesmen of the liberals, in the following passage, which is also a reply to Tvardovsky's remark about the rehabilitation of writers liquidated under Stalin: "there are still . . . morose compilers of memoirs who look to the past rather than to the present day or to the future and who because of their distorted vision, with zeal worthy of a better cause, rake around in the rubbish dump of their very fuddled memories in order to drag out into the light of day moldering literary corpses and present them as something still capable of living." He then referred to the young poets of the type of Yevtushenko in the following terms: "we also have some poetic, and also prosaic, chickens who have still scarcely lost their yellow down, but who are desperately anxious to be thought of as fierce fighting cocks." But the most astonishing passage in Kochetov's speech was one in which, in total contradiction to the spirit of the Congress, he virtually called for a purge of the leadership of the Union of Writers, which the "liberals" have dominated since the removal of Alexei Surkov as General Secretary three years ago: "It should be said in all frankness that the Congress should have been told about the state of our literary affairs by the leadership of the Union of Writers, but this leadership . . . to put it in military language, has, as you can see yourselves, lost its combative spirit and is in need of a radical regroupment. Yet it would have a lot to report, if it had not consigned to oblivion the main questions of our ideological and creative life."

Finally, again clearly replying to Tvardovsky, Kochetov hotly defended the concept of *lakirovka,* i.e., the typically Zhdanovist practice of emphasizing only the positive features of Soviet life. In this connection, too, he appealed to some remarks made by Khrushchev at the Third Writers' Congress in defense of the "embellishers," who at that time were less discredited and were better able to command some political support.

To sum up, the Twenty-second Congress brought further encouragement to the "liberals." Kochetov was patently out of tune with the general mood and indeed, according to a number of reliable reports, he was constantly interrupted and heckled from the floor with shouts of "Enough!" and "Shut up!" For the time being at any rate, it is clear that the liberals, as represented by Tvardovsky (who is now a candidate member of the Central Committee), have greater political influence, and have little to fear from the desperate rear-guard action of the neo-Stalinists. The latter, however, evidently still have their powerful protectors. Kochetov was given the Order of Lenin on his fiftieth birthday, and his new novel, *The Obkom Secretary,* has received some support, even though it has enraged the liberals by its clearly neo-Stalinist tone. There is the passage, for instance, in which the hero of the novel returns home after attending the secret session on Stalin at the Twentieth Congress and has the following conversation with his wife: " 'Sonya, Sonya,' he said, 'all our life we spent with him, life was unthinkable without him. We thought: We will die but he will live on and on, because in him we loved Lenin. Do you remember how he taught us to love Lenin? Do you remember *Questions of Leninism?*' Then they took out *Questions of Leninism* and read again the inspired chapters of Vladimir Ilyich. 'Sonya, Sonya,' he said, 'in him we loved the Party, our dear Party which brought us up, which taught us, which armed us with an idea which made life three times more sensible and more contented. Sonya!' " The novel was scathingly attacked in *Literaturnaya Gazeta* on December 16, 1961, by Y. Surkov (no connection with Alexei Surkov) for, in effect, apologizing for Stalin: "[Kochetov] confines criticism of the cult of personality . . . only to the admission that 'there was a time when Lenin's name was overshadowed by the name of Stalin,' and then, having admitted this, he returns to the old song: 'Then came years of struggle against the deviationists, then the war years. During our common ordeals Stalin's name rose to untouchable heights.' " Soon after this, however, Kochetov was defended in *Sovietskaya Rossiya* (December 22, 1961) and by a party secretary writing in *Partiinaya Zhizn* (February 1962). It is quite evident from the latter that Kochetov has a considerable following among all the innumerable jacks-in-office who cannot accept the implications of the exposure of Stalin, because of their own past involvement in his crimes.

The affair of Yevtushenko's poem "Babi Yar," published in the *Literaturnaya Gazeta* of September 19, 1961, was an even clearer indication of the division in the ranks of Soviet writers. The reactions to Yevtushenko's vehement denunciation of Russian anti-Semitism were an ominous expression of the Great Russian chauvinism which characterizes the neo-Stalinists. It was wrongly assumed in the West at the time that these reactions were officially inspired. In fact, however, it seems as though the authorities were far less distressed by Yevtushenko's poem than by the embarrassing display of scarcely veiled anti-Semitism which it provoked. It is an encouraging sign of the relative lack of influence of the neo-Stalinists that, while no sanctions appear to have been applied to Yevtushenko, the editor of *Literatura i Zhizn* was

dismissed for having published anti-Semitic attacks on him. From all this and much similar evidence it would seem that Khrushchev, if not the party as a whole, continues to lean toward a neutrality which is favorable to the "progressives." It is of course impossible to say how long this state of affairs will continue, since it obviously depends on obscure groupings at the center of power, of which we can have no real knowledge.

In a passage at the end of *Doctor Zhivago,* Pasternak says: "Although the enlightenment and liberation which had been expected after the war had not come with victory, the presage of freedom was in the air throughout these post-war years, and it was their only historical meaning."

We have seen that there has indeed been a growth of freedom in the years since Stalin's death. The writers have played a great part in this. In this brief and necessarily inadequate survey I have dwelt on some of the more unsavory aspects of Soviet literary history, but I should like to end by saying that the majority of Soviet writers have acquitted themselves with honor in a situation which required more courage, patience, intelligence, and fortitude than could ever be imagined by people who live in more fortunate circumstances. One day it will perhaps be shown that not only Russia, but the whole world, is indebted to Soviet literature for keeping alive, in unimaginable conditions, that indefinable sense of freedom which is common to all men.

4

"Themes and Variations in Soviet Literature" displays Hayward's remarkable understanding of the political factors at play in the production of contemporary Russian literature. This short essay, covering fifty years, is a virtuoso performance that touches upon the illustrative moment and the characteristic author or work in each period without distracting the reader with the mass of supporting detail Hayward commanded. It was read as a paper at Stanford University in 1967 at a conference marking the fiftieth anniversary of the Bolshevik Revolution. The essay later appeared in Fifty Years of Communism in Russia, *ed. Milorad Drachkovitch (University Park, Pa.: Pennsylvania State University Press, 1968).*

"The Decline of Socialist Realism" is one of several articles Hayward wrote for his friend Leopold Labedz, the editor of Survey. *Published in the Winter 1972 issue of that journal, it is a critical examination of Soviet literary doctrine in theory and especially in practice. His conclusion is that the relaxation of controls and the political exigencies of the post-Stalin era had led to the "virtual dissolution" of socialist realism. The centerpiece of the article is a negative though by no means scathing review of A. Ovcharenko's writings on socialist realism. An ideologist and critic, Ovcharenko had attempted to reconcile the old dogma with the new realities of the age.*

In Moscow, the custodians of socialist realism got very excited, responding to Hayward's article in Literaturnaya Gazeta *(October 4 and November 15, 1972). The agitated Ovcharenko replied at length in* Molodaya Gvardiya *(No. 9, 1973) and later in his* Socialist Realism *(Moscow, 1972), where Hayward is characterized as a "bourgeois Sovietologist" who had slandered Soviet literature by saying that it descended into a "blackened night" during the*

*late 1930's. In spite of the rude tone of some of the replies, it seemed clear that the ideologists were not displeased to find that a Western scholar was at least devoting some attention to socialist realism. Plainly, Ovcharenko wanted to provoke Hayward into pursuing the debate. He declined, observing privately that socialist realism was so moribund in Russia that even critical comment abroad—however hostile—was welcomed by its custodians.—*ED.

Themes and Variations in Soviet Literature, 1917-1967

One can say without much fear of contradiction that the only significant work produced in the first fifty years of the Soviet period is in the Russian language and is a continuation of the prerevolutionary Russian tradition, however distorted or mutilated it may at times have been. The Soviet claim to have created a "multinational" literature must be disputed. Only Russian literature had the metropolitan concentration, the inherited richness and variety, to survive in the rigorous postrevolutionary climate. Other cultural traditions within the Soviet Union faced impossible odds, and any promise that they might have resisted strong pressure to assimilate to Great Russian models was extinguished in the late 1920's and early 1930's by brutal campaigns against "bourgeois nationalism" and the application of the principle "nationalist in form and socialist in content."

Neither is there much sign, in the Soviet period, of any fructifying influences on Russian literature from the non-Russian periphery, except for a certain Jewish element (notably Isaac Babel)—but this, too, has been basically Great Russian in its roots and modes of expression. It is only quite recently that there have been discernible stirrings in the Ukraine (which suffered particularly from the campaigns against "bourgeois nationalism"), the Baltic states, the Caucasus, and elsewhere.

Despite the continuity (particularly in formal terms) with prerevolutionary Russian literature, there are certain features of the literary response to the Soviet experience which are specific to this particular historical setting. The present paper will focus mainly on such distinguishing features. This means looking at Russian literature of the Soviet period for the light it may throw on the thinking of the Russian intelligentsia during this time when it was violently wrenched out of the mainstream of European development and all but physically destroyed. From the contrast between certain typical attitudes of the 1920's and moods that have been articulated in literature in the years since Stalin's death, one can draw useful conclusions about the effects of Soviet cultural policy over the last five decades. It is only during these two periods that one can be reasonably certain that ideas expressed in literature were more or less freely arrived at, and not merely the result of intimidation or opportunism.

There is no doubt of the genuineness of the immediate reactions to the October Revolution, and of the attitudes underlying much of the prose and poetry through NEP to the "great turning point" of 1929, and even beyond this into the early 1930's. But apart from a slight relaxation during the war, the succeeding years until 1953 saw the development of a literature which offers no insight into the real thoughts or feelings of those writers who still published. There was no way of telling a true conformist from a false conformist, and only after Stalin's death was it possible once again to discern faces behind the masks.

It was not until the early 1930's, with the promulgation of the doctrine of socialist realism, that the party began to insist that literature and the arts should fulfill a crudely defined political and social function. The ineffectual search in nineteenth-century literature for social ideals and perfect human beings to embody them provided antecedents for an aesthetic theory which demanded of writers the portrayal, for avowedly inspirational purposes, of "positive heroes." But the attempt to impose this doctrine by external pressure was a total failure. Those responsible for cultural policy in the 1920's (including Lenin and Trotsky) were intelligent enough to see this. They realized that the application of mechanical controls and doctrinaire pressures would result only in *false* conformism. Being intellectuals themselves, they understood that the most satisfactory way of controlling and harnessing the intelligentsia, would be to allow it to develop with *comparative* latitude some of its own spontaneously generated delusions.

The Lure of Revolution

Of course, for many Russian intellectuals the October Revolution was politically sordid. One did not have to be committed to a non-Bolshevik party to see Lenin's seizure of power as a usurpation which could have frightening consequences. Maxim Gorky, as is clear from his famous articles denouncing Lenin in *Novaya Zhizn,* saw it in this light.[1] If statistics were available, one might discover that a majority of the Russian intellectuals were similarly skeptical of the October Revolution, if not hostile to it.[2] We are interested, however, in the minority whose accept-

---

[1] For example, on November 10, 1917: "Lenin is, of course, a man of exceptional force. . . . He has all the qualities of a leader, including the indispensable amoral quality and an aristocratic merciless attitude to the lives of common people. . . . Life in its real complexity is unknown to Lenin. He does not know the masses of the people. He has never lived among them. Only from books he learned how to raise this mass on to its haunches, and how most effectively to rouse its instincts to a fury. . . . He is working like a chemist in his laboratory—with this difference—that the chemist employs dead matter to gain results valuable for life, whereas Lenin works on living material and is leading the revolution to disaster." Quoted by Richard Hare, *Maxim Gorky: Romantic Realist and Conservative Revolutionary* (London, 1962).

[2] In December 1917 the newly appointed cultural "commissar" Lunacharsky invited more than 120 writers and artists to a conference in Petrograd; only five appeared including Blok, Mayakovsky, and Meyerhold. See Yu. Yelagin, *Temny Genii* (New York, 1955), p. 209.

ance of October as some kind of millennial event made it possible for the architects of Bolshevik cultural policy to feel that they could win over the intelligentsia, through the medium of art and literature, and incorporate it more or less painlessly, as an ally, in the new scheme of things.

It was soon realized by the Bolshevik leaders (Lenin and Trotsky were specific on this point) that the attempt to create a proletarian culture was bound to fail, resulting at best only in the assimilation of a few talented workers and peasants to already existing cultural standards. A. Bogdanov's Proletkult was soon condemned and disbanded. The proletariat might in time be able to produce its own writers and artists, just as it would certainly produce engineers and scientists—this was only a matter of education—but in the meantime, there would obviously have to be considerable reliance on "bourgeois specialists" in this field as in others. Hence was born the concept, in art and literature, of the "fellow travelers" whose cooperation, or at least benevolent neutrality, was sought in the first few years after the Revolution by guarantees, such as those given in the famous party resolution of 1925, that there would be no undue interference with the creative process.

Not all Russian writers accepted this compromise and some saw clearly enough that in conditions of half-freedom the intelligentsia would only help to prepare the ground, seemingly of its own free will, for its own future subjection. But a significant part of the literary intelligentsia in the 1920's sought to interpret the Revolution in such a way as to make possible some degree of intellectual and moral accommodation with it. These attempts at rationalization were often (as in the case of Alexander Blok and Sergei Yesenin) short-lived and swiftly ended in disillusionment that brought tragedy in personal terms, but not before they had contributed to the creation of a cultural climate which facilitated the abject surrender of later years. In some measure the literary ferment in the Soviet Union today can be seen as a revolt against attitudes more or less freely arrived at by the fellow-traveling intelligentsia of the 1920's.

Some immediate poetic reactions to the October Revolution had already established the archetypes of the fellow-traveling pattern of thought, and there can be no question that they were spontaneous and genuine. Blok's "Twelve" was not written to order, but it gave a kind of higher sanction to the Bolshevik seizure of power by investing it with metaphysical, mystic qualities which put it in a traditional framework of Russian historio-sophic speculation. Blok was consciously paying tribute in his poem to the exalted ideas associated with the noted historian of the Russian intelligentsia, Ivanov-Razumnik,[3] and the Scyths. This group, which also included Andrei Bely and the "peasant" poets Yesenin and Nikolai Klyuyev, was brought together on the basis of a common acceptance of the October Revolution. As a symbolist Blok had always tended to find cosmic meaning even in the most squalid reality, and he was attracted by an interpretation of the revolutionary events in terms of familiar Russian messianism. The idea of the Russian people as a God-bearer *(narod-bogonosets)* endowed with higher instinctive wisdom before which the intelligentsia must bow, was congenial to Blok as to many other Russian intellectuals who were tormented by their feeling of estrangement from the people.

Ivanov-Razumnik wrote about "The Twelve," in an essay that appeared in 1919, in a way which convincingly relates it to his Scythian ideology. He described the October Revolution as, in effect, a sequel to the revolution begun by Christ. Christianity— we are here on familiar Dostoyevskian territory—had gradually been frustrated by the power of the old world, by Rome which had penetrated and taken it over. The role of Russia, whose hour was now at hand, was to renew the gospel of spiritual freedom and to ensure its triumph by translating it on a world scale into terms of political and social freedom:

---

[3]Ivanov-Razumnik (R. V. Ivanov) was a Social Revolutionary whose direct influence on Blok and Yesenin was considerable. He was arrested by the Cheka in 1919, after the assassination of Count Mirbach, ostensibly by the left S. R.'s, and spent a good part of the following two decades in jail. See R. V. Ivanov-Razumnik, *Memoirs* (London, 1965).

Twenty centuries ago there came the good tidings of the spiritual liberation of mankind, but it is clear that apart from the inner freedom proclaimed by Christianity, the world must have *external* freedom, complete political and social liberation. The old world of our times has received the good tidings of universal social revolution just as the old world in the days of Petronius received the good tidings of the spiritual revolution.[4]

In Ivanov-Razumnik's view—also of course a commonplace among a section of the Russian intelligentsia—Russia was uniquely qualified to complete mankind's unfinished revolution (of which October had ushered in the final stage) by virtue of her spiritual maximalism, her capacity for total commitment, her ability to embrace and assimilate the cultural values of the whole world, her *vsechelovechnost.*

With specific reference to "The Twelve"—and his interpretation was never repudiated by Blok—Ivanov-Razumnik expounded a "symbolic" view of the October Revolution which was breathtaking—but probably no less appealing to some intellectuals—in its audacious universalism. Elaborating on the imagery of the twelve Red Guards taking pot-shots at the old Russia and led by an invisible Jesus Christ, Ivanov-Razumnik wrote:

"The Twelve" is a poem about revolutionary Petersburg at the end of 1917 and the beginning of 1918. It is a poem about blood, dirt, crime, and the fall of man, but that is on one level. *On the other level* [italics supplied] it is a poem about the eternal universal truth of the Revolution, about how the new good tidings of the liberation of man come into the world through these blood-stained people. For were not the twelve apostles also murderers and sinners?

In reply to this startling question he quotes the fifth chapter of the Acts of the Apostles about how Peter caused Ananias and Sapphira to drop down dead for having hidden part of their

---

[4]*Alexander Blok, Andrei Bely: Sbornik Statei* (Petrograd, 1919). The essay quoted here is dated April 1918.

property from the Christian commune. The killing of the prostitute in the poem by a Red Guard (also Peter!), because she had been tempted by the material goods offered her by counterrevolutionaries, is thus found to be paralleled in the Gospels, and Bolshevik violence against the bourgeoisie is made to appear not to contradict Christian teaching.

From this it is a short step to the insidious idea that the twelve sinful Red Guards (i.e., the Bolsheviks) are the unconscious instruments of a higher truth. They embody the instinctive "God-bearing" rightness of the people and, although in words they reject Christianity ("freedom, freedom, without the cross!"), they are really led by Jesus Christ, because they are completing His revolution. This idea of a higher truth temporarily obscured by the ugliness of everyday reality, the belief that there can be an ultimate, hidden good that is unwittingly served by evil means—at least as expressed in Blok's poem and in Ivanov-Razumnik's exegesis of it—was the most sophisticated of the early intellectual attitudes to the Revolution. It subsisted in more secular forms for a long time. It was quite compatible with the Marxist dialectic, except that the will of God (or "providence") was substituted for the inevitable historical process, and everything that happened in its name could be thought of as ultimately justified.

It is pathetic to see the millennial view of the revolution reflected in the simpler mind of Yesenin. He also embraced the theories of the Scyths, but without dialectical subtlety. With childlike innocence and wholeheartedness, in verse marked by very concrete imagery, he spoke of the Revolution in strongly religious language, associating the figure of Christ with the Revolution, paraphrasing events in terms of the Passion, and totally misunderstanding the intentions of the Bolsheviks by presenting October as the dawn of a rural utopia in which the power of the accursed machine (identified of course with the West) would be broken. He seems actually to have believed in the imminent establishment of God's kingdom on earth—he spoke of the Revolution as no less than the second coming of Christ, and the beginning counterrevolution as the threat of a new crucifixion. In his poem "Jordan Dove" (June 1918) he proclaimed himself a

Bolshevik and drew a picture of a village paradise in which the Virgin Mary was a familiar everyday figure.

This extreme state of self-delusion fostered by the heady sophistries of his intellectual friends was bound to be followed by bitter disenchantment, and it is the disillusioned verse of Yesenin, in the few years before his suicide in 1925, that most affected the mood of his contemporaries. His reaction to the disappointment of grotesque hopes was one which only encouraged a feeling of resignation toward the revolutionary *fait accompli.* In 1918, in his long poem "Inonia," he tried to secularize his earlier vision of heaven on earth, violently rejecting Christianity and extolling the cosmic potentialities of man as his own savior. But this was only a rhetorical flourish which was soon followed by verse in which he dwelt on his sense of being pathetically irrelevant in the new society. In the famous poem "Soviet Russia" (1924) he describes his return to his native village only to find that people are singing "other songs" (those of the brash proletarian rhymester Demyan Bedny) and that he is not needed.

Yesenin was the first to give effective artistic expression to the idea of the defeated and disillusioned individual who meekly accepts the image of himself as an ineffectual, unwanted alien body who has been "thrown on the rubbish heap of history."[5] This contagious attitude of surrender to the supposedly inevitable was not quite complete. In one important respect he showed defiance, namely in a refusal to give up his integrity as a poet: "I'll take what comes. / Accept things as they are / I'm ready to follow in their steps. / To October and May I'll offer up my soul, / But never surrender my beloved lyre." Yesenin did not live to see the end of the decade when he would have been expected to give up his lyre too.[6]

---

[5]Yesenin's importance as a symbolic figure is brilliantly defined by Georgi Ivanov in *Peterburgskiye Zimy* (New York, 1952), Chapter 18.
[6]It is the "resigned" verse of Yesenin which gained the widest currency, but there are lesser known works in which he gave vent to a rebellious mood. He wrote an unfinished play in blank verse, *The Country of Scoundrels* (1922–23), in which the Revolution appears almost as a foreign plot against the Russian people. The hero is the anarchist leader

It is almost a relief to turn to the only significant Soviet poet, Vladimir Mayakovsky, who accepted the Revolution in the same spirit as its makers. It is true to say that he was the only poet of the Soviet era—Stalin knew what he was doing when he "canonized" him in 1935—who gave original artistic expression, in Marxist and Leninist idiom, to the Revolution. He no doubt represented as significant a minority among the Russian intelligentsia of the 1920's as those who resignedly accepted their own rejection by the times, or those who claimed to perceive a "higher" reality behind the new scheme of things. Boris Pasternak, his antipode, who was fascinated by him, saw in him an outstanding representative of a traditional Russian type that is fanatically devoted to chaos.

It has been suggested that in *Doctor Zhivago* the strange figure of Klintsov-Pogorevskikh (in the chapter "Farewell to the Past") may have been intended as a portrait of the Mayakovsky type. This provincial intellectual, a deaf mute who has been trained to speak (Mayakovsky once said of himself that an elephant had trod on his ear so that he perceived the world only visually), puts his view very plainly: "What you call disorder is just as normal a state of things as the order you are so keen on. All this destruction—it's the right and proper preliminary stage of a wide constructive plan. Society has not yet disintegrated sufficiently. It must fall to pieces completely, then a genuinely revolutionary government will put the pieces together on a completely new basis." His radical views and the vehemence with which he expounded them remind Zhivago of the nihilists in Dostoyevsky, in particular of Peter Verkhovensky.

This type of intellectual, of whom there are enough in all societies, came into their own as Russia disintegrated in war and revolution, and Mayakovsky was their most eloquent spokesman.

Makhno (thinly disguised as Nomakh). The Bolshevik villains are Chekistov (a German from Weimar whose ambition is to turn all Russia's churches into lavatories) and a Chinese sleuth. The play has a combative "counterrevolutionary" flavor about it. It is astonishing that it got through the censorship in the early 1920's, and still more that it was published in the latest Soviet edition of Yesenin's works.

He had no time for the metaphysics of the Scyths and he was specifically anti-Christian. His great epic on the Revolution, *Mystery Bouffe*, performed in 1918 on the first anniversary, was a cheerfully blasphemous paraphrase of the story of the Flood, after which heaven on earth, in which there is no place for Christian humility or forgiveness, is built by proletarian toil: "My heaven is for all except for the poor in spirit, / Who from fasting have swollen up to the size of the moon, / It is easier for a camel to go through the eye of a needle, / Than for such an elephant to come to me, / Let him come, Who has calmly planted a knife / Into the enemy's body and walked away with a song! / Come, you who have *not* forgiven! / You shall be the first to enter my earthly kingdom."

Mayakovsky was, at least to outward appearances, the perfect literary ally of the Bolsheviks. He had boundless faith in a crude and schematic rationalism according to which Man could "scientifically" refashion himself and his society, vanquishing nature with machines ("If even [Mount] Kazbek gets in the way, pull it down!"). It is true that the outrageousness of his public performance masked private anguish and that in all the bravado and insolence of both his early and his late verse, there was a note of pain, but the other Mayakovsky rarely got a hearing from the drumbeater of the Revolution.

The Fellow Travelers

Between the Scythian affirmation of the Revolution for what it patently was not (shortly before his death in 1921 Blok was to say, "It was not these days we summoned") and the Mayakovskian glorification of its literal, surface ideals, there were other, more mundane attitudes amply represented in the prose of the 1920's. This prose was for the most part concerned with recent revolutionary history or the contemporary scene, the nature of the drastically changed fabric and texture of Russian society, particularly as these changes affected the behavior and status of the individual. In contrast to later socialist realist writing it carried conviction because of its undoubted "truth to life," its relative detachment, and its occasional undertones of distaste for the new order. A lot of it tended, like the vatic utterances of some of the poets, to invest the Revolution and its aftermath with a kind of "legitimacy" as the expression, when all was said and done, of the *Volksgeist*, as something flowing naturally from Russian history in which a "Bolshevik" (though not a Marxist) current could easily be furnished with the credentials of tradition: the "Russian rebellion merciless and senseless" had good antecedents.

A typical and influential stance in this spirit was that of Boris Pilnyak, the author of the first Soviet novel, *The Naked Year* (1920), in which he depicted the Revolution as an unleashing of "dark" and "elemental" (a favorite word of the period) forces. The raw vigor of the "people" was tellingly contrasted with the degeneracy of a moribund "Westernized" society. The Bolsheviks were seen, in a formative image which gained wide currency, as the iron-willed, "energetically functioning men in leather jackets" who appeared, at least in the early stages, to be an emanation of the anarchic, cleansing forces of the Revolution, which were inevitably represented, in another characteristic metaphor of the time, as a raging blizzard. Before long (for example in Pilnyak's later novel *Machines and Wolves*, 1923) it became more fashionable in fellow-traveling literature—this because of increasing awareness of the actual, prosaic role of Leninist party organization —to lay more emphasis on conflict between "elemental" anarchy and the organizing will of the "men in leather jackets."

By the mid-1920's it is no exaggeration to say that Soviet literature was predominantly concerned, in one form or another, with an antagonistic confrontation of forces variously presented as a clash between old and new, town and country, man and machine, anarchy and discipline, even (in Leonid Leonov's *Soviet River* between engineers and monks. In this contest, which seemed less and less grandly apocalyptic as the unheroic years of NEP went by, the attitude of most fellow travelers was that of spectators—sometimes benevolently neutral, at other times skeptical or hostile. Common to all the fellow travelers, however, was a feeling, nearly always discernible in their work, that they were witnessing a process which was somehow beyond good and evil —a clash of implacable historical forces which it was impossible for human beings to influence, except as collective embodiments of them. This acceptance of the idea of society as an arena for the interplay of impersonal "forces," in which individual self-assertion was a futile, romantic gesture, was of more direct advantage to the new regime than the positive affirmation, later extracted from writers, of its ideology and goals. This resignation among the leading writers of the 1920's (those, like Yevgeni Zamyatin,[7] who refused to see themselves as impassive witnesses to the Cyclopean struggle found it increasingly difficult to publish) did much to create a public mood in which individual dissent, the clinging to personal idiosyncrasy, appeared quixotic, irrelevant, comic, and reprehensible.

It is striking that even in novels where the author is plainly sympathetic to him, as in the one artistically outstanding novel of the first decade after the Revolution, Yuri Olesha's *Envy* (1927), the lone, romantic rebel against "history" is a doomed figure, conscious of his own hopelessness and futility, wallowing in his own debasement. Olesha's romantic antihero says: "We envy the coming epoch. This is the envy of old age." Furthermore, this last-ditch individualism is identified with *meshchanstvo* (a word always calculated to arouse feelings of guilt among intellectuals)—a petty concern with one's own private life and feelings, a longing to hide in the "musty mattresses of time," to borrow Mayakovsky's phrase. The "coming epoch" is presented, through the eyes of the brash "new men," as a bright vista of ever increasing efficiency in the organization of industry and mass consumption, an era dominated by youthful vigor, collective

---

[7]Zamyatin is best known as the author of the novel *We*, an antiutopian nightmare, in which—evidently as the ultimate consequence of the trend he saw in Soviet life of the early 1920's—he prophesies the extinction of the free personality. In his literary essays, published in Russia before his emigration in 1931, he spoke of the need for heresy and of its social utility: "Heretics are the only remedy for the entropy of human thought. . . . Heretics are necessary to health. If there are no heretics, they have to be invented" (*Literature, Revolution, and Entropy*, 1924). His play on the Spanish Inquisition, *The Fires of St. Dominic* (1922), was an obvious cautionary tale for his times.

sport, uninhibited participation in public life—the new harmony of disciplined, purposeful activity crowds out the untidy, amorphous world of private feeling. There will no longer be any such thing as a private act, as Olesha tries to show in a little touch which betrays the residual squeamishness of one fated to live in the transitional period between past and future: his "positive hero," the representative of this future, is a "healthy man, full of the joy of life, who sang in the lavatory in the mornings."

This irony of Olesha's, which only underlines an awareness of defeat on the part of his pathetic "rebels," nevertheless brings out a certain ambiguity in the attitude of the fellow travelers. Throughout the 1920's there was often an undertone of doubt as to whether the "new" would really triumph. In Leonov's *Badgers* (1924), for instance, the victory of the leather-jacketed Bolsheviks from the towns seems by no means certain. Breathtaking as it was in its audacity (the actions of "strong men" had then, as always, a fatal attraction for intellectuals), there was something foolhardy about their challenge to peasant Russia, which seemed to know only the two poles of inertia or anarchy. It is never quite clear whether Leonov, whose ambivalence in this respect was fairly typical, was more impressed by the iron will of the men from the towns, or by the capacity of the peasants to withstand their encroachments. The awesome problem of "who—whom?" was still unresolved. Leonov put his doubts (disguising them as the skepticism of one of his peasants) in the form of a parable about the Czar Kalafat who built a tower "up to heaven" only to find, when it was completed, and he stood on the top to survey the natural world he thought he had vanquished, that he was surrounded by rustling forests as before: his tower had sunk into the ground (Chapter 15 of *Badgers*).

Socialist Realism

But with the first Five-Year Plan and the beginning of collectivization, the possibility of overwhelming the inertia of nature, together with the human masses who had seemed to be just as unyielding, suddenly became real in the eyes of many Russian intellectuals. There is little doubt that Gorky's decision around this time to return to Russia and lend his authority to the Soviet regime was prompted by a genuine feeling that the "revolution from above" might well succeed not only in the construction of an industrial society based on social justice, but also in ending the cultural schism between the people and the intelligentsia.

Dazzled by this glorious vision, a number of Soviet writers abandoned the "wait-and-see" attitude of the NEP period and declared themselves—almost with the millennial fervor of the earliest revolutionary days—for the "splendid surgery" by which not only the material world but human nature itself would now be transformed (for instance, Leonov in *Soviet River*, 1929, and Valentin Katayev in *Time, Forward!*, 1932). In his Candide-like novel *The Extraordinary Adventures of Julio Jurenito and His Disciples* (1922), the sardonic Ilya Ehrenburg prophesied that communist prisons would not differ greatly from bourgeois ones, and in *A Street in Moscow* (*V Protochnom Pereulke*, 1927) had shown the Revolution hopelessly bogged down in the mire of NEP, but even he was now carried away by the vision of Russian society being hurled into the future—into a new Promethean era in which, among other things, the twilight of a jaded intelligentsia, henceforth redundant except for its technical and professional skills, would be lit up by the garish but warming glow of blast furnaces. The old search for an eternally elusive solution to the "accursed questions" which had traditionally beset the "critically thinking section of society" would be blissfully abandoned, and the voice of doubt would be drowned out by the symphony of a revolutionary upsurge unknown in history—men and machines working in harmony, an end to the estrangement of man from man, as well as from his natural environment and the processes and product of his labor.

This attitude on the part of some writers and of a section of the intelligentsia at large was by no means, in the early 1930's, merely a response to *force majeure*. It is true that Pilnyak and Zamyatin had been hounded and publicly arraigned in 1929, and that this intimidated rank-and-file members of the existing literary organizations which were to be "Bolshevized" with as little ceremony as the peasants were to be collectivized.[8] A reign of terror by the "proletarian" writers' association (RAPP) was openly designed to force literature into specific ideological confines, and life became very difficult for writers who hesitated to make a positive political commitment.

But in a way characteristic of the Stalin period, this campaign of intimidation was followed by a "liberal" breathing space: in April 1932 the party suddenly disbanded RAPP and announced its intention to form a "unified" writers' organization which, in an apparent gesture of reconciliation, would be open to all, irrespective of their class antecedents (i.e., whether they had been proletarians or fellow travelers) as long as they were prepared to give their support to the party and to assent to the literary doctrine of socialist realism. This latter was suddenly sprung on the literary community, without any previous public debate, in May 1932.[9] While this appeared at the time as an attempt to provide a relatively loose organizational and doctrinal framework which would accommodate and give scope to vastly different individualities—ranging from, say, Alexander Fadeyev to Boris Pasternak—it became increasingly clear after the fairly easy-going First Writ-

[8]For a detailed account of this affair, see my article "Pilnyak and Zamyatin: Two Tragedies of the Twenties," *Survey*, April–June, 1961.

[9]The first use of the term "socialist realism" was almost casual. It appeared in a leading article entitled "Down to Work!" in *Literaturnaya Gazeta* of May 29, 1932: "Truthfulness in the depiction of the Revolution—this is the demand we have the right to put to all Soviet writers without exception. . . . The masses demand from the artist sincerity, truthfulness, revolutionary *socialist realism* in portraying the proletarian revolution." The literary scholar Valeri Kirpotin has recently revealed (in *Voprosy Literatury*, May 1967) that he was the author of this lead article. As secretary of the Organizational Committee of the Union of Soviet Writers, he also drafted, together with Fadeyev and Pavel Yudin, the Union's statutes *(ustav)*, which included a clause requiring members to be guided by socialist realism. Pavel Yudin, the "philosopher" who later edited the Cominform journal in Belgrade and became Soviet Ambassador to Peking in 1953, again figured as an expert in literary matters in 1966 when he wrote a report for the prosecution of the trial of Sinyavsky and Daniel. In it he testified that the work of the latter showed him to be a "consummate and convinced anti-Semite." See *On Trial: The Soviet State versus "Abram Tertz" and "Nikolai Arzhak"* (revised and enlarged edition, New York, 1967), p. 190.

ers' Congress held to inaugurate the new Union of Soviet Writers in 1934, that the new arrangement was really meant to homogenize the writers both ideologically and artistically, and to convert them gradually into an obedient adjunct of the Central Committee's propaganda apparatus.

But in the early 1930's this was not apparent to everybody. It was a time of confusion in which nobody can be blamed for thinking that the political situation was still fluid and that no irrevocable choices had been made. In any case, some major writers evidently felt that to be yoked, however ignominiously, to what appeared to be a great national enterprise involving the masses, offered at last a release from the particular hell of the Russian intelligentsia—the sense of having been severed from the "people." The sacrifice of one's intellectual and moral independence did not seem too high a price to pay—though in fairness to those Soviet intellectuals who succumbed to this particular temptation, it must be said that it happened in an era when all too many intellectuals in Western societies were easily beguiled into shedding the burden of individual responsibility. The tragedy of the Russian intelligentsia in the 1930's was made more poignant by the fact that, after 1929, they had no free choice in the matter, and could only pretend to themselves that they had. It is painful now to read the novels of the late 1920's and early 1930's in which the hitherto self-evident right to make one's own moral or intellectual judgments was virtually equated with treason to the higher cause of humanity.

The most memorable and subtle work on these lines was Ehrenburg's *The Second Day* (*Out of Chaos*, 1933–34), whose effect was no doubt at the time all the greater for its having been written in Paris; there could be no question of external constraints on the author. It was also distinguished by a "European" smoothness of style which made it palatable to Western readers and hence positively dazzling to more ingenuous Russian ones. It can still be read as a good summary of most of the delusions of the first postrevolutionary decade. The inevitable biblical parallel suggested already in the title is developed in such a way as to liken the building of socialism to Genesis ("Kuznetsk was like the creation of the world"). The hero—or rather the antihero in the new topsy-turvy scale of values—is a hereditary intellectual, Volodya Safonov, who, as much as he would like to accept the social and political ideals of October, is by temperament incapable of going against his conscience—the "old disease" which had afflicted his father, a man who got into trouble both before and after the Revolution for protesting against injustice. After several attempts to overcome this affliction—he is, needless to say, envious of those who are able to do so without qualms—Volodya drifts into the despairing state of an outcast whose virtues of mind and character are a source not of strength but of guilt. He becomes a spiritual émigré.

Because it is clear that Ehrenburg was thrashing out what he genuinely fancied to be his own dilemma, the portrait of Safonov is full of insight and one gets a vivid idea from this novel of what it was like, in the tightening vise of early Stalinism, to be a lone intellectual clinging to moral and aesthetic standards at variance with those of the "collective." With terrifyingly perverse logic Ehrenburg argued, obviously intent most of all on persuading himself, that the only alternative before his sensitive and independent-minded hero was either to submit to the general will or to become an "enemy," a traitor. The author has him commit suicide, but in the endless variations on this theme in Soviet literature right up to the death of Stalin, he would more likely have found grace by "seeing the light" and making his submission. Alternatively he would be unmasked and destroyed. In retrospect, it may be seen that the achievement of socialist realism was not in creating positive heroes to serve as inspiring models to the reader (they were far too wooden and contrived), but in playing on a natural feeling of guilt, particularly among intellectuals, and making it appear that there was something shameful about having a mind of one's own. The constant harping on this theme, like all preaching by negative example, was not without effect. Whether or not it increased the production of the blast furnaces, it certainly contributed to the desolation of the spirit by which thinking Russians were even more sorely tried than by physical terror.

The Genre of Silence

The promise of the early 1930's, which found such persuasive expression in the work of leading fellow-traveler writers such as Ehrenburg, Leonov, Katayev, and the now broken Pilnyak (in *The Volga Flows to the Caspian Sea*, 1930), quickly proved to be a mirage. Those who chose, like Isaac Babel, to practice what he called at the Writers' Congress in 1934 the "genre of silence" were the wiser and, oddly enough, had about as much chance of escaping physical extinction as those who, for whatever reason and however abjectly, chose the path of conformity. I have so far laid stress on those writers who "accepted" the Revolution and its consequences and were able to find some mode of accommodation with it. In drawing up a balance sheet of the last fifty years, they are clearly crucial to any consideration of the extent to which the cultural policy of the new regime was successful. It could only be successful insofar as it was able to produce true conformists, i.e., people who had really persuaded themselves that submission was right and necessary, and who were able to convey this conviction in artistically effective terms. Only through such spokesmen could literature be expected to play its "educational" role with any authority. But the gradual increase in external constraints failed to achieve anything but a conformity whose genuineness was increasingly in doubt.

This was underlined in the 1930's and (except for a short interlude during the war) until Stalin's death by the stubborn silence of Anna Akhmatova and Boris Pasternak, two poets who became symbolic figures, a last source of moral authority for the Soviet intelligentsia. In the worst of times they were most eloquent when they said nothing. There is an astonishing consistency—almost to the point of monotony in the case of Akhmatova—about their lives and their poetic response to the times in which they lived. Neither, unlike Blok, Bely, or Yesenin, affected to perceive a "higher" meaning in the October Revolution. Akhmatova saw it with prophetic matter-of-factness as the beginning of a long time of troubles in which the life of the poet would be difficult, if not impossible: "Now nobody will want to listen to songs, / The days foretold have come to pass . . . Not long ago, as free as a swallow, / You made your morning flight, / But now you will be a hungry beggar, / Knocking at the door of strangers who will not open up."[10]

Pasternak's attitude toward the Revolution was a little more ambiguous, and not easy to read out of his work. Judging by his hero Zhivago's momentary exhilaration at its "splendid surgery," Pasternak was himself perhaps not unaffected for a time by the mood of the left-wing intelligentsia. But this was certainly short-lived and on the evidence of his prose sketch "Without Love" (1918), which prefigures *Zhivago*, he evidently soon decided that the revolutionary zeal of some of his contemporaries was like a state of trance in which they had lost their sense of proportion.[11]

Revaluation of All Values

The trance turned into a nightmare, and when it slowly began to fade after 1953, such central questions in Soviet literature as the place of the individual in society were reexamined in the light of

---

[10]This poem, dated by the author 1917, was first published in February 1918. Akhmatova had a true prophetic quality, as one sees in the last four lines (not yet published in the Soviet Union) of her poem "Voronezh," written in 1936 after a visit to Mandelstam, who was in exile there: "In the banished poet's room / terror and the muse watch by turn, / And a night is coming / that has no dawn."

[11]As Sinyavsky shows in his introduction to Pasternak's verse (Moscow, 1965), Pasternak's relative immunity to the blandishments of "historical" reality was rooted in his conception (set out in his article "The Black Chalice," 1916) that poetry and history are separate universes which exist side by side, the one in eternity, the other one in time. This idea is expressed in his famous line defining the poet as "eternity's hostage captive to time" *(vechnosti zalozhnik u vremeni v plenu)*.

a grim experience which had scarcely been envisaged in the 1920's or the early 1930's. Only a chosen few of the older surviving writers could stand by what they had written previously, without revising their own past. Akhmatova, for example, had said as much as needed to be said at the height of the nightmare in her *Requiem,* which she lived to see published abroad.[12] Pasternak completed *Doctor Zhivago* not long after Stalin's death and defied the most fearsome of Soviet taboos by deliberately arranging for its publication abroad. The continuing embargo on it inside the country is self-defeating, as is clear from the constant echoes of Pasternakian ideas and beliefs in the work of younger poets.

Of almost equal significance in the post-Stalin period have been those writers, such as Ehrenburg, Leonov, and Katayev, who survived to write work in which the values urged by them in the late 1920's and early 1930's are drastically reviewed in the light of their subsequent experience. This "defection" has contributed a great deal, in the crude terms of literary politics, to the establishment of conditions in which younger writers, for the most part unknown before Stalin's death, have been able to achieve— fighting every inch of the way—a surprising measure of creative autonomy. What we have witnessed in Russia in the last ten years or so must be historically unique: an inexorable "revaluation of all values" in which a contrite older generation has been an ally of the younger one.

The process of reassessment was begun, fittingly, by Ehrenburg in *The Thaw* (1954), which, despite its jejune manner, must now be regarded as a document of historical importance. The chastened Ehrenburg of the early 1950's seems to be replying to the eager fellow-traveling Ehrenburg of the early 1930's. If, in the

---

[12]It will be impossible to give a balanced account of the 1930's and 1940's until more of these "delayed reports" come to light. They will certainly be an important corrective to the present dreary picture. Lydia Chukovskaya's *Deserted House* is a courageous pendant in prose to *Requiem.* It is a hopeful sign that Mikhail Bulgakov's great comic philosophical novel *The Master and Margarita* (completed just before the author's death in 1940) has at last been published (with cuts) in Moscow.

earlier novel, the lone nonconformist had been presented as a socially harmful element who was doomed to be destroyed during the forced march to socialism, in *The Thaw* this judgment is reversed and the reader is made to feel that the only honorable course in a society where public dissent is not tolerated is to hold to one's beliefs (which are here, needless to say, not political, only aesthetic) and wait for better times. The characters in *The Thaw* who are out of sympathy with prevailing artistic standards are quite passive and keep their thoughts to themselves—precisely what Volodya Safonov was condemned for doing. What he might have become, had he "conformed," is conveyed in the portrait of the cynical young artist in *The Thaw*, Volodya Pukhov, who paints socialist-realist canvases because this is the only way to make a career ("with ideas you will only break your neck"), but hates himself for it and secretly envies another painter who, at the price of being a social outcast, paints as he pleases.

In the few years after *The Thaw* the character of the lone dissident established himself in Soviet literature, despite furious opposition from orthodox critics and occasional attempts to reverse the trend by political intimidation (notably in 1957 and 1963). In *Not by Bread Alone* (1956)—another poor novel which is historically important—Vladimir Dudintsev went a stage further than Ehrenburg by suggesting that a person who goes against the current ought to perform an active function in society. He implied that it is the duty of a good citizen—and this goes for "true" communists in particular—to fight for what they believe to be right. The guardians of official ideology have been peculiarly helpless to prevent the development of this theme, which displaced or made ludicrous the Stalinist concept of the positive hero.

But even the Dudintsev kind of hero is now old-fashioned. In recent years a frequent complaint against the young prose writers is that they have ceased to be interested in any kind of hero. Certainly, in many of the stories and novels of Kazakov, Aksyonov, Tendryakov, Voinovich, and others, the exploration of human behavior and motive tends to revolve less around the "civic" functions of their characters and much more around their

socially undirected acts and thoughts or their private moral dilemmas. No amount of fulmination against the "deheroicization" of
literature, against preoccupation with small trivial "truths" instead of the "major truth" (which has not been redefined since
Stalinist days as consisting in a broadly optimistic view of progress
toward communism), has had any effect.

It is an indirect confession of failure that there is now a tendency to try to make it appear that socialist realism is a much
broader and more elastic doctrine than formerly appeared. When
it is in decay and can no longer be enforced by terror, a dogmatic
system has little choice but to present itself as being in reality
more accommodating than it was thought to be. As time goes on,
points of view, even large concepts such as cybernetics and sociol-
ogy, previously denounced as "bourgeois," are being subsumed
into the "treasure house of Marxism-Leninism." In line with this
general trend, socialist realism is gradually being "liberalized" so
that at times it appears tolerant of any literary phenomena (this
now includes such imports as Kafka and Ionesco) which, in the
face of initial opposition, gradually gain currency in the Soviet
literary community.[13] Another sign of the new tolerance is the
relatively moderate tone of "conservative" literary criticism.
Younger prose writers are rebuked for "factography." Not many
years ago the charge would have been "naturalism" and "distortion of Soviet reality." The boundary between "critical" and
"socialist" realism has become hopelessly blurred, as the facts of
life in the *pays réel* have gained admittance to literature. It was
impossible to expect even the most complaisant of Soviet writers
to draw overoptimistic conclusions about Soviet life in the ac-

---

[13]This, of course, particularly applies to the past. So far it is chiefly a matter of grudging
tolerance. But this does now extend to allowing (or rather not preventing) the selective
publication of such hitherto submerged figures as Marina Tsvetayeva and Osip Mandelstam. Even more symptomatic is the offhanded mention, in lists of Soviet "achievements"
in literature and art, of work by people whose lives were spent—and sometimes lost—in
tragic conflict with socialist realism. *Literaturnaya Gazeta* of November 1, 1967, has a
panoramic "jubilee" drawing of Soviet writers over the last fifty years in which Akhmatova,
Pasternak, and Tsvetayeva are shown in the company of such as Alexei Surkov and
Vsevolod Kochetov.

counts they were allowed to render after the Twentieth Party Congress in 1956.

The death, from inanition, of the positive hero, the dislodgment of neat romantic projections by disorderly and disconcerting facts, the tolerance of literary influences formerly denounced as "alien," the uncomfortable (though still controlled) treatment in literature of some of the consequences of the "cult of personality" —all this has eroded the basis of official cultural policy. The result is a comic discrepancy—particularly noticeable in the jubilee year —between the otiose incantations in "authoritative" journals[14] and the actual practice of the literary journals—not only *Novy Mir* but also *Znamya, Moskva, Neva,* and others.[15]

What has really made nonsense of official literary doctrine, however, was the appearance (in one case with the highest approval) of several notable works which question the validity of the Soviet historical experience, *in toto* or in large essential aspects such as collectivization.[16] The best known such work was Alexander Solzhenitsyn's *One Day in the Life of Ivan Denisovich* (1963). Of course, Solzhenitsyn's novel would never have been published if Khrushchev had not permitted it for tactical reasons in his struggle with his right-wing opponents. In his usual blunder-

---

[14]An almost random example, from an article by V. Ozerov in *Kommunist,* August 1967: "Honorable is the mission of the artists, called on to show the strength and beauty of the institutions of socialism, which are developing a new communist morality. . . . In the last few years moral-ethical [*sic!*] themes are being elaborated by Soviet literature very intensively." This is followed by the inevitable, grotesquely understated, rider: "However, their correct solution is hindered by moods of abstract humanism which have made themselves felt in certain books, plays, and films."

[15]One reason for the spread of liberalism from *Novy Mir* to other central journals is the need to compete commercially: editors take political risks in order to boost circulation. An interesting development in the past few years has been the liberal editorial policy of two Russian-language literary journals in non-Russian republics: *Literaturnaya Gruziya* in Georgia and *Prostor* in Kazakhstan, both of which on occasion give "literary asylum" to Moscow writers.

[16]A lot of writing on the kolkhoz theme, almost by the nature of the subject, must lead Soviet readers to the conclusion that collectivization was a fearful mistake. This can even be so if the author's intention was the opposite (e.g., Ivan Stadnyuk's *People Are Not Angels,* 1962–65). One remarkable but curiously neglected novel on collectivization is Sergei Zalygin's *On the Irtysh* (*Novy Mir,* No. 2, February 1964).

ing impetuosity[17] he did not stop to think of the irreversible damage he was inflicting on the very socialist realism he aggressively upheld a little later at the famous Manège art exhibition. Since the novel has the unassailable finality of a true work of art, it cannot be hidden, ignored, or explained away. What makes it peculiarly awkward and unassimilable is that its existence "on the record" as a published work of Soviet literature has forever confused the issue—to put it mildly—of what is "permissible" in print. The piecemeal intrusion into literature of unpleasant detail about the seamy side of the Soviet past and present could always, up to a not easily definable point, be made to appear compatible with a reformed socialist realism, but Solzhenitsyn destroyed the basis for rough-and-ready theoretical compromise with a neorealism which, though "critical," could be presented as something helpful to the party in its never-ending battle with recalcitrant human nature.

Solzhenitsyn is no mere "factographer." The "facts" in *One Day* are not self-contained—they are built into a compact symbolic pattern and prompt ironic reflections on all the cherished features of the Soviet "image." Indeed, the whole "building of socialism" is likened to the setting up of a concentration camp. In the context of the story there is no mistaking the implication of the passage about the prisoners building a new "Socialist Community Development": "But so far it was nothing more than bare fields covered with snowdrifts, and before anything could be done there, holes had to be dug, posts put in, and barbed wire put up—by the prisoners for the prisoners, so they couldn't get out. And then they could start building." Pasternak used exactly the same metaphor in the epilogue of *Doctor Zhivago*, where one of the hero's friends, who had survived the holocaust of the 1930's, describes what happened when he was brought with a transport of prisoners to an open field in the

---

[17]A similar intervention, about a year later, resulted in the publication of Tvardovsky's *Vasili Terkin in the Other World*, a mordant satire on ideological humbug in general. Perhaps there were moments when Khrushchev himself saw through it all.

middle of a forest: "They told us: 'Here is your camp. Settle down as best you can.' . . . We cut down saplings with our bare hands in the frost to build huts. And would you believe it, we gradually built our own camp. We cut down the wood to build our own dungeons, we surrounded ourselves with a stockade, we equipped ourselves with prison-cells and watch-towers—we did it all by ourselves."

Pasternak explicitly took issue with the tragic delusions which had ended for so many Russian intellectuals in the way described by Zhivago's friend, an epitome of the fellow-traveling intellectual of the 1920's who, in Zhivago's words, had "broken himself in like a circus horse." It is clear that Pasternak had in mind some of the leading Soviet writers of the 1920's when he wrote: "A man who is not free always idealizes his bondage. This is how it was in the Middle Ages and the Jesuits always made play with it. Zhivago could not stand the political mysticism of the Soviet intelligentsia."[18]

The similarity of these two passages, which both make the same symbolic reference to the sense of Soviet history as it appears to the authors (and to many of their generation), shows how incongruous it is to try to maintain a division between the best work in post-Stalin literature published in the Soviet Union and the considerable body of prose and verse that has been published only abroad (apart from Pasternak, one may mention Andrei Sinyavsky and Joseph Brodsky). Of course very few works published inside the U.S.S.R. have broken through the continuing (but increasingly capricious) constraints on free expression as radically as Solzhenitsyn. Only he has been able to match, in direct utterance, the outspokenness of works so far published only in the West. It is fascinating, however, to see how Soviet writing in recent years has naturally reverted to the celebrated Aesopian techniques of an earlier age. There is almost nothing that cannot be said between the lines in the elusive manner which some Soviet writers

---

[18]For a discussion of *Doctor Zhivago* and the Soviet intelligentsia of the 1920's, see my article in *Survey*, April–June 1958.

even seem to prefer, because of the challenge it offers to their ingenuity.[19]

Most of the surviving fellow travelers have now confronted, however obscurely, their "political mysticism" of the 1920's and early 1930's. An excellent example, worth giving at length, of how convoluted this can be is the case of Leonid Leonov. In 1963 he published a remarkable parable, *Yevgeniya Ivanovna,* which was favorably received by conservative critics and caused scarcely a stir among the reading public. The ambiguity that Leonov practiced so successfully for many years under Stalin proved, in this one extraordinary case, to be a fatal impediment to a repentant fellow traveler trying to settle accounts with his past. There is something tragicomic in this failure to communicate.

The story is about a Russian woman who at the end of the Civil War leaves the country together with her husband. After a few months of destitute émigré life in Constantinople, her husband suddenly abandons her and disappears. Some years later, having heard persistent rumors that her first husband is dead, Yevgeniya Ivanovna marries an English professor of archaeology whom she meets by chance in Paris at a moment of total despair, when she is contemplating suicide. The professor takes her on an archaeological expedition to the Middle East, and while they are in Turkey, Yevgeniya Ivanovna suddenly feels acute nostalgia for Russia and urges her new husband to take her there, via the Caucasus, so that she can visit her mother's grave in Rostov. Because of his international standing, the professor, most unusually, is given a visa by the Soviet consul in Turkey to enable him

---

[19] It is clear that there is now an elaborate game between censors, editors, and authors. It is unlikely that the former are deceived by the sometimes blatantly Aesopian techniques used to put across dissident ideas. One suspects that, as in liberal periods under the czars, some censors are by no means unsympathetic to the censored. But the first rule of the game is that authors should adopt some disguise—even if it is as intentionally obvious as the masks of classical drama—so that the censor can also "cover" himself if called to account. The jubilee year has been notable for direct and indirect attacks on the censorship. Solzhenitsyn sent a strong denunciation of it (dated May 16) to participants at the Fourth Writers' Congress which, however, took good care not to discuss this or any other controversial issues.

to go to Russia through Georgia. The time is evidently in the mid-1920's. The couple are accorded a warm official welcome in Tiflis and are told that the best Intourist guide in the Soviet Union will be attached to them during their stay in Georgia and their subsequent journey to Russia proper. When the guide presents himself he turns out to be Yevgeniya Ivanovna's first husband, Stratonov.

The purpose of this curiously contrived melodramatic situation is clearly to make it possible for the author to put into the mouth of an utter scoundrel the *sub specie aeternitatis* view of the significance of the October Revolution which had been typical of the fellow travelers in the 1920's. Stratonov justifies his return to Russia and his betrayal of his wife in terms of a higher loyalty to Russia's historical destiny, which he talks about as follows:

> The great minds of Russia have always prophesied for her a special, heroic—because she is free of European egotism—historical mission. . . . It is a matter of the most ancient, universal human longing for peace, goodness, and truth, that is, of establishing on earth a higher level of humanity. . . . Vast Russia has taken upon herself her predestined task. In essence it is just another way to the stars, but unlike previous ones, which were devious and via heaven, the idea now is to thrust forward by the shortest possible, earthly route. . . . I agree that this may require victims, but the inspiration of such eras as this gives those who live in them cataleptic powers of endurance and prolonged insensibility to suffering.

Filled with horror at this encounter with the man who had betrayed her and who has now reappeared suddenly as a kind of harbinger of the "new Russia," and nauseated by his brand of messianic Bolshevism, Yevgeniya Ivanovna begs her English husband to take her *home* to England—though she has never been there before. She no longer wishes to travel on to Russia.

Thus, in the context of the novel, England seems to embody a type of historical experience and a view of the world antithetic to those now prevalent in Russia. Like the Slavophile Alexei Khomyakov before him, Leonov evidently sees in England a pattern of organic social growth which has not been interrupted or violently distorted by "revolutionary" change. As in *Doctor Zhivago*, the betrayal of a woman becomes a symbol for the attempt to transform life in accordance with preconceived notions which, in any case, speedily degenerate into the "ideological" pattern of the timeserver.[20]

The younger prose writers, and particularly the poets who have made their mark since 1956, are less obsessed with the Stalinist past, but it weighs too heavily on the national conscience to be ignored by them. Andrei Voznesensky, to take the best example, is the author of a historical allegory, "The Skull Ballad," in which he considers the sense of what happened in 1937 (though he appears to be speaking of Peter the Great), and in which (again an echo of *Doctor Zhivago*) the fate of a woman is the counterpoint to preoccupation with reshaping the world. ("Love is so small who cares for love / In times like these men build and set a world on fire.") In general, the writing of the younger generation often betrays a brooding concern with the sense of Russia's destiny. Moreover, in considering the wider problems raised by Soviet history—such as the relationship of means to ends—they clearly find the flexible, "dialectic" ethic of Marxism-Leninism unacceptable, and innumerable articles in recent years rebuking them for "abstract humanism" have had no effect. It is unlikely

---

[20]There is a good portrait of the sort of timeserver who began to thrive in the 1930's in the latest work by a repentant fellow traveler: Valentin Katayev's *The Holy Well* (1966). The figure of a "modern version of Bulgarin," the "human woodpecker" Prokhindeikin, almost seems intended to represent the author's alter ego of former years, as in the following description of him: "Like a shadow he never left me but followed a step behind. This most rare cross between a man and a woodpecker, a heavily built swine, a real animal, a buffoon, a timeserver, an archracketeer, an informer, a bootlicker, an extortioner, and a bribetaker—a monstrous product of those far-off days. Yet I remembered him as a slim, hard-up young man, with a tiny spark in his breast." Katayev also tries to convey something of the unspeakable indignities to which he and the other writers of his generation were subjected if, like Zhivago's friend, they had "broken themselves in." In *The Holy Well* writers who committed themselves in the 1930's to socialist realism are symbolized by a talking cat which has been trained by its Georgian owner to mouth human words. For a brilliant examination of the fellow traveling ethos, see the article by B. Sarnov on Katayev's latest work in *Voprosy Literatury*, January 1968.

that Soviet writers could again be induced or forced to ignore the existential dilemmas which troubled the "critical realists."

Back to the Accursed Questions

In his essay *On Socialist Realism*, Sinyavsky has argued that in its heyday, before the onset of its slow decomposition after 1953, socialist realism involved a return to a kind of eighteenth-century classicism for which certainty in the rightness of the Purpose was so strong that the role of literature was mainly to proclaim and propagate it (as Derzhavin and Mayakovsky did) and sing the praises of its apotheosized instruments (Catherine the Great or Stalin). The nineteenth century, on the other hand, was a time of skepticism, irony, moral ambiguity, but also of a thirst for faith which is seen in almost all the figures—from Pushkin to Tolstoy —who still dominate the Russian consciousness. In Sinyavsky's view, the perfect image of the nineteenth-century Russian intellectual was Lermontov's Demon ("I wish to make my peace with heaven / I wish to love, I wish to pray. / I wish to believe in the good."). This craving for faith and anguish at one's consignment to a moral limbo was, as Sinyavsky points out, an admirable preparation for a reckless leap into some supposedly liberating commitment. It is only this that can explain the way in which Alexander Blok and other intellectuals in 1917 embraced the Revolution with the ardor of religious converts. The more corroded they were by irony and self-doubt, the more prone they were to take the plunge. As Sinyavsky says: "The hunger of the nineteenth century prepared us Russians, perhaps, for the way in which we so greedily threw ourselves on the dish cooked by Marx, and swallowed it without bothering to examine its taste or smell, or think about the consequences."

In the freedom of an enquiry not intended for immediate publication inside the country (just as, in his fiction, he has explored the effects of the "cult of personality" in terms of abnormal psychology, an area still largely off limits to Soviet writers),

Sinyavsky has spelled out what is implicit in many significant works of post-Stalin literature: that the basic questions, far from being solved by Marx's recipe and its Leninist application, were only temporarily pushed out of sight. The Demon, after his fatal love affair with the beautiful Tamara, was thrown back into his old tormented state, his anguished search for faith.

It is difficult to say whether the renewed search for answers to the old "accursed questions" will find any very forceful expression in present-day Soviet literature (only Solzhenitsyn, of the partially published prose writers, shows signs of measuring up to prerevolutionary standards), or to speculate as to what direction it will take. It is enough for us to note, in general conclusion, that the mere fact of Soviet literature now being dominated by uncertainty about past, present, and future, speaks eloquently of the total failure of Soviet cultural policy. It has failed to harness literature and the arts (except by debasing them) to its aim of the social and moral transformation of man in a new image. It has failed to enlist the support of anyone truly gifted in the younger generation. It has failed even to retain the allegiance of those of the older generation who once thought of service to it, not as bondage, but as a kind of higher spiritual freedom.

Looked at from the point of view of its dominant themes, Soviet literature (at least in some of its best and most genuine representatives) has moved from qualified acceptance of the Revolution through a period of meaningless and artistically barren lip-service to it, back to its starting point in traditional Russian literature, whose genius was always expressed in its insights into moral and psychological ambivalence. Looked at from the point of view of form, the Soviet experience has been utterly destructive. Early attempts at innovation (e.g., the Serapion Brothers, the formalist critics, not to mention the many individual poetic and artistic styles of the 1920's) were destroyed and replaced in the late 1930's by an empty, bombastic pseudo-popular style which reminded many Russians of the folksy, nationalist vulgarity of the age of Alexander III. The acolytes of this official style are still numerous and powerful. The Soviet ruling class still insists, for the most part, that literature and art should confirm it in its own crassness and mediocrity, and in the sterility of its social ideals. Perhaps, if it ever becomes more confident of itself, it might, like other ruling classes, cease to regard true aesthetic values as a threat to its power. Only the next fifty years will show.

The Decline of Socialist Realism

Even in the later years of Stalin, who was a past master in aligning theory and practice, there was never a perfect congruence between the two in literature and the arts. The ragged edges of the practice that occasionally peeped out from under the blueprint were ruthlessly snipped away, sometimes together with the heads of the guilty, but all the same there were anomalies—even licensed by the great Engineer of Human Souls himself—to remind one of the underlying tenuity of the doctrine. A case in point was the posthumous canonization of Mayakovsky, which was hard to square with the all-encompassing condemnation of "formalism" in the years after the war.

Such anomalies, as one can see now, were of great importance in the preservation of some vestiges of an alternative culture. The constant availability of Mayakovsky to the younger generation was a prime factor in the revival of poetry after Stalin's death— Yevtushenko and Voznesensky would be unthinkable without him, in moral as well as formal terms. Various other "undermining" influences survived—some from prerevolutionary times, others from the early years of the Soviet regime—despite frenetic attempts in the later Stalin years to minimize them. It was awkward to ban Dostoyevsky and Yesenin,[1] though everything possible was done to limit access to them. Even so, the minds of the innocent young and the terrorized old could not be totally insulated from them and other "harmful" voices from the past. On the whole, however, it was undeniable that by the end of Stalin's reign the official picture of Soviet literature fitted the visible reality pretty well—though rather in the way that a shroud may be said to fit an amputated corpse.

The doctrine of socialist realism[2] was launched out of the blue in 1932 after virtually secret preparations linked with the drafting of the statutes of the Union of Writers. During the following years it took shape in several pronouncements at the highest level (by Zhdanov in his speech to the First Writers' Congress in 1934, and then again in 1947 in his "report" on the journals *Zvezda* and *Leningrad*) and, more importantly, through the gradual establishment of an illustrative canon which started with Maxim Gorky's *The Mother* (1906) and came to include some of the prose of the 1920's, adopting further works *passim* during the 1930's, 1940's, and early 1950's. At first sight it was a motley collection, embracing work of very varied type and quality. But there was a certain consistency in the choice and, with the notable exception of Mayakovsky, it conformed well enough to the official theory; by the time of Stalin's death, theory and practice could be said to match each

---

[1]Dostoyevsky was denounced in an article in *Pravda* in 1948 by the notorious Vladimir Yermilov, "Against the Reactionary Ideas in Dostoyevsky's Writings." (Ironically, the immediate pretext was a book by Valeri Kirpotin—see below—entitled *Young Dostoyevsky*). After this, none of Dostoyevsky's work was reprinted until after Stalin's death, his museum in the Bozhidomka was closed, and school textbooks of literature mentioned him only in passing, as a figure of no great importance who had lapsed into obscurantism after his progressive early work, *Poor Folk*. But he was never formally banned, so that secondhand copies of his collected works remained available—at prohibitive prices. The same was true of Yesenin, who became something of a cult figure in the *bas-fonds* of Soviet society in the later Stalin years. (See in this connection the fascinating note by V. Shalamov, "Sergei Yesenin and the World of Thieves" in *Grani*, No. 77, 1970.)

[2]The term was first used in print in an anonymous leading article in *Literaturnaya Gazeta* in May 1932. It was written by Valeri Kirpotin.

other in a fairly stabilized relationship. Even foreigners, such as Howard Fast and Andersen Nexø, could be adapted into his canon, though the casualty rate was high. The detailed story of the elevation of foreign writers to the status of honorary socialist realists, and the subsequent "disgrace" of some of them, is the best illustration, if any is needed, of the political opportunism to which literary theory was at all times subject.[3]

But to take it at its face value, what was socialist realism in its heyday—from about 1934 to 1953? At the risk of repeating the all too familiar, it may be well to attempt a summary of what now seem to have been its essential features, as a prelude to a discussion of its position at the present day.

Its ancestry has always been a cause of some embarrassment for Soviet critics, since it is difficult to equip it with a Marxist pedigree (the "revisionists" are more easily able to find support, for their arguments in favor of the autonomy of art, in the writings of Marx and Engels), and they had to seek justification for it mainly in the views of nineteenth-century radical critics—in particular Belinsky, Chernyshevsky, and Dobrolyubov, who are an abundant source of quotations for anyone wishing to buttress the contention that art and literature must serve social or didactic purposes.[4] Of the three elements—*narodnost* ("national character"), *ideinost* ("ideological expression"), and *partiinost* ("party spirit")—which have always been considered basic to socialist realism, the first two are derived from the utilitarian aesthetics of the last century, and the third is the special contribution of Lenin.

---

[3]Almost all the foreign socialist realists have fallen from grace, unless, like Theodore Dreiser, they died in good time. Upton Sinclair, once prized for his exposures of American capitalism, was suddenly dropped at the end of the 1940's (*Krokodil* had a caricature of Sinclair showing a bloated frog croaking anti-Soviet slanders in a bog). Howard Fast was excommunicated in 1959 at the Third Writers' Congress by his old friend Boris Polevoy (whose lying assurances about the fate of the Soviet Yiddish writers had finally disillusioned Fast).

[4]In particular, Chernyshevsky's study *The Aesthetic Relations of Art and Reality* (1855) and Dobrolyubov's articles on contemporary literature ("What Is Oblomovshchina?," "A Ray of Light in the Kingdom of Darkness," etc.).

Providing the sanction for party control over literature as well as for the writer's enforced commitment to aims not necessarily of his own choosing, *partiinost* is the feature which marks off socialist realism from any other kind of realism. By virtue of it, what for Belinsky and Chernyshevsky was only a moral imperative became in Soviet times an externally imposed obligation, an ordinance enjoined by holy writ. When, in 1956, the historian Y. M. Strochkov made an attempt to cast doubt on the meaning of Lenin's words by suggesting that his article "The Party Organization and Party Literature" had been intended to apply only to political and publicist writing, the official reaction was very sharp indeed: it was at once recognized that the removal of this keystone would have brought the whole edifice of Soviet literary doctrine tumbling down. No one has ever dared raise this issue again.[5]

The best way of defining the kind of literature which met the three chief requirements of socialist realism is to list some of the principal works—what may be called the Soviet classics—firmly established in the canon by the end of Stalin's life, and then to decide what they have in common. In more or less chronological order, they included Maxim Gorky's *The Mother* (1906); Dmitri Furmanov's *Chapayev* (1923); Konstantin Fedin's *Cities and Years* and Leonid Leonov's *Badgers* (both 1924); Fedor Gladkov's *Cement* (1925); Alexander Fadeyev's *The Rout (The Nineteen)* (1927); Mikhail Sholokhov's *Quiet Don* (in four books, 1928–40); Leonov's *Soviet River* (1929); Sholokhov's *Virgin Soil Upturned (Seeds of Tomorrow)*, Valentin Katayev's *Time, Forward!*, and Leonov's *Skutarevsky* (all three 1932); Nikolai Ostrovsky's *How the Steel Was Tempered* (1932–34); Ilya Ehrenburg's *The Second Day (Out of Chaos)* (1933–34); Alexei Tolstoy's *Peter I* (three books, 1929–45); Ehrenburg's *The Fall of*

---

[5]For a discussion of Strochkov's interpretation, see my article "The Thaw and the Writers" (*Daedalus*, Summer 1960). I am now inclined to think that Strochkov was using the device common in the mid-1950's of "opposing" Lenin to Stalin, and that Lenin probably did intend his words to apply to literature of every kind—or at any rate would not have minded their wider application.

Paris (1941–42); Polevoy's *The Story of a Real Man* (1946); Ehrenburg's *The Storm* (1946–47); Fadeyev's *The Young Guard* (1947; rewritten version, 1951); and Kochetov's *The Zhurbin Family* (1952), which as a working class saga, appropriately, and on a distinct note of degeneration, closes the cycle of classical socialist realism begun by Gorky's novel on a similar theme.

This list is by no means complete, but it is representative enough for the purposes of definition. It is a very mixed bag from several points of view. In their social or class origins, for instance, the authors of these works range from the aristocrat Alexei Tolstoy to the worker's son Nikolai Ostrovsky (the majority being of an in-between "bourgeois-intellectual" background). In terms of their earlier literary allegiances, some were fellow travelers (Ehrenburg, Leonov, and Fedin, for example), while others, such as Fadeyev, were members of RAPP, or of other militant left or proletarian groups subsequently liquidated in 1932 (writers belonging to these last were lucky to escape denunciation as Trotskyists, which is perhaps one reason why fellow travelers seem to predominate among the older generation of socialist realists). Not all of them were party members (e.g., Leonov), failing to join even at times when the "best people" usually found themselves under overwhelming pressure to do so (this is significant only as an indication that a chosen few were instructed to remain outside the party to make it easier to refute the recurrent bourgeois "slander" about all writers having to be party members). The work of some of them was not adopted in its entirety into the canon. Leonov's *The Thief* (1927), for example, was excluded from the collected works that were published in 1953–55, and appeared in a dutifully rewritten form only well after Stalin's death, in 1959. Ehrenburg's *Extraordinary Adventures of Julio Jurenito and His Disciples* (1922) was under a ban in Stalin's lifetime, and his *Stormy Life of Lazik Roitschwantz* (1927) has not only never been republished but appears to be one of the few works of Soviet literature that remains unmentionable. *How the Steel Was Tempered*, one of the most lauded classics of socialist realism, creates the impression of almost having been made to measure as an illustration of the theory.[6] Several other celebrated novels in the list (*Quiet Don* among them) were extensively revised by their authors in the postwar period to bring them into line with the more exacting standards of Stalin's later years.[7] It will be seen from the dates of publication that at least half the books in the list were actually written before the concept of socialist realism had been born or received a name, and that one was co-opted from prerevolutionary times. Almost all of them relate to the "heroic" eras of Soviet history: the Civil War, the first Five-Year Plan and collectivization, the Second World War, and postwar reconstruction. A few are set, at least partially, in other countries *(The Fall of Paris)*, or even in other eras *(Peter I)*.

Socialist realism of the Stalin years consisted preponderantly of novels, stories, and plays. Only a few writers of agitational or epic verse were admitted to full status within the canon—for instance, Mayakovsky, thanks to Stalin's praise of him in 1936, and Demyan Bedny, until his temporary fall from grace in the same year.[8] Several poets were at least partially admitted on the strength of romantic ballads about the Civil War: Nikolai Tikhonov for such calls to revolutionary duty as *The Ballad of the Blue Packet* (1922), Eduard Bagritsky for *The Lay of Opanas* (1926), and Nikolai Aseyev for his *Twenty-six* (1925), about the martyred Baku commissars. Even Pasternak occasionally got an indulgent mention by the critics for his unfinished attempts to

---

[6]The novel was the object of unprecedented propaganda in the Soviet press, and its hero, Pavel Korchagin, is still held up to the young as an inspiring example. In view of the work's glaring literary inadequacies, there is a certain cynicism in this. A leading literary functionary in the Soviet Union once candidly described it to me as a pathetic work, totally devoid of talent *(bezdarneisheye, bespomoshchneisheye proizvedeniye).*

[7]The extraordinary details of this unparalleled operation are given in Maurice Friedberg's article "New Editions of Soviet Belles Lettres: A Study in Politics and Palimpsests," *The American Slavic and East European Review* XIII, No. 1 (February 1954).

[8]Bedny's disgrace (caused by Stalin's displeasure with his libretto for Borodin's opera *The Bogatyrs [Heroes of Antiquity]*, although according to Nadezhda Mandelstam in *Hope against Hope* an attendant reason may have been his imprudent complaint about the grubby finger marks left on books he had lent to Stalin) was short-lived, and in the late 1940's and early 1950's he was often bracketed with Mayakovsky in school textbooks as a great Soviet poet.

deal in epic fashion with revolutionary themes (*Lieutenant Schmidt*, 1926–27, and *1905*, 1925–26), but his lyrical "sins" always debarred him from real acceptance as a Soviet poet.[9]

Some older poets were co-opted as precursors of socialist realism in poetry—notably Alexander Blok, on the basis of a willfully one-sided interpretation of "The Twelve," and, more justifiably, Valeri Bryusov, for his poetic offerings to the Revolution and Lenin (not to mention his gesture of joining the party as early as 1921). But it was not until the second half of the 1930's that a group of younger poets, formed entirely under the Soviet system (Alexander Tvardovsky, Konstantin Simonov, Alexei Surkov, Margarita Aliger, and others), came, at least nominally, to fill the void left by the effective exclusion from the Soviet literary scene of almost all of the older poets who mattered (apart from the "balladeers"). It is apparent that by its very nature socialist realism was inimical to poetry as such, scarcely tolerating true lyricism and accepting only narrative, declamatory, or occasional verse (i.e., political satire, eulogy, etc., in the manner of Mikhalkov or Bezymensky). Lyric poetry, it is true, made a brief appearance during the war (Simonov, Surkov, Aliger, and others) but was snuffed out when its usefulness as a release for the overriding sorrows of war had come to an end. The reemergence of Akhmatova and Pasternak was equally short-lived and served as one of the pretexts for the cultural pogrom begun by Zhdanov in 1946.

In addition to the full-fledged works of socialist realism of the type mentioned above, there were many others which, because of a certain ambiguity, were consigned to a gray zone, tolerated as a part of Soviet literature but not accepted into the canon (these generally came under a virtual ban in the last years of Stalin's life). A most outstanding example was Yuri Olesha's *Envy* (1927). The

---

[9]One of the reasons for Pasternak's survival may have been the hope that he might one day fulfill the slight promise of his long poems and be won over. Nadezhda Mandelstam quotes Fadeyev as once having said, "You know, Pasternak is not one of us either, but all the same he is a little closer to us, and we can come to terms with him in some things" (*Hope against Hope*, p. 152).

same applied to most of Babel's and Pilnyak's writings, until they were proscribed after the authors' disappearance in the purges. Andrei Platonov, though never arrested, was virtually excluded by the mid-1930's. Mikhail Zoshchenko, Mikhail Bulgakov, and Ilf and Petrov, tolerated during the 1930's, were cast out in the postwar years. Through the curious quirk of Stalin's having taken a fancy to *The Days of the Turbins*, the stage version of his *White Guard*, Bulgakov was spared physically, but his work disappeared from sight after his death in 1940. Zoshchenko's concessions to the demands of the age, such as his "biographical tale" *Kerensky* (1937)—actually somewhat double-edged—did not save him from anathematization in 1947. Ilf and Petrov were posthumously outlawed in 1949, during the campaign against "rootless cosmopolitans," after the publishing house Sovietsky Pisatel had rashly brought out a one-volume edition of *The Twelve Chairs* and *The Golden Calf* (originally published in 1928 and 1931); it is a miracle that they survived so long, and did so perhaps only because of the inglorious end of the villain Ostap Bender. In general, few gray-zone writers survived the last years of Stalin's life and were only gradually rescued from oblivion after 1956.

What, then, was the common denominator among the canonical works mentioned that determined their admittance to socialist realist status? What was it, conversely, that disqualified those in the gray zone? It is clear that the decisive feature shared by all of them was their authors' attitude to the historical process. It did not matter whether they were Marxist, or even whether they wrote from inner conviction (some probably did not), as long as they presented the course of events and the development of society in such a way as to lead the reader to conclude that ultimately victory was certain. The arena chosen to demonstrate this could be microcosmic (say, at its crudest, the struggle to raise production in a factory or farm), or national (the fight for survival in the Civil War or Second World War), or international (as in Fedin's *Cities and Years* and Ehrenburg's *The Fall of Paris*); indeed, it could be cosmic: Alexei Tolstoy's *Aelita* (1922–23), which describes the triumph of revolution on Mars, was frequently reprinted in later years as one of the rare examples of socialist realist science fiction. The same author's major novel on Peter the Great showed that socialist realism—particularly in the second half of the 1930's—could also embrace distant epochs, depicting them as a necessary preparation for the revolution to come, even though it meant implying that Peter the Great and Ivan the Terrible were enlightened forerunners of Lenin and Stalin.

This central requirement that the author display a certain historical optimism was less restricting than might be thought, at least in the early period. Some of the retrospectively adopted novels, such as Leonov's *Badgers* and Sholokhov's *Quiet Don,* still strike the reader by their objectivity, particularly in the light of the more stringent standards of socialist realism in the postwar years. Both Leonov and, at least in the first two parts of *Quiet Don,* Sholokhov portrayed the Civil War and its aftermath in an almost neutral way—both sides committed atrocities; honorable and courageous people could be found in both camps; it was quite possible for an ordinary person, like Sholokhov's hero Grigori Melekhov, to become confused and change sides, eventually ending up on the wrong one. The crucial point is, however, that at the end Melekhov appears as a tragic, broken figure, and the Soviet critics could thus point to the implication that his total defeat and abandonment were the result of having been unable, through weakness, blindness, or *force majeure,* to grasp the nature of the struggle, failing to make the "right" choice—and being "thrown on the rubbish heap of history" as a consequence.

If one substitutes historical force for gods, this was tragedy in the Greek sense—a man could anger History as he could Zeus and be punished accordingly. It is certainly not true, as is sometimes said, that there was no place for tragedy in socialist realism. Several of its better specimens were even tragedies ending in defeat for the "right" side (for example, Gorky's *The Mother* and Fadeyev's *The Rout*), but to qualify as a socialist realist the author of such tragedies had to make it plain that defeat was but a temporary setback on the road to certain victory in the long run. There were, of course, two kinds of tragedy: the tragedy of defeat and death for those representing "progress" (Pavel Vlasov in *The*

Mother and Levinson in *The Rout*), and the tragedy of those who failed to see the light (Melekhov in *Quiet Don*, and particularly the type of wavering intellectual exemplified by Andrei Startsov in Fedin's *Cities and Years* and Volodya Safonov in Ehrenburg's *The Second Day*).

As the inclusion of *Quiet Don* in the canon shows, "positive heroes" were not obligatory (though, like Fadeyev's Levinson, desirable) at the center of the action. Sholokhov's Bunchuk and Stokman, as the conscious representatives of "progress," are both marginal and artistically unconvincing.

In the late 1930's, and particularly in the postwar years, however, socialist realist orthodoxy demanded a schematic contrast between positive and negative characters—which destroyed the sense of tragedy. Even in novels on the war, such as Fadeyev's *The Young Guard*, individuals who found themselves on the wrong side were treated as mere criminals, and never as the victims of historical circumstance; defeat and death in the service of the cause, on the other hand, was robbed of its tragic pathos by the sententious way in which the moral was drawn. In the last years of Stalin's life, socialist realism degenerated into the final absurdity of the "lack of conflict" theory and the "varnishing of reality" (defensive responses to the Zhdanov decrees), with the result that the novels and plays of that time, now mercifully forgotten by common consent, were devoid of either plausibility or dramatic tension.

Taking an implicit (or better still, explicit) declaration of faith in ultimate victory as the essential criterion, it is easy to see the consistent principle behind the incorporation of fellow-traveler novels into the canon. Indeed, this criterion was felt to be so important that features totally impermissible by the later standards of socialist realism were overlooked or forgiven for its sake: for example, the even-handedness with which Leonov treats the Bolsheviks from the town and the anarchist partisans in *Badgers*, the stark description of Red atrocities in *Quiet Don*, the brutally frank account of the human cost of industrialization at the beginning of *The Second Day* (much toned down in postwar editions), and the general tendency in novels of the 1920's and early 1930's to give due weight to the ordeals and cruelty of the struggle and to the squalor of everyday life. (There was, of course, less indulgence for this kind of thing as the years went by; Fadeyev paid dearly for his description in the first edition of *The Young Guard* of the chaos on the Soviet side at the beginning of the Second World War.) It was even found expedient to overlook unresolved ambiguities in the attitude of an author—such as Leonov displayed in his earlier novels—as long as the balance was tipped at least slightly in favor of belief in victory for the "new." There were clearly degrees of optimism, and a writer's subsequent record was certainly taken into account in assessing the socialist realist potential of his earlier work; indeed, progress from a certain skepticism to absolute faith was a useful illustration of the power of "truth."

It is in itself a telling comment on Soviet literary doctrine that the more ambiguous a work in its all-important conclusion about the final historical outcome, the more successful it tends to be as literature. *Quiet Don* is a good example of this general rule. There is much in the first two parts that gainsays the message of the ending. The novel can easily leave the reader with the feeling, as *Doctor Zhivago* does in a way consciously intended by Pasternak, that ultimately history and the doings of men take place on a low level when compared with the eternal process of nature—that they are a finite part of the infinite, and so victory in any human conflict is never final or complete.[10]

It is easy to see why works at first consigned to the gray zone and later suppressed altogether did not pass the vital test for acceptance in the canon. Babel's *Red Cavalry*, for instance, despite the fact that it dealt with the same sort of heroic Civil War

[10]There is a strong undercurrent of nature symbolism in a lot of Soviet writing. Whether consciously so intended or not, it tends to contradict the belief in historical "victory." Leonov employed this device in *Badgers* (the legend of Czar Kalafat) and in *Russian Forest* (1953), where, despite the camouflage of praise for Stalin's great afforestation schemes, the wanton destruction of the forests is subtly identified with ruthless exploitation of the Russian people under the Soviet regime. Nature, as a symbol for something at once pure and invincible, plays a large part in the "new wave" post-Stalin fiction (notably Kazakov and Tendryakov).

material as did *Quiet Don,* and despite a highly fortunate defense by Gorky from Budenny's attack, was nevertheless debarred because of its lack of any message—except the dispiriting one that cossacks are cruel, as is life itself, with no end in sight to the miseries of the human condition. Nearly the only time that Babel expressed a general view about the future—and then only indirectly, through the old Jew Gedali in the *Red Cavalry* story of that name—it was to put forward the scarcely optimistic, and certainly un-Marxist, idea that it would take an "Internationale of men of good will" to save the world from its own wickedness."[11]

Babel's efforts in the 1930's to adapt led only to the production of unfinished fragments (for example, "Kolyvushka," 1930, announced as a chapter from a novel to be entitled *Velikaya Staritsa*), so that he was never able to expiate the "sins" of *Red Cavalry.* He thus remained in the gray zone until he was expunged from the record after his arrest in 1939. The same was true of Olesha's *Envy,* where the author's own ambivalence in dealing with the struggle between old and new is less latent than in, say, Leonov's *Badgers.* Although Olesha's quixotic survivors from the past are defeated and humiliated in resounding fashion and made to wallow in their own impotence, the reader is nevertheless left with the feeling that some ghost in the machine may yet haunt, if not one day confound, the bold engineers who think that the whole world can be run like a model sausage factory.

It seems probable that Olesha's novel—like a good deal of Yesenin's later verse—was tolerated not least for its demoralizing effect on the representatives of the "old," even though it cast doubt on the permanence and wisdom of the "new." In this sense some gray zone literature could fulfill an important sociopolitical function. Leonov's *The Thief,* to take an example of a gray zone

---

[11]The Gedali story was used to mount a fantastic provocation against Babel in 1929. The Polish communist novelist Bruno Jasieński wrote a letter to *Literaturnaya Gazeta* calling attention to an article in the Warsaw literary journal *Wiadomości* which alleged that Babel had admitted to a Polish writer he had met in France that Gedali's idea represented his own philosophy. Babel vehemently denied the suggestion in a letter to the paper.

work by a writer the bulk of whose remaining output was accepted into the canon, was too obviously pessimistic, too full of disillusionment (on the part of both the author and his leading character, Mitya Vekshin, the disenchanted Civil War veteran who takes to crime during NEP) to fulfill Soviet literature's task of "helping to turn the whole planet into a beautiful home for man, united in one family," in Gorky's words at the First Writers' Congress in 1934.[12]

A number of other prose works of the 1920's and early 1930's were of course eventually banned because of their outright hostility. Andrei Platonov's *The City of Gradov* (1929), a satire on bureaucratic degeneration (the same author's *Foundation Pit* [*Kotlovan*], a nightmarish tale of "socialist construction," was not even published, like most of his later fiction); Ehrenburg's *Stormy Life of Lazik Roitschwantz*, with its *leitmotiv* that all is for the worst in the worst of all possible worlds; Bulgakov's "The Fatal Eggs" (1925), with its Wellsian vision of doom in a society controlled by overweening bureaucrats; and of course books by Soviet authors that appeared only abroad, such as Zamyatin's *We* (written in 1920 and published in France in 1924) and Pilnyak's *Mahogany* (Berlin, 1929).

From the very nature of the main criterion applied to prose, it is obvious that nearly all poetry worthy of the name—particularly lyric poetry—was automatically disqualified. With the best will in the world, a poet could hardly be expected to deploy the necessary social and historical arguments—except, as already pointed out, in epic or narrative verse, but few genuine lyric poets could sustain this kind of effort, as Pasternak's example shows. The result of a real poet's attempt to force himself to write an ode

---

[12]*The Thief* was also objectionable because of the influence of Dostoyevsky, particularly *The Possessed*. One of the characters, Chikilev, is a clear borrowing from Dostoyevsky's Shigalev, who looks forward to a society in which the chief binding force will be universal fear and mutual distrust. When Pasternak, in his *Sketch for an Autobiography*, wanted to find an adequate word for Stalin's terror in 1937, he invented the term *shigalevshchina*. Leonov's introduction of this prophetic idea into a novel published in 1927 shows how narrow was the dividing line between a future socialist realist and a counterrevolutionary.

in praise of Stalin is powerfully described by Nadezhda Mandelstam in Chapter 43 of her memoir *Hope against Hope*. The only poet who was capable of making the eventually crippling effort to suppress his own lyricism ("stepping on the throat of his song") in favor of *partiinost* was Mayakovsky. Perhaps it was only possible because it satisfied certain quirks of character, but even so it cost him his life and required genius, of a kind, to do at all. Stalin, with a shrewdness that does him credit, recognized this by canonizing him in 1936—there *had* to be a socialist realist poet of real stature, and Mayakovsky was the only candidate; this was his ironic and incongruous posthumous service to a doctrine yet unborn at the time of his death. All other poets either perished early (Blok, Gumilev, Yesenin) or were reduced to silence, not necessarily by censorship alone—the "dumbness" by which Akhmatova, Pasternak, and Mandelstam were stricken in the second half of the 1920's is mentioned by Nadezhda Mandelstam (p. 162 of *Hope against Hope*) as a factor that arose well before external pressures became intolerable.

Prose, then—and in particular the long novel (sometimes in verse, like Tvardovsky's *The Land of Muravia*, 1936, which was divided into nineteen "chapters")—was the form most adapted to socialist realism. Only with the discursiveness of the traditional Russian novel—as Babel understood when he made his vain attempt to fulfill the "social contract" at the beginning of the 1930's—was it feasible to provide the extensive social background and portrayal of character in relation to which the "truths" involved had necessarily to be demonstrated (Soviet writers, said Zhdanov in 1934, must depict reality in its revolutionary *development*).

All other features of "classical" socialist realism were secondary —both in the sense that they derived logically from the main criterion described and in the sense that the party set far less store by them. The insistence on a realist style, for instance, was based on the correct assumption that the message would all the more readily be understood by a mass readership. (It was natural, of course, that the aesthetic demands of the theory should bear the imprint of the personal tastes and prejudices of Gorky, the author of the first socialist realist novel. But he was not fanatical, as witness his tolerance of Babel's conscious revolt against Russian realism.) The fact is, however, that nonrealist forms were frowned upon and denounced as "formalism" only because, like lyric poetry, they were ill adapted to delivering the message. The comparative unimportance of form is shown both by the acceptance of Mayakovsky, whose incomprehensibility to the masses was compensated for by the perfection of his sentiments, and by the fact, pointed out by Andrei Sinyavsky, that even realism became inadequate as a vehicle for the cruder demands of Stalin's later years.

In the eighteen years since Stalin's death the relationship of Soviet literary theory to current practice has altered radically. There is no need, for the purposes of this paper, to detail the stages by which this has come about. It suffices here to state the obvious general conclusion that in the post-Stalin years literary theory, that is, the doctrine of socialist realism, has been overtaken by events and constantly belied by actual trends beyond the control of its keepers. The gradual introduction into literature of previously forbidden themes; the rehabilitation of almost all of Stalin's victims and in many cases their republication; the general ideological havoc wrought by the Twentieth Party Congress and some of Khrushchev's pronouncements and actions (notably at the Third Writers' Congress in 1959); the flood of influences from abroad (not least from the People's Democracies and the revisionist Marxists of Western Europe); the partial, if erratic, relaxation of censorship; the spectacular growth of uncensored *samizdat* publication; the crystallization of a variety of conflicting political moods and their public expression, however muffled—all these factors have put an impossible strain on the theory of socialist realism, which was, after all, developed at a time when the power to enforce it was not in doubt. Indeed, it was posited on the existence of firm control over literary practice. Its rhetoric was suited only to what Zamyatin termed a state of entropy, a static situation of imposed unanimity. In other words, it was adequate to a policy of forced convergence, but it is hopelessly thrown out of kilter by the present trend toward differentiation.

It is not surprising that since about the mid-1960's the theory has at last begun to show a slight sensitivity to all the changes that have taken place in real life and has even itself been subject, on a minor scale, to the general process of segmentation. If the exercise were not too tedious, it would now be possible to plot "left-wing," "right-wing," and "centrist" trends in the current writing about socialist realism. The custodians of the doctrine—that is, those critics-cum-ideologists who regularly write theoretical articles on literature in *Kommunist, Voprosy Literatury,* and the "fat" journals, such as A. Metchenko, V. Ivanov, B. Suchkov, Y. Barabash, V. Ozerov, G. Lomidze, L. Novichenko, and A. Ovcharenko—have been debating among themselves in recent years in a way that betrays unmistakable apprehension about the glaring, no longer concealable, gap between theory and practice, as well as the infiltration of "alien" viewpoints.

One such exchange took place on the pages of *Novy Mir* in a series of articles begun in October 1970 and continuing into 1971. Several of these critics have also written books in which the differences between them are very apparent, though it is a low-key polemic among people who recognize their basic solidarity in the defense of the doctrine against those many Soviet literary scholars and writers who no longer even bother to pay lip service to socialist realism. The majority of them are, needless to say, more or less conservative, and the nuances between them are hardly worth discussing, but one of them, A. Ovcharenko, has come forth in his book *Socialist Realism and the Contemporary Literary Process* (1968), and in his contribution to the debate in *Novy Mir* (May 1971), as the advocate of a cautious *aggiornamento.* It is difficult to say how authoritative this may be, but Ovcharenko's standing, as a frequent contributor to *Kommunist,* must be fairly high. It is also noteworthy that in February 1970 he was appointed to the editorial board of *Novy Mir* with the evident assignment of helping to wean it away from the excessive "liberalism" of the Tvardovsky years. He probably represents a middle-of-the-road orthodoxy, thus reflecting, at the level of theory, the general policy of the present party leadership toward literature, and steering a course between the "right," which wants no modification at all, and the "left," which, as is darkly hinted by

Ovcharenko himself, would gladly jettison socialist realism as something utterly compromised by its dogmatic interpretation under the cult of personality, and accept in its place Garaudy's revisionist *"réalisme sans rivages."* Garaudy and the "Austrian renegade" Ernst Fischer are at present the particular bogeymen of the Soviet literary establishment; their doctrines were denounced by Vitali Ozerov at the Fifth Writers' Congress in June 1971 as a call for ideological pluralism, a denial of *partiinost,* and, *horribile dictu,* an attempt to substitute Trotskyism for Leninism.

In his book, Ovcharenko moves away from the rigid Stalinist definition of socialist realism while trying to draw the line one may not cross without lapsing into "revisionism" and going over to the camp of the ideological enemy. The contorted postures which this balancing act involves often make Ovcharenko's arguments difficult to follow, but through all the hedging and backtracking one can discern significant rethinking on three central points: the question of form, the application of doctrine to the Soviet literary heritage, and the nature of current writing in the Soviet Union.

Time and time again Ovcharenko insists that the essential demand of socialist realism remains what it was: namely, that literature should only be written in the spirit of the party *(partiiny)* and must help to lead men to the bright horizons of the millennium by expressing faith in its history-ordained advent. But, having made his position on this central point clear, he goes on to say that socialist realism is hospitable to any literary techniques or devices which may further its main purpose. Stream of consciousness, fantasy, the deliberate distortion of reality[13]—all these may be employed in its service. Moreover he claims, in the face of all the evidence, that this has always been so, and quotes Lunacharsky as once having said: "If, in order to accentuate a

---

[13]Ovcharenko suggests that some of the techniques claimed by modernism in fact belong to the general development of literature and may therefore be incorporated into socialist realism as part of its rightful heritage. He quotes a study by the French scholar M. Aucouturier showing that stream of consciousness, for instance, was anticipated in Russian realism by the inner monologue of Tolstoy, Dostoyevsky, and Chekhov.

certain social feature more effectively, it is necessary to show
. . . what lurks beneath a façade of propriety by means of a
distorted, caricatured image, then such a procedure is profoundly
realistic." Even more tellingly, the progenitor of socialist realism,
Maxim Gorky himself, had said in 1932: "If you are hindered by
the techniques of realism in depicting the hero of our age in the
way he deserves, then seek other techniques." Undoubtedly aware
that this advice could not have been quoted for the guidance of
Soviet writers in the later Stalin years, Ovcharenko comments:
"Today Gorky's words take on new force. Our art is called upon
to depict both communist man and the very complicated process
of the evolution of the man of the old world, which turns out to
be more involved and lengthy than might have been imagined.
To show communist man in all his grandeur, it will be necessary
not only to exploit the best that has been achieved by artists of
all times, but constantly to create something new as well. Therefore one can only welcome the explorations [*poiski*] characteristic
for the literature of all socialist countries, as well as for progressive
writers in capitalist countries."

The real sense of this apparent concession (characteristically
disguised as something that was always inherent in the doctrine)
is that it would be wise, in the present hard times, to yield on a
secondary point in the hope of safeguarding the cherished core
of socialist realism: its extraliterary function. What Ovcharenko
is saying, in effect, is, "Be 'formalists' if you like, only please serve
the cause!" This is, in fact, merely an extension of the license that
Stalin posthumously granted to Mayakovsky.

Apart from raising tricky logical problems that even the dialectic would be hard put to resolve (how would one classify a nonrealist work of socialist realism?), such a minor concession about form
is irrelevant to the problems besetting Soviet literary theory at the
present day (though it has some importance for the past). In
prose, few of the young writers have shown much inclination to
indulge in formal experiment (except for Sinyavsky and Daniel,
who went to prison for employing fantasy and deliberate distortion of reality in order to show "what lurks beneath a façade of
propriety"); on the contrary, they have displayed a marked prefer-

ence for the techniques of old-fashioned realism. This makes their challenge to accepted theory all the more insidious: it is, one might say, "realism with a vengeance." As regards poetry, the right to considerably greater freedom in the choice of formal devices has in any case been won (in the teeth of opposition) over the last decade and a half, so that Ovcharenko's doctrinal "concession" comes too late to be meaningful. In poetry, too, the main headache for the theorists is *what* is said, not *how* it is said.

The second aspect of Ovcharenko's *aggiornamento*, which emerges in his gentle debate with other exegetes to the right of him, concerns the problem of examining the heritage of Soviet literature in the light of official theory, especially that considerable part of it that was either consigned to the gray zone or suppressed altogether. This question overlaps, of course, with the third and even more contentious one of how to deal with the variegated phenomena of contemporary Soviet literature.

The view of the conservatives (as expressed, for instance, by A. Metchenko, a senior contributor to *Kommunist,* in his book with the eloquent title *Krovnoye, Zavoyovannoye* [Bloodied and Victorious], 1971) is that in the early days of Soviet literature there was a linear development from critical realism (and the "progressive" strands in futurism and symbolism) toward socialist realism. According to this notion, through a process of struggle during which alien and hostile trends were eliminated—together with those representatives of them who failed to mend their ways in time—there was an inexorable movement from "lower" to "higher," until socialist realism became established as the *only* method. Since there were difficulties on the way, the career of individual writers could be like an obstacle race—some, like Leonov, came through to the state of grace; some like Olesha, Platonov, and Pasternak, remained in limbo; and other hapless wretches, like Pilnyak and Zamyatin, were cast into outer darkness.

Ovcharenko's view is a more subtle one which, insofar as it reflects actual practice (having to a considerable extent been dictated by it), amounts to proposing that the belated sanction of modified theory be applied to what for years now in the writing of Soviet literary scholars has been a pragmatic approach to the past. Instead of seeing the history of Soviet literature in terms of a simple convergence toward socialist realism, Ovcharenko maintains that both in the past and at present *different* trends have always coexisted—generally in a state of conflict with each other —and that not to recognize and take account of this plain fact is to adopt an "unhistorical" point of view, with disastrous methodological results. While socialist realism and its ultimate triumph is still the highest desideratum, the fact must be faced that, in the wicked state of the real world, what one finds at any given moment (including the present day in the Soviet Union) is not the imminent triumph or undivided reign of socialist realism, but a confused jumble of conflicting tendencies, which it is the prime task of literary scholarship and criticism to analyze in "concrete historical" terms.

In other words, socialist realism has to compete for attention in literary scholarship and fight it out in current literary practice with other approaches. Ovcharenko even implies that this is not a bad thing, inasmuch as socialist realism may be strengthened in the process of its struggle to establish itself as the only valid method. (If this particular argument in favor of pluralism were carried further, there is no knowing where it would end—as the conservatives are quick to point out.) The corollary is, of course, that socialist realism cannot logically be imposed by force. If it is to hold its own and eventually sweep the world, it must do so because of an intrinsic superiority, which cannot be imparted to it by administrative means (as Ovcharenko admits, its present difficulties are indeed largely caused by the "narrowly dogmatic" way in which it was applied in the past).

In the usual interpretation, socialist realism had supposedly arisen out of the actual practice of "progressive" writers, going back to Gorky's *The Mother,* and had merely been codified and given a name in the early 1930's. Its triumph had been formally signalized in 1934 by its adoption into the statutes of the Union of Writers as the "basic method" *(osnovnoi metod)* to be employed by Soviet writers. Thereafter, during a further period of *Gleichschaltung* in the 1940's and 1950's, it became virtually identical with the concept of "Soviet literature" as such.

Opposing this traditional Stalinist idea, Ovcharenko contends, interestingly, that the concept of socialist realism is both older and narrower than the concept of Soviet literature. It is older because its roots may go back a good deal further than Gorky (to the literature of the Paris Commune, for instance), but at the same time it is narrower because it does not, and never did, contain the *whole* of Soviet literature—being only, as it were, an optimum toward which all should strive, until in the distant communist future it comes to be the sole form of literature.

We need not concern ourselves with the logical problems raised by the universal triumph in literature of what is a moral rather than an aesthetic principle (it is, indeed, a vision worthy of one of Saltykov's insane *gradonachalniki*, or municipal bureaucrats), but Ovcharenko's remarks, as applied to the present, enable him, if not all of his colleagues, to get out of the theoretical impasse into which events since Stalin's death have gradually driven them. It is in effect a plea for the legitimization of what now actually happens in the practice of Soviet literary criticism —among other things, the discussion of early works of Soviet literature for what they were, rather than as examples of socialist realism *avant la lettre*. There is no need, in Ovcharenko's words, to "shamefacedly gloss over the fact that in the first years of the Soviet regime some writers made attempts, often unsuccessful, to express communist subject matter not only in realist or romantic forms. . . . For me," he continues, "Mayakovsky's *Mystery Bouffe* is an example of expressionism, and Bryusov's "Vesnyanka" and "Russia" of symbolism."[14]

By the same token, it should now be possible—as indeed it is —to talk about Akhmatova, Pasternak, Bulgakov, Tsvetayeva, Platonov, and others almost on their own terms, as part of Soviet literature, however alien or contradictory they may have been in

---

[14]These two atrocious poems are symbolist only in the crudest sense; the first (1918) compares the Revolution to the awakening of springtime.

terms of socialist realism (and, incidentally, however much some of them might have objected to being considered "Soviet" writers). There is also theoretical justification in Ovcharenko's *aggiornamento* for the treatment in "concrete historical" fashion of the creative careers of those writers—particularly old fellow travelers like Leonov and Fedin—whose works are still held up as models of socialist realism. This, he implies, is preferable to selecting and twisting the facts in such a way as to "prove" that these classics progressed in a more or less straight line to the high plateau of socialist realism, where they now reside in Olympian serenity. (This kind of approach still inhibits proper study of the early work of Leonov, Katayev, and Ehrenburg, and in particular of their post-Stalin writings. Such a study would no doubt show that only the work of their middle—that is, their worst—periods belongs, properly speaking, to socialist realism.)

The extent to which this *aggiornamento* only reflects the well-established practice of Soviet literary scholarship can be seen in the pages of *Voprosy Literatury* and *Novy Mir* (which occasionally deviate well to the left of it[15]); in the four-volume *History of Soviet Russian Literature,* put out by the Gorky Institute (1967–71); and especially in *The Concise Literary Encyclopedia* (Vols. 1–6, 1962–71). This last has established a remarkably high standard of objectivity and tries to avoid question-begging labels (one of its techniques is to report as a matter of fact that so-and-so has been attacked in the Soviet press for such-and-such errors or deviations, without itself expressing any editorial opinion). The encyclopedia has, of course, distinguished itself as a stronghold of liberalism in the sphere of literary scholarship, and has found itself fairly constantly under fire as a result (see, for example, the article by V. Ivanov, "The Methodological Zigzags of the Literary Ency-

---

[15]A remarkable example from *Novy Mir* (No. 9, 1969) is the article "The Future of Russian Literature," by the venerable historian of ancient Russian literature D. Likhachev, who, looking at things in the perspective of a thousand years, concludes that the only basic feature of the development of Russian literature is its search for ever greater freedom from formal constraints, despite occasional attempts to reverse the trend (for example, under Ivan the Terrible and Peter the Great).

clopedia," in *Kommunist*, No. 14, 1969). Nevertheless the recently published sixth volume shows every sign of maintaining the same high standard as the first five—if not throughout, then at least in part. In a sense this is possible because, ironically, the interests of the liberals and the interests of the influential middle-of-the-road theoreticians of socialist realism (such as Ovcharenko) happen at a certain practical level to coincide—or rather, they can be expressed in such a way as to appear the same at first sight. The point is that the liberals have long used the Aesopian device of mentioning in the same context writers who would formerly have been strictly separated, such as introducing the discussion of less "acceptable" writers within the discussion of "safe" ones: Tikhonov, Mayakovsky, and even Demyan Bedny can serve as an umbrella, as it were, for Pasternak, Akhmatova, or Mandelstam. This results in a tendency to blur distinctions and gloss over polarities in a manner that infuriates critics on the right (though it can work both ways: there are cases in which the names of orthodox writers are linked with those of their antipodes in an evident attempt to confer respectability by association).

Ovcharenko's motive for mentioning formerly incompatible names in the same breath is different: it is to escape the theoretical dilemmas of socialist realism by admitting the need for discussion of the conflicting phenomena that coexist within Soviet literature. But he insists on a rigorous analysis to differentiate them—something that is often lacking in the encyclopedia, as its critics point out. The blandness with which "incompatible" names are lumped together by the author of the article on Russian literature of the Soviet period in the sixth volume is well illustrated by the statement that during the Second World War "the old masters D. Bedny, Akhmatova, and Pasternak came out with patriotic calls for struggle and victory." The same lack of discrimination occurs in lists of writers and works that have been rehabilitated in recent years: "An active part is played [*sic!*] in contemporary literary life by works written many years ago but not republished for a long time. In the first instance there are the works of A. Vesely, I. Babel, P. Vasilyev, B. Kornilov, M. Koltsov, I. Katayev, V. Kirshon, and others. Together with them the reader has had restored to him [*chitatelyu vozvrashcheny*] the verse of Akhmatova, the works of Zoshchenko and Platonov, the prose of Bulgakov, including such important books written in the 1930's as his *Theatrical Novel* (published in 1965), and particularly the satirical-philosophical novel *The Master and Margarita* (published in 1966–67)." Koltsov and Kirshon, loyal supporters of the regime who perished through the vagaries of Stalin's terror, are odd company for Akhmatova and Bulgakov. But though the motives for admitting all and sundry to "Soviet literature" may not always be the purest, the practical result, insofar as it entails a tolerance unheard of by the standards of fifteen years ago, can only be welcomed.

The recent controversies about the meaning and scope of socialist realism have also revealed profound differences among the theorists about how to deal with current Soviet literature. Obviously the conservatives would like to exclude everything that is not socialist realist, but this would mean narrowing the definition of Soviet literature in a way that is simply no longer possible. The alternative, as for the past, is to admit the existence of different trends, but this leads to a recognition of the very awkward fact, condemned by some and condoned by others, that a good deal of the most significant work published in the Soviet Union in the years since Stalin's death has to be qualified as *critical* realism. As Ovcharenko tells us, this has been said of "individual works" by Solzhenitsyn, S. Zalygin, V. Bykov, V. Voinovich, and V. Semin. He does not commit himself to this view of them, saying only that it is a complicated problem which cannot be "waved away," and that the relationship of these writers to critical realism needs further study. But in another connection he says that the description of socialist realism in the statutes of the Union of Writers as the basic method must be taken literally to mean that there are *other* methods, even at the present day, which cannot be *simply dismissed*. In other words, there exist alternatives to socialist realism that form a *legitimate* part of contemporary Soviet literature.

As a recognition of fact, this represents the most far-reaching of Ovcharenko's concessions. Inasmuch as it reflects quasi-official thinking (as I believe it does), it provides doctrinal support for the flexible attitude which is in actual fact shown toward present-day Soviet writing, however much such flexibility may on occasion succumb to administrative pressures, censorship, and so on (but these too are variable nowadays). Once again it must be emphasized that these suggested adjustments to the theory spring less from a change of heart than from a sober recognition of the bitter truth that, in its classical form, the doctrine patently fails to account for the reality that everybody can see. This is the covering up of the emperor's nakedness as practiced by all keepers of a decaying ideology that is no longer properly enforced by a secular arm. The essence of this subterfuge—for such it is—consists in claiming that your doctrine has never been so rigid as its enemies make out, but that it is on the contrary a developing, living system, capable of adapting itself to the times. In the case of socialist realism this means, among other things, that having for decades abused and proscribed them and in some cases killed them in its name, you now "accept" Akhmatova, Babel, Platonov, Bulgakov, Pasternak, Mandelstam, Kafka, and so on.

Even a cursory inspection of the literature that in the last decade *has got into print* (that is, leaving aside *samizdat*, which is often only work rejected by the censorship) shows that Ovcharenko's solemn recognition of the coexistence in present-day Soviet literature of different trends is nothing but a *vérité de la Palisse*. Worse still, from the point of view even of modified literary theory, most, if not all, of contemporary writing of quality is a denial of socialist realism, since it fails to meet what we have seen to be the crucial ideological test of affirming belief in ultimate victory and giving readers positive examples of how people may and should consciously work to bring it about. On the contrary, the best of Soviet prose in the post-Stalin years has tended, using realism as the appropriate method, actually to undermine its readers' faith—if they had any—not only in future victory but also in the historical rightness of the chosen path. This is most manifestly so in the case of those writers mentioned by Ovcharenko, whom some Soviet critics regard as critical realists. Solzhenitsyn's *One Day in the Life of Ivan Denisovich* (1962) and

"Matryona's Home" (1963) describe a mournful reality stemming from a disastrous past—the building of socialism was expressly likened in the first to the setting up of a concentration camp—and promising no good in the future. The message of both is that the world lies in evil and, though it may be graced by righteous persons, it will not be redeemed by the purposeful movement of the masses in a direction foreordained by history.

Sergei Zalygin in *On the Irtysh* (*Novy Mir,* No. 2, 1964), shows collectivization to have been a national catastrophe, starkly symbolized at the end of his tale by a peasant house being pushed into the river in a senseless gesture of self-destruction. Vasili Bykov's novels on the war *The Dead Feel No Pain* (*Novy Mir,* No. 1, 1966) and *The Ordeal* (*Novy Mir,* No. 5, 1970) are far removed from the heroics of previous years, picturing the war for what it was as a tragedy beyond redemption in human accounting. After reading Bykov one is not inclined to feel that bestiality on such a scale can be made good by the achievement of a social purpose, however lofty. Most awkward of all, given the nature of the social purpose in question, are the studies of the Soviet working class by Vladimir Voinovich and Vitali Semin. Nothing more authentic on this theme has appeared in print. Voinovich, in such stories as "I'd Be Honest If They'd Let Me" and "Two Comrades" (*Novy Mir,* No. 2, 1963, and No. 1, 1967), and Semin in his novel *Seven in One House* (*Novy Mir,* No. 6, 1965) convey an impression of an alienated proletariat which contradicts the clichés of the standard Soviet "production" novel in unanswerable fashion.[16]

The drift toward a prose that ignores or flouts the central premise of socialist realism began, of course, in the 1950's with

---

[16]In "Two Comrades" Voinovich paints a picture of alienation, in the original Marxist sense, that it would be difficult to better as an extreme instance of the modern industrial worker's lack of personal involvement with the processes and product of his labor: the two young comrades of the story's title work in a factory that is so secret that nobody knows the purpose of the spare part they produce. When asked where they work, the youths reply, "*V yashchike*" (In the box)—because the factory has no address, only a post office box number.

Ehrenburg's *The Thaw* (1954), in which the eloquent contrast between the two artists Pukhov and Saburov was rightly seen by the critics as a challenge to the principle of *partiinost*, and continued with the crop of works in 1956—Vladimir Dudintsev's *Not By Bread Alone*, Alexander Yashin's "The Levers," and Daniil Granin's "A Personal Opinion"—all of which, after being much fought over, gradually became accepted as a legitimate part of Soviet literature, finding a more or less honored place in the encyclopedias and histories of literature. The early battles after Stalin's death prepared the way for the younger prose writers such as Vladimir Tendryakov, Yuri Nagibin, Yuri Kazakov, Vasili Aksyonov, and Alexander Gladilin, whose "neorealism" (or whatever one calls it) has dominated Soviet prose, such as it is, in the last decade and a half.

It is significant that these "new wave" writers have even abandoned the preferred genre of classical socialist realism—namely, the long novel—having found that the short story or novella (*povest*) exempts them from the need to supply a broad social setting for their characters. Within the restricted compass of the shorter form they are able to show people only in the context of personal or moral problems which could arise in *any* society (hence the accusation by hostile critics of "abstract humanism"). In this low-key fiction, Soviet society is generally taken for granted as the indifferent, even hostile, backdrop against which small private dramas are enacted. Since the younger prose writers have never known any other, it is hardly surprising that they accept Soviet institutions not as the manifestation of a higher order of things but only as the banal, sometimes even slightly comic, framework of daily life. In most cases their heroes (or antiheroes) are at odds with society, or have lost their place in it (e.g., Kazakov's "Silly-Billy" [*Trali-Vali*], 1961, and "Adam and Eve," 1962). They are never identified with its long-term aims, and its values are sometimes implicitly questioned—in Tendryakov's "The Trial" (1961), for instance, the *summum bonum* of industrial development is seen as a factor estranging man from his natural environment. The story was much attacked for this at the time of its appearance.

The only outstanding long novels written in the post-Stalin era, Pasternak's *Doctor Zhivago* (1958) and Solzhenitsyn's *The Cancer Ward* and *The First Circle* (both 1968), have exploited the scope of the genre to provide historical and social perspectives for purposes directly counter to those of socialist realism. These three novels in the grand tradition could not, therefore, be published in the Soviet Union, because their authors deliberately set out to show that the whole Soviet interlude was an aberration (indeed, in Pasternak's view, the result of a counterrevolution) whose cost in human sacrifice and moral degradation has already negated its aims.

A further blow to the doctrine of socialist realism has been the virtual defection of some of the old fellow travelers whose earlier work is still held up as a model: Ehrenburg, Katayev, and Leonov have written works (including short ones, of *povest* length!) in which they go back on the romantic illusions (to describe them charitably) which once earned them their place in the socialist realist canon.[17]

At the Fifth Congress of Soviet Writers, held in June 1971, there was ample recognition in several speeches that the essential demand of socialist realism had not been met in the practice of Soviet prose during the 1960's. Fedin's successor as first secretary of the Union, G. M. Markov, repeated the usual assurances that socialist realism is "our only artistic method" and that the distinctive feature of Soviet literature is its "unitary ideological and artistic sense of purpose *(ustremlennost).*" He also maintained, no doubt mainly for the benefit of Brezhnev and the other high party and government guests sitting behind him in the seats of honor, that "literature has become *even more* [author's emphasis] imbued with a sense of historical optimism and insight into the social prospects of mankind." But, in a manner typical of Soviet rhetoric, this assurance was belied in the later part of his report, when he came to a more concrete review of the present situation:

---

[17]I have discussed the works in question in my "Themes and Variations in Soviet Literature" [pp. 119–49].

"If we are to sum up all the various shades of dissatisfaction with the state of contemporary literature, then, in our view, they add up to the fact that Soviet man of the 1960's and beginning of the 1970's has not yet been depicted in all the fullness of his historical deeds and high purpose." In other words, as Markov implies in another passage of his speech, the purposeful sense of historical mission no longer finds embodiment in the sort of classical heroes who formerly provided such inspiration: Pavel Vlasov (in Gorky's *The Mother*); Chapayev (in Furmanov's novel of the same name); Chumalov (in Gladkov's *Cement*); Korchagin (in Ostrovsky's *How the Steel Was Tempered*); Davydov (in Sholokhov's *Virgin Soil Upturned)*; Meresyev (in Polevoy's *Story of a Real Man);* the young guard (in Fadeyev's *The Young Guard*); and the Zhurbin family (in Kochetov's novel of that name). The only hero of a post-Stalin Russian novel whom he finds worthy of inclusion in this roster is Baluyev, from the novel *Let's Get to Know Each Other, Baluyev* (1960), by Vadim Kozhevnikov, the editor of *Znamya*. As the Russian proverb says, "When there are no men, even Foma [a common peasant name] is a nobleman."

One of the conservative speakers at the Congress, Nikolai Gribachev—without breaking the evident unspoken agreement to avoid name-calling—was more explicit about the general sense of a loss of purpose in the prose of the last decade or so: "In the recent past our prose has been in a visibly precarious state. In the treatment of the war the main emphasis has been on human suffering, which has overshadowed [the theme of] principled re-sistance to fascism . . . in the treatment of the countryside there has also been constant emphasis—also in a 'suffering' vein—only on the difficulties and excesses of collectivization, in the artificial playing up of which you lose sight of the self-sacrificing deeds of communists, class-conscious peasants and workers, and even of the historical inevitability of collectivization itself." Having de-nounced such writing as the "bearing of historical false witness," Gribachev then noted signs for the better in recent works—most of them on the wartime theme, which lends itself most readily to the depiction of heroes—by Anatoli Ananyev, Yuri Bondarev, Alexander Chakovsky (editor of *Literaturnaya Gazeta*), Ivan Stad-

nyuk, and the Uzbek writer Askad Mukhtar.[18] Few of Gribachev's listeners can have found this evidence of the resurgence of
socialist realism very heartening. (It was left to the Kirghiz writer
Chingiz Aitmatov—one of the few Central Asian writers who
refuses to join the pathetic claque from which the Moscow conservatives expect moral support at literary gatherings—to defend
by name some of the leading representatives of the trend denounced by Gribachev. He said that Nagibin, Tendryakov, Kazakov, and Aksyonov had done "excellent work" in Soviet prose, and
that Vasili Bykov had been subjected to "one-sided criticism."
His criterion for excellence in prose is a touchingly simple one:
"I dream of seeing in the pages of our press a story after reading
which I cannot sleep at night. There were times when this happened fairly often . . . this was in the days of Gorky, Chekhov,
Bunin, and Kuprin." It is clear that Aitmatov is not robbed of
his sleep by the reading of Ananyev, Chakovsky, and the
others.)

On the evidence of the speeches representing various points of
view at the Writers' Congress, one might well conclude that
socialist realism in the traditional sense has now become a minority trend in such Soviet prose as merits the name of literature (this
is to stretch a point in favor of Chakovsky, Kozhevnikov, Mikhail
Alexeyev, Lipatov, and others on the conservatives' "approved
list").

A fascinating development in the last few years is that the prose
of some of the leading Stalinists, whose work can scarcely be
regarded as literature (and is not uninfluenced, incidentally, by
the Western trash they affect to abominate), also betrays a radical
departure from socialist realism. This is evident in Kochetov's
What Is It You Want? (*Oktyabr*, Nos. 9, 10, 11, 1969), Oles
Benyukh's priceless *Jaws of the Locust* (*Oktyabr*, No. 1, 1969),

---

[18]Yuri Bondarev is the author of an anti-Stalinist novel, *Silence* (*Novy Mir*, Nos. 3–5,
1962), but he has found favor with the conservatives for his later novels on the war, during
which he served as an artillery officer. Ivan Stadnyuk is the author of *People Are Not
Angels* (1962–65), a novel about collectivization which gives a horrifying picture of the
resulting famine. Nevertheless, he is careful to vindicate the policy as such.

and Ivan Shevtsov's *Love and Hate* (Voyenizdat, 1970—in 200,-000 copies!). The candid message of these masterpieces of *kitsch* is that, far from marching on to even greater heights, the country is going to the dogs and will continue to do so until the political leadership pulls itself together. These novels are in fact an expression of right-wing dissidence which reflects and plays on the nostalgia of countless *apparatchiki* for the good old days. There are indications that the party leadership (including Brezhnev himself) fears this Stalinist longing for a strong hand even more than it does opposition from the left, which is numerically weaker and hence much more vulnerable.

An important consequence of this growth of oppositionist Stalinism is that the party still clings to the "centrist" policy inherited from Khrushchev (but without his violent lurchings from one side to another). It is only thus that one can explain why the liberal view got some sort of hearing at the Writers' Congress (from Aitmatov, Yevtushenko, and Simonov), and why Voznesensky and Yevtushenko were elected to the new presidium (though both they and the extreme right, as represented by Kochetov, were excluded from the more powerful secretariat, whose "centrist" behavior is thus guaranteed). It is also the only way to explain the continuing balance between the literary journals which have come to be identified with the opposing factions— this despite the departure of Tvardovsky from *Novy Mir.*

The latest authoritative statement of a centrist policy came from Brezhnev himself at the Twenty-fourth Party Congress, and was quoted by Markov at the Writers' Congress and incorporated in the final resolution: "Some people have tried to reduce the manysidedness of contemporary Soviet reality to a few problems irrevocably consigned to the past by the party's work in overcoming the consequences of the cult of personality. The opposite extreme, current among certain other writers, is represented by attempts to whitewash phenomena of the past that have been subjected to decisive and principled party criticism, to preserve concepts and views which run counter to the new, creative [spirit] introduced by the party into its practical and theoretical activities in the last few years." Translated into plainer language, this means that the condemnation of Stalin at the Twentieth Congress is still endorsed by the party leadership, but that his legacy must neither be harped on by the diehards nor represented in too favorable a light by the liberals. In other words, extremes must be avoided.[19]

When it comes to poetry, the declining relevance of socialist realist theory to what is actually published in the Soviet Union appears even more striking. As suggested earlier, socialist realism is by its very nature inhospitable to lyric poetry, and the extraordinary explosion of verse after Stalin's death can be seen in retrospect as a spontaneous reaction against it and all it stood for. Nadezhda Mandelstam has spoken in *Hope against Hope* about the revival of poetry as the outward sign of a certain spiritual emancipation among the young. Voznesensky made the same point in his long poem "Oza" (*Molodaya Gvardiya*, No. 10, 1964): "Why, when we pack the Luzhniki, / Do we crave verse like a cure for scurvy, / Our souls bursting shyly forth like buds?" There is little in the poetry of Bella Akhmadulina, Viktor Sosnora, Yunna Morits, Novella Matveyeva, Alexander Kushner, Gleb Gorbovsky, Vladimir Soloukhin, Yevgeni Vinokurov, or David Samoilov, let alone in the unpublished Joseph Brodsky, that can give any comfort to the custodians of socialist realism. The only exception among the younger poets is perhaps Robert Rozhdestvensky—it is difficult to think of anyone else who combines

---

[19]The message has since been hammered home in more specific terms. N. Yevchuk, in his article "Contemporary Problems of the Ideological Struggle" (*Kommunist*, October 1971), writes: "The party press and literary public opinion have condemned the one-sided and erroneous approach to previous periods of history—for example, the mistakes permitted at one time in the journal *Novy Mir*, where too much emphasis was put on the so-called camp theme, attempts were made under the flag of deheroicization to denigrate the heroism of Soviet soldiers, and in certain works such as [Solzhenitsyn's] "Matryona's Home" and [Boris Mozhayev's] "From the Life of Fedor Kuzkin," the kolkhoz village was painted in dark and unrelievedly gloomy colors. . . . At the Twenty-fourth Party Congress it was also noted that . . . there have been attempts to whitewash the phenomena of the past. . . . Certain works (such as, for example, the not unknown compositions of I. Shevtsov . . . and a few others) display lack of faith in the Soviet intelligentsia and youth, and a peculiar nostalgia for those phenomena of the past connected with arbitrary rule."

such formal skill with almost uniformly "correct" sentiments.[20]

The long epic poem, which formerly sometimes met the aims of socialist realism in verse, has now become the almost exclusive preserve of the kitschmongers, who use it in the same spirit and for the same purposes as Kochetov and Shevtsov do the novel; an example is S. V. Smirnov's *I Myself Stand Witness* (*Moskva*, No. 10, 1967).[21] On the other hand, a genuine epic poet like Tvardovsky, who once made important contributions to the sparse canon of socialist realist verse—*The Land of Muravia*, 1936; *Vasili Terkin*, 1941–45; *The House by the Road*, 1946—has turned to lyric poetry, as witness *Lyric Poems of Recent Years*, 1967,[22] and particularly the moving cycle of poems in *Novy Mir*, No. 1, 1969, which conveys a poignant sense of disillusionment in a man of outstanding courage and sensitivity. (They also contain an oblique expression of sorrow—probably the only one to appear in print in the Soviet Union—at the invasion of Czechoslovakia.) Tvardovsky's sequel to his wartime epic on Vasili Terkin —*Vasili Terkin in the Other World*—circulated in manuscript for several years before being allowed to appear in print by an impulsive gesture on the part of Khrushchev[23]; it cannot be said

---

[20]Rozhdestvensky also occasionally writes propaganda pieces, which sound odd coming from a poet of his generation. See, for example, his note on Brezhnev's visit to France: "In the Name of the Future" (*Literaturnaya Gazeta*, November 3, 1971).

[21]This contains the following extraordinary comment on the trial of Sinyavsky and Daniel:

> I can positively say
> —It's plain as plain could be—
> That the notion of "Fifth Column"
> Is still topical today,
> And while such creatures stink,
> Appealing to the country's foes,
> Weaken not nor wither,
> Dear dictatorship of ours!

[22]*Lyric Poems of Recent Years* was awarded the State Prize in literature in 1971 (*Literaturnaya Gazeta*, November 10). This, considering Tvardovsky's sponsorship of one of the extremes denounced at the Twenty-fourth Party Congress, must be seen as a sop to the liberals.

[23]In *Izvestiya*, August 18, 1965. It appeared anonymously a little earlier in the émigré journal *Mosty*, August 10, 1963.

that it fulfills the first condition of a socialist realist work, an affirmative attitude to the future prospects of mankind under socialism.

The same is true of the occasional long poems written by lyric poets. Voznesensky's "Oza" is a lament about our destiny under the heel of modern technology (whether communist or capitalist makes little difference), and Yevtushenko's two epics, "Bratsk Station" (begun in 1964) and "The University of Kazan," his offering on the hundredth anniversary of Lenin's birth (*Novy Mir*, No. 4, 1970), were denounced by his critics as ideologically ambiguous. Thus, if genuine lyric poetry is now (as it always has been) beyond the ken of socialist realism, narrative poetry, once its special province, is also slipping outside its terms of reference.

In conclusion, then, it is evident that the development of Soviet literature during the past eighteen years has led to the slow dissolution of Soviet literary theory. The main reason, apart from the erosion of administrative control over literary practice, has been the inner weakness of basing literary theory not on an aesthetic principle but on an ideological one subject to changing political requirements. The canon used to substantiate the theory was held together only by this principle, not by any literary method or quality shared by the writers in question. The basic weakness of socialist realism was further underlined by its inability to accommodate poetry (this has proved particularly damaging in view of the eclipse of prose—Solzhenitsyn apart—by poetry in the post-Stalin years), and by the fact that the best work included in the canon antedated the birth of the doctrine. Much of this work (the early novels of Leonov, the first two books of Sholokhov's *Quiet Don*, etc.) begins to look more as though it belongs in the company of some of the gray zone and even "hostile" writing, a good deal of which has been republished in the past decade, since the rehabilitation of its authors. Ovcharenko's proposed modifications to the theory even allow for the possibility of detaching the early novels of some of the fellow travelers from the old canon. This would leave socialist realism only with those works it can legitimately lay claim to: *How the Steel Was Tempered, The Zhurbin Family,* and all that vast corpus of later Stalinist writing whose function, as Vera Dunham has shown in her fascinating study of it, was to propagate a system of values for the class that Stalin knew he had to create in order to perpetuate his rule. This class still exists, and its tastes are extensively catered to by a redoubtable army of graphomanes who produce the requisite paraliterature for popular consumption, and who received their marching orders at the Fifth Writers' Congress from G. N. Markov:

> There is no doubt that the writers will deepen their interest in the activity of the production collectives, the life of workers in factories, construction sites, and electric stations. They will closely study the transformation of agricultural activity, the formation of new features in the village toiler, the historical process of rapprochement between town and country, the conversion of the peasant's toil into a form of industrial work. . . . Our literature has particular obligations toward the men of the Soviet Army and Navy. . . . Writers have created many vivid works about the heroic past of the Komsomol, but the feats of the present-day Komsomol still await their proper depiction in literature.

And so on.

This may be socialist realism, but is it literature?[24]

---

[24]Since this paper was written there have been signs of an attempt to "restore discipline" on the ideological front. Recent pressure on *samizdat* and the arrest of Bukovsky are reportedly part of a concerted drive launched in accordance with a Central Committee resolution at the end of 1971. A plenum of the Union of Writers in February 1972 discussed the need to strengthen *partiinost* and develop the "fruitful traditions of socialist realism." It will require more than this kind of pressure to halt the decline of socialist realism described above (indeed, it can only accelerate it), but it is probable that there will be increased administrative and censorship restrictions on the writers for a time.

PART 2

5

Max Hayward frequently wrote about Boris Pasternak and even more frequently referred to him. From the time of Hayward's immersion in Doctor Zhivago, which he translated with Manya Harari in 1957, Pasternak was the touchstone by which Hayward assessed the quality and determined the historical weight, as it were, of a work of Russian literature. His most brilliant essay on Pasternak was written as the introduction to Alexander Gladkov's Meetings with Pasternak (London: Collins and Harvill Press; New York: Harcourt Brace Jovanovich, 1977). In Hayward's remark about what Pasternak meant "for Russia, as a whole" may be discerned what the poet meant to his most devoted interpreter in the West: "A man who seemed childishly innocent and ineffectual in his practical dealings not only withstood, almost alone, the intolerable pressures of the times, but also came to be seen by many as a last surviving focus of moral resistance to the infinitely cruel and merciless master of the country's destiny."

Hayward's devotion to Pasternak extended to the poet's beloved friend Olga Ivinskaya, for whose release Hayward labored so wholeheartedly after she was arrested in 1960. "An attack on her is in fact a blow at me," Pasternak had written in a letter shortly before his death. As Hayward says, Olga Ivinskaya, like Lara in Doctor Zhivago, "personifies the whole country's betrayal, captivity, and defenselessness." He translated her memoir, A Captive of Time (London: Collins and Harvill Press; New York: Doubleday, 1978) and provided the introduction which is reproduced in this volume under the title "Life into Art: Pasternak and Ivinskaya." It is essentially an elaboration of his earlier essay on Pasternak. The fact that Hayward scarcely mentions Ivinskaya is suggestive: he had *mixed feelings about some of the more intimate aspects of her memoirs.*

Hayward's early love of Pasternak awakened his interest in Anna Akhmatova, Marina Tsvetayeva, and Osip Mandelstam. His short essay on Akhmatova is characteristically less concerned with analyzing her poetry than with reflecting on her life—her martyr-dom, "her courage and steadfastness," and her sovereign intelligence. His essay serves as an introduction to Poems of Akhmatova *(London: Collins and Harvill Press, 1974; Boston: Little, Brown, 1973). Hayward also acted as the linguistic interpreter for the American poet, Stanley Kunitz, who translated the verse in that volume.*—ED.

Meetings with Pasternak

Like rafts down a river, like a convoy of barges,
The centuries will float to me out of the darkness.
And I shall judge them.

Meetings with Pasternak is the first important memoir of the poet to have emerged so far from the Soviet Union, where it has been in limited circulation as a *samizdat* manuscript for several years.[1] It was published in Russian in Paris in 1973. The author,

---

[1]It is referred to in Nadezhda Mandelstam's *Hope Abandoned,* and there is even a brief quotation from it in the discussion of Pasternak in the *History of Soviet Russian Literature* published by the Academy of Sciences of the U.S.S.R. (Vol. 3, 1969).

Alexander Gladkov, who died in Moscow in 1976, was a play-wright at one time associated with Meyerhold's theater. He is best known for a play in verse, *Long, Long Ago*, about Napoleon's invasion of Russia, which had its premiere in Leningrad in 1941.

Gladkov first met Pasternak in Meyerhold's apartment in 1936. After this they saw each other only fleetingly until the war years, when they both lived for several months in the small town of Chistopol on the river Kama (November 1941–March 1942). Pasternak, together with many leading Soviet writers, was evacuated here during the German threat to Moscow in the autumn of 1941, and in this comparatively relaxed provincial environment he often talked to Gladkov at length, sharing his inner reflections with him in a way which, even for someone so unusually trusting and spontaneous, would have seemed unthinkable in the capital city.

Gladkov recorded their conversations in a diary he kept at the time. Their contact continued, more intermittently, during the remaining years of the war, after both returned to Moscow in 1942. In several meetings after the war, Pasternak again showed a remarkable degree of confidence in Gladkov, speaking his mind about the state of affairs in the country with astonishing frankness. Gladkov provides the first direct testimony that *Doctor Zhivago*, which Pasternak began writing in 1946, was deliberately conceived as a challenge to everything Stalin and his regime stood for.

In 1948 Gladkov, like countless other Soviet intellectuals in those years, was arrested and sent to a forced labor camp, from which he was released only after Stalin's death. He now again met Pasternak on a number of occasions, and gives a vivid idea of his mood during the campaign of persecution launched against him after *Doctor Zhivago* had been published abroad in 1957. The memoir ends with an account of Pasternak's funeral in June 1960 when in death, as he had sometimes done in life, he brought together a large number of his fellow countrymen for whom he represented a unique "repository of other values"—to quote the words of one of the poets of the younger generation influenced by him.

One of the most important aspects of Gladkov's memoir is that, through his account of the part played by Pasternak in his own intellectual and spiritual development, he conveys a sense of what the poet meant for Russia as a whole, of the way in which a man who seemed childishly innocent and ineffectual in his practical dealings not only withstood, almost alone, the intolerable pressures of the times, but also came to be seen by many as a last surviving focus of moral resistance to the infinitely cruel and merciless master of the country's destiny. It is still not easy to explain why Stalin should have spared Pasternak when so many others were done to death, imprisoned, or reduced to abject silence for much less. There was a conscious, if for the most part unspoken, confrontation between the two. As we see from some passages in Gladkov's book, Pasternak was much preoccupied with his own attitude to Stalin—and Stalin clearly had the supreme tyrant's fascination for those very few poets and writers (Mandelstam, Pasternak, Bulgakov, Akhmatova) who could be destroyed but never completely bent to his will, whose genius, in his brutish way, he perceived and recognized.

Pasternak had always been thought of as an ivory-tower figure remote from the immediate concerns of his age. The volumes of lyric poetry that first established his reputation, sometimes even by their titles—*Above the Barriers, My Sister Life*—marked him off as the antipode of a contemporary such as Mayakovsky with his active involvement in the Revolution. Pasternak's principal themes—love, nature, life at its most everyday and ordinary— seemed to suggest that he was quite aloof from the great events taking place in the world. In the very early days of the Revolution he pictured himself in a poem shouting through the window of his study to the children in the street: "What millennium is it out there?"—a line which has often been quoted as proof of his detachment from the history which was then in the making.

His early verse (which in later life, somewhat unjustly, he tended to dismiss because of what he regarded as its abstruseness and lack of deeper content) is notable for its sheer exultation in the words themselves. With an unusually plastic language such as Russian it is easy enough for a poet of Pasternak's temperament to be carried away by the positively sensuous joy that comes from handling his material. He reminds one of a happy child marveling at the world and his discovery of it, conveying his delight in a language which is as tangible a part of it as the sky, the trees, the snow, and all the familiar objects of domestic life. For Pasternak nothing is so extraordinary as the ordinary, and he constantly tries to make us see it through his eyes by an exuberant use of metaphors of the kind quoted by Gladkov—raindrops are as weighty as cufflinks, and a branch of wet lilac blossom looks like a sparrow caught in a rainstorm. Many people, including Gladkov, have noted Pasternak's "self-centeredness" and it was true in a literal sense: he stood at the center of a perpetually astonishing universe, and his poetry is the tale of how, in all its diversity, it related to himself, the only fixed and immutable point. It was this "self-centeredness," as much as his natural integrity, which made him impervious—though not indifferent—to the terrors and temptations of the age. From his unassailable vantage point he looked out at what was going on in the new millennium and found that most of it could not be assimilated to his poet's vision.

Like Osip Mandelstam, he was dominated by an inborn sense of rightness; the world could only be as he saw it, not as others might have wanted him to see it. Under a "normal" tyranny it would probably not have been difficult for Pasternak to have lived his life without much concern for the "history" he originally thought outside his province, but, like all his compatriots, he was confronted by a reality which forced itself on the attention with insistent, baleful malignance, demanding total subservience to itself, and never to be propitiated by mere acquiescence or tokens of compliance. The final human embodiment of this reality was, of course, Stalin. Since Pasternak could not accept it, he was driven into a conflict which did violence to his nature by compelling him to take issue with a conception of the world so warped and narrow that, in the ordinary way of things, it would have lain completely outside his field of vision.

Whether he liked it or not, he eventually felt bound to respond to this aggressive "deutero-reality" which had intruded itself through the sheer force of its hostility, by putting it in the perspective of his own world, thereby showing what an alien and transient thing it was. To do this he had to depart from his habitual lyrical mode and adopt a form which came far less naturally to him, that of an extensive prose narrative. (I shall return later to the problem of defining it.) *Doctor Zhivago* was the result of Pasternak's determination to meet, in the only way he thought appropriate, a challenge which had to be answered as a matter of overriding duty, even though it conflicted, to some extent, with his beliefs about the nature of poetry and his own place in it. Already at the time of his first important conversations with Gladkov in the first few months of the war, Pasternak had resolved to speak out if Stalin—as he evidently foresaw would be the case—began to rule even more harshly after the victory over the Germans.

But in the earliest days of the Revolution Pasternak had been by no means totally unsympathetic toward it. He could not but be impressed by the grandiose sweep of events. His feelings at the time are reflected in a passage in *Doctor Zhivago* where his hero, Yuri, speaks of the atmosphere in the country, after the fall of the monarchy, in images which suggest that Pasternak saw no inevitable dichotomy between revolution and the eternal real world of nature and art he knew as a poet:

> Last night I was watching a meeting in the square. . . . Mother Russia is on the move . . . she's talking and she can't stop. And it isn't as if only people were talking. Stars and trees meet and converse, flowers talk philosophy at night, stone houses hold meetings. It's like something out of the Gospels. . . . The revolution broke out . . . like a breath that's been held too long. Everybody was revived, reborn, changed, transformed. You might say that everyone has been through two revolutions— his own personal revolution as well as the general one. It seems to me that socialism is the sea, and all these separate streams, these private individual revolutions are flowing into it—the sea of life, of life in its own right. I said life, but I mean life as you see it in a work of art, transformed by genius, creatively enriched.

Even Lenin's usurpation of the Revolution had its momentary appeal for Yuri Zhivago—and hence, we may infer, for Pasternak: "Such a huge event cannot be asked for its credentials, it has no need to give dramatic proof of its existence, we'll take it on trust. It would be mean and petty to try to dig for the causes of titanic happenings." In 1921 Pasternak saw Lenin in the flesh as he spoke at the Ninth Congress of Soviets in the Bolshoi Theater, and evidently recognized him as a genius who was indeed capable of transforming life, but when he described the occasion in a poem written toward the end of the 1920's (not long before Stalin finally established himself in supreme power), it was in full and prophetic consciousness of the tragic fate of all revolutionary beginnings: "A genius comes as a harbinger of betterment, and his going is avenged with tyranny."

It is apparent from this, and from much else he wrote during the first decade and a half after the Revolution, that Pasternak's reputation as an ivory-tower poet was in fact quite undeserved, and that his professed ignorance of what millennium he was living in could only be understood in an ironical sense. Although nature is the dominating theme of his lyric poetry, he frequently shows his acute awareness of history as the other dimension of human existence. As Andrei Sinyavsky has pointed out,[2] already well before the Revolution Pasternak had arrived at a precise, almost schematic notion of the relationship between nature and history which remained with him, in one form or another, to the end of life, and was at the center of his understanding of his own position as a poet. In *The Black Goblet,* an essay published in 1916, Pasternak distinguished between eternity and time as separate spheres of being. Our lives run their course in time, which we experience as history—the arena of heroes or men of action. Transcending and enfolding it, as a not directly knowable category, eternity is the concern of the lyric poet, who enables us to

---

[2]In his introductory article—a miracle of suggestiveness, considering the circumstances in which it was written—to Pasternak's *Poems* (Moscow, 1965). See also Olga R. Hughes, *The Poetic World of Boris Pasternak* (Princeton, 1974).

glimpse it fleetingly in nature and art. The poet, as the temporal representative of eternity, is thus always the antithesis of those who "make history." In Russia, ever since the days of Pushkin and Nicholas I, the opposition of poet and czar has seemed particularly stark and tragic, a drama always awaiting reenactment, and forty years after writing *The Black Goblet* Pasternak had more than theoretical reasons to revert to the same language in defining his role as a poet:

> Poet, keep watch, keep watch,
> You must not fall asleep—
> You are eternity's hostage
> A captive of time.

Through history absolute rulers have sometimes felt a certain awe before poets and philosophers—the hostages of eternity defenseless in the face of their temporal might. In the case of Stalin, the word awe would be misplaced, but he undoubtedly had a kind of superstitious appreciation of the supreme worth of those very few who in every generation stand outside and above their age. It is significant that, with the exception of Osip Mandelstam, none of the indisputably great writers who had been recognized as such before Stalin's assumption of supreme power were killed or even imprisoned by him—although he knew very well how inimical they were to him by their very nature. Hosts of lesser writers—including some distinguished by little else but their expressions of doglike devotion to the new order—were swept away in successive waves of terror, quite indiscriminately, with casual contempt.

The case of Mandelstam was anomalous. The miracle is that he was not summarily executed in 1934 for the poem in which, in words shorn of any allegorical circumlocution, he described Stalin as a murderer surrounded by braying and whinnying "half-men." In an unprecedented and never subsequently repeated act of clemency, after Bukharin, Akhmatova, and Pasternak had pleaded for his life, Stalin contented himself with having Mandelstam exiled to a provincial town. In the circumstances it was a fate not much worse than what had befallen Ovid or Pushkin. When

Mandelstam returned to Moscow in 1937, it was at the height of the Great Terror, and it is scarcely to be wondered at that someone who had committed such blatant *lèse-majesté* only three years previously should now have been rearrested—to die, this time, on the way to a concentration camp.

It may be that Mandelstam's second arrest was the result of direct orders from Stalin, but it could equally well have been owing to a zealous initiative at a lower level—such initiatives were not lacking in those days, when Stalin could hardly have concerned himself with one individual among the vast numbers being rounded up. But on the other hand, when the death of Mandelstam came to his attention, it could possibly have occasioned a slight displeasure: this much we may judge from the rumors, reported by Nadezhda Mandelstam in her memoirs, that the end of Mandelstam was quoted in high official circles in 1939 as an example of the "excesses" committed by Yezhov. It is not inconceivable that Pasternak's survival during the postwar years, when —as Gladkov and others clearly show—he made no secret of his intention to speak his mind, was due to Stalin's unwillingness to see the case of Mandelstam repeated. If this is so, then it may not be fanciful to believe that Pasternak's dossier bore some specific indication that he was not to be touched without permission from Stalin himself.

Although they were physically spared, neither Pasternak nor Akhmatova went unmolested in the years after the war. In both cases (apart from odious campaigns of abuse in the press), attempts were made to break them by the persecution of people dear to them. With Akhmatova a partial success was achieved: her son, Lev Gumilev, was arrested (not for the first time) in 1949 and sent to a camp, and a year later—obviously in the hope of obtaining clemency for him—she published several poems in praise of Stalin. But when applied to Pasternak, this same tactic failed. In 1946, as Gladkov reports, "a great new love entered his life." This was Olga Vsevolodovna Ivinskaya, a literary editor and translator then in her mid-thirties, who became Pasternak's companion and was with him till the end of his life. She managed his practical affairs, collaborated on translations with him, and provided the inspiration for Lara, the heroine of *Doctor Zhivago*. In 1949 she was arrested, held in the Lubyanka, and sentenced to five years in a forced labor camp—from which she was released after Stalin's death. As one can judge from several of the poems (such as "Parting") in the *Zhivago* cycle devoted to her, Pasternak was infinitely distressed by this cruel blow. But it did not have the desired result. He made no concessions and went on writing the book in which, as no one had ever done before, he was to settle accounts with the epoch through which he had lived.

It could be that Stalin spared Pasternak himself for no other reason than that he hoped eventually to exact a poetic tribute from him as well. This would obviously have been of triple advantage, as he no doubt calculated in his cynical fashion: he would be "immortalized" by a real genius, the rebel poet would be punished far more excruciatingly than by death or imprisonment, and the many Russian intellectuals who, cowed and demoralized as they were, still looked to Pasternak with secret hope ("Everything changes under our zodiac, only Pasternak remains Pasternak," as the saying then went) would finally despair and inwardly submit if this last bastion fell.

Perhaps, however, it was not quite as simple as this. There is some slight evidence of a special element of some kind in the relationship between Stalin and Pasternak. Nothing else can explain the extraordinary immunity enjoyed by Pasternak between 1946 and 1953, when on various occasions he read chapters of *Doctor Zhivago* to small private gatherings, and even lent parts of the manuscript to a number of people. In 1948, as Gladkov tells us, he read the opening poem of the *Zhivago* cycle, "Hamlet," with its clear declaration of his intention to speak out, to a group of actors at one of the Moscow theaters. All this, needless to say, provided a rich harvest for the secret police. It is known that the then head of the Ministry of State Security, Abakumov, took a personal interest in Pasternak, and that a case was ready on the basis of which he could at any moment have been arrested and charged as a British agent (it was, of course, enough that his two sisters lived in Oxford). There can be little doubt, therefore, that he can only have survived in those years (not to mention his equally miraculous survival in 1937) because he was under Stalin's personal protection.

It might be thought that, in general terms, Pasternak enjoyed a peculiar kind of "fool's license." His extreme spontaneity, the almost childlike directness and lack of guile so vividly described by Gladkov, could possibly have impressed the morbidly suspicious Stalin more than all the protestations of loyalty he was so used to hearing—and of which, like any despot, he knew the true worth. But this can scarcely be the whole explanation. The most plausible single reason was suggested some years ago in a remarkable article published in a Russian-language journal in New York by an émigré writer and ex-Red Army officer, Mikhail Koryakov.[3] Koryakov draws attention to a highly unusual circumstance connected with the death of Stalin's second wife, Nadezhda Alliluyeva, in November 1932. There were many rumors about this at the time—according to some, Stalin had murdered her. The truth appears to be that she shot herself, probably in a fit of depression over the terrible consequences of collectivization, or as a protest against it. The official version was that she had died of peritonitis. If Stalin ever showed himself capable of normal human feelings, it was probably only in his relations with Alliluyeva. There is at any rate a good deal of evidence (in his daughter's memoirs, for instance) that he was shattered and grief-stricken by her death.

It also seems certain that the pathological side of Stalin's nature was accentuated by this tragedy in his personal life. The frenzied paranoia that overwhelmed him in 1937, and then again in the postwar years—culminating in the violent anti-Semitic paroxysm of the Doctors' Plot—may easily have had its roots here. The cult of his personality was already then well under way, and the announcement of Alliluyeva's death was naturally followed by fulsome and stereotyped expressions of condolence from leading representatives of various professional and other bodies. A letter to Stalin from the Union of Writers was published in *Literatur-*

---

[3]*Novy Zhurnal*, New York, 1958.

naya Gazeta of November 19, 1932. It was signed by thirty-three people (of whom six were liquidated a few years later), and was as trite in style as it was manifestly insincere in sentiment: "Accept our grief at the death of N. S. Alliluyeva, who devoted all her strength to the cause of the liberation of the millions of oppressed humanity, the cause which is headed by you, and for which we are ready to sacrifice our lives in confirmation of its unbreakable, life-giving force."

Pasternak evidently refused to sign this letter, since it is followed by a brief separate message from him which is astonishing both for its laconic, almost casual manner, and for what it says: "I share the feelings of the comrades. The day before [the announcement of Alliluyeva's death] I thought deeply and intensively about Stalin; as a poet—for the first time. Next morning I read the news. I was shaken, as though I had been there, living by his side, and had seen it. Boris Pasternak." It is impossible to convey the quality of the original in translation. There is an absolute minimum of words—pronouns and auxiliary parts of speech are left out, as in a telegram. Yet—perhaps because of this, and the total lack of sycophancy—it creates an impression of genuine compassion.

To anyone familiar with the stylized manner of such pronouncements in the Soviet press, even in those early days of the cult of personality, it will seem well nigh incredible that something as eccentric as Pasternak's message could have appeared in print. Quite apart from the pointed gesture of dissociation from the other comrades, there is an almost sacrilegious note in the phrase about having thought of Stalin "for the first time." And why "as a poet"? Most extraordinary of all is the suggestion that Pasternak had a premonition of Alliluyeva's death—a hint of "mysticism" surely unparalleled in a context of such a kind. Koryakov believes that it was this which must somehow have awakened in Stalin a superstitious feeling that Pasternak, as a poet, was gifted with second sight. It is hard to say whether this was literally so, but one may readily agree with Koryakov's claim to have found here an important clue to the mystery of Pasternak's survival in later years. Such an oddly phrased message from

Pasternak must have caught Stalin's eye at this critical moment in his personal life, marking him off from other men in a way that, for whatever unfathomable motives, prompted Stalin to grant him the kind of protection enjoyed by almost no one else.

This strange incident was the beginning of an obscure and distant, but nonetheless definable, relationship between the two, the main stages of which may be clearly traced, at least on Pasternak's side. Almost two years later, in July 1934, it was followed by the famous telephone call from Stalin to Pasternak which has been described by Akhmatova and Nadezhda Mandelstam.[4] Stalin's purpose was to let it be known that he had heeded Pasternak's and Akhmatova's pleas on behalf of Mandelstam, which had been conveyed to him by Bukharin, then editor of *Izvestiya*. (Bukharin still retained a vestige of influence with Stalin, or at least had access to him, after his political defeat a few years earlier.) After an exchange about Mandelstam, Pasternak said he would like to meet Stalin and talk with him. "About what?" Stalin asked. "About life and death," Pasternak replied. At this point Stalin hung up. Pasternak's desperate and rather comic attempt to get back to Stalin via the Kremlin switchboard was fruitless, and for a long time afterward he was deeply upset at what he regarded as his failure to make proper use of this unique opportunity of a personal contact with Stalin. It is clear that in his ingenuous and trusting way he felt he might somehow have been able to influence Stalin, to open his eyes to what was going on in the country.

At that time, in the breathing space between collectivization and the horrors of 1937, Stalin seemed in some ways to be pursuing a more moderate policy, curbing the excesses of Marxist militancy in cultural and other spheres; the aggressive proletarian writers' organization had been disbanded, and a more conventional approach to the teaching of Russian history had been introduced on Stalin's personal initiative. Most significant of all, no doubt, in Pasternak's eyes was that Stalin had listened to the

---

[4]See *Hope against Hope*, Chapter 32.

voices of two poets and shown mercy to a third who had mortally insulted him.

It is with this in mind that one must read an even more astounding message from Pasternak to Stalin which appeared on New Year's Day, 1936, in *Izvestiya*—this time in verse, under the title "Two Poems." The last part of the second poem is clearly addressed to Stalin, though he is not actually mentioned by name. Superficially, it reads like a tribute to the Great Leader who lives behind the ancient Kremlin Wall—not so much a man as the personification of "action on the whole globe's scale"—who has been appointed by fate to do what others before him had dreamed of, but had never dared put into effect. To some extent the poem is an expression of the hope, widespread among the intelligentsia in the mid-1930's, that Stalin might lead Russia back from revolutionary insanity into more traditional paths: one line notes pointedly that, while carrying out his "fabulous deeds," Stalin had kept the "old ways" intact, and "the centuries have grown as used to him" as they are to the chimes of the Kremlin's bells.

This is a clear allusion to Stalin's seeming wish at that time to restore at least some of the outer forms of Russia's past, if not its substance. A whole stanza is devoted to emphasizing that, despite the vastness of what he was doing, this "genius of action" remained a human being. The image chosen to convey this is a very odd one and, indeed, implicitly casts doubt on it. In what is perhaps a remarkable example of poetic intuition, if not of studied ambiguity, Pasternak tells us that when Stalin goes out hunting a hare, his gun echoes round the woods "just like that of any man." This detail betrays an actual knowledge of Stalin's tastes: he was indeed fond of shooting. It is curious, however, that the blood-lust of the hunter—and in pursuit of such a frightened and defenseless quarry as a hare—should be alluded to as an illustration of Stalin's common humanity. It is hard not to see here a premonition of what was to happen only a little over a year after the poem was published. Even so, it was evidently written not without optimism and with some faith in the possibility of a kind of partnership ("a fugue for two voices") between the "extreme polarities" represented by the poet and the man of action. Pasternak was thus harking back in these lines to his old idea about the lyric poet and the hero belonging to utterly different spheres. Throughout the poem there is an implication that the poet, though "infinitely small," can absorb the "genius of action" as he absorbs so many other things "like a sponge"—rather, perhaps, as eternity absorbs or swallows up time. In the last line the poet proclaims his belief in the knowledge these two "extreme polarities" may have of each other, implying that if the genius of action heeds the voice of eternity (as Stalin had done, apparently, in pardoning Mandelstam), then all could be well even on the temporal plane.

It was a vain hope, soon to be rudely disappointed. Only Pasternak was capable of speaking to Stalin in this spirit. One wonders what Stalin made of the poem. Perhaps he was pleased to see himself described as a "genius of action." Bukharin would hardly have printed it in *Izvestiya* if he had not been certain that it would be well received. He may have thought that Stalin would simply see in it an oblique expression of gratitude for the sparing of Mandelstam, but as an admirer of Pasternak's work he would also not have failed to appreciate the underlying meaning, which doubtless accorded well with his own pious hopes in those days.

The next few years showed the utter futility of imagining that Stalin could be "humanized." The great manhunt of 1937–38—one of the cruelest and most senseless of all times—resulted in the death or disappearance of many people close to Pasternak. He was terribly affected by the fate of the two Georgian poets Paolo Yashvili and Titian Tabidze, whom he had come to know during his first visit to Georgia in 1931, and he felt an almost personal responsibility for the hounding to death of Mandelstam in 1938, and the suicide of Marina Tsvetayeva in 1940—this, in particular, preyed on his mind till the end of his life. Long after Stalin's death he expressed his feelings in a poem (one of the many still not published in the Soviet Union), of which Gladkov quotes the first lines:

> My soul, you are in mourning
> For all those close to me,

Turned into a burial vault
For all my martyred friends . . .

In the increasingly nightmarish atmosphere of the second half of the 1930's Pasternak, like many others, found it harder and harder to write work of his own. His last volume of poetry *(Second Birth)* had been completed in 1931, and although he wrote a few poems in the mid-1930's, none—except the ones published in *Izvestiya*—appeared in print until the collection *On Early Trains* came out in 1943. For most of the 1930's he devoted himself almost exclusively to translation. In 1935 he published a volume of Georgian lyric poets, and his *Selected Translations* (of Kleist, Byron, Keats, Verlaine, Shakespeare, and others) appeared in 1940. At the time of his meeting with Gladkov early in the war, he was already working on *Romeo and Juliet,* which eventually came out with other Shakespeare plays in a two-volume edition in 1949. In the postwar years he did the first complete version of *Faust* to be published in the Soviet Union (1953), and also Schiller's *Maria Stuart,* which was produced on the stage in Moscow in 1957.

For many writers in those years, translation—and also writing for children—served as a refuge: it was a way of earning a living without the compromises or loss of integrity which the publication of original work increasingly entailed. But for Pasternak it had a much more positive significance. In many instances, he chose for translation works which said things he could no longer publicly express in his own name. In this respect his version of *Hamlet* was particularly important and must be seen almost as an essential prologue to *Doctor Zhivago,* which he started writing in earnest six or seven years later. Contrary to his temperament and his whole philosophy Pasternak, like Hamlet, found himself compelled by circumstances to respond, in whatever way lay open to him, to the outrages of which he was a witness and which touched him so closely. As he makes plain in his essay on translating Shakespeare, he looked on Hamlet not as a weak and vacillating character but as a man who steeled himself to play a role alien to his nature. This view of himself as a tragic actor in the literal sense, forced despite himself to walk out onto the stage of history, was the subject of his poem "Hamlet" (probably written in 1946, when he began work on *Doctor Zhivago*):

> The noise is stilled. I come out on the stage . . .
> The darkness of the night is aimed at me
> Along the sights of a thousand opera glasses.
> Abba, Father, if it be possible,
> Let this cup pass from me . . .

The image of the opera glasses aimed at him out of the darkness aptly conveys the agonizing sense he had of being the focal point of a myriad obscure expectations among the many readers of his verse who looked at him, in mute hope, as the last person able to express, perhaps, what few even dared to think. In his conversations with Gladkov during and after the war, he spoke often of his feeling of being "in debt" to his readers. As he put it in a poem, it was "shameful to be a legend on all lips, and an empty name." In the later war years, when there seemed a slight prospect of easier times after victory, he was already casting around for a suitable way of speaking more directly to his readers than was possible in lyric poetry or translations. His first attempt to do so took the form of an audacious narrative poem, *Nightglow*, a fragment of which was actually published in *Pravda* in October 1943. Inevitably it was cut short and had to be abandoned, but it showed, in hardly veiled language, the startling lengths to which he was prepared to go once he had any opportunity of making himself heard.

But with the renewal of the terror against the intelligentsia in 1946, he was soon as effectively isolated from his readers as he had been before the war. Until 1949, when Ivinskaya was arrested, he got off comparatively lightly. There was no attempt to starve him into submission (as in the case of Akhmatova and Zoshchenko, who were expelled from the Union of Writers), and the worst that happened to him was the publication of a vicious attack by Alexei Surkov in the newspaper *Kultura i Zhizn* (March 1947). He was able to continue work on his version of Faust, which, needless to say, he intended should speak as eloquently for himself as Hamlet had done. At the same time, assured of a livelihood by his contract for this and other translations, he wrote *Doctor Zhivago* and courted arrest by reading parts of it to private gatherings.

During this period when most people, naturally enough, thought only of how to save their skins, Pasternak on one occasion showed his defiance in public, at a poetry reading in what was then the largest auditorium in Moscow, the Polytechnic Museum.[5] It is worth describing at length, since it undoubtedly had enormous significance for the Moscow intelligentsia and for Pasternak himself. The event was announced several days beforehand, in January or February 1948, in the newspaper *Vechernyaya Moskva* and was billed as "An Evening of Poetry on the Theme: 'Down with the Warmongers! For a Lasting Peace and People's Democracy' "; this was already after the establishment of the Cominform and the beginning of the massive Soviet campaign against the "aggressive North Atlantic Treaty." The score or more poets listed in the announcement as due to take part included Pasternak. This seemed doubly incredible: incredible that, after recent attacks on him in the press, he should have been invited by the organizers to attend, and even more incredible that he himself should have agreed to be associated with what was obviously going to be a crude manifestation of support for official propaganda.

The immediate thought was that Pasternak might at last have succumbed to all the pressures, and was now going to be produced in public to demonstrate the fact. This, as soon appeared, was anything but the case, and it seems likely that he was invited only in the hope that he might avail himself of this chance of showing himself a "true Soviet poet." Even if he failed to do this, his mere presence on such a platform, it was no doubt felt, would compromise him in the eyes of the many people who looked upon him as almost the last remaining poet who had not "fallen." An incidental calculation was, perhaps, that the appearance of his

---

[5] I was then in Moscow as a member of the British Embassy, and had a seat in the front row. It was the only time I was able to see Pasternak.

name in the list of participants would draw a much larger audience than could otherwise be expected to attend such undistinguished and predictable proceedings. It was only on this last point that the organizers were not disappointed. The large hall, often used for major propaganda lectures, was quite remarkably crowded: people were squatting on the steps in the aisles, and large numbers who had not been able to get tickets stood on the street outside, desperately hoping to buy one at the last moment. There was a perceptible air of excitement, most unusual for the apathetic Soviet audiences of those days.

About twenty poets trooped out onto the stage and sat down dutifully on chairs facing the audience. In front of them was a table, and a rostrum with a microphone. But Pasternak was not among them. One chair at the back of the stage remained empty. The tense expectancy in the hall gave way to what was quite evidently a mixture of disappointment and relief—after all, what would *he* have been doing in this company? It seemed probable that he had been excluded at the last moment, or had simply decided against it himself.

The reading was presided over by the novelist Boris Gorbatov, who took his seat at the table. He had a little bell in front of him. The first poet summoned to come forward was Surkov. He stood at the rostrum and declaimed into the microphone some verse which went straight to the point, denouncing the North Atlantic Treaty, the warmongers, and Churchill, who at that time was regarded as the prime mover in the Cold War because of the famous Fulton speech in which he first used the phrase about an Iron Curtain between Eastern Europe and the West. As Surkov was halfway through his last line, the audience suddenly burst into loud applause and when he glanced over his shoulder, startled at this ovation which was so clearly not for him, he saw what everybody else could see: Pasternak had slipped in from the wings and was just taking his seat in the back row. He looked a little flustered, but was visibly very gratified as he made imploring gestures with his outstretched palms until the crowd eventually quieted down. The recital continued, with each of the successive poets delivering his rhymed invective in the accepted sub-Mayakovskian manner, perhaps uncomfortably aware of how out of place it now was, and grateful for the thin, impatient applause of the audience, which was restless and ill at ease. What could Pasternak possibly say that would have the slightest relevance to warmongers and the North Atlantic Treaty? At last Gorbatov called his name and motioned him toward the rostrum. The audience again went wild, clapping and shouting. As he advanced from his chair to the edge of the stage, he smiled rather shyly and again gestured with his hands as though begging people not to go too far in expressing their feelings about him.[6]

Instead of walking up to the microphone into which all the others had spoken, he came down some steps at the side of the stage and stood below, directly in front of the audience, shifting his feet slightly as he waited for the applause to die away. At last there was dead silence. He looked exactly as Gladkov describes him—extremely young, with a strikingly handsome face, on which there now appeared a rather mischievous, almost puckish, yet at the same time invincibly innocent expression. In his peculiarly nasal voice, drawing out the Russian vowels to at least twice their normal length, he said: "Unfortunately, I have no poem on the theme of the evening, but I will read you some things I wrote before the war." The tension was broken and there was renewed applause. Beads of sweat appeared on Gorbatov's bald head.

Pasternak then recited several poems which were obviously known to the audience from his volumes of poetry published years before. After each of them there was tremendous applause. At one moment he forgot a line and was immediately prompted from various parts of the hall. People began to shout out requests for particular poems, and he was clearly ready to oblige, but things were getting out of hand, and Gorbatov looked more and more distressed, though he too was affected by the general mood; at one point his lips could be seen moving as he followed the words of

---

[6]He was well aware, as Mrs. Mandelstam reports in *Hope Abandoned*, of what Stalin is supposed to have said when he heard of a similar reception in this same place for Akhmatova a few years previously (in 1944): "Who organized this standing ovation?"

one of the poems. Somebody shouted *"Shestdesyat shestoi davai!"* (Give us the Sixty-sixth!)—this was a request for Pasternak's version of Shakespeare's sonnet, which had been included in his volume of selected translations published in 1940. Perhaps it was fortunate that he did not recite these lines which so perfectly defined the general state of affairs, and his own situation in particular:

> And art made tongue-tied by authority,
> And folly, doctor-like, controlling skill,
> And simple truth miscall'd simplicity,
> And captive good attending captain ill:
> Tir'd with all these, from these would I be gone,
> Save that, to die, I leave my love alone.[7]

The meeting was developing into an unheard-of public demonstration and Gorbatov started to ring his bell frantically, trying to bring the crowd to order. But for a long time the applause went on, and Pasternak stood there, smiling awkwardly and patently enjoying his dangerous triumph. At last Gorbatov managed to make himself heard and declared an intermission. (There were many empty seats during the second half of the program. The only other noteworthy person on the platform was Ilya Ehrenburg, who sat there listening sardonically. When his turn came, perhaps emboldened by Pasternak's example, he said: "I must admit that I am more accustomed to cursing in prose, but I will read you some verse I wrote during the Spanish Civil War.")

Almost anybody but Pasternak would certainly have been arrested for such a "political provocation"; he had virtually sabotaged an important public meeting devoted to the "struggle for peace." His immunity, however, still held good and, although the indirect sanctions against him continued to be relentless and cruel

---

[7]The *Sixty-sixth* was one of only two Shakespeare sonnets selected by Pasternak for translation (the other was the *Seventy-third,*) and his rendering is remarkably powerful and trenchant. A blander (but fairly close) version by Samuil Marshak appeared in a full collection of Shakespeare's sonnets which was awarded the Stalin Prize in 1949. (An interesting illustration of what a difference the context can make!)

beyond words, he was not himself touched. Right until Stalin's death in 1953 he was able to go on writing the work which he considered to be of infinitely greater significance than anything he had written previously, and whose publication abroad in 1957 may be seen as the final stage in his relations with the dictator: a posthumous settling of accounts, an act of poetic justice in the literal sense.

When Gladkov read *Doctor Zhivago,* he was disappointed by it, and he devotes several pages of his memoir to explaining why. He is at pains to emphasize that what he says about it must be set against the background of his unbounded affection and respect for the author, and that his misgivings are based on purely aesthetic grounds: "As a gesture it is brave and heroic; its moral premises are impeccable. But the literary result is doubtful and a matter for debate."

Doctor Zhivago has, of course, never been the object of a genuine debate in Russia. If it is ever published there, it may one day receive the kind of critical appraisal that a work of literature can be given only in the course of free public discussion in its country of origin (as happened, for instance, in the case of Bulgakov's *The Master and Margarita,* a quarter of a century after it was written).[8] It is, of course, impossible to say what the result of a fair and dispassionate exchange of views would be in Russia. Some would presumably share Gladkov's opinion that Pasternak was attempting to write in a genre unsuited to him, and that—in form, at least—*Doctor Zhivago* therefore appears weakly derivative of the nineteenth-century Russian novel; others would certainly accept Pasternak's own view (which it will be easier to substantiate when the correspondence of his last years becomes more fully available) that he was breaking new ground and deliberately departing, in important respects, from the canons of the classical Russian novel. I believe myself that—whether one thinks

---

[8]There has, of course, been some fruitful discussion in the Russian emigration. Most noteworthy are the brilliant essays by the late Victor Frank in *Selected Articles,* edited by Leonard Schapiro (London, 1974).

it for better or for worse—the latter is in fact the case, and that *Doctor Zhivago* is, within the Russian tradition of prose writing, *sui generis*—and was consciously intended to be.

It is perhaps to be regretted that it is called a novel. The word inevitably invites comparison with the great Russian novels of the past, and this has often bedeviled discussion of it. The general scope of the work, the time span covered, and the fact that it has a narrative structure of sorts (a story which could even be used to make a film in the West), has likewise led to its being judged by the same standards as such vast synoptic portraits of an age, with a large cast of elaborately drawn characters, as Tolstoy's *War and Peace*. Needless to say, anything judged by inapplicable criteria is bound to be found wanting.

Like Gladkov, Nadezhda Mandelstam was also led by the choice of the word "novel" and the superficial resemblances to Tolstoy to speak in a critical vein of *Doctor Zhivago*, judging it a failure from the point of view of what Pasternak himself said he had set out to achieve. But in the course of taking him to task, she does, it seems to me, brilliantly define what he was actually trying to do—and might more unquestionably be thought to have succeeded in, if the issue had not been confused by terminology and comparisons of dubious validity:

I understand Pasternak better now—he was drawn [i.e., in writing *Doctor Zhivago*] by the need to "externalize," to look at things from the outside, "objectively." As a poet, he was wholly dominated by his feelings, and his lyrics are essentially part and parcel of his ordinary, workaday life; this indeed is their charm. In the everyday life around him, he only rarely glimpsed "objective" factors beyond, such as history and the country as a whole, and even then he saw them chiefly in the perspective of the immediate present. But he was prey to a nagging urge to analyse, to look at things from a distance, to see them in larger perspective. This was because he felt that for someone like himself who lived by inner feeling there was an unfortunate cleavage between subject and object. Pasternak's novel is a remembrance of things past, an attempt to determine his own place in the swift-flowing movement of days, and to seek understanding of this movement itself.

This is a perfectly true description of Pasternak's intentions, and could not be better put, though, as we have seen, his "nagging urge to analyze" was born of a sense of imperative duty, and his concern with broad historical issues and the fate of the country at large had always been greater than Mrs. Mandelstam allows. The essential point is that once Pasternak had been forced by extraneous circumstances to deal with matters he would normally have thought outside the purview of a lyric poet, he had to face the difficult question: by what means was it to be done? It was a question that had exercised him long before his own experiences in later years made it almost literally a matter of life and death for him. In the immediate aftermath of the Revolution, during the 1920's, he had already approached broad historical themes in long narrative poems, but he was clearly not yet very sure of his ground. As for many of his contemporaries (including Mandelstam), it was still too early for him to resolve the ambiguities in his attitude to what was going on. These poems were unfinished and, as Sinyavsky says, they create the impression of long "lyrical digressions."

The same is true of the various prose fragments he wrote during the 1920's and 1930's. Some of them anticipate *Doctor Zhivago* in general manner, themes, and occasionally in certain precise details. Already in "Without Love" (published in a newspaper in November 1918), we find one name later used in *Doctor Zhivago* and the makings of a plot which would have centered on the fate of intellectuals in the Revolution. From this alone it is clear that *Doctor Zhivago* was not the caprice of a poet who late in life decided to try his hand at writing a novel, but that it was something which in form as well as in content had matured over many years. When, after the terror of 1937 and its renewal in the wake of victory over the Germans, Pasternak felt in duty bound to make some extensive statement or comment on his times far beyond the scope of lyric poetry, it was natural for him to revert to his earlier "experiments" in prose. He certainly did so not only in full consciousness of his limitations as a novelist in the ordinary sense. He was even more aware of the inadequacy of the classical novel as such to portray what Akhmatova called "the real, not the calendar, twentieth century," which began in Russia in 1905 and somewhat later in the West.

It is possible, as Gladkov suggests, that Pasternak would have achieved his aim better by means of a more direct autobiographical account of the era (as in his much earlier *Safe Conduct*, 1931) without any of the trappings or fictional devices of the novel. But if he considered this, he must have rejected it for several reasons. In the first place, he did not want to be tied by the literal facts of his own life. A very important and perhaps overlooked aspect of *Doctor Zhivago* is that though the central character is largely based on the author's own life,[9] it is at the same time a projection into the past of what this life *might*, or indeed *should*, have been, had it been more typical of what happened to Pasternak's generation. Yuri Zhivago dies of a heart attack in a suffocating Moscow street car (the "locomotive of history"?) in 1929. This very effective image for the death of the Russian intelligentsia as a whole at the end of the 1920's, in the year when Stalin achieved supremacy over his rivals, would have been impossible in a straightforward autobiographical narrative. What came later, in the 1930's, for those who like Pasternak survived to see them, was a life in the tomb. In *Doctor Zhivago* this is indicated by the devastatingly simple device (perhaps unprecedented of its kind in literature) of passing over those years in silence: the unspeakable cannot, by definition, be spoken of. Only in the Epilogue, set in the wartime interlude when, paradoxically, Russia again began to breathe in the midst of death, is there a backward glance at the 1930's in a conversation between two friends of the poet who have survived. This too would have been impossible in an autobiography, where the author would have had to account for a whole decade of his life.

Perhaps another, more incidental, reason for the choice of the

---

[9]And in some externals on that of his friend from university days, Dmitri Samarin.

novel form was that the very conditions under which Pasternak wrote *Doctor Zhivago* imposed a fictional disguise: he could scarcely have given the manuscript to read to other people in the Moscow of 1947–53, if the many crucial reflections on history, art, and the meaning of the Revolution had been set down in his own name, instead of being presented as dialogue between invented characters living in Russia before the war or in the 1920's.

Then there is the problem of Lara. It was Pasternak's love of Ivinskaya that sustained him throughout the period when he was at work on *Doctor Zhivago,* including the four terrible years after her arrest in 1949. Without her, and her fate, the book would probably never have been completed. It might well have petered out and remained a fragment, like several previous attempts to write a lengthy piece of narrative prose. Yuri's relations with Lara (that is, Pasternak's with Ivinskaya) are the keystone of the work, and she personifies the whole country's betrayal, captivity, and defenselessness. The arrest of Lara, with which the book ends, is of course a direct allusion to Ivinskaya's arrest in 1949—though by an extraordinary kind of prophetic anticipation it was more closely paralleled in real life by her second imprisonment in 1960, a few months after Pasternak's death. (The fear that the Soviet authorities would take posthumous revenge on him through her, when he was no longer there to protect her and his relative immunity no longer extended to her, haunted him constantly during his last unhappy years of persecution under the Khrushchev regime: "Tir'd with all these, from these would I be gone, / Save that, to die, I leave my love alone.") It would obviously have been out of the question in those years for Pasternak to describe his relations with "Lara" in other than some kind of fictional form, as a story transferred to a previous decade.

If one is to judge a work of literature by the extent to which it fulfills the author's intentions, then there is no doubt that *Doctor Zhivago* is a successful embodiment of what Pasternak set out to do, and this must *ipso facto* apply to the form as well. In his choice of means, he was of course concerned to find a way of overcoming what Mrs. Mandelstam calls the "cleavage between subject and object." He accomplished this by the very straightforward procedure of subordinating the objective narrative of the conventional novel to the paramount subjective vision of the author; as in his lyric poetry, he remains at the center of his universe. This may sound somewhat arbitrary, but I believe that the effect of such a characteristically "self-centered" approach was, curiously, to legitimize (in aesthetic terms) the use of extensive narrative prose after decades of its misapplication in the Soviet era.

The main consequence of socialist realism, when it was forcibly imposed in the 1930's, was to revive and perpetuate (increasingly as an empty shell) the conventional novel as it had evolved in the nineteenth century. Ludicrous as this was, it was comprehensible as a reflection of a desire for stability once the revolutionary upheaval was over: it was all part of the general trend in the Stalin years to bring back some of the outward appurtenances of the old bourgeois society. The canon of socialist realism was therefore based not on the truly revolutionary prose writers of the preceding decade (Babel, Zamyatin, and others), but on those who had already then, often consciously taking Tolstoy as their model, depicted the Revolution and its aftermath in long, panoramic novels (Sholokov, Fedin, and to some extent Leonov). In both Russia and the West, the nineteenth-century novel was the product of relatively settled, hierarchical societies which it was possible to survey at leisure, in sometimes vastly comprehensive fashion, and often from the vantage point of a tranquil, well-to-do existence. Of the great Russian novelists perhaps only Dostoyevsky, in the frenetic quality of his writing, gave a foretaste of the disintegration to come. But, as Mrs. Mandelstam so rightly says, it is hard to think of Dostoyevsky as a mere novelist.

After the old Russian society had exploded, never to be reconstituted except (by Stalin) in a few of its most vicious and hollow aspects, it became absurd—and, what is more, an offense against realism—to continue writing a kind of prose appropriate only to the seemingly eternal way of life under which it had flourished. Babel understood this (in *Red Cavalry*, 1923), when he showed the Civil War much as it was seen by those who were caught up in it—as a series of brief, cinematic glimpses of savage and meaningless activity which went on autonomously, having no visible connection with any wider social or historical background such as a classical novelist would have supplied. The simple fact of the matter is that when a society disintegrates, it is self-evidently impossible for anyone to have an overall view of it. The tremendous, frenzied movement of people, the breakdown of normal communications and accustomed relationships, means that nobody, not even the new rulers, know what is going on in the country or the world at large. It has been said very aptly that the individual experience of a revolutionary upheaval is like a dream: reality no longer impinges on the mind in an orderly, coherent fashion, but rather in grotesquely fragmented, apparently alogical sequences. The pattern of human contacts, normally so predictable and for the most part subject to prior coordination, dissolves away and life appears instead to be ruled mainly by irrational coincidences.

One of the chief criticisms of *Doctor Zhivago* in the West was that it relies too much on coincidences, but in this, as in other respects, Pasternak was only emphasizing the realism of his approach: anyone whose life has been catastrophically dislocated will confirm that coincidence plays a much larger part than in an ordinary, settled existence. During a revolution, or as a homeless refugee, you are always running into people at the most unlikely moments and in the most unlikely places, and such chance meetings come to seem much more natural than when they occur in the context of the stable relationships they have replaced.

Doctor Zhivago is less a novel in the usual sense than what might be called a lyrical kaleidoscope: persons, events, and places pass rapidly before the reader, and there is rarely any attempt to elaborate them, let alone to place them against a general background. But that is how life was for most people during all the years of war and revolution and throughout the subsequent Soviet era. There was no "general background," either to individual lives or to the life of the country as a whole. Nobody could have the broad picture which previously, like so much else, had always been taken for granted. Other things—also once taken for granted (and not only by the privileged)—move into the foreground: the simple business of staying alive is no longer a routine, and the actual processes of daily existence assume inordinate importance.

It is also part of Pasternak's truth to life that he devotes so much attention to apparently trivial matters like gathering fuel, laying in supplies of potatoes for the winter, or obtaining food by barter from a peasant woman. Such things loomed infinitely larger than "events" or the personalities supposedly in control of them: it is significant that of the three who made the Revolution, only Lenin is mentioned directly (and then in passing), while Stalin is referred to obliquely as a "pockmarked Caligula" in a conversation that takes place in prerevolutionary times, and Trotsky appears once under a Russified Yiddish form of his first name: "Leibochka." Another striking aspect of the disruption of reality in a revolutionary epoch is the blurring, in retrospect, of chronological distinctions. The suicide of Strelnikov in Chapter 14 of *Doctor Zhivago* is something that might seem to have belonged more plausibly to the later 1930's, but its displacement to the early 1920's only enhances the sense, tellingly conveyed in *Doctor Zhivago* as a whole, that for those who, like Pasternak, survived to look back on the period from later decades, it had been like living in a trance, at some "bewitched crossroads" in history.

Doctor Zhivago, as Mrs. Mandelstam says, was Pasternak's attempt to "determine his own place in the swift-flowing movement of days," and it must be judged primarily from this point of view.

Life into Art:
Pasternak and Ivinskaya

*. . . life became converted into art, and
art was born of life and experience.*

Boris Pasternak was born in Moscow in 1890, and died in the
country not very far from it seventy years later. Apart from a few
brief intervals, all his life was spent in or near the city.

His father, Leonid Pasternak, had grown up in the Black Sea
port of Odessa and came to Moscow, originally to study medicine
at the University, shortly after his marriage in 1889 to Rosalia
Kaufman, the daughter of a manufacturer. (Leonid Pasternak's
father had been an innkeeper, one of the few callings open to Jews
in the Pale of Settlement in southwest Russia, to which they were
largely confined by law.[1]) After settling in Moscow, he abandoned
medicine for art and went on to achieve great distinction as a
teacher and painter.

Four years or so after the birth of Boris, his first son, Leonid
was appointed to a professorship at the Moscow College of Painting, Sculpture, and Architecture. The College was under the
patronage of the Imperial court, and the appointment was ap-

---

[1]The Pasternaks were apparently not Ashkenazi, like most of the Jews in southern Russia,
but were descended from a Sephardic family that had settled there in the eighteenth
century. Leonid believed that one of his forebears was Isaac Abarbanel, the celebrated
theologian (1437–1508) who served for a time as treasurer to Alfonso V of Portugal.

proved even though Leonid did not go through the usual formality of conversion to Russian Orthodoxy in order to remove the technical liability of being officially "of Jewish faith." (Before the Revolution citizens of the empire had their religion entered in their identity papers, not—as later in the Soviet Union—their race.)

The Pasternak family lived in quarters allotted to them in the handsome eighteenth-century building of the College on one of the principal thoroughfares of central Moscow, not very far from the scene of many of the events described in Olga Ivinskaya's memoir, *A Captive of Time*. Boris, his younger brother Alexander (later to become an architect), and his two sisters Josephine and Lydia, spent their childhood years there.

In his *An Essay in Autobiography* (written in 1956), Pasternak has given an account of his early life, and it is also portrayed in many sketches and paintings by his father. He seems to have had an entirely Russian upbringing, hardly distinguishable from what it would have been in any middle-class home in the Moscow of those years. Formal religion apparently played little or no part in the family, as for the liberal intelligentsia in general. But at an early age Boris was taken to church by his nanny to be baptized, and throughout his life he attached much significance to this, particularly in his later years when the symbols and liturgical language of Christianity (outwardly embodied in childhood memories of the gold-and-blue-domed churches of Moscow) came to occupy an important place in his poetry.

The Pasternak household was dominated by art, music, and literature. Before her marriage Boris's mother had intended to become a concert pianist, and she sometimes gave private recitals in the apartment at the College. One of his earliest memories was of an occasion in 1894 when Leo Tolstoy came to hear his mother play. Tolstoy was a family friend and, as Pasternak was later to put it, "our whole house was permeated by his spirit." His father visited Tolstoy at his country estate in Yasnaya Polyana, where he made a series of notable drawings of him, and—at Tolstoy's request—he also did the illustrations for *Resurrection* as it was serialized in a Petersburg magazine during 1899. In November

1910, when Tolstoy fled from his home and died in the station-master's house at Astapovo, Leonid Pasternak was informed by telegram. He went there immediately, taking Boris with him, and made a drawing of Tolstoy on his deathbed.

Although Pasternak was not appreciably influenced by Tolstoy in his work, he always looked on him as a tutelary spirit, and this early personal connection with the great writer must have given him a paramount sense of the legitimacy of his place in Russian literature when, many years later, attempts were made by detractors with no such credentials to banish him from it.

His education, like his upbringing in general, was on completely Russian lines. For a moment it seemed that he might go to the Lutheran school in Moscow (much favored by Jewish parents), for which he was intensively prepared in German. As a result, German became the foreign language in which he was most proficient; until the end of his life he was able to write it with old-fashioned elegance. In the end, however, he was sent in 1901 to a Russian grammar school where he received a good grounding in both modern and classical subjects, including Greek. Vladimir Mayakovsky, two years Pasternak's junior and later to be ranked with him as one of the great poets of the era, went to the same school, but they do not seem to have been aware of each other's existence at that time.

Pasternak's overriding passion during his school years was music. As he has described in his two autobiographical works, it came to him like a revelation during the summer of 1903, when the family happened to rent a dacha near where the composer Scriabin was living. Of all the many illustrious figures who visited his parents' home in those years, Scriabin was the one who had the most immediate effect and influence on Pasternak. Sometimes to the detriment of his work at school, he began to study composition at the Moscow Conservatory. His parents were delighted, and it seemed a foregone conclusion that he would become a composer. (Three piano pieces composed by him in his last few years at school have recently come to light and were publicly performed in Moscow in 1976.)

But quite suddenly, and at first sight unaccountably, he gave it all up. This happened in 1910, shortly after Scriabin's return to Moscow after a six-year absence abroad, when Pasternak went to play his compositions for him: "Scriabin's reaction surpassed all my hopes. He approved . . . encouraged me and gave me his blessing." Pasternak's explanation for having nevertheless abruptly decided against devoting his life to music is that he did not feel it was his true vocation: it did not come to him with the miraculous ease he believed necessary to the expression of a natural gift, and he had been increasingly tormented by what he considered his inability to bring effortless technical skill to it. "For six years," he wrote much later, "I had lived for music. Now I tore it up and flung it from me as you throw away your dearest treasure. For a while I went on improvising by habit, but I was gradually losing my skill. Then I decided to make a clean break —I stopped playing the piano and going to concerts, and I avoided meeting musicians." It was, as he said, as painful as an "amputation." But this total ban did not last, and throughout his life he was a familiar figure among the audience at concerts in the Moscow Conservatory.

It was impossible to grow up in Moscow in those years without being affected by the great revival of poetry which began at the turn of the century. The decade and a half before the First World War, often referred to as the "Silver Age," was a time of extraordinary ferment in all the arts. It was one of those moments in history when a sudden quickening of the consciousness coincides with vigorous economic growth. The newly rich Moscow merchants (such as the celebrated sugar or textile kings, whose fathers or grandfathers had sometimes been serfs) patronized the arts in lavish fashion, and often with strikingly good taste not always exhibited by their counterparts in the West. In retrospect there seems little doubt that, but for the war and the Revolution, Russia would have developed into a liberal bourgeois democracy in which Moscow and Petersburg might easily have come to outshine the capitals of Western Europe. (The way in which this promise, soon to be aborted, arose out of the abolition of serfdom and the other reforms of 1861, was the theme of Pasternak's last work, his unfinished play *The Blind Beauty.*)

Ironically, the impatient questing of the Silver Age was not only a symptom of the fatal strains in Russian society, but also helped to accentuate them. When they became intolerable under the impact of a virtually lost war in 1917, the fabric crumbled. At the age of fifteen Pasternak witnessed the first ominous signs: the demonstrations in 1905 that led to the establishment of a limited parliamentary system could be seen from the balcony of the College, and some of the fiercest street fighting went on nearby. He received a glancing blow from a gendarme, and his father made a drawing of a girl wounded in a skirmish. The events and mood of that time were to be graphically recalled in poems and prose written in the 1920's, and in *Doctor Zhivago.* Like most liberal intellectual families (and some of the merchant tycoons), the Pasternaks sympathized with the revolutionaries.

But for Boris Pasternak the perturbations of the era were refracted mainly through art and the kind of speculative thought so appealing to the Russian intelligentsia; here too there had been a revival, marked by a strong movement away from the somewhat shallow materialism of the preceding age. In 1909 Pasternak entered Moscow University to study philosophy (after at first wishing to study law), but during his student years poetry began to take the place of music as an object of major interest, though still not as an overwhelming passion. A few years previously he had begun to read modern verse and, like all his contemporaries, had been particularly affected by Alexander Blok, the dominant figure in the symbolist movement, and of the Silver Age in general. (At about the same time, Pasternak was also greatly impressed by the work of the German poet Rainer Maria Rilke, whose portrait his father had once painted.)

By 1912 symbolism had been challenged by two rival movements, futurism and acmeism, and most of Pasternak's contemporaries—such as Mayakovsky, Akhmatova, and Mandelstam—were associated with one of these conflicting trends, though as major poets they naturally soon came to rise above them. Pasternak was never much concerned with "programs" of any kind and, apart from a brief involvement with a late offshoot of futurism just before and during the First World War, he always stood alone.

Rigorous independence was an essential component of his idea of what it meant to be a poet. This was as much a personal or moral ideal as an aesthetic one, and was embodied for him by Blok: "He had all the qualities which go to make a great poet—passion, gentleness, dedicated insight, his own conception of the world, his own gift of transforming everything he touched, his own reserved, restrained, self-effacing destiny."

These words were written by Pasternak toward the end of his life, but they well sum up what was undoubtedly his instinctive feeling from the beginning: that to be a great poet it was not enough to write poetry. It was essential—by responding submissively to a high and lonely destiny—to contribute in some vital way to the life of the times. For this reason there could be no question of choosing poetry or anything else as a vocation; it was a matter, rather, of being singled out by destiny in some unmistakable fashion.

When he understood that philosophy could not be the vehicle of his genius and his fate, he gave it up as abruptly as music, just at the moment when a brilliant future in it seemed to be assured. In 1912, on the urging of one of his closest friends at Moscow University, Dmitri Samarin (who later served, to some extent, as the prototype of Yuri Zhivago in the novel), he traveled to Marburg to spend the spring and summer studying in the seminar of Professor Hermann Cohen, a neo-Kantian philosopher of international renown to whose lectures people flocked at that time from all over Europe. In Pasternak's first autobiographical work, *Safe Conduct* (1931), he has described how a disappointment in love —the subject of one of his best known poems, "Marburg"— precipitated the abandonment of his studies. It happened just as he had been invited to lunch with Professor Cohen on a Sunday —a summons which normally augured a successful academic career in the field. Instead of going, Pasternak went off to see a cousin who had unexpectedly arrived in Frankfurt from Petersburg. Despite this, Professor Cohen persisted in suggesting he should stay in Marburg and then settle down to teach philosophy in Germany. But he had lost interest in it and was now, for the first time, overcome by an irresistible urge to write poetry; it had seized possession of him in the days after his rejection by a girl whom he had first got to know in his last year at school. He began to write poetry in his student lodgings in Marburg, as though in a trance: "Day and night . . . I wrote about the sea, dawn, southern rain, the coal of the Harz." Before returning home to Moscow, he traveled to Italy, stopping for a short time in Venice and Florence.

The next few years confirmed him in his overpowering sense that poetry came naturally to him. In the summer of 1913, staying with his parents in the country, he wrote all the verse for his first published collection, *The Twin in the Clouds* (a title he later described as pretentious, in the spirit of the times). He was inevitably drawn into the literary life of Moscow with its competing coteries, and he got to know some of the leading figures of the older generation, symbolists such as Valeri Bryusov, Vyacheslav Ivanov, Andrei Bely, and others. But it is significant that he was not under the personal influence of any of them. There was no question of the sort of dependence which may well have played a part in his decision to give up music and philosophy. The two living poets whose work had made the greatest impression on him remained remote figures: it was not until 1921 that he met Blok briefly for the first (and last) time, and his only significant contact with Rilke was by correspondence in years when Pasternak's own absolute originality was not in doubt.

He was, however, tremendously affected by one of his almost exact contemporaries, Mayakovsky, whom he first met in the summer of 1914. After seeing him on one occasion in 1917, Pasternak even seriously thought for a moment of giving up poetry himself, and says he would have done so if he had not been too old by then to change direction yet again. It was not a case of jealousy, but of genuine humility: in the presence of Mayakovsky he felt he was utterly without talent. But at the same time, he instinctively recoiled from the bohemian posturing and flamboyant style of public declamation cultivated by the futurists, most of all by Mayakovsky himself.

Pasternak was by temperament incapable of playing the role of the romantic poet and never thought of writing verse as an exclusive way of life, or as a profession in the ordinary sense. If poetry at times possessed him, he never allowed himself to be consumed by the fact of being a poet, or to project himself as one. All his life he thought soberly—not only out of necessity, but as an article of faith—of the need to support himself and his dependents by the industrious exercise of a craft. In his later years he was often forced by circumstances to devote himself almost entirely to translation, but already well before the Revolution he evidently looked on it as a skill which—in the doubtless regretted absence of any professional training—would enable him to earn his living. (In a letter written to a friend in Moscow from Marburg in 1912, he spoke of translating a work by the Swiss writer Gottfried Keller in order not to be a burden to his by no means wealthy parents when he returned home.) While a student he had also sometimes found employment as a private tutor in rich Moscow families. In the early summer not long before the outbreak of the First World War, he stayed with the family of the poet Baltrushaitis, coaching his son and working on a translation of Kleist's *Broken Jug* which had been commissioned by a theater.

An injury to his leg as a child had made Pasternak permanently lame and he was exempted from military service. In the first three years of the war (apparently only in the summer months) he worked as a tutor in the family of a merchant called Philipp (whose foreign name made him the object of anti-German riots after the outbreak of war; all Pasternak's books and manuscripts were lost in the sacking of Philipp's house). This enabled him to maintain his literary interests and contacts in Moscow, which centered round a small, mildly futurist group started on the initiative of Sergei Bobrov in 1913 and calling itself Centrifuge. The only poets of note to be associated with it were Nikolai Aseyev and Pasternak, who contributed to the several volumes of poetry and criticism put out by it, and whose second collection of lyrics (*Above the Barriers*, 1917) appeared under its imprint. But it is clear from recently published correspondence with Bobrov and other members of Centrifuge that he was lukewarm toward his involvement in collective literary activities, and was altogether skeptical about what he called (in a letter of December 1915) the "poor, sterile epoch" and his own "meanderings and delusions." Pasternak's letters of those wartime years also betray his characteristic dissatisfaction with the idea of an existence based on the writing of lyric poetry ("scribbling," as he put it), which could only be the product of intermittent inspiration. Already then he was anxious to attempt something more substantial and of a different order: a work in prose or a long narrative poem.

Evidently as a form of civilian war service Pasternak spent two consecutive winters (1915–16 and 1916–17) in the Ural Mountains and on the river Kama, where a number of major Russian ordnance factories were located. This was his first important experience of life away from the literary and intellectual environment of Moscow, and his impressions of the region and its people provided the basis, many years later, for several chapters in *Doctor Zhivago*. His duties were administrative and mainly involved the obtaining of military exemptions for men recruited to work in the local war industry. Toward the end of the second winter he found himself at a chemical factory in a mountain area about two hundred miles from the nearest railroad station, at Kazan on the Volga, and it was here that he heard the news of the fall of the monarchy and the Revolution in February 1917. His first piece of prose to be published (early the following year) was the opening part of a never-completed story entitled "Without Love," in which he described his hectic nighttime journey by horse-drawn sleigh through the snowdrifts down from the mountains to Kazan —the first stage of his return to revolutionary Moscow. This fragment is remarkable evidence of how, at the very outset of the new era, he was already preoccupied by the central narrative theme to be unfolded decades later in the novel which made him world-famous: the fate of his generation of the Russian intelligentsia as it would be shaped by the time of great upheavals whose first beginnings in 1905 he had witnessed as a boy.

In the interlude between the February Revolution and the Bolshevik seizure of power in October 1917, it is clear that Pasternak was affected by the general feeling of exhilaration created by the sudden downfall of the autocracy: the description in the novel of Yuri Zhivago's jubilant acceptance of the Revolution during the summer of 1917 is obviously based on his own feelings at the time. But there is no evidence that he was actively involved in what was going on in the country. The summer of 1917 was significant in his own life less for any external events than for a sustained lyrical mood which gave rise to the series of poems later published in 1922 under the title *My Sister Life*. These immediately established him as a poet of supreme quality and achievement. At the same time they created an impression of such detachment from everything except his own feelings and experiences that he was never able to shake off the reputation (sometimes, in the later Stalin years, held against him in menacing fashion) of a figure largely aloof from the great issues of the day. It is true that the poems contain very few topical references. There is a mention of Kerensky and of "soldiers' mutinies." The word "revolutionary" occurs once—as the epithet for a haystack.

The poems nevertheless convey the same heady sense of freedom and of rebirth which in *Doctor Zhivago* was to be described more explicitly in terms of the general mood of intoxication with the great historical changes then taking place. For Pasternak these happened to coincide with a love affair which brought his emotions and perceptions to an exceptional pitch of intensity, releasing an impetuous flow of language hardly to be matched again in his verse for over a decade. By their nature such lyrical eruptions are short-lived and can rarely be repeated, but *My Sister Life* served as the first triumphant assertion of what was always to remain Pasternak's distinctive manner, only slightly modified with the passing years by a serener, more reflective tone, and a conscious striving after greater simplicity.

The months chronicled in the poems of *My Sister Life* were apparently spent between Moscow and various places in the Volga region near Saratov, which accounts for a typical blend of images drawn from both town and country. In many ways this slender volume is a compendium of Pasternak's themes and poetic devices. Although he had his darker moments (in *An Essay in Autobiography* he confesses that as a child he had at times been "close to suicide," and in later life he was no stranger to sharp bouts of melancholy or depression), it shows him in his usual and most characteristic mood of eager communion with the world, of grateful acceptance of life as it is. His own changing state of mind is mirrored in nature and merges with it, in this case during the kind of incomparably luxuriant Russian summer, constantly refreshed by sudden downpours and thunderstorms, which is nowhere more nostalgically evoked than in these poems. It is always a domesticated nature, never suggestive of cosmic despair or brooding anguish, but soothing emotional turbulence by its closeness to ordinary, familiar, and human things: the Milky Way leads over toward Kerch, like a dirt road across the steppe with a herd of cattle raising the dust on it; dead branches resemble the sleeves of a damp shirt hung up to dry; rain weaves like a silkworm as it beats against the windowpanes, cocooning those inside. These are some of the more obvious of the metaphors in which his poetry abounds. His use of language is exuberant and sometimes he is carried away by it, sacrificing clarity to intricate patterns of assonance which enchant the Russian ear and defy the translator, but he is never guilty of banality and continually surprises by introducing expressive colloquialisms into the most poetic contexts—one of his several ways of humanizing the natural scene. As Nadezhda Mandelstam has said, *My Sister Life* is a "book of knowledge about the world, of thanksgiving and joy."

Pasternak remained in Moscow throughout the Civil War (1918–21), making no attempt to escape abroad or to the White-occupied south, as a number of other Russian writers did at that time. No doubt, like Yuri Zhivago, he was momentarily impressed by the "splendid surgery" of the Bolshevik seizure of power in October 1917, but—again, to judge by the evidence of the novel, and despite a personal admiration for Lenin, whom he saw in the flesh at the Ninth Congress of Soviets in 1921—he soon began to harbor profound doubts about the claims and credentials of the new regime, not to mention its style of rule.

The terrible shortages of food and fuel, and the depredations of the Red Terror, made life very precarious in those years, particularly for the bourgeois intelligentsia. In a letter written to Pasternak from abroad in the 1920's, Marina Tsvetayeva reminded him of how she had run into him in the street in 1919 as he was on his way to sell some valuable books from his library in order to buy bread. He continued to write original work and to translate, but after about the middle of 1918 it became almost impossible to publish. The only way to make one's work known was to declaim it in the several literary cafés that then sprang up, or—anticipating *samizdat*—to circulate it in manuscript. It was in this way that *My Sister Life* first became available to a wider audience.

In 1921, however, with the end of the Civil War and the beginning of the New Economic Policy (NEP), the situation changed radically. The partial restoration of a free market meant that private publishing firms could be launched, and for a time it seemed that Russian literary life had a chance of resuming on much the same lines as before. Several writers (such as Ilya Ehrenburg and Alexei Tolstoy) who had emigrated now returned home, and some of the prewar literary trends and movements began to reconstitute themselves, often advancing rival claims to special relevance under the new dispensation. Links with the West were reestablished, and for a few years it was possible to come and go with relative ease. At the beginning of NEP there was a particularly close connection between Moscow and Berlin. Being the nearest West European capital, Berlin served as a convenient halfway house for those Russian intellectuals and writers who at this time hesitated between permanent emigration or return home to a Russia now apparently in retreat from the revolutionary stringencies of the Civil War. Several émigré Russian publishers in Berlin established connections with Moscow, and for a few years new books were often published in both capitals under the imprint of one of these Berlin firms. The arrangement symbolized the ambiguities of the period, and did much to encourage the more optimistic in the hope that the new Russia would not be isolated from the outside world.

Nobody could really know whether NEP, with the limited economic and cultural diversity it allowed, might lead to permanent relaxation, or whether it was to be merely a breathing space. This indeed was the main question which came to divide the opposing factions in the Bolshevik leadership after Lenin's death in 1924. Several leading writers and poets (such as Tsvetayeva) took no chances and emigrated as soon as it was possible. In August 1921 Pasternak's father (who had retained his position at the College throughout these years) obtained permission to travel to Berlin on the grounds that he and his wife required medical treatment not available in Russia. Although he did not apparently intend to stay abroad for good and later thought of returning, he and his wife and two daughters in fact remained in Germany for a number of years, and then moved to England not long before the Second World War. Toward the end of 1922 Boris also went to Berlin, and for a moment he seems to have toyed with the idea of staying there with his family. He visited Marburg again, but Professor Cohen was dead and only his former landlady recognized him. In general the sight of postwar Germany was not inspiring—"like a beggar with outstretched hand," as he was to describe it in *Safe Conduct.* Around this time *My Sister Life* was published in Berlin by the same firm which had already brought it out a few months previously in Moscow, to which he now returned early in 1923. He never saw his parents again.

That same year he married his first wife, Yevgeniya Vladimirovna Lurye, a painter. His son Yevgeni was born the following year, and he began a more or less settled existence as a writer and poet already of some considerable reputation, and was widely considered to be the equal of such contemporaries as Akhmatova, Mandelstam, and Mayakovsky. He shared the general material hardships of the time—a cramped apartment and an uncertain income—but it was at least possible now to make some kind of living by literary work. For a time in the mid-1920's, in addition to advances from publishers for his books and translations, he even received a salary as a researcher in the library of the People's Commissariat for Education, where his task was to read through foreign journals and clip out all references to Lenin. The birth of his son had made this regular employment essential, and it also had the incidental advantage of keeping him in touch with Western European literature, since in the intervals of hunting for Leniniana he was able to read Proust and Joseph Conrad, among others.

Much of the original verse and prose he wrote in these conditions was in form and content as inconclusive as the times themselves, and thus reflected not only his own inner uncertainties, but those of most of the intelligentsia during NEP. As before, it was his ambition to write a substantial work in verse or prose. Apart from translations (of Kleist, Goethe, Hans Sachs, and others) and a further volume of lyric poems (*Themes and Variations,* 1923), he published a lengthy but fragmentary soliloquy in verse on the relation between art and revolution (*A High Illness,* 1923), and attempted a novel of which only a first part appeared (*The Childhood of Luvers,* 1922). In the second half of the 1920's he brought out the unfinished narrative poems *Lieutenant Schmidt* (1926–27) and *1905* (1925–26). Their incomplete state underlines how unready he still was for the task he had set himself. This was to give an account of the revolutionary era he had lived through, trying to draw up a balance sheet of what it meant in terms of its effect and claims on uncommitted individuals of his own kind, and on the agents of revolutionary change themselves.

Unlike Mayakovsky, whom he had so much admired in the previous decade, he was divided in his mind about the new order, and the nearest he came to a nominal display of support for it was by joining Mayakovsky's combative LEF (Left Front of Art), together with other former members of Centrifuge. But this was, perhaps, more a gesture of solidarity with old associates than an act of wholehearted self-identification with LEF's revolutionary program. As much as he had been impressed by the inimitable verve and audacity of the earlier Mayakovsky, he was now repelled by the blustering hyperbole of such long-winded encomia to the Revolution as *150,000,000* (1921) and *Vladimir Ilyich Lenin* (1924). In 1927 Pasternak formally broke with Mayakovsky by leaving LEF. It is noteworthy that during the years of increasing estrangement from Mayakovsky he began to correspond with Marina Tsvetayeva, who had supported the White cause in the Civil War before she emigrated. This did not, of course, signify any political preference on Pasternak's part, but only that he now found in Tsvetayeva the same qualities which had once so much attracted him in Mayakovsky: overwhelming poetic strength and verbal brilliance in the service of truth to oneself.

In his necessarily unfinished narrative poems of those years Pasternak showed a much greater awareness of the real dilemmas of history than those of his contemporaries who supposed themselves to be marching in step with it. While by no means denying the imperatives of social justice, he knew too well how readily victims turn into bullies and liberating ideas congeal into tyrannical institutions, and how easily revolutionaries may lose control of the processes they set in motion. (As early as 1918 he had published an intriguing dramatic fragment in verse about Saint-Just and Robespierre which suggests how deeply he must have pondered the tragic lessons of the French Revolution for the Russian one.)

Yet there is nothing gloomy or pessimistic in his vivid poetic impressions of 1905, in his epic portrait of Lieutenant Schmidt (one of the heroes of the naval mutiny which helped to spark off the events of 1905), or in *Spektorsky*, his semiautobiographical account of the complex relationship of a Russian intellectual (Spektorsky) to the troubled and uncertain times. (The latter was planned as an ambitious "novel in verse" on the general theme which was much later fully elaborated in *Doctor Zhivago*.) What is common to all three works is the evident belief that the Revolution would be justified and fulfill its promise as long as it remained in harmony with the overriding claims of life as such, furthering rather than stultifying them, and did not demand the total sacrifice of the individual personality. There was nothing deliberately insidious about the doubts implied in posing the question like this, but it needed the experiences of the following decade to resolve them.

The end of NEP and the opening of a completely new phase in Soviet history at the close of the 1920's happened to coincide with major developments in Pasternak's personal life and, as in the summer of 1917, the resulting mood found expression in a series of lyrical poems—the last such cycle for many years. These poems, written between 1930 and 1931, were published in 1932 as a volume under the eloquent title *Second Birth*, and they offer fascinating insights into Pasternak's view of himself and the world at that crucial turning point.

For all its relative latitude—and to some extent because of it

—NEP had been morally debilitating. The suicide of Mayakovsky in 1930 (about which there is a remarkable poem in *Second Birth*) was a stunning comment on the toll which its essential ambivalence had taken. It was dispiriting both to those who hoped for a return to the old freedoms and to those who, like Mayakovsky, during its "gray weekdays" had continued to crave the radical transformations it had deferred. For this reason there was a widespread feeling akin to relief (naturally not unmixed with trepidation) when the situation was clarified by Stalin's defeat of his political rivals and the consequent launching of his "revolution from above": the forced march to industrialization begun by the First Five-Year Plan, and the collectivization of agriculture. For a moment, before it turned into unprecedented bloodletting, it looked to many like a return to the "splendid surgery" of October 1917. The huge sacrifice in life it involved, and the somber political consequences of Stalin's assumption of absolute power, were not to become fully apparent for some little time.

Pasternak was affected by the singular euphoria which at that moment came over many intellectuals, including some who had originally been opposed to the Bolsheviks. But the prime source of the lyrical bravura so evident in *Second Birth* was ·the ending of an equivocal situation in his own life. By 1929 his marriage to his first wife had virtually collapsed; in the summer of the same year he met and fell in love with Zinaida Nikolayevna, the wife of a well-known pianist, Genrikh Neigaus. Despite the domestic and emotional upsets involved, the whole spirit and tone of the poems of 1930–31 show that the metaphor "second birth" accurately defined Pasternak's state of mind at that time. Even the lines addressed to the wife he was soon to divorce, remarkable for their touching candor and elegiac tenderness, do not detract from the buoyancy induced by a passionate new love and the overall sense of a fresh beginning in his own affairs, as well as in those of the world at large. Less frenetic and more disciplined in language than *My Sister Life*, *Second Birth* thus similarly arose from a conjunction of Pasternak's private mood with what he perceived as a public one.

There was a third, and less ephemeral, element in his feeling of regeneration: his discovery of the Caucasus, to which he went for the first time, together with Zinaida Nikolayevna, in 1931. Their journey over the Georgian Military Highway (probably the most breathtaking mountain road in the world) to Tiflis—where they stayed with the poet Paolo Yashvili, later a victim of the terror—is described in poems which have not been equaled since Pushkin and Lermontov wrote on the same theme. For Pasternak the Caucasian peaks, receding in an infinite panorama of unexampled grandeur, offered a simile for a vision of what a socialist future might be like. But, as before, most of his images are domestic and intimate, even in this prodigious setting: the rugged lower slope, for instance, reminded him of a "crumpled bed." Although the use of such topical words as "plan," "commune," and "construction" indicates a greater direct concern than in *My Sister Life* with what was afoot in the country, the paramount source of life and renewal—as usual in Pasternak's eyes—is still nature, and nobody could have been further from seeing socialism in the Marxist terms of its conquest by man. If it was to succeed, he often seemed to be saying, socialism would have to emulate nature and coalesce with it. What is more, he still insisted on those moral aspects of building a new society which had long been disregarded and were soon to be blatantly trampled on: "labor in common," he said in one line, must go hand in hand with a "rule of law." In view of the future events related by Olga Ivinskaya in *A Captive of Time,* there is a particular irony in a passage where he declares his acceptance of the "revolutionary will" because it had supposedly put an end to the oppression of women—something which had exercised him from his childhood days.

People have occasionally seen naiveté in all this, and it is undeniable that Pasternak shared certain of the misplaced hopes of the moment. But it is also clear that the historical wisdom and prescience displayed in the narrative poems of the previous decade had not in fact deserted him. This appears with particular force in his paraphrase of some famous lines of Pushkin addressed to Nicholas I in 1826 with the evident intention of moving the czar to show mercy to the rebellious officers arrested after the

Decembrist uprising in the previous year. Using the same veiled language as Pushkin, Pasternak expressed the hope that Stalin would likewise spare his defeated opponents. In both cases such a plea was proved by events to be wishful thinking, but of the kind patently aimed at warding off or exorcising clearly perceived dangers. The fact is that in 1931, as in 1917, Pasternak was still prepared to accept the Revolution only on his own terms, and if (in the last poem of *Second Birth*) he elaborately compared it to the spring, this was clearly in the conviction that it would only be worthy of its name if it lived up to the high promise implicit in this and his other figures of speech for it.

In the first half of the 1930's it was still possible to harbor illusions in connection with Stalin's emergence as the unchallenged master of the country. By 1932 or 1933 it had become obvious that collectivization—during which at least five million peasants died—had been a terrible and irreversible disaster. As Pasternak commented through the mouth of one of the characters in *Doctor Zhivago:* "I think that collectivization was both a mistake and a failure, and because that couldn't be admitted, every means of intimidation had to be used to make people forget how to think and judge for themselves, to force them to see what wasn't there, and to maintain the contrary of what their eyes told them." Yet at one moment Stalin himself condemned the excesses that had occurred, and for a while he seemed anxious to appease various sections of the population, and to create the impression of a return to "normalcy." On his personal initiative a more traditional approach to the teaching of Russian history was adopted in the schools, and the militant doctrinaire application of Marxism was expressly discouraged in a number of other fields. At the same time, the revolutionary quality of life in the 1920's was modified by a seeming restoration of certain conventional values (especially marked in family life), and class warfare began to give way to some degree of social reconciliation. But by the time this changed attitude came to be enshrined in the new Constitution of 1936—vaunted as "the most democratic in the world"—the terror had begun. Stalin himself was soon calling for an intensification of class warfare.

To many writers it at first seemed a positive step that the proletarian literary organization known as RAPP was disbanded by decree in 1932 and a Union of Soviet Writers set up in place of all previous literary groupings and associations. The so-called fellow travelers—those who, like Pasternak, had accepted but not actively supported the Revolution—were henceforth to be recognized as legitimate participants in the tasks of creating a Soviet literature whose formal continuity with the classical tradition of the nineteenth century was stressed in the new official doctrine of socialist realism (first launched in 1932). The rise of Hitler and the consequent policy of seeking the support of noncommunist public opinion in the West also seemed initially to work in favor of a liberal approach to writers and intellectuals in the Soviet Union. Stalin was not unaware of the useful prestige to be derived from a show of tolerance for writers such as Pasternak, who by now had a certain reputation in the West as well. The avowed strategy was, in a word, to win over the hitherto uncommitted intelligentsia by displaying relative indulgence toward their past attitudes, and—even more importantly, perhaps—by allowing them to share the material privileges of the ruling elite.

During the 1930's (particularly in the second half) the genuine egalitarianism and informal social behavior of the previous decade —when even the leaders could occasionally be glimpsed walking in the streets—yielded to an increasingly noticeable inequality in the distribution of goods and services. High officials began to move about in the sleek chauffeur-driven and discreetly curtained limousines produced by the new Soviet automobile industry, and obtained their supplies in special stores open only to them. Luxury apartment blocks with their own private facilities were built in Moscow for various groups of functionaries, and they were also allotted dachas in the beautiful wooded areas around Moscow. Members of the Union of Writers gradually found themselves being co-opted into this new establishment and given access to its bounties, including the medical services of the Kremlin Hospital and its several branches. Leading writers were offered apartments in a twelve-story building put up for them in one of Moscow's most pleasant streets, and dachas with generous allotments of surrounding land were set aside for them in the particularly agreeable country district of Peredelkino, about twenty kilometers southwest of Moscow, and easily reached by train or road. In 1936 Pasternak settled here with Zinaida Nikolayevna, whom he had married two years before. (It is interesting to note that Peredelkino had been the estate of the family of Dmitri Samarin, Pasternak's friend from his student days who, as previously noted, was to some extent the prototype of Yuri Zhivago.)

After the difficult existence of earlier years it was perilously easy to succumb to such inducements. A few of Pasternak's friends and neighbors (such as the novelist Konstantin Fedin) found it impossible to resist the temptation of accepting important positions in the apparatus of the Union of Writers, which rapidly became one of the lesser but nonetheless beguiling avenues of power and influence, if not of glory, in the Soviet system. By the end of the 1930's it had grown into an awesome corporation which watched over its members and administered literature on behalf of the state, making its views and wishes known through its newpaper, *Literaturnaya Gazeta.* In the 1920's there had been several private or cooperative publishing firms and a number of journals representing the various competing trends in literature, but all this had now come to an end. There was no longer any substantive difference between monthlies such as *Novy Mir, Znamya,* and others, and the publication of works of literature in book form was monopolized by Goslitizdat (an acronym formed from the Russian words meaning "State Publishing House for Literature"), and several smaller enterprises all under the same control. Overall supervision of culture and the arts was exercised by a department of the party's Central Committee, and Stalin himself was notoriously inclined to keep a personal eye on them as well. During NEP, censorship had been mainly concerned to prevent the open expression of political dissent and had in any case been relatively lax, but in the 1930's strict editorial control and surveillance made actual censorship almost a formality: very little that was "unacceptable" reached the anonymous officials who made the final check.

Whatever grounds there may have been for hopefulness in the

early 1930's vanished completely when the terror began in earnest in 1936–37. (It had started already after the assassination of Kirov in 1934, but it was not until the show trial of Zinovyev and Kamenev in August 1936 that it developed into the frenzied campaign of extermination which literally decimated the party and government apparatus, the military, and the intelligentsia.) By this time Pasternak had certainly lost any illusions he may have had. He was shaken by the arrest of Osip Mandelstam in 1934, and after a further veiled attempt to reason with Stalin in two extraordinary poems published in *Izvestiya* at the very beginning of 1936, he drew the melancholy conclusions about the era that were eventually to lead him to the writing of *Doctor Zhivago*.

Ironically, just as he was irrevocably making up his mind as to the nature of the situation, he found that he was the object of attempts to lure him into the role of a literary public figure. He was evidently thought fitted for the part in view of his generally acknowledged status as the greatest surviving poet of his generation who was not in some way politically compromised (like Akhmatova, by the execution of her husband as a counterrevolutionary, and Mandelstam, by his poem denouncing Stalin). In 1934 he was invited to take part in the First Congress of Soviet Writers, at which he heard his praises sung by the official party spokesman. He knew perfectly well that he was being "got at," and the behavior of some of his fellow writers showed clearly enough what the price of giving in to such seductive approaches would be.

In a remarkable letter written to his Czech translator at the end of 1935 (and first published in Prague in 1965), he wrote: "All this time, beginning with the Writers' Congress in Moscow, I have had a feeling that, for purposes unknown to me, my importance is being deliberately inflated . . . all this by somebody else's hands, without asking my consent. And I shun nothing in the whole world more than fanfare, sensationalism, and so-called cheap 'celebrity' in the press."[2] In June 1936 he was sent, against his will,

---

[2]As quoted by Olga R. Hughes in *The Poetic World of Boris Pasternak* (Princeton, 1974).

as an official Soviet delegate to an international writers' congress in Paris (his last journey abroad). By now the general state of affairs in the country and the pressure on Pasternak to lend his name to it had brought him, as he says in *An Essay in Autobiography*, to "the verge of mental illness."

In the following year he resolved the ambiguity of his situation in a bold and unparalleled fashion. At another writers' meeting held in Minsk (February 1936), he told his assembled colleagues how profoundly he disagreed with their view of literature as something that could simply be produced in the way one pumps water. He spoke of the need for a new Tolstoy capable of exposing their barren rhetoric for what it was. He then served notice, in so many words, that he intended to part company from them. It was an astonishing performance, clearly born of desperation and occasionally marked by a caustic tone otherwise quite uncharacteristic of him: "I am not aware of anything in our legislation that forbids genius—if so, some of our leaders would have to forbid themselves." Nothing like this was heard again from a public platform until long after Stalin's death—or at least it has not been recorded. He seemed to be deliberately inviting the virtual ostracism to which he was indeed subjected during the following years. A few months later such plain speaking could have cost him his liberty or his life. Perhaps he was saved on this occasion by the mildly complimentary tone of his poetic message to Stalin published in *Izvestiya* the month before. At any rate, as Madame Ivinskaya makes clear in *A Captive of Time*, there is little doubt that he survived the terror of 1936–38 (and then again the equally savage persecution of the intelligentsia in the postwar years) only because it was Stalin's personal whim not to allow his destruction.

After his Minsk outburst Pasternak was left more or less alone. There seem to have been no further serious efforts to draw him into the literary establishment, and he was certainly never again invited to make a public speech. Yet at the same time he was allowed to retain the material privileges of membership in the Union of Writers, including the one he prized most: the house in Peredelkino, which served as a haven for the rest of his life. The chief disability he suffered was probably to experience greater difficulty in publishing original work. But it is likely that inspiration for lyric poetry was in any case lacking during the second half of the 1930's: after *Second Birth* he neither wrote nor published any verse to speak of except the *Izvestiya* poems and a cycle on a second visit to Georgia which appeared in *Novy Mir* in October 1936. (These poems were subsequently attacked by Stavsky, the secretary of the Union of Writers, who ominously denounced them as "slander on the Soviet people"; part of the price Pasternak paid for his Minsk speech was that he was no longer relatively exempt from this kind of scurrilous abuse.)

Almost the only original work he published in the late 1930's consisted of unfinished pieces of prose fiction (*From a New Novel about 1905*, 1937; *Journey to the Rear*, 1938; *Aunt Olya* and *The Proud Pauper*, 1939). All these foreshadow *Doctor Zhivago* and show how largely preoccupied he now was by the themes and ideas which were to find their embodiment after the war in the novel he considered to be the ultimate justification of his whole life as a poet.

During the 1930's he also turned increasingly to translation. Besides providing an independent means of livelihood, it also often served as an indirect way of giving public expression to what he himself thought or believed. His versions of a number of Georgian lyric poets came out in 1935, and in 1940 he published his *Selected Translations* (two Shakespeare sonnets, verse by Byron, Keats, Verlaine, and others). By the beginning of the war he had completed his version of *Hamlet,* which so pointedly conveyed his view of the times he lived in that he tended to look on it as an essential part of his own work. During and after the war he went on to translate other plays of Shakespeare which were eventually published in two volumes in 1950. (After the war he brought out the first full version of Goethe's *Faust* to be completed in the Soviet Union, and his rendering of Schiller's *Maria Stuart* achieved a notable success on the stage in 1957.)

The Nazi invasion of the Soviet Union in June 1941—as Pasternak was to put it in *Doctor Zhivago*—"broke the spell of the dead letter." Demoralized and unprepared, the country at first suffered hideous defeats, but for Pasternak, as for many of his compatriots, the real terrors of war in a desperate struggle for national survival were almost welcome, after the senseless horrors of 1936–39. As the war went on and the tide began to turn, there was also a widespread conviction among Soviet citizens of all classes that there could be no reversal to the past.

In October 1941, when Moscow was threatened by the lightning German advance, Pasternak was evacuated, with many other members of the Union of Writers, to the small town of Chistopol on the river Kama, not very far from the places where he had spent two winters during the First World War. He remained there for about a year with his wife and young son Leonid (who had been born in 1937), but in 1942 returned to Moscow, where he lived for the remainder of the war. In his *Meetings with Pasternak,* Alexander Gladkov has drawn a most revealing portrait of him during those years. While he continued to work hard at his translations, he confided to Gladkov that he was anxious most of all to write and publish something of his own which would justify the hopes he believed were being placed in him by the many admirers of his poetry. One of the striking features of the wartime period was that people no longer felt totally afraid to speak their true thoughts and feelings to each other. In this franker atmosphere it was borne in on Pasternak that he would meet with an eager and grateful response if he could find some way of talking directly to his fellow countrymen. He began to regard it as his duty not only to help sustain their patriotism, hatred of the enemy, and will to victory (which he did in a series of poems published in the newspapers between 1941 and 1944), but also to voice their expectations of better times once there was peace again. He first tried to do this in a narrative poem, of which a fragment was even printed in *Pravda* in 1943, but he was forced to abandon it. A plan to write a play also came to nothing. But he vowed to Gladkov that if things did not change after the war, he would speak his mind, whatever it cost him.

Within a year and a half after the victory over Nazi Germany, all hopes for a relaxation in Stalin's regime were shattered (in August 1946) by the notorious party decree denouncing Akhmatova and Zoshchenko—the first of a number of brutal measures deliberately aimed at reducing the Soviet intelligentsia to the same cowed state as before the war.

It was shortly after this that Pasternak met Olga Ivinskaya for the first time, and her book is a detailed account of the years that followed, until Pasternak's death in 1960. Her eloquent, moving, and often dramatic testimony gives an intimate portrait of him as he was during the last, crucial years of his life when he wrote *Doctor Zhivago,* and the magnificent verse that goes with it. Here he finally achieved the "unheard-of simplicity" he had promised in *Second Birth.* Madame Ivinskaya was a direct source of inspiration to him in this crowning achievement: the heroine of the novel, Lara, is in many respects modeled on her, and a number of the poems are about her or addressed to her.

For the most part *A Captive of Time* speaks for itself, but it may be helpful to give here a brief outline of the author's life, and of the structure of her book.

Olga Vsevolodovna Ivinskaya was born in 1912 in a provincial town where her father was a high-school teacher. The family moved to Moscow in 1915. In 1933 she graduated from the Faculty of Literature of Moscow University. Her two marriages ended in tragedy: her first husband, by whom she had a daughter Irina (born in 1938), committed suicide, and her second husband, the father of her son Mitya, died after an illness. During the war (in 1943), she began to work for the monthly literary journal *Novy Mir,* where she was in charge of the section for young authors. Soon after meeting Pasternak toward the end of 1946, she left the journal and became a freelance translator of poetry, working in collaboration with him.

In October 1949 she was suddenly arrested and detained for many months in the Lubyanka (the headquarters of the secret police), before being sentenced to five years in a forced labor camp. Following Stalin's death in April 1953, she was released under amnesty, having served four years of her sentence, and came back to Moscow. She now resumed her life with Pasternak and their relationship ended only with his death in May 1960.

About two months later, in August 1960, she was arrested a

second time and again held in the Lubyanka under interrogation for several months. Her daughter Irina was also arrested. At a secret trial in Moscow on December 7, 1960, she was sentenced to eight years' forced labor, and Irina to three.

When news of this act of posthumous vengeance on Pasternak leaked out to the West, there was a worldwide outcry. The first official Soviet response came only in January of the following year, in a scurrilous English-language broadcast beamed to the West, by which time the two women had been transported to a camp in Siberia. The Soviet authorities were deaf to all pleas on their behalf. After a few years, however, both were quietly released: Irina in 1962, and her mother in 1964. Since then Madame Ivinskaya has lived in Moscow, still working as a translator. She finished writing her book about her years with Pasternak in 1972.

Anna Akhmatova

Anna Akhmatova was a reticent woman, and even if she had not lived in the extraordinary isolation to which the circumstances of her time condemned her, we would doubtless still know little of her life, except what she chose to say in her verse and in the brief autobiographical note published in Moscow not long before her death. Reticence was part of her style. It was reflected in her poetry as extreme economy, not to say brusqueness: an imperious take-it-or-leave-it which at once drew attention to her when her work was first published and marked her off from the fashionable poetesses of the day (*poetess* was a word she loathed). Reticence went naturally with the regal manner that caused Marina

Tsvetayeva—the only contemporary woman poet she recognized
—to call her "Anna Chrysostom of all the Russias." Future biog-
raphers will certainly tell much more than she ever let her readers
glimpse, but in the meantime enough is known of the bare facts
to heighten appreciation of her genius and to suggest the measure
of her courage and steadfastness.

Although Akhmatova was born in a suburb of Odessa on the
Black Sea, she is indelibly associated with Petersburg and the
small town of Tsarskoye Selo ("Czar's Village"), the imperial
summer residence. She was brought to Tsarskoye Selo at the age
of one and spent the first sixteen years of her life there. The palace
built by Rastrelli, the park, and the lyceum founded by Alexander
I and attended by Pushkin, are constantly mentioned in her
poetry. There could be no more inspiring place for a Russian poet
to grow up in. Pushkin was a familiar spirit to her. "A swarthy
youth rambled / by the forlorn lakeshore," she wrote in 1911, and
when she returned there in 1944, just before the end of the war,
she already had no doubt that she belonged in his company:
"Though the branches here are hung with many lyres / a place
has been reserved for mine, it seems." In her autobiographical
note she recalls it as it was in the 1890's, when she was a little
girl: "The green, damp magnificence of the parks, the paddock
where my nanny took me, the old railway station." The mention
of a nanny suggests that her family was comfortably off (her father
was a naval engineer), but there was no question of opulence or
luxury, and in any case she was notably indifferent to material
possessions in later life. Her parents separated in 1905 and her
mother took her, with four brothers and sisters, to live in Yev-
patoriya in the Crimea, where she continued her education at
home, after having attended the girls' high school in Tsarskoye
Selo. She did her last year of high school in Kiev in 1907 and then
went on to the law faculty of the Higher Women's Courses there.
She enjoyed the history of law and Latin, but soon got bored
with the strictly vocational subjects. More important than
her formal education was evidently the fact that from an early age
her mother read Russian poetry to her: Lermontov, Nekrasov,
Derzhavin.

In 1910 she married Nikolai Gumilev. The marriage also marked the beginning of a literary association that proved fateful for her later on. Gumilev was one of the most colorful figures in Russian poetry before the Revolution. He was the first Russian poet to introduce exotic themes from non-European countries into his work. His travels to Africa (particularly to Abyssinia, in the year after his marriage to Akhmatova) provided material for manly tales and sentiments. There was always, however, an undertone of tragic stoicism and religious awe that lifts his verse above the merely picturesque. His marriage with Akhmatova was not a happy one; many of her poems at that time speak of their wretchedness together ("I wrung my hands . . ."), and there is a trenchant sketch of him and their relationship in "Three Things Enchanted Him."

Akhmatova got her first taste of Western Europe on her honeymoon with Gumilev in Paris, which she visited a second time in the following year (1911). She was impressed by the new boulevards, which were just then being finished, and by the fact that nobody bought poetry unless it was illustrated by vignettes—poetry, as she puts it, had been "gobbled up" by painting in France. She met Modigliani when he was still poor and unrecognized. They sat in the Jardin du Luxembourg and recited Verlaine to each other. He drew sixteen portraits of her, of which only one survives. She preferred it to any other and kept it hanging in her room to the end of her days. She describes these meetings with Modigliani in a memoir of him published in 1965, and notes with evident nostalgia that the city in which they took place was *"vieux Paris et Paris d'avant guerre,"* where the principal means of transport was still the fiacre. The Russian ballet was all the rage—*The Firebird* was put on in June 1910—and Chagall had already arrived "with his magical Vitebsk."

It must have seemed to her, then, that Paris could easily have been added to Petersburg as the other pole of her existence. Nothing would have been easier and more natural, in later years, than to take refuge there, as so many of her compatriots did. She stayed in Russia by deliberate choice (as is clear from her poem "I am not one of those who left the land . . . ," 1922), but throughout the years of terror her brief visits to Paris in 1910 and 1911 must have remained in her mind as a fleeting vision of what could have been an alternative to the "cold and darkness of the days to come" which had been foretold by Alexander Blok. She says as much in a poem written in 1944 ("This cruel age has deflected me, / like a river from its course"). In Paris, as she relates in her autobiographical note, she also had her first glimpse of some of the forces preparing "this cruel age": a man called Werner ("a friend of Edison") pointed out two tables in the Taverne du Panthéon: "These are your social democrats—the Bolsheviks here, and the Mensheviks over there."

On her return to Petersburg she began to write verse in a serious way (what she had written earlier, as a schoolgirl, she describes as "feeble"), though her husband was skeptical of her efforts and urged her to go in for the ballet: "You have just the right figure for it," he told her. She was not herself sure what she wanted to do. While Gumilev was away in Abyssinia, she happened to read a proof copy of a posthumous volume of verse, *The Cypress Box*, by Innokenti Annensky, a poet better known as a classical scholar—he taught Greek at the lyceum in Tsarskoye Selo—and translator of Euripides, Horace, Mallarmé, and Baudelaire, among others. He had died the previous year (1909). Although the symbolists had claimed him as their own after the appearance of his first volume of verse in 1904, he had very little in common with them. Both in language and themes he was notably down-to-earth, and though he could be cryptic, it was the obscurity of extreme precision. Unlike other symbolists, he had no interest in "other worlds" or in mystical "correspondences"; one recognizes the qualities and temperament that so much appealed to Akhmatova and made Annensky the only avowed modern influence on her. Reading *The Cypress Box* she was, as she records, "oblivious to the world." This sudden illumination was decisive: she had found her voice, and what she now wrote impressed even Gumilev on his return from Abyssinia (it was the verse which was to appear in her first collection, *Evening*, published two years later in 1912). As she makes plain in "To the Muse," she was henceforth wedded only to poetry.

The influence of Annensky was one of the catalysts which had been working for some time to hasten the disintegration of symbolism, the dominating force in Russian letters for well over a decade. Symbolism was more than just a literary school or movement. It was an all-pervading climate of thought, the expression of the Russian Zeitgeist in the years before the historical upheavals ushered in by the First World War. As such, it was also a symptom of the age, a precursor—and some would say an accomplice—of the coming disasters. There were many different strands, often incongruous or conflicting: end-of-the-century decadence, Nietzscheanism, Christian mysticism (stemming largely from Vladimir Soloviev), and so forth. Geniuses, dabblers, and charlatans were involved side by side in a very diverse and changing movement. The only thing they all recognizably had in common was an urge to escape—from themselves, their society, their culture, the present, their very being—into other worlds, Christianity, anthroposophy, or paganism, into the past or the future, into cults (of Beauty, Art, etc.).

It was essentially a romantic impulse, but one that prefigured and anticipated great historical change, instead of following in its wake. The symbolists believed that the visible here-and-now was illusory and that everything was in any case fated to shatter or decompose—a prospect that filled them with fearful presentiment or longing. Alexander Blok thrilled at the very thought of apocalyptic events. Valeri Bryusov wrote a poem in which he proclaimed his welcome to "the coming Hun." For the symbolists, poetry was the vehicle of their prophecies, forebodings, and insights into the "beyond." Since things were not what they seemed to be, words were often used as symbols instead of in their accepted, everyday senses, and poetry acquired a vatic quality. Some of the leading symbolists—notably Vyacheslav Ivanov, at the famous Wednesday gatherings in his fifth-floor apartment, called the Tower—behaved almost as high priests.

By 1910, however, the movement had lost its cohesion, and in 1912 two dissident groups came out in open revolt against it: the futurists and the acmeists. Futurism (of which the best known representatives were Velemir Khlebnikov and Vladimir Mayakovsky) was outwardly the more radical and aggressive of the two challenges to symbolism, advocating contempt for "poetic" language and demanding autonomy for the word. Khlebnikov ingeniously made up his own words from existing roots. In addition to daring neologisms, Mayakovsky freely employed the language of the street to create a provocatively "antipoetic" effect. Needless to say, the futurists rejected mysticism in all forms, though Khlebnikov created a fantastic etymological universe of his own, somewhat like Joyce's. Mayakovsky, despite the original futurist demand for autonomy of the word, put his poetry at the service of protest, both personal and social, and later, after the Revolution, he eagerly lent his gifts to the outright political purpose of propaganda for the new regime. Thus, though it was launched as a movement of emancipation from symbolism, futurism was in effect a crude derivative of it: poetry was eventually treated as a means to an end and, sharing the same romantic impulse, futurists tended as naturally as symbolists to become fellow travelers of the Revolution.

Acmeism—it was first called this by unfriendly critics—was a more total break with symbolism. Its three leading exponents—Gumilev, Akhmatova, and Osip Mandelstam—called into question the very attitude toward life on which symbolism was based. The breach came after Vyacheslav Ivanov, at one of his Wednesday gatherings, had denounced a new poem by Gumilev. But this was only the formal pretext. With Mandelstam, Akhmatova, and a few other "dissidents," Gumilev founded a rival group which he called the Poets' Guild. Like symbolism, acmeism meant different things to different people—for some it was classical precision of language, as opposed to the blurred, polysemantic usage of the symbolists; to others it implied formal elegance and aestheticism (this was so in the case of Mikhail Kuzmin, who was close to the acmeists—he wrote a preface to Akhmatova's first volume—though he never joined them); Gumilev seems to have thought of it mainly in terms of a straightforward narrative style. What they all had in common was a revulsion against the hectic romanticism of the symbolists, their "ideological" preoccupations, and high-priestly pretensions. Most of them believed that language possesses a logic and structure of its own that must not be arbitrarily tampered with (here they differed radically from the futurists), but treated rather with the respect a craftsman accords his materials; it was not for nothing that the acmeists first referred to themselves as the Poets' Guild, or *tsekh*—the word in Russian can also mean workshop. Language was like any other material, and in fashioning poetic artifacts from it one had to take account of its natural qualities and limitations.

It is significant that the leading acmeists were all fascinated by architecture, in which they plainly saw the best analogy to their view of the poetic function. On her second journey to Paris, in 1911, Akhmatova had made a brief trip to northern Italy, visiting Genoa, Florence, Venice, and other cities. The impression made on her by Italian painting and architecture, as she says in her autobiographical note, was "enormous"—it was "like a dream you remember all your life." In the 1920's, when she could no longer publish original work, her two main preoccupations were Pushkin and the architecture of old Petersburg. In 1910, in an important article that was symptomatic of the crisis of symbolism and presaged the break with it, Kuzmin used architectural imagery to make his point: "I beg you," he said, addressing his fellow poets, "be logical in the design and structure of your work, in syntax . . . be a skillful builder, both in small things and in the whole . . . love words, as Flaubert did, exercise economy in your means, thrift in the use of words, precision and authenticity—then you will discover the secret of a wonderful thing: beautiful clarity." Though this was written before the acmeists formed into a group, it could well have been their manifesto. Mandelstam, who called his first volume of verse *Stone* (1913), also spoke of poetry in terms of the builder and his materials (as in the quotation below).

But acmeism—at least for Akhmatova, Gumilev, and Mandelstam—was not only a matter of form, or of greater respect for language. This was simply the external aspect of a general attitude or temperament that predisposed them to accept things as they are—not in a complacently conservative sense, but in a spirit of awe and humility before life as it presents itself to the human mind and senses. They thought it almost blasphemy to regard poetry as a means of probing (let alone escaping from) the reality within which man is confined. Gumilev pointed out that the unknowable cannot, by definition, be known, and Mandelstam considered that knowledge of what is hidden can come only through revelation, not through poetry. At the same time, the acmeists did not accept the division of the world into poetic and nonpoetic—any experience or perception, however lowly, legitimately came within the poet's sphere. Nadezhda Mandelstam, in her memoir *Hope against Hope,* writes as follows:

The poets and artists who rejected symbolism do not look down on ordinary, everyday life—on the contrary, it is a source of beauty for them whether they are poets or painters. The symbolists—such as Vyacheslav Ivanov and Bryusov—assumed the role of high priests standing above everyday life, and for them beauty was something apart from it. By returning to earth, the generation that followed them [i.e., the acmeists—M.H.] considerably enlarged its horizon, and for it the world was no longer divided into ugly prose and sublime poetry. In this connection I think of Akhmatova, who knew "from what trash poetry, quite unashamedly, can grow," and of Pasternak, with his passionate defense of the "daily round" in *Doctor Zhivago.* For Mandelstam there was absolutely no problem here: he did not . . . seek to escape into some realm of pure spirit from the earthly confines of our here-and-now. In his essay "The Morning of Acmeism" (1913), he tried to give a poetic justification for remaining attached to the earth with its three dimensions: "The earth is not an encumbrance or an unfortunate accident, but a God-given palace." . . . In the same essay, which was a kind of manifesto, he asked: "What would you think of a guest who, while living at the expense of his host and enjoying his hospitality, actually despises him in his heart of hearts and thinks only of ways to outsmart him?" *Outsmart* here means to escape from time and three-dimensional space. To Mandelstam, as a self-styled acmeist, three-dimensional space and life on earth were essential because he wanted to do his duty by his "host"—he felt he was here to build, which can only be done in three dimensions. This explains his attitude toward the world of things. In his view, the world was not hostile to the poet or—as he put it—the builder, because things are there to be built from.

This was in essence a religious approach, or at least it implied acceptance of life as a gift and the conviction that it could best be lived within a traditional culture from which religion is inseparable. Gumilev and Akhmatova were Russian Orthodox Christians. Mandelstam, a Jew, believed that the highest achievement of human society was in the Judeo-Christian values which had first evolved in the Mediterranean world: they constituted the basis of our art and culture. In a remark he made in the 1930's, Mandelstam is reported to have defined acmeism as "nostalgia for world culture." This was said with hindsight, but it probably sums up what the acmeists were really concerned with before the First World War and the Revolution: namely, to defend Russia's always precarious hold on the essential features of her own culture, which ultimately derived from the same Mediterranean matrix as that of Europe as a whole.

The apocalyptically minded symbolists (and the futurists, *a fortiori*) were in a curious way hypnotized by the chaos from which this culture had been so arduously won. The thought of its destruction in a holocaust thrilled as much as it may have appalled some of them. Blok, Bely, and Bryusov all to varying degrees believed that, by ridding himself in a Dionysian frenzy of the accretions of civilization, man could be mysteriously reborn or transfigured.

In the eyes of Akhmatova, Mandelstam, and Gumilev, this was the terrible heresy of the age—just how terrible, they were all three to experience with a vengeance. To quote Mandelstam: "One cannot launch a new history—the idea is altogether unthinkable; there would not be the continuity and tradition. Tradition cannot be contrived or learned. In its absence one has, at the best, not history but 'progress'—the mechanical movement of a clock hand, not the sacred succession of interlinked events." It was the aim and effect of the Bolshevik Revolution to put an end to history, understood in this way, and to usher in a millennium of "progress."

The acmeists were not reactionaries, in the sense of opposing social betterment, but they felt that Russia could hardly further her development in any sphere by abandoning the heritage of the previous millennium; in a poem dated 1917, Akhmatova spoke of the country committing "suicide" when "the stern Byzantine spirit abandoned our Russian church." Neither were they cosmopolitans. They abhorred the romantic nationalism in the name of which the symbolists—even Blok—tended to make a virtue out of the self-destructive trait in the Russian character, but they passionately believed in Russia as a rightful heir to the ecumenical values that had been materialized in stone in the churches of Moscow and the architecture of Petersburg; it was up to the poet, using the materials of his craft, to build in the same spirit.

In October 1912, the same year in which the Poets' Guild was formed and her first book of poetry appeared, Akhmatova's son, Lev, was born; she had no other children. The moderate success of her first book, followed by acclaim for her second, *Rosary,* two years later in 1914 (which went through three editions in as many months, just before the outbreak of war) established her as a figure of consequence on the literary and social scene of Petersburg. In 1911 and 1912 she frequently read her verse at both the Poets' Guild and the Tower (it was here she first met Mandelstam, in 1911). In the autumn of 1913 she found herself together with Blok at a public meeting in honor of the Belgian poet Émile Verhaeren and was asked, to her embarrassment, to read immediately after him. At the end of that year she called on Blok to ask him to sign some volumes of his poetry for her. In one he wrote "To Akhmatova—Blok," and into another he copied out a madrigal about her that he had written a couple of weeks earlier, in which he depicts her in a Spanish shawl with a red rose in her hair —details which, as she revealed fifty-two years later in a talk on her meetings with him, were completely fictitious.

Akhmatova never became close to Blok, and for the reasons already outlined could not sympathize with a good deal of what he stood for, but he was a figure of enormous importance to her as a poet and as an epitome of the ill-fatedness of the Russian intelligentsia. She later referred to him as "the tragic tenor of the age," and in the culminating work of her life, *Poem without a Hero,* he appears as the demonic genius presiding over the ghoulish harlequinade that comes back to her, in 1940, as a nightmare vision of Petersburg society in 1913, the last year before the beginning of the "real, not the calendar, twentieth century."

Apart from literary salons and gatherings, there was another place at which the Petersburg intelligentsia met: the celebrated Stray Dog, a *cabaret artistique* opened by Boris Pronin in 1912. Often described in the literary memoirs relating to this period, it consisted of a basement which had been decorated by a leading set designer, Sergei Sudeikin. There was a small stage from which poets of all the contending schools came to read their verse to an after-theater crowd. Blok, Bely, Bryusov, Khlebnikov, Mayakovsky, Kuzmin, Gumilev, Akhmatova, Yesenin—all appeared here before a larger public than was possible in the more intimate and ingrown literary gatherings. The Stray Dog probably did a good deal to establish the somewhat theatrical element in Russian poetry reading that persists to the present day. The public often went there just for the "show," and it was the scene of many notable encounters. (In her memoir of him, Akhmatova says that Mandelstam introduced her to Mayakovsky here; she also relates how Mandelstam once went up to Mayakovsky while the latter was declaiming in his usual stentorian fashion and silenced him by saying, "Mayakovsky, stop reading your verse. You are not a Rumanian orchestra.")

The atmosphere of the place, the decor, and Akhmatova's feelings at a certain moment about the society for which it was a venue are poignantly evoked in her poem "We're all drunkards here . . . ," dated, very precisely, 1 January 1913. The poem obliquely refers to a tragic event at the very end of 1912 which involved some of the visitors to the Stray Dog and which haunted Akhmatova for decades until, in *Poem without a Hero,* it assumed symbolic contours. The actual facts are saved from triteness only by the identity of some of the actors in the drama. A young officer of the dragoons who wrote poetry, Vsevolod Knyazev, was in love with Sudeikin's wife, Olga Glebova-Sudeikina, one of the great beauties of her day, who often appeared in miniature theatrical performances on the stage of the Stray Dog and was a close friend of Akhmatova (they lived in the same house in Leningrad for several years after the Revolution, until Glebova-Sudeikina emigrated to Paris in 1923). On the eve of the New Year, Knyazev shot himself on the stairway of Glebova-Sudeikina's apartment after discovering that his rival for her affections was Alexander Blok. (This at least is what happened if certain details in *Poem without a Hero* are taken literally, as they are clearly intended to be.)

Although the exact circumstances remain obscure, it appears that Akhmatova herself was involved in the affair—sufficiently to assume some of the burden of guilt, while partly absolving Glebova-Sudeikina. (What Akhmatova felt about her immediately after the event is suggested in the last line of "We're all drunkards here. . . .") Whatever the real facts may have been, they now matter less than the poetic truth—that this event became, in Akhmatova's eyes, a parable for the sins of a world on which, with the outbreak of war in 1914, a long and terrible retribution began to be exacted.

Akhmatova's second volume of poetry, *Rosary*, is concerned mainly with the intensely personal emotions of this period: the anguish of her unhappy marriage to Gumilev, a gnawing sense of guilt, resignation, and a hint of penitent self-renunciation, which perhaps explains the title of the volume. The *amor fati*, already expressed in the first volume in "To the Muse," grows into a conviction that she is above all the embodiment and instrument of her poetic voice. There was nothing of the sibylline affectation of the symbolists about this, only a matter-of-fact sense of being fated to speak as she does.

With her third volume, *White Flock*, which appeared a month or so before the October Revolution, the lyricism of her early work begins to yield to an epic tone, reflected sometimes in a slightly archaic, Derzhavin-like diction; personal experience and memory provide the authority for majestic utterances about things that affected all her compatriots. This tendency reached its climax in the long poems of her later life: *Requiem* and *Poem without a Hero*. According to Nadezhda Mandelstam, Akhmatova became increasingly preoccupied with her mission to endure and bear witness. Her own view of her role and situation as a poet under the Soviet regime is obliquely conveyed in such poems as "Dante" (1936), "The Death of Sophocles," and "Alexander at Thebes" (1961).

At the outbreak of the First World War, Gumilev immediately volunteered for service at the front. Toward the end of the war he was attached to the Russian expeditionary force in France, but he returned home after the October Revolution. This enforced separation led to a final breakdown of the marriage in 1916 and to divorce in 1918, after which she went to live with the eminent Assyriologist V. K. Shileiko. During the next two hungry years of the Civil War she earned her meager ration (supplementing Shileiko's rather better academic one) by working as a librarian at the Institute of Agronomy in Petrograd.

Very little is known about Akhmatova's life in the subsequent few years. In her memoir of Mandelstam she mentions having met him frequently in 1917 and 1918, when they sometimes rode in a horse cab together "over the unbelievable potholes of the revolutionary winter, among the famous bonfires which were kept alight almost till May, to the crackle of rifle fire coming from Lord knew where." They went together like this several times to the Academy of Arts, where they took part in poetry readings for the benefit of the wounded. She also recalls the appearance of the city a little later, in 1920, when she says she lived "in complete isolation," not even seeing Mandelstam: "The Petersburg shop signs were still there, but behind them was nothing but dust, darkness, and gaping emptiness. It was a time of typhus, famine, shootings, pitch-dark apartments, damp firewood, and people so swollen up as to be unrecognizable. In the Gostiny Dvor you could pick a large bunch of wild flowers. The famous wooden blocks with which the streets of Petersburg had been paved were finally rotting away. You could still smell the chocolate from the basement windows of Kraffts. All the cemeteries had been pillaged. The city had not merely changed; it had turned into the

antithesis of itself. But people, particularly the young, loved poetry almost as much as they do today" (written in 1965). The
demand for poetry, despite the cruel hardships of the Civil War,
was shown by the publication of her third volume, *Plantain*, in
1921.

In the same year Gumilev was shot by the Bolsheviks for his
alleged part in a conspiracy (the details of which are still obscure)
against the new regime. His execution, which profoundly shocked
and frightened the Russian intelligentsia, stigmatized his ex-wife
and son, particularly during the later Stalin years. It also compromised the acmeists as a group; one of them, Sergei Gorodetsky,
another founder of the Poets' Guild, only saved his skin by losing
no opportunity to revile Gumilev's memory.

A further volume of Akhmatova's verse, *Anno Domini
MCMXXI*, incorporating the poems of *Plantain*, came out in
1922 and was followed by a slightly expanded second edition in
1923. After this, scarcely anything more of hers was published in
the Soviet Union until 1940. In private conversation many years
later she revealed that in 1925, at the height of the "liberal" New
Economic Policy, the Central Committee of the Communist
Party had issued specific instructions that none of her original
work be published. She continued to live in Leningrad, as her
beloved Petersburg was now called, except for a brief period in
1925 when she moved to Tsarskoye Selo. At this time she began
to see Mandelstam again and started the close friendship with his
wife, Nadezhda, that was to last to the end of her life. In the
mid-1920's she also left Shileiko for Nikolai Punin, an art historian and critic.

Although she was later to deny rather indignantly the suggestion that she wrote no poetry during the years when she was
banned from publication, there is little doubt that in the second
half of the 1920's and the first half of the 1930's Akhmatova was
affected by the same "dumbness" with which both Mandelstam
and Pasternak were stricken at that period. Apart from the Pushkin studies that occupied a good deal of her time in those years
(two of her articles on this theme were even published in the
1930's), she earned her living by translation, as did many other

proscribed or semiproscribed poets from that time onward. (Her translation of Rubens's letters appeared in Leningrad in 1933. In later years, particularly after the war, she translated a great deal from numerous languages, including Chinese, Korean, ancient Egyptian, Bengali, Armenian, Georgian, and Yiddish, working for the most part with the aid of literal versions. Very few of her original poems are in fact known from these ten "dead" years: they hint at greater despair and bitterness, sufficient in itself to explain her silence, than she ever voiced in the worse times to come. (In "The Last Toast," for instance, dated 1934: "I drink to our ruined house, / to the dolor of my life, / to our loneliness together . . . / to lying lips that have betrayed us, / to dead-cold, pitiless eyes, / and to the hard realities: / that the world is brutal and coarse, / that God in fact has not saved us.")

There was plenty to be despairing about. Apart from official ostracism, the gathering gloom of Stalinism, and her evident personal unhappiness, she suffered constant material hardship and was intermittently ill with tuberculosis. She had lost touch with her family—not that she had ever been very close to them, but their fate can only have increased her distress and loneliness: one brother had been brutally shot during the Civil War, and another had committed suicide in the mid-1920's.

In May 1934 she went to stay with the Mandelstams in their Moscow apartment—to raise her return fare to Leningrad she had to sell two objects of sentimental value—and she was there when the secret police came to arrest Mandelstam for his poem denouncing Stalin. In 1935 her son, Lev Gumilev, was arrested during the wave of terror which followed the assassination of Kirov: the name he bore was sufficient reason. In the same year, presumably in the same connection, Nikolai Punin was also arrested. The line "At dawn they came and took you away" in *Requiem* refers to Punin. Both were released a year or two later; Punin is known to have been out of prison by 1937, but Lev Gumilev was rearrested in 1938.

Under the stress of these events, as Stalin's Great Terror began, Akhmatova moved into an intensely creative period, thus bearing out a remark by Mandelstam to the effect that great poetry is often a response to total disaster. Apart from *Requiem* (composed mainly between 1935 and 1940), she wrote a remarkable tribute to Boris Pasternak and the poem "Voronezh," inspired by her visit in 1936 to Mandelstam, who had been exiled to Voronezh after Stalin temporarily reprieved him. (He returned to Moscow in 1937, was again arrested in 1938, and died in a concentration camp near Vladivostok at the end of that year.) By 1940 Akhmatova's personal circumstances could not have seemed worse. With the Cleopatra of her poem she could say: "Darkness falls, / The trumpets of the Roman eagle scream." In her poem on Mandelstam in Voronezh she had prophesied the horrors of 1937–38, when Stalin gave his demented commissar of internal affairs seemingly unlimited license to kill and imprison: "In the banished poet's room / terror and the muse watch by turn, / And a night is coming / that has no dawn."

Miraculously, however—even though her son remained in prison—she benefited from the curious breathing space which the country briefly enjoyed after the abatement of the purges and the signing of Stalin's pact with Hitler in 1939. At the beginning of 1940 a few of Akhmatova's new poems—including the one addressed to Pasternak and "Voronezh" (though, needless to say, without the last four lines quoted above)—were published in two Leningrad literary journals. Even more remarkably, a small selection of her earlier verse, with the addition of some hitherto unpublished items, appeared later in the year under the title *From Six Books*. At this time, too, she appears to have been allowed to join the Union of Soviet Writers—the essential condition for a recognized literary existence.

It is noteworthy that in the same year, when the Soviet Union was for a brief moment peacefully allied with Nazi Germany, Akhmatova's thoughts turned to occupied Paris, and to London under bombardment by the Luftwaffe. Perhaps nothing more moving has been written on this theme than "In 1940," which could not of course be published in Russia at the time. This cycle of five poems is an excellent example of her later manner: personal emotions and memories merge with the momentous events of the era and history is refracted, as though in a prism, through the images stirred in her mind by a sudden thought of the past. In 1940—the end of an era, as she says at the beginning of the first poem—her mind dwelt on an earlier year that had similarly been the last of a whole age: 1913. Thus, London in 1940 was associated in her mind with Petersburg in 1913, and the living link between the two was a friend from that vanished era, Salome Andronnikova (the "beauty of the year '13"), who had left Russia after the Revolution and now lived in London.

An even greater flood of memories about 1913 was unleashed toward the end of 1940. As she described it in a letter to a friend in 1955: "In the autumn of 1940, going through my old papers (which were later destroyed in the Blockade), I came across some letters and poems which I had had for a long time but had not read before. . . . They related to the tragic event of 1913, the story of which is told in *Poem without a Hero*." As she records in a prose preface to *Poem without a Hero,* she wrote the first part, "A Petersburg Tale," during one sleepless night (December 27, 1940, which must have been close to the anniversary of Knyazev's suicide), when the vision described evidently came to her in her apartment in the old house on the Fontanka Canal, which had once belonged to the Sheremetev family and still displayed their coat of arms, with the motto *Deus conservat omnia.* (Punin had apparently brought her to live there in the mid-1920's.)

Poem without a Hero continued to preoccupy her long after its completion in 1943, having become something of an obsession. As she says in the letter just quoted: "For fifteen years, again and again, this poem would suddenly come over me, like bouts of an incurable illness (it happened everywhere: listening to music at a concert, in the street, even in my sleep), and I could not tear myself away from it, forever making amendments or additions to a thing that was supposedly finished."

Like Lot's wife looking back on her "native Sodom" in her poem of 1925, Akhmatova looked back "from the year nineteen forty / as from a high tower" and was transfixed by her sudden glimpse of what she had left behind in another era. Why did Knyazev's suicide, of all the events of prerevolutionary Petersburg, come back to haunt her so intensely throughout the Second

World War and after? The episode had not been uppermost in her mind, if the keen recollection of it was triggered only by the chance discovery of some old papers (the poems she mentions were no doubt Knyazev's, some of them addressed to Glebova-Sudeikina, and published after his death). It was perhaps to be explained in part by a natural inclination to cast around in her mind, as one of the very few of her generation to survive until the breathing space of 1940, for something in her own past life to which she could in some way relate the unspeakable calamities that had befallen her and her contemporaries. It could scarcely have been a question of expecting to find a rational cause, but the thought that these visitations had been without meaning would have been intolerable. A woman of her temperament would readily have accepted that ultimate meaning is hidden and not accessible to human reason, but there is a lesser kind of meaning which involves interpretation within a more or less familiar framework. This is often the only way in which the mind can protect itself against insanity, unless it is blessed with the lack of imagination that shields most.

It is understandable, therefore, that Akhmatova should have seen the events of her life in terms of sin and expiation: this at least offered the hope and possibility of redemption. It is significant that there are many echoes of Dostoyevsky in the *Poem;* in the later stages of her work on it, while living in Tashkent in 1942–43, she spent a good deal of time reading and rereading him, and she must have been profoundly impressed by his reflections on such matters, as well as by his premonitions of the disasters that would flow from unbridled "self-will." There is more than a hint of the "possessed" in the masked revelers—"prattlers and false prophets"—who visit the author on New Year's Eve 1940, reminding her of the follies that had led, among other things, to the death of a young poet whom she alone is now left to mourn.

Akhmatova had every reason to know the truth of Pasternak's famous statement that the overriding sorrows of war, as opposed to the contrived horrors of the purges, came almost as a relief. After the German invasion, when Stalin, on the verge of tears, addressed his subjects over the radio as "brothers and sisters," there was a temporary respite inside the country. Stalin made his peace with the Russian Orthodox Church and, in the face of the threat to Russia's existence, even sought the cooperation of some of his innumerable victims. Akhmatova's son, like many others, was released from imprisonment and sent to serve at the front. In March 1942 *Pravda* published a poem by Akhmatova under the title "Courage." Written in her gravest and most solemn manner, it was no doubt more effective than anything else of its kind to appear at that critical time. Other poems on war themes were written by her during the next two years. In September 1941, as the blockade of Leningrad began, she spoke over the radio to the women of the city: "The enemy is threatening death and disgrace to the city of Peter, the city of Lenin, of Pushkin, Dostoyevsky, and Blok." After spending the first winter of the blockade in Leningrad, she was evacuated by plane—clutching the score of Shostakovich's Seventh Symphony—to Tashkent, in Central Asia. Here she lived for the next two and a half years in part of an Uzbek-style house, a *balakhana,* which she shared with Mandelstam's widow. A volume of her selected works appeared in 1943 and was immediately sold out. Apart from completing the first draft of the *Poem without a Hero,* she wrote some fascinating verse on local themes, such as "Your lynx eyes, Asia . . ."

By the time she returned to Leningrad in June 1944, she had regained some of the public standing she had enjoyed before the party had deliberately tried to drive her into obscurity. In fact she had never been forgotten, and her enforced silence of the previous years only served now to heighten her moral authority. For many, indeed, she was quite simply the true voice of Russia. This was demonstrated by an extraordinary and fateful incident in May 1944 in Moscow, where she stayed for a while on her way back to Leningrad from Tashkent. When she appeared at a meeting in the Polytechnic Museum (the largest auditorium in Moscow, where Mayakovsky had often declaimed after the Revolution) and read her poetry from the stage, the audience of three thousand rose to their feet and gave her the sort of ovation normally reserved for the highest in the land. It must have seemed like an act of homage and reconciliation, in the spirit of the eager expectation many Russians now had for a better life after the victory over Germany. But Stalin was already sharpening his knives again. Two years later he is reported by Zoshchenko to have asked, "Who organized this standing ovation?"

On her return to Leningrad she was horrified, as she says in her autobiographical note, by "the specter pretending to be my city." She tried to describe her impressions in prose and wrote two pieces which she later destroyed. Her comment on them is worth quoting: "Prose had always seemed to me mysterious and seductive. From the very beginning I had always known about verse, but I had never known anything about prose. Everybody was full of praise for my first experiment, but of course I was skeptical. I called Zoshchenko. He told me to take out a few things and said that he approved of the rest. I was pleased."

At the end of the war she was evidently full of hopes and plans. The publication of a note she wrote in *Literaturnaya Gazeta* (the newspaper of the Union of Writers) in November 1945 showed the extent of her acceptance into the Soviet literary community: she announced that at the beginning of the following year the State Publishing House in Leningrad would be bringing out a large volume of her collected works that would include all her previous volumes (*Evening, Rosary, White Flock*, etc.), her new wartime poems, and a small cycle on Central Asia. She also reported that she was putting together her notes and essays on Pushkin to make a book, and that she was still at work on a long poem, *Triptych*, "begun in 1940 and finished in draft form in 1942" (this was in fact *Poem without a Hero*, which she continued to rewrite, changing and adding, almost to the end of her life).

But the volume of her poetry never appeared (though it is said to have gotten as far as being set up in proof, one or two copies of which may have survived). On August 14, 1946, the Central Committee of the party, with all the stilted formality that was one of the eeriest features of such pronouncements, issued a decree expelling her from the Union of Soviet Writers and forbidding any further publication of her work in the Soviet press. The decree appeared in all the Soviet newspapers and was accompanied by a report from Andrei Zhdanov, a member of the Politburo and Stalin's lieutenant in Leningrad. It was the signal for a witches' Sabbath which went on unremittingly until Stalin's death in March 1953. Zhdanov said, in part:

> Akhmatova's subject matter is utterly individualistic. The range of her poetry is miserably limited: it is the poetry of an overwrought upper-class lady who frantically races back and forth between boudoir and chapel. She is mainly concerned with amorous-erotic themes which are intertwined with elements of sadness, nostalgia, death, mysticism, and doom. . . . A nun or a whore—or rather both a nun and a whore who combines harlotry with prayer . . . Akhmatova's poetry is utterly remote from the people. It is the poetry of the upper ten thousand in old, aristocratic Russia. . . . A Leningrad journal has opened wide its pages to Akhmatova and given her full freedom to poison the minds of our youth with the pernicious spirit of her poetry. . . . What can there be in common between this poetry and the interests of our people and state? Nothing whatsoever. Akhmatova's work belongs to the distant past; it is alien to contemporary Soviet life and cannot be tolerated on the pages of our journals. . . . There is no room in Leningrad for various literary hangers-on and swindlers who want to exploit it for their own purposes. Akhmatova and her like have no time for Soviet Leningrad. They see in it the embodiment of a different social and political order, another ideology.

After accusations of this kind, most people in the Soviet Union in those years would automatically have been arrested. But Stalin had devised a more refined punishment for Akhmatova: though she was henceforth ostentatiously followed by two police agents, she was not otherwise molested. In 1949, however, her son was arrested for a third time. The next day, fearing the kind of delayed search she had witnessed after the arrest of Mandelstam in 1934, Akhmatova burned her papers in the stove of her apartment: a notebook with her verse, the stories mentioned above, and the text of a play she had written in Tashkent. The discovery of this material—particularly the play—would certainly have made her son's position even worse and led to her own arrest as well. The verse—including, no doubt, *Requiem*—was preserved in her memory and later written out again without difficulty, but she was unable to reconstitute the original text of the play, which had been in prose. Many years later, toward the end of her life, she wrote some verse fragments as part of a projected new version, but according to Mrs. Mandelstam this, even if completed, would have borne little relation to the play actually written in Tashkent in 1942. All that remains is Mrs. Mandelstam's description of it as performed in front of a few close friends, with Akhmatova playing the leading part in a dress she had designed of sackcloth.

The play—or rather, playlet—was called *Prologue: A Dream within a Dream* and was about the trial of a woman poet before a tribunal of fellow writers in the presence of representatives of the people. The heroine is never quite sure what she is guilty of; she mumbles pathetic lines of poetry about "a world in which there are air and water, earth and sky, leaves and grass," but her accusers cut her short, saying that nobody has given her the right to mumble verse like this, that she should pause to consider whose mill her verse provided grist for, and that she must answer for it to the people. Those privileged to attend this remarkable performance were reminded of Kafka, Gogol, and Sukhovo-Kobylin (a nineteenth-century Russian playwright who wrote a trilogy about a man trapped in the judicial processes of the bureaucratic state). Akhmatova, on the other hand, thought that she had done no more than compose a perfectly realistic tableau about what had been the actual situation of poets in Russia since the mid-1920's. In this sense the play was not prophetic, but it would have infuriated the public officials dealing with her son's case in 1949.

She reacted to the party decree of 1946 and the subsequent campaign of vulgar abuse "without any emotion" (according to Mrs. Mandelstam), but she naturally feared the possible consequences, particularly to her son. The main point in arresting him in 1949 was to use him as a hostage, eventually to bring irresistible pressure to bear on her. The worst punishment Stalin inflicted on poets was not to kill and imprison them but to make them praise him. This Akhmatova did in 1950, in a series of fifteen poems under the general title "Glory to Peace," published in the weekly illustrated journal *Ogonyok*. They have nothing of Akhmatova in them and were couched in a language which makes it impossible to regard them as anything but a deliberate pastiche of the standard doggerel of the time. One of them, for instance, contains the lines: "And he hears the voice / of his grateful people: 'We have come / to say: Where Stalin is, there is freedom, / Peace and the greatness of our land.'"

Lev Gumilev was released in May 1956, two months or so after the Twentieth Party Congress, at which Khrushchev denounced Stalin in his secret speech. After this, Akhmatova began to benefit from the selective rehabilitation associated with the "thaw." She was under no illusions about the precarious nature of this improvement in her conditions (in the second half of the 1950's she remarked to Mrs. Mandelstam that there are good Caesars and bad Caesars; she was lucky to have lived to see a good one), but it did mean that she was able to spend her last years in relative serenity with even a modicum of carefully calculated official recognition. Twenty-two of her poems were republished in an anthology of Soviet poetry which appeared in 1958, and three years later, in 1961, a volume of her verse came out with an afterward by Alexei Surkov, then the secretary of the Union of Writers. Even better, a major new edition of her work, in the preparation of which she had some say, *The Flight of Time*, was published in 1965 with a Modigliani portrait of her on the cover. She was restored to membership in the Union of Writers, and at its congress in 1964 she was even elected to the presidium.[1]

In the same year she was allowed to travel abroad for the first time in half a century; the occasion was the award to her of the Etna-Taormina prize in Sicily. In her letter of acceptance to Giancarlo Vigorelli, written in Italian, she expressed her joy at

[1]This election, one among many others, was purely nominal and honorific, but it has given rise to the misconception that she ended her days as president of the Union of Writers. The idea seems to originate with a misunderstanding based on the use of the word *présidente* in the excellent study of Akhmatova by Jeanne Rude.

receiving this distinction from a country "which I have loved tenderly all my life," particularly as she was about to undertake a translation of Leopardi into Russian and would now have the opportunity "of immersing myself in the Italian language and seeing the house in which the great poet lived and worked." In her autobiographical note she mentions something that must have given her the greatest pleasure of all—that the prize was awarded to her "on the eve of Dante's anniversary."

In June 1965 she was allowed abroad a second time and traveled to England and France. She received the honorary degree of D.Litt. at Oxford and was able to meet old friends in London and Paris.

When she died the following year on March 5, it was in the consciousness of having fulfilled her destiny. She could feel that, with Osip Mandelstam, Boris Pasternak, and Marina Tsvetayeva, she had—in the words of her wartime poem "Courage"—preserved "Russian speech" and kept it "pure and free." It was something she had set out to do when she first joined Mandelstam and Gumilev in the Poets' Guild in 1912. She could scarcely have envisaged how hard the going would be, but she never flinched and would not have wished her life to be otherwise: "If I could step outside myself / and contemplate the person that I am, / I should know at last what envy is."

6

It was Max Hayward's devotion to Pasternak that first led him to take an interest in Andrei Sinyavsky (in his guise as a Soviet literary critic). Hayward had been struck by Sinyavsky's critical review in Novy Mir (No. 3, 1962) of a bowdlerized Soviet edition of Pasternak's verse and deeply impressed by Sinyavsky's introduction to a more acceptable edition of Pasternak (Poems, Moscow-Leningrad, 1965). It seemed plain to Hayward that Sinyavsky shared the same values as Pasternak. The fact that Sinyavsky had been one of the pallbearers at the poet's funeral appeared to have been a symbolic act of great importance. "There could have been no clearer public confession of faith," Hayward wrote.

At the same time, he was mesmerized by an underground, pseudonymous Russian writer, Abram Tertz, whose fiction he had begun to translate. It was not until Sinyavsky was arrested in 1965 that the two writers were revealed to be one and the same. Hayward's concern for Sinyavsky was such that he devoted a year to helping gather signatures of protest against the harsh sentences given Sinyavsky and his codefendant Yuli Daniel, and to collaborating with Leopold Labedz on a book about the case, On Trial (London: Collins and Harvill Press, 1967).

"A Voice from the Chorus" was Hayward's introduction to Sinyavsky's book of that name (London: Collins and Harvill Press; New York: Farrar, Straus & Giroux, 1976). This dense, contrapuntal piece of writing provided him with one of his greatest challenges as a translator.

"Pushkin, Gogol, and the Devil" is Hayward's review of two of Sinyavsky's books that had appeared in Russian in the West, following the author's emigration (Times Literary Supplement, May 28, 1976). The review illustrates how deeply grounded Hayward was in Russia's nineteenth century, though he could scarcely ever be brought to write about its authors. The review also tells us that he regarded Russian literature as "a single enterprise in which no one writer can be separated from another. . . . A later generation consciously takes up the motifs of its predecessors, responds to them, echoes them, and sometimes consummates them in the light of the intervening historical experience." It was the mark of Hayward's generosity, and of his vision, that he could discern so much in Soviet literature that belongs to this "single enterprise," in spite of the continual, forcible attempts to atomize it.

He had been thrilled by the appearance of Alexander Solzhenitsyn's One Day in the Life of Ivan Denisovich in the Soviet Union in 1962. He set out to translate it, regarding it as a literary masterpiece. This assessment was questioned by Victor Erlich, who pleaded for "a viable balance between literary and political considerations" in making critical judgments. In an exchange in the Slavic Review (XXIII, No. 3, September 1964), Hayward concurred with Erlich about the need for balance, adding what might be termed his credo as a critic of contemporary Russian literature. He argued that man's situation in his society—his relation to the polis—was eminently fit material for literary exploration, disputing the view that "any emphasis on the political context in which works of literature may be produced is somehow vulgar and unworthy of a serious student of literature."

In 1975 the publishers Little, Brown asked Hayward to write an introduction to From under the Rubble, a collection of provocative essays on Russia's present and future, edited by Solzhenitsyn, who also provided three of the essays (London: Collins and Harvill Press; Boston: Little, Brown, 1975). Hayward's introduction traces the ideas expressed by Solzhenitsyn and his colleagues back to the contributors to Vekhi (Landmarks), published in 1909. By so doing he was quite consciously attempting to disabuse Solzhenitsyn's critics of the view that his ideas represent some bizarre anomaly in Russian intellectual history.

Hayward was disappointed when Solzhenitsyn decided to cut down his essay to a few pages in From under the Rubble. His text is published here in full for the first time. —ED.

Sinyavsky's
<u>A Voice from the Chorus</u>

For spring, my child, you'll wait—
You'll find it lies.
You'll call out for the sun to rise—
It will not rise.
When you begin to cry, your cries
will sink like lead . . .

Then be content with life today,
Stiller than water, lower than grass.
Oh children, if you only knew
The cold and gloom of days ahead!
(From Alexander Blok's "A Voice from the Chorus,"
February 1914)

Few writers, in this or any other age, can have had such a bizarre literary career as Andrei Sinyavsky, otherwise known as Abram Tertz, the author of *A Voice from the Chorus*. A decade has now gone by since the trial in Moscow at which he and his fellow defendant, Yuli Daniel (Nikolai Arzhak), attracted worldwide attention; it may, therefore, be helpful to give here some account of the events, and of the background to them.

Until his arrest in the autumn of 1965, Andrei Donatovich Sinyavsky was known only as a teacher and writer who, though still young, had already established a modest reputation in Moscow literary and academic circles. As a member of the Gorky Institute of World Literature (a dependency of the Academy of

Sciences of the Soviet Union), he had published a number of scholarly essays and studies on modern Russian writers and poets —contributing, for instance, signed chapters on Maxim Gorky and Eduard Bagritsky to a three-volume history of Soviet Russian literature published by the Academy in 1958. The range and depth of his learning was demonstrated in *The Poetry of the Revolutionary Era* (1964; written together with A. Menshutin), the first work in the field after Stalin's death to revive many forgotten or suppressed names of the early years of the new epoch.

Even more significant was Sinyavsky's lengthy introduction to a selection of Pasternak's poetry that came out in 1965; it was passed by the censors for publication only three months or so before Sinyavsky and Daniel were arrested. Nothing better has ever been written on the nature and sense of Pasternak's work: it is illuminating in the precise meaning of the word. The achievement was all the more impressive in that Sinyavsky was unable even to mention, let alone discuss, many of the poems included in *Doctor Zhivago*, particularly the religious ones, which—together with the novel itself—are still under a ban in the Soviet Union. Although the mere fact of the publication of this new and somewhat fuller selection marked a further stage in the gingerly process of rehabilitation that had been going on since his death in 1960, Pasternak's unprecedented act of defiance in having deliberately published *Doctor Zhivago* abroad, and the consequent award of the Nobel Prize to him in 1957, had still not been forgotten or forgiven by the Soviet authorities, least of all by the rancorous, backward-looking literary establishment associated with them. Sinyavsky had already given public proof of his allegiance to Pasternak at a time when it was decidedly even less healthy to do so. At Pasternak's funeral in May 1960, which was attended—despite the best efforts of the authorities to head them off—by many members of Moscow's liberal intelligentsia, he and Yuli Daniel had played a conspicuous part as pallbearers—there is a photograph which shows them leaving Pasternak's house with the coffin. The policemen later involved in the investigation of their "crime" must have been struck at how the pair thus boldly associated themselves, at his death, with the great poet who had shown them the way. In the light of the revelations to come, it was indeed a breathtaking gesture.

Side by side with his scholarly publications Sinyavsky wrote articles and reviews for a much wider audience in *Novy Mir*, the monthly literary journal which, under the editorship of Alexander Tvardovsky, became the chief forum and rallying point for the liberal intelligentsia during the Khrushchev years. Sinyavsky made his first appearance in this journal in 1962 with a strongly critical review of an unrepresentative and biased volume of Pasternak's verse (some of it actually tampered with!) that had come out a couple of years after the poet's death and could only be seen as a preliminary step, now that he was out of harm's way, in a familiar process of falsely making him out to have been, despite everything, a loyal son of the age. This attempt to protect Pasternak's memory from a posthumous affront naturally did nothing to endear Sinyavsky to the more retrograde section of the literary community—which in those years, thanks in part to Khrushchev's erratic policies, was somewhat on the defensive. Even worse from this point of view were other subsequent articles in *Novy Mir*, where Sinyavsky wrote with a gentle but nonetheless devastating irony about some of the shoddy literary products of several conservative or neo-Stalinist writers. In other articles written at this time Sinyavsky left no doubt where his sympathies lay by his very choice of subject: Anna Akhmatova, Isaac Babel, and other such authentic representatives of Russian literature who had been silenced or persecuted, and could be partially restored to their rightful place only in the post-Stalin years.

In the first half of the 1960's—indeed, until the time when Sinyavsky's and Daniel's arrest and trial precipitated an abrupt change in the climate—there was nothing unusual in such a display of liberal sentiment. The process set off by Stalin's death and the revelations about him at the Twentieth Party Congress in 1956 had affected most intellectuals of Sinyavsky's generation in much the same way: disillusionment, not to say disaffection, was all but universal. In this respect Sinyavsky could scarcely be said in those years to have stood out particularly among the many other young scholars and writers who hastened to express themselves in cautiously worded (and often heavily censored) articles written for learned periodicals, for *Novy Mir,* and for certain other journals where liberal influence predominated. But in Sinyavsky's case there were some special features.

First of all, there was the circumstance—later to prove fateful —that in 1947, as a student at Moscow University, he had become acquainted with Hélène Pelletier, the daughter of an attaché at the French embassy, who by way of a diplomatic courtesy had been given permission to attend courses in Russian literature. In the late Stalin years, when truly fantastic measures were taken to isolate the Soviet population from corrupting outside influences, and when the few Westerners resident in Moscow as diplomats or newspapermen were treated as pariahs (even though materially privileged ones), this was a very rare concession, granted to only one or two other foreigners; it would certainly have been unthinkable a year or so later, when the last of the token goodwill generated by the wartime alliance had vanished.

In an account of her meetings with Sinyavsky in those days, Hélène Pelletier (later, by marriage, Zamoyska) recalls that he seemed to share the basic articles of faith to be expected at that time in one of his age and background: "The son of an active revolutionary, he shared his family's cult of the Revolution . . . he belonged to the Komsomol and was, needless to say, an atheist." Although curious about the outside world and relatively open-minded, he was not impressed (nor is he still!) by any claims on behalf of Western humanism and its institutions. He believed in a kind of ideal communism (whose remoteness from Stalinist practice, however, was certainly dawning on him already then) and felt that Christianity had nothing to offer: "Christianity has been going downhill ever since the Renaissance, ever since it made personal salvation the only thing that mattered. Modern Christianity is individualist; communism is concerned with the good of mankind, so its moral meaning is higher." With all this, he was already delving into virtually forbidden areas of the Soviet past, particularly the literature of the 1920's, which would inevitably raise fundamental doubts in his mind. But, as in the case of many younger Russian intellectuals, it was a sudden personal confrontation with an act of arbitrary injustice that first really jolted him: in 1951 his father—whom he several times fondly recalls in *A Voice from the Chorus*—was arrested on a trumped-up charge; though released after the end of the Stalin terror in 1953, he died shortly afterward.

Khrushchev's secret speech on Stalin at the Twentieth Congress demolished the very foundations of the beliefs on which Sinyavsky and his contemporaries had been reared. Many of them, however, had become emotionally and intellectually dependent on faith in an all-embracing system of values of the kind that communism claimed to be. The only alternative to despair or cynicism was to set about immediately on the search for a substitute. But what? And where to begin looking? The collapse of the old had been as total as its continuing pretension to undivided predominance; only a small minority felt able to try and salvage something from the debris—it was easier to return to "pure" Marxism in the West, far away from the inescapable evidence of what an impure form had wrought in practice. There was no question at that moment of fruitful contacts with the external world. Russia was still effectively sealed off, and the "half-men" —as Osip Mandelstam once called them—who inherited Stalin's power were determined to keep it so. Any hope of spiritual renewal could only come from an internal source, from somewhere close at hand.

It may seem barely credible, but it is a literal fact that in the period after Stalin's death—and as a consequence of his vast depredations—there was only a single figure alive in the whole of the Soviet Union who enjoyed any wide measure of genuine authority and to whom at least some section of the educated or thinking community could look for guidance in their sudden perplexity, and who could serve, if only in silence, as a moral exemplar—and hence as a potential source of alternative values. This solitary figure was Pasternak. The reason for Pasternak's lonely eminence was that he was the only indisputably great poet of his generation who had lived through and survived the whole of the Soviet era on his own terms: he had made no concessions of principle and had never yielded to the blandishments, intimidation, or direct coercion that had led almost everybody else to various degrees of compromise, of which the least was to lie low in the usually vain hope of being spared. But Pasternak made no effort to bargain for his life, even on these minimal conditions.

Already during the war, as Pasternak confided to friends, he had determined to speak out if the Stalin regime continued unchanged after victory over the Germans. It was at this time that *Doctor Zhivago* was conceived at least partly as something which would place his own age in the perspective of the whole Christian era and, beyond that, of eternity. In this light the Soviet epoch, with its Great Leader ruling over the anonymous masses, was seen in effect as a reversal to Imperial Rome where "you had blood and beastliness and cruelty, and pockmarked[1] Caligulas untouched by the suspicion that any man who enslaves others is inevitably second-rate." In the late 1940's, at the height of the postwar terror, Pasternak gave draft chapters of the novel to friends and acquaintances—an act of unimaginable courage, not to say foolhardiness, in those years. When copies inevitably found their way into the hands of the secret police, Pasternak was subjected to unspeakable tribulations, the full story of which is still to be told.

It was a strange, largely silent duel between the "pockmarked Caligula" and the poet, who even perpetrated unheard-of acts of public defiance: on one occasion in 1948, for instance, at a poetry reading in Moscow's largest auditorium (to which he had only been invited in the expectation or on the understanding that he would demonstrate his loyalty), he explicitly dissociated himself from the other poets present and the propaganda topic ("Down with the Warmongers!") to which, according to the advertised program, they were all supposed to address themselves. It was this —his last public appearance in the Stalin years—that showed the packed audience of Moscow intellectuals in the hall that he had not surrendered. If Stalin's hand was stayed in this unique instance, it was partly because he undoubtedly planned a sweeter revenge than mere physical removal of the rebellious poet would

---

[1] Stalin's face was pockmarked.—ED.

have afforded, calculating that by a combination of unbearable pressures he could still force him to sing his praises in verse—as he had forced Akhmatova to, by using her son as a hostage.

When Zamoyska (the former Hélène Pelletier) returned to Russia after Stalin's death and renewed her contact with Sinyavsky, she learned that, like other leading dissidents of the future, he had found his way to Pasternak's house in the writer's colony at Peredelkino near Moscow. He read *Doctor Zhivago* in manuscript and was particularly struck by the religious poems, though at that time he did not agree with all of Pasternak's ideas. As Zamoyska writes, Sinyavsky "was even more impressed by him as a person than as a writer." This was not surprising, for if freedom from convention and affectation is unusual in the West, it was rarer in the Soviet Union so soon after Stalin's death. There was no prudence in Pasternak, not the slightest attempt at evasion or concession to political expediency and conventional jargon. The fear of what others might think, distrust, and the terror fostered by Stalinism seemed to have passed him by, leaving him as full as ever of enjoyment of life and of confidence in his fellow men. Pasternak's courage in sending his manuscript abroad, his deep conviction that he had a perfect right to do so, as well as a positive duty to "bear witness to his time"—none of this did anything but enhance his reputation and stimulate others to follow his example. Certainly Sinyavsky was influenced by the example of a man he admired as "a great patriot and a great poet."

Thus inspired by the way Pasternak had acted in defiance of all the taboos, Sinyavsky now asked Zamoyska to arrange for the appearance of his own work abroad. Not being protected by the fame that Pasternak enjoyed both in Russia and the outside world, Sinyavsky knew of course that his attempt to publish free of censorship would immediately be cut short if he did so under his own name. He therefore chose the pen name "Abram Tertz," the hero of an underworld ballad in the tradition of the romantic Jewish freebooters of the Moldavanka, the thieves' quarter of Odessa immortalized in the early stories of Isaac Babel. Ballads like the one about Abram Tertz became popular in Moscow after Stalin's death, partly, perhaps, because the criminal underworld had achieved a certain autonomy unique in Soviet society, and also because of the extraordinary fact that under Stalin there was honor *only* among thieves: their peculiar "law" emphasized loyalty to each other as the supreme virtue. As Sinyavsky shows in his account of them in *A Voice from the Chorus,* they constituted a kind of chivalry which contrasted very favorably in some respects with the rest of society. The choice of this pseudonym was also appropriate, needless to say, in its implied allusion to the way in which the untrammeled exercise of the writer's craft is regarded in official Soviet circles.

The first Abram Tertz manuscript, an essay entitled *On Socialist Realism,* was printed in the French literary journal *Esprit* in February 1959, and was followed shortly afterward in 1960 by a short novel, *The Trial Begins,* published in the original Russian in the Paris émigré Polish journal *Kultura* (and a little later in English translation in *Encounter*). A collection of five stories under the general title *Fantastic Stories* came out in Paris the next year and was soon translated into the major Western languages. Another short novel, *Lyubimov,* appeared in 1964 (in English translation as *The Makepeace Experiment,* 1965). *Unguarded Thoughts,* a small book of notes and reflections—a kind of inner monologue almost in diary form—was published in America a few months before the arrest of the author, and a final story, "Pkhentz," appeared in *Encounter* in 1966, a month after his trial.

The stylistic accomplishment of Sinyavsky's writings, and the unusual literary culture patently lying behind them, led one or two Western specialists in Russian literature to surmise that Abram Tertz must surely be an émigré pretending to write from inside the country. In its very few references to the matter before the truth came out, the Soviet press did what it could to foster this view of the shadowy Tertz as a "white émigré bandit of the pen," and it seems possible that the Soviet authorities may actually have believed this themselves for a time. It did indeed seem well-nigh incredible not only that any living Soviet author should possess this degree of literary sophistication, but that—even more unaccountably—he should also have the ingenuity to evade detection for so long (nearly five years by the end of his clandestine career) in a country where police informers are as numerous and inconspicuously ever-present as sparrows.

In *On Socialist Realism,* after showing up official literary doctrine for the poor, hollow thing it is, Tertz-Sinyavsky concluded that realism of any stripe, whether genuine or pretended, was inadequate as a means of representing the improbable present, and he invoked Hoffmann, Dostoyevsky, Goya, and Chagall as necessary teachers in the creation of a "phantasmagoric art" to replace it. What he meant is illustrated by some of the stories he composed during the following years in the precarious secrecy of his Moscow apartment, ever mindful of the Draconian penalties he would incur if found out. In the *Fantastic Stories* the familiar surface of everyday life is often suddenly shattered and then reassembled in the manner of surrealist painting. In one of them ("The Icicle"), for example, the tramcars racing along a Moscow street are transformed by the fantasy of a bystander into mammoths charging through a prehistoric canyon. Time and place are no longer stable categories to be taken for granted: in *The Makepeace Experiment* a small Russian provincial town suddenly slips into a different dimension and becomes the scene of occult happenings. Sinyavsky's phantasmagorias are disciplined, tightly constructed narratives which never descend to mere whimsicality and are always geared to the serious purpose of conveying, by unexpected dislocations and shifts of focus, the otherwise unimaginable quality of life in the Soviet era, at the same time commenting, with a profundity lightly disguised by humor, on its ideological assumptions.

The only modern Russian writing to compare in this use of comic inventiveness as a means of bringing home the deadly earnest, is that of Mikhail Bulgakov, whose *The Master and Margarita* (published in Moscow in 1966–67, twenty-seven years after the author's death) also depicts Soviet "reality" as something surely conjured up by a magician with the power and genius of Satan himself. This is as much as to say that Sinyavsky belongs in the Gogolian tradition of Russian literature—a debt of affinity handsomely acknowledged by him in a brilliant study of Gogol written in the forced-labor camp. As in Gogol's tales of the Ukraine and Petersburg, nightmare constantly obtrudes; in Sinyavsky's stories, however, it takes the form not of the phantom emanations of the subconscious (these, like other Gogolian devices, are sometimes wittily parodied—the strange bird, for example, in *The Makepeace Experiment*), but of the hallucinatory mental disorders endemic in a populace ruled for decades by fear and mutual distrust: there can be no more telling study in modern literature of what by understatement must be called paranoia than "You and I," one of the *Fantastic Stories*.

The special conditions that made such obsessive terrors so all-pervasive are given the sharp immediacy of a bad dream in *The Trial Begins*, where the leaden oppressiveness of Stalin's last years receives its literary deserts in a fashion unlikely ever to be rivaled —unless, as may be hoped, by Abram Tertz himself in his new incarnation. Perhaps the most affecting of the stories is "Pkhentz," the last of them. To some extent inspired by the author's own situation, it is about a being from another planet, the sole survivor of a spaceship that had crash-landed on Earth some years previously in the wilds of Siberia, who now lives in a Moscow communal apartment—that is, sharing a kitchen and bathroom with other tenants. Since his biology and metabolism are nonhuman, this involves elaborate disguise and constant vigilance, and hope is sustained only by the dream of one day meeting another creature similar to himself, or of an eventual return to the nostalgically remembered culture from which he has been separated with such finality.

Unguarded Thoughts is in a very different vein from the stories —so much so that it was at first believed by some people to have surely come from another pen than Abram Tertz's. In form—and to a lesser extent in substance—it is the precursor of *A Voice from the Chorus*, consisting of the author's ideas and musings on a variety of topics, and written down just as they came to him; the mode of expression thus tends to the aphoristic, and the book has no preconceived structure except the loose one imposed by the recurrence of certain dominant themes. If *The Trial Begins* and *Fantastic Stories* often show preoccupation with the consequences of loss of faith in Soviet Marxism as a debased product of Western humanism (itself transplanted to Russia, it should always be borne in mind, in a predigested form, and in such an imperious way as to provoke enduring social, cultural, and psychological distress), *Unguarded Thoughts* is largely the record of how Sinyavsky came to find himself under the spell of the God so rudely ousted in the few years before he was born to make way for the new idols which he and his generation were brought up to worship.

Perhaps the key to Sinyavsky's new sense of the world (if it is a sense rather than a view) is to be found in the following passage: "I never know what liberal philosophers mean by the 'freedom of choice' they are always talking about. Do we really choose whom to love, what to believe in, what illness to suffer? Love (like any other strong feeling) is a monarch, a despot, who dominates us from within, capturing us to the last remnant and forbidding us to glance back. How can we think of freedom when we are *swallowed whole,* when we see nothing, are aware of nothing except the One who chose us and, having chosen, torments us or bestows favors on us? The moment we wish to free ourselves (whether from sin or from God), we are already swayed by a new ruler who whispers about liberation only until the day we have totally surrendered to him." The words about being "swallowed whole" are perhaps especially significant: they suggest that Sinyavsky's theology is intimately related to his artistic perception of things, indeed as his aesthetics already summed up in *On Socialist Realism,* where he wrote of the rapture we may feel at "the metamorphoses of God taking place before our eyes, at the giant peristalsis of His viscera, at the convolutions of His brain."

Sinyavsky's dual existence came to an end in September 1965 when he was arrested. The KGB had possibly picked up the scent because of an indiscretion in the West and had soon been able through a little detective work, aided by the installation of listening devices which monitored conversations in Sinyavsky's apartment, to gather all the evidence they needed. At the same time they arrested Yuli Daniel, whose manuscripts had also been smuggled out of the country by the same channels. For several months the two were held in almost solitary confinement, seeing no one except their interrogators, stool pigeons put in the same cells with them, and material witnesses occasionally brought in for a confrontation. In these post-Stalin times, no physical brutality was used, but the usual array of sometimes even more effective torments was deployed in full—playing on the prisoner's anxiety about his family, hints at supposed betrayal by friends, and so forth. Each of them could have made things easier for himself— and received a shorter sentence when the case came to trial—by admitting that what he had done was wrong, and by indicating willingness to express public repentance. But neither yielded.

The three-day trial which eventually took place in February 1966 was unique in Russian history: neither under the czars nor even under Stalin had there ever been proceedings in which the main corpus delicti consisted of the actual contents of works of imaginative literature. The trial was hopelessly prejudiced by vituperative and grossly misleading articles in the press, and reports from the courtroom (to which access was severely restricted) were meager and flagrantly biased.[2] The verdicts—seven years for Sinyavsky and five for Daniel—provoked a storm of protest in the outside world which, for a case of this kind, was unprecedented in its intensity and in the degree of unanimity between communists and noncommunists alike. The result of the trial also gave rise to the first widespread and organized protests in Russia itself: this was the beginning of large-scale dissidence and *samizdat*. But it did not help. Sinyavsky and Daniel were sent off to forced labor camps, and both served their sentences almost to the end.

The area to which they were sent is about three hundred miles due east of Moscow, near a small town called Potma, at a junction of the main railway line from Moscow to Kuibyshev. On both sides of a branch line (not marked on the maps) running off north from Potma for about thirty miles are the numerous camps and other installations of the extensive "corrective labor colony"—to

---

[2] A proper record was made by Sinyavsky's wife and several friends who afterward collated their notes; no one person was allowed to attend all the sessions of the court.

use the official term—which is still called by the code name *Dubrovlag* ("oak-forest camp") assigned to it in 1947, the year when Stalin personally ordered the establishment of special camps with bucolic and geographically anonymous designations such as *Ozerlag* ("lake camp") and *Rechlag* ("river camp"). All political prisoners were to be concentrated in these camps with a view to their speedy murder in the event of a new war.

After the winding down in the post-Stalin years of many of the much larger and remoter camp complexes of the Gulag in the far north and east, Dubrovlag remained as one of the major camp areas for all categories of prisoners, including political ones.[3] It has certain advantages. It is conveniently situated for receiving convicted prisoners from the big Moscow jails, where people are held only during their interrogation and trial. Moreover, it is an old, established camp complex with about fifteen subcamps of the familiar kind: barracks surrounded by compounds with searchlights, watchtowers, and forbidden zones round the perimeter, all administered by experienced personnel and located in a region where the population has long been schooled in mistrust toward the occasional escapee. Last but not least, Dubrovlag has an industry in which the prisoners can be productively employed: a furniture factory, served by its own sawmill, foundry, etc.

The exploitation of prison labor in the economy thus continues, though it is now a question of consumer goods rather than of such primary industries as mining and lumbering; the railway brings fuel and other materials—together with prisoners—to the stations along the Potma branch line. Back to Moscow go the products of the factory, such as cabinets for television sets, to be sold in the capital's shops at a profit to the state. A pittance is paid to the prisoners from which they can supplement their meager rations by purchasing extras in the camp store.

Sinyavsky and Daniel—kept apart from each other in different

---

[3]There are still many other camps throughout the country; those of Dubrovlag are simply the ones about which most is known. As in the past, there is no official information about the scope of the Soviet penal system.

camps because they had been "accomplices"—were put to work at the various kinds of manual jobs mentioned in *A Voice from the Chorus*. Estimates of how many prisoners there were in Dubrovlag in the 1960's vary, but the lowest puts the total at about fifteen thousand. The majority were common criminals and persons convicted of white-collar offenses, but there were also many prisoners sentenced for alleged anti-Soviet activities, including nationalists from non-Russian minorities (such as Ukrainians—a large and growing category) and members of religious sects, including one thought to be extinct until Sinyavsky encountered representatives of it among his fellow prisoners. Although common criminals no longer virtually run the camps, as they did at times in the Stalin years, the politicals are by no means segregated from the others, so that a Jewish intellectual, for example, may well find himself rubbing shoulders with anti-Semitic Russians who were sentenced many years ago for collaborating with the Nazis during the war. As we see from his book, Sinyavsky came to know a motley range of humanity, and the contact is reflected in numerous ways, though he attempts no systematic account of his fellow inmates, nor indeed of any other aspect of the camp and his life there.[4]

As already indicated, *A Voice from the Chorus* is not a descriptive narrative in the ordinary sense and is based almost entirely on the lengthy letters written by the author to his wife Maria twice a month—all that was allowed under the regulations. The contents of all letters were examined by the camp authorities, and any detail or comment thought to be too outspoken could result in a letter not being passed, and in the writer being put in the punishment cells into the bargain. This is, therefore, not just another book about the camps, written after the prisoner's release, but a record of the author's own inner preoccupations as he actually noted them down during his long sojourn in the "house of the dead." The title is borrowed from the poem by Alexander

---

[4]Important descriptions of Dubrovlag written by prisoners who were there in the mid-1960's include Anatoli Marchenko's *My Testimony* and Mykhaylo Osadchy's *Cataract.*

Blok quoted earlier here. Written not long before the outbreak of the First World War, these are some of Blok's most cheerless lines, full of characteristic foreboding of the horrors to come, "the cold and gloom of days ahead." Blok put "A Voice from the Chorus" as the first item in an anthology of his work which he published the year before his death,[5] when he had already understood that his own cries would indeed "sink like lead," and that his poet's voice would be drowned out by the rising din of the postrevolutionary "chorus."

As a child of the Revolution and a Russian intellectual, Sinyavsky was fated to endure in actual fact what Blok and some of his contemporaries had only foreseen and summoned forth in apocalyptic premonitions, not, for the most part, living to see them come to pass in full. In choosing his title, Sinyavsky may also have had in mind the reference to a similar poem of Blok's by a surviving friend of Yuri Zhivago in the epilogue to Pasternak's novel: "A thing which has been conceived in a lofty, ideal manner becomes coarse and material. Thus Rome came out of Greece, and the Russian revolution came out of the Russian enlightenment. Take that line of Blok's: 'We, the children of Russia's terrible years'—you can see the difference of period at once. In his time, when he said it, he meant it figuratively, metaphorically . . . now the figurative has become literal, the children are children, and the terrors are terrible."

The chorus which Sinyavsky himself supplies at certain points in his book as a background to his own voice is picked out of the general hubbub around him in the bleak, overcrowded barracks, the camp compound, or the factory to which the prisoners were taken out under escort for the daily grind of "corrective" labor. The chorus serves at most times as a confused demotic counterpoint to the author's silent thoughts on art, literature, the human condition, and many other topics. Since most of the chorus sentences (given in italics in the English translation) are devoid of

---

[5]I am indebted for this detail, as well as for the translation of the poem, to Sergei Hackel's *The Poet and the Revolution* (Oxford, 1975).

specific context, representing isolated snatches of talk which invaded the author's ears from the surrounding Babel, their individual import is frequently left to the imagination, though it can generally be inferred from its connection with neighboring phrases, or from the reflections sometimes set in train by them. The meaning of what the chorus says is, however, of less concern than its tone or flavor; in vocabulary and phonetic coloring, it vividly echoes the submerged vernacular of the Russian lower depths into which the author was cast; it is a speech abounding in malapropisms, non sequiturs, grotesquely garbled forms, pathetically inadequate attempts at "educated" parlance, slang words from the criminal underworld, camp jargon, etc. To a Russian ear (and, alas, in all the nuances *only* to a Russian ear) this verbal flotsam and jetsam evokes—not with condescension, always with compassion and wonderment—a whole world in which language mirrors a desolation of the spirit such as is everywhere closer, perhaps, to the essence of society at large than may be readily avowed.

With the difference, then, that his voice is no longer unaccompanied, Sinyavsky now continues in much the same manner as in *Unguarded Thoughts*. But we see a distinct shift of emphasis in the burden of his meditations: there the main themes were God and Christianity. By the time he arrived in Dubrovlag, this matter had been settled. As a believing Russian Orthodox Christian, he could now pass on to other subjects, secure in a faith which embraced all else (including art, the other redeeming link that besides his religion means most to him) and made him in the core of his being invulnerable to the ordeal ahead. As he had written before his arrest in *Unguarded Thoughts*: "Truly Christian feelings are against human nature, they are abnormal, paradoxical. You are beaten, and you rejoice. Misfortunes shower on you, and you are happy. Instead of running away from death, you are attracted to it and assume its likeness in advance. To any normal, healthy person it seems mad . . . but here everything is in reverse —unnatural, say the humanists; supernatural, say the Christians . . . we don't overcome our nature—it is replaced by some other, unfamiliar nature which teaches us how to be ill, suffer and die, and relieves us of the obligation to fear and hate."

The predominant theme in *A Voice from the Chorus,* the theme from which nothing distracts the author for long, is art in all its forms. It was the subject of many of the books he ordered from home (two packages a year, under the regulations), or borrowed from fellow prisoners. Apart from miniature essays on the general nature of art, literature, myths, and folklore, we find vignettes devoted to an astonishingly wide range of individual writers, artists, works, and styles: Swift and Defoe, Akhmatova, Rembrandt's *Prodigal Son,* Hamlet, Hogarth, Stevenson's *Dr. Jekyll and Mr. Hyde,* Matisse, Kipling, and Javanese shadow theater, Mandelstam, the Irish legend of Cuchulainn (inspired by the perusal of a rare work by Alexander Smirnov, the only Russian Celtic scholar), Yoshida Kenko and early Japanese painting, the myths of Oceania, Russian church architecture, and many others which the reader may browse among at will; as the author himself emphasizes, his book is not the usual purposeful affair that progresses in one direction to a final destination. There is no lack of topics of a different kind: the code of the Russian criminal underworld, the theory of evolution, the importance of the Holy Ghost for the Russian national character, the reason for the ten years' war over Helen of Troy (what an illumination to come from Dubrovlag!), and—particularly dear to the heart of Abram Tertz —a great deal on magic and fairy-tale transformations, which are assigned no less credibility and certainly not held in lower esteem than all the monkey tricks of the prideful technology they anticipated.

There is an element of what can almost be called drama in the contrast between the scholarly, contemplative nature of these notes and the circumstances in which they were written. But the truth is that Sinyavsky—at one point he says as much—did not really think of himself as being under the constraint normally implied by such circumstances. In a word, he remained beyond the reach of his judges and jailors, and in a vital sense it is perhaps they, rather than he, who were and are in the captive state.

During his time in the camp, he managed to write a superbly original essay on Pushkin, now published in Russian in the West.[6] Here he quotes what Pushkin remarked in 1836 about Silvio Pellico's account of his prison life: "Silvio Pellico spent ten years in various dungeons and, when he was released, he published his notes. There was general astonishment: people were expecting bitter complaints, but instead they read touching reflections full of serenity, love, and benevolence." The same could be said of Sinyavsky's letters *de profundis.*

Pushkin, Gogol, and the Devil

During his six years in the Dubrovlag forced labor camp, to which he was sent in 1966 for his stories published abroad under the pen name "Abram Tertz," Andrei Sinyavsky wrote long letters home to his wife which form the basis of his *A Voice from the Chorus.* He also managed, in his first two years, to complete a study of Pushkin and then to do the preliminary work for a much lengthier book on Gogol which he began to write in the camp, but finished only after his release. Both these works have now been published in Russian in London under his subversive pseudonym.

Walks with Pushkin is a literary study par excellence, being least of all concerned with Pushkin's life as such, but rather with his poetic nature in its deepest essence. It assumes the familiarity with Pushkin's work of most educated Russians, and much of it is concerned to overthrow the commonplace notions that often

---

[6] *Walks with Pushkin* (London, 1975).

accompany this familiarity. In this sense it is a revolutionary study, one which, by exploring deeper layers and recesses, challenges accepted ideas and preconceptions. Pushkin's place is unique: for the Russians he is a dominating presence, all-encompassing and all-pervasive, the creator not only of their literature, but of the national consciousness, the measure of all things. Needless to say, there has always been a good deal of contention about how to interpret a figure so universal and many-sided, and a natural tendency to emphasize one aspect at the expense of others. Perhaps most commonly and insistently he has been presented as a "progressive" poet, a friend of the Decembrist rebels of 1825, a foe of tyranny, a sympathizer with the common man, the first Russian realist, and a great Russian patriot. To some degree he was no doubt all of these and there is enough in his work to bolster such a view to the exclusion of all others, as of course happened in later Soviet times.

In a less blatant form, the same view of him was held by many liberals before the Revolution, though some more extreme radicals instinctively understood that, as a poet first and foremost, he was not ultimately on their side, and they execrated him as an irrelevance, or even a hindrance, on the path to social transformation. Pisarev, for instance, denounced him as "an obsolete idol." In the wake of the literary revival in the first decade and a half of this century, there was some attempt at a reinterpretation of Pushkin aimed at separating him from the progressive image established by the previous generations of critics. In his *Wisdom of Pushkin*, Mikhail Gershenzon even went to the opposite extreme of suggesting that in reality, imbued with aristocratic hauteur, he was an aesthete disdainful of what he correctly anticipated would be his posthumous fame as a supposed apostle of enlightenment. Sinyavsky is likewise concerned to free Pushkin from the incrustations of traditional criticism, but he does so without Gershenzon's polemical, not to say provocative, tone. He shows that Pushkin is beyond the reach of any partial standard of judgment: he cannot be seen as believing or standing for this, that, or the other, because he was a law unto himself. In this sense he was not only an aristocrat (which he was, of course, by descent), but a sovereign, conscious of the awesome distance between himself (as a poet) and ordinary mortals.

His fascination with Peter the Great (the subject of one of his greatest poems, *The Bronze Horseman,* and of several other works) was based not only on the fact that Pushkin's African ancestor had been Peter's godson, but also on the awareness that, like Peter, he was an elemental force, bringing a new universe into being. If Peter, single-handed, created modern Russia, Pushkin created her literature: he dictated its language and much of its subject matter, and he is omnipresent in it. He was chosen by fate and prepared by his very genealogy (a recurrent theme in his poetry, as Sinyavsky emphasizes) to perform this task. As an instrument of destiny, he was not strictly responsible for what he did, nor was he answerable to anyone. Pushkin's famous "secret freedom," therefore, did not consist in occasionally thumbing his nose at the czar (he was himself a czar!), but in a supreme lack of ordinary restraints in the pursuance of the task imposed on him by forces outside his own control. He was nobody's spokesman, he held no particular views pertaining to moral, political, or suchlike questions. Insofar as he touched on them it was because, as an overwhelming fount of poetic energy, he was bound to enter all the pores of the life around him. He impinged on everything and his overt opinions could be quite conventional on either side of the fence: liberals can point to his epistle of solace to the Decembrists in their Siberian exile, and conservatives to his denunciations of "Russia's slanderers."

He was much given to reproducing ideas and even clichés from the common stock of the times—in Anna Akhmatova's words, "he echoed every sound"—but this was never indicative of any overriding attachment or commitment, being incidental to his task as a demiurge. To create a poetic universe almost from scratch you have to take stock of all the materials at your disposal, to catalogue and muster them in Aristotelian fashion: *all* elements in Russian life and history, and in the world outside, had to be assembled and incorporated into his new poetic cosmos, much as Peter had to forge the new Russia out of everything that came to hand both inside and outside the country. All the accessories from surrounding reality in Pushkin's poetry thus formed the material of his art, bearing the same relation to it as bricks and blocks of masonry to a building. The crucial thing was the poetic urge, overpowering and involuntary, that imposed form and order on these materials. He was conscious of creating harmony out of chaos, out of the jumble of things around him. It was the act of creation that was all-important, and in this sense his work was *pure* art—as Sinyavsky puts it—because it was unattached, at the service only of itself ("the spirit moves where it will"). This is shown to account even for the apparent frivolity of much of Pushkin's subject matter: his anacreontic poems, his many light verses written for ladies' albums, his epigrams and satirical epistles to friends, and most particularly, his extensive digressions on the trivia of society life in his masterwork, the novel in verse *Eugene Onegin* (which led the contemporary critic Belinsky to describe it as an "encyclopedia of Russian life").

All this was a natural consequence of his declaration of *total* freedom, as the first Russian poet to claim complete independence and to exist in his own absolute right. At the same time it served as a kind of disguise for this freedom, and—more importantly—as a necessary concession to Pushkin's own human weakness. In one of the most interesting parts of his argument, Sinyavsky demonstrates that Pushkin was fully aware of the unavoidable duality of a poet as epoch-making (in the literal sense!) as himself: the instrument of destiny resided in a frail vessel and could thus be as humanly fallible and insignificant as any mortal. This he expressed in a famous poem which begins: "Until called by Apollo / to holy sacrifice the poet / is immersed, fainthearted, in the world's vain cares, / his lyre muted, his soul wrapped in sleep, / most worthless of all the worthless children of the world." In an original interpretation of *The Bronze Horseman*, Sinyavsky suggests that the "poor Eugene" who impotently threatens Peter's statue, when all he possesses has been swept away by the flood (a reminder that Peter's city had been created only by imposing order on the elements), is meant to stand for Pushkin's own sense of his worthlessness as an ordinary "child of the world" —that is, when not in the grip of inspiration, when not serving as an instrument (like Peter) of forces outside himself. Similarly, the eponymous hero of *Eugene Onegin* mirrors the trivial and frivolous side of Pushkin's own nonpoetic existence as a man about town.

Pushkin's reference to Apollo in the poem quoted above is not a mere figure of speech, but an indication of his belief that as a poet he was "possessed" and that his inspiration sprang from deep, elemental sources; when "called by Apollo," the poet runs —as he says in the final stanza of the same poem—"wild and stern / full of sound and tumult, / to the shores of desolate waves, / to broad-rustling groves." (It is significant that, in *The Bronze Horseman,* Peter, as he contemplates the founding of his city, stands sunk in thought "on the shores of desolate waves"— exactly the same phrase as in the Apollo poem. Sinyavsky points out that there could be no more cogent illustration of Pushkin's identification of himself with Peter as a fellow "maker," who contrived harmony out of the unbridled forces that possessed both him and nature.) Thus, the serene and classical surface of Pushkin's work is deceptive—harmony is only the counterpart of chaos.

Sinyavsky's essay goes far to explain the uncanny power that poets have exercised not only over the minds of the Russian nation, but also over the minds of even its most oppressive rulers. It was Pushkin who first created the aura of authority which surrounds them: Stalin hesitated to kill Mandelstam (and, on some slight evidence in Nadezhda Mandelstam's memoirs, may have had second thoughts about his death), and shrank from touching Pasternak and Akhmatova. It was thanks to Pushkin that the Word, embodied in poetry, became almost sacrosanct in the literal sense, evoking a feeling akin to religious awe: the poet is high priest, wielding a spiritual power equal to the czar's in the temporal domain. For this reason, in the Soviet period one or two poets were able to survive as the repositories of alternative values. It would have been impossible without Pushkin, the supreme legislator even in death: he laid it down that the spirit, whose voice he was, is *absolutely* free. Sinyavsky's general conclusion is that Pushkin's true significance lies here, and in reading the last pages of this remarkable essay one sees why Pushkin should have been the chosen companion in Sinyavsky's walks around the camp compound, because of the secret freedom bequeathed by the poet to all Russian writers. This is essentially a study of the spirit of Russian literature at its origins and, by implication, of what led Sinyavsky himself to court the fearful punishment that overtook him.

It has always been tempting to think of Gogol as Pushkin's antipode. In a way it is true: Gogol might well seem to have been the one who diverted Russian literature from the path of poetry to prose, which it was not to forsake until the end of the century ("we have all come from under Gogol's 'Greatcoat,' " in Dostoyevsky's celebrated phrase). At the same time, if Pushkin breathed life into the pagan forms borrowed by a previous generation, and established literature as a secular, autonomous realm in its own right, it might be argued that Gogol was the first to desecularize it again: after his comic masterpieces *The Inspector General* and *Dead Souls,* he renounced literature for preaching and prophecy in his *Selected Passages from a Correspondence with Friends,* which struck his contemporaries as the ravings of a crackpot suddenly afflicted with religious mania. In retrospect he thus seems to have initiated the tendency of leading Russian writers to remember, perhaps atavistically, their remoter origins in pre-Petrine times when, unless employed for ordinary practical purposes, the word was the word of God alone and its use for mere entertainment would have been a sinful perversion, to be denounced by the church together with the antics of wandering clowns and minstrels.

Ever since Gogol's day Western Europeans may be forgiven for thinking that in every major Russian writer there lurks a lay theologian. With Gogol himself the idea that literature for its own sake is sinful had a tragic outcome: he burnt most of the second part of *Dead Souls,* was overwhelmed by the horrors, and died miserably. Dostoyevsky had the good grace to keep literature and preaching in separate, if parallel, spheres; Tolstoy embarked on prophecy in a serious way only when he had finished with literature; Blok was tormented by a sense of the sheer depravity of his poetic calling, but fortunately he did not, or could not, bring himself to renounce it (nor, on the whole, did he try to "redeem" it by putting it at the service of a cause).

Gogol may indeed be regarded as the initiator of this trend. But at first sight it looks almost as though he was prompted by his older contemporary and friend, or that he virtually carried on at a point where Pushkin left off. Pushkin's genius was so all-embracing that it even seemed to contain the seeds of a later line of development inimical to literature in his conception of it. The fact is that Pushkin, even if he never played it himself, had anticipated the prophetic role of the Russian writer, and even, as it were, licensed it—in "The Prophet" ("And God's voice called out to me: / Arise, Prophet, and see and hear . . . / and burn with your Word the hearts of men"), and even more strikingly in a lesser-known poem, "The Wanderer," written only two years before his death. This draws a remarkable picture of a man overcome by indefinable anguish and suddenly haunted by a vision of the world's end—so much so that, appearing to take leave of his senses, he deserts his wife and family and goes off, in the tradition of the Russian religious wanderer, to prepare his soul for Doomsday and seek the salvation which he sees, in the form of an ineffable light, on the distant horizon. Pushkin could here almost have been describing, in a flash of premonition, Tolstoy's flight from home seventy-five years later. Gogol was profoundly affected by this poem, which appeared in the very year when (with Pushkin's encouragement) he was embarking on the first volume of *Dead Souls:* Pushkin, it might thus seem, gave Gogol his cue— as he had earlier supplied him with the theme of *The Inspector General.*

Pushkin himself, it could be said, launched Russian literature on the path of the "natural school," or of "realism"—whose paternity is imputed to Gogol in every textbook—with its inborn propensity to abjure belles-lettres for the serious business of saving one's soul and the world's. It looks, then, as though there was a single thread of development from Gogol to Tolstoy (and beyond). As Sinyavsky points out, in their respective "Confessions" both Gogol and Tolstoy depicted in remarkably similar terms the melancholia that presaged their abandonment of literature for earnest moral sermonizing; both attempted to distill rationalist precepts from Christian teaching, losing touch with its true spirit in the process.

But there is a great difference, and one of Sinyavsky's many achievements is to have clearly brought it out. With Tolstoy (and even to some extent with Dostoyevsky), literature and prophecy were compartmentalized, representing different phases or disparate spheres. Tolstoy's later prophetic phase was not an inevitable outgrowth of his great novels. In the case of Gogol, however, there is a direct and fateful connection between *The Inspector General, Dead Souls,* and the *Selected Passages,* which still seems, as it did to many of his contemporaries, like a betrayal of himself: how could the great humorist, the incomparable satirist of the ills of Russian society, turn into a gloomy, humorless fanatic? In fact Gogol was never concerned to satirize a society from which he stood largely aloof, as from his fellow men in general.

The comic types he created issued out of the laboratory of his own soul and mind. He was like an alchemist who actually saw homunculi crawl from his retorts and was terrified by them— literally to death. Gogol was consumed by his own creations; he felt his art to be a form of demoniac possession which compounded the evil it conjured from the depths by perpetuating and intensifying it. *Selected Passages* was, therefore, not prophecy in the Tolstoyan or Dostoyevskyan sense, but a desperate, belated attempt at expiation and exorcism. For Russia's greatest humorist, literature, like the black arts, was no laughing matter; indeed, it was allied with them in sinister fashion. If his successors generally made a distinction between life and literature, for Gogol there was a fatal blurring of the boundary—literature invaded life, taking satanic possession of it. Any glimmering of an understanding of him, as Sinyavsky makes brilliantly clear, must be sought in this sense that Gogol had of himself as a sorcerer's apprentice. In his astounding final chapter, Sinyavsky speculates that Gogol's mind represented an extinct formation: that it was, so to speak, a psychological coelacanth, a unique survival (at least in European culture) of the time when magic was a living, potent force, and when there was no dividing line between words (or any form of representation) and deeds—when in fact, art was magical conjuration.

Hence Gogol's fascination with the visual; in "Portrait" a painted image becomes an apparently autonomous presence—a kind of zombie. (Sinyavsky does not introduce the analogy, but his description of what art meant for Gogol suggests something almost exactly like voodoo.) This archaic, prehistoric quality of Gogol's sensibility, his magical intuition, made him a true seer (not just a *Weltverbesserer*) who on the threshold of the modern technological age, when the potential of the new sorcery of science was dimly beginning to penetrate the consciousness, had a sudden hallucinatory vision of something latent in the reality around him: man as an automaton, an animated corpse, manipulated by forces unleashed (as he thought) by himself. Gogol already saw this reality as a macabre marionette show orchestrated by the Devil, a world of despiritualized humans "radio-controlled from Hell" (in Sinyavsky's suitably anachronistic phrase).

Superficially, Chichikov is a beguiling picaresque rogue, but why is there such an unremittingly sinister aura about this venturesome dealer in dead souls and the seedy provincial world he seems to control with the dexterity of a puppet master? One of the reasons, Sinyavsky suggests, is that for the reader in our time he may well appear to be a visionary prefiguration of both the capitalist entrepreneur and the commissar—twin emanations and instruments of the same sorcery. (Seen in such a light, the Revolution was thus nothing but Satan's mock remedy for his own mischief.) Of course the evil of the world, in Gogol's horrorstruck perception of it, was ontological, and to reduce it to the particular social manifestations still only looming on the horizon in his day would be to simplify impermissibly; but all that has happened in the century since his death in 1852 nevertheless brings his intuitions into sharper relief, lending them, as we look backward, an undeniable quality of clairvoyance.

It is a striking feature of Russian literature—which it perhaps owes, along with so much else, to the presiding genius of Pushkin —that it is, as it were, a single enterprise in which no one writer can be separated from another. Each one of them is best viewed through the many-sided prism constituted by all of them taken together. A later generation consciously takes up the motifs of its predecessors, responds to them, echoes them, and sometimes consummates them in the light of the intervening historical experience. Gogol, for instance, has been "consummated" in the Soviet era by the most fantastic—literally and in all other senses —prose work of the twentieth century: Mikhail Bulgakov's *The Master and Margarita.* By a baleful inversion, Bulgakov's Woland stands in a hypostatic relationship to Chichikov resembling that of Father to Son. The obsessive theme of evil in Russian literature is in this way at last represented in truly adequate fashion by the Prince of Darkness himself, who is able to realize some of the vast possibilities only glimpsed by Gogol in the age of Nicholas I, but actually lived through by Bulgakov in the age of Lenin and Stalin.

Bulgakov adds a millennial perspective to Gogol's vision by wedding it to the story of the Passion (in his own splendid, neo-apocryphal version) and the Faust legend, heightening in the process whatever sense one may already have of the dreadful pertinence of all three. *Dead Souls* and *The Master and Margarita* exist in the same literary historical continuum, and neither can be fully appreciated without the other. (This is not a topic developed by Sinyavsky, only a reflection prompted by his chapter on *Dead Souls.* One may hope that in good time he will turn his attention to Bulgakov: no one could speak about him with greater authority than Sinyavsky, who in his own imaginative writings— *Fantastic Stories, The Makepeace Experiment,* etc.—in some respects carries on where Bulgakov left off at his death in 1940.)

Compared with Gogol, and even though he encompassed within himself the whole future of Russian literature, Pushkin was by temperament a man of the past; he regarded the world as something to be ordered, believing that chaos could be contained by harmony, as surely as Peter had tamed the treacherous waters of the Neva with his granite embankments; but Gogol, the younger man, saw only a world that was by its nature fatally disordered and was bound to revert to a primordial state of nonbeing, an "antiworld" theologically perceived as the contiguous and constantly encroaching realm of Satan, and subject only to a faint hope of redemption (in which Gogol himself had little faith, to judge by the loudness of his Christian protestations). The only thing left to do was to pray hysterically, in the manner of a savage trying to ward off evil spirits.

To lure Gogol out of his magician's den into the light of day is almost by definition impossible. It is not the least of Sinyavsky's merits that he knows he is defeated from the start and can only, like others before him, circle round this strange, elusive figure in bafflement, occasionally catching him in the sudden flare of a metaphor or paradox, but always seeing yet another perspective dissolve or blur. The performance is, by its nature, dizzying, and in parts even more virtuoso than the essay on Pushkin, though inevitably lacking its concentrated energy: the author sometimes flags, as though exhausted by his fantastically sustained effort. He understands that Gogol, like a nuclear particle in the cyclotron, is automatically distorted by the observing instrument, that he is protected by an indeterminacy principle (a powerful charm, this!) which excludes or frustrates any single approach.

He dismisses the psychoanalysts in a sentence. He is unimpressed by the "noseologists," those who see the root of Gogol's art in his obsession with his "priapic nose" and all that it supposedly betokened. He is equally unimpressed by the pedants and academicians (one of whom, as Sinyavsky mentions in what must surely be the most startling footnote ever penned in this kind of context, furnished expert testimony to the KGB on his "subversive" literary style as he awaited trial in the Lubyanka). Yet knowing there can be no conclusion, no crossing over the magic line drawn round his subject somewhere near the center, he comes breathtakingly close—perhaps closer than anyone else. He insists on trying to make us see the import of Gogol's work as a whole, and with the elective affinity of his kindred imagination, he is able to survey it in its entirety, grasping the structure, if not the unknowable core, and charting the grotesque topography of the mind that engendered it.

While it may be possible to reproduce the bare bones of some of Sinyavsky's arguments, there is no hope of conveying the extraordinary quality of the style inseparable from them. The subtlety of his insights is matched by a use of language hardly encountered in Russian literary criticism since the early years of the century. Both studies are in themselves works of literature which inspire as well as illuminate. Reading Pushkin and particularly Gogol will never be the same again. And in future, anyone thinking of staging *The Inspector General* would do well to acquaint himself with what Sinyavsky has to say on the matter.

Solzhenitsyn and the Russian Tradition

From under the Rubble is a collection of eleven essays edited by Alexander Solzhenitsyn, who wrote three of the essays as well. It opens with a brief foreword by Solzhenitsyn indicating that its purpose is to stir debate, after over half a century of enforced silence, on matters of fundamental principle concerning the present state of Russia. The intention is to suggest a diagnosis of the evils and difficulties that beset the country, and to point to possible long-range solutions, if only tentative ones. Although the issues are discussed primarily in Russian terms, the contributors show themselves to be not uninformed about the outside world and fully conscious that the problems of the planet now override those of any one part of it.

From under the Rubble has a forerunner in prerevolutionary Russia, namely a famous collection of articles by a group of prominent scholars, writers, and thinkers which was published in 1909 under the title *Landmarks (Vekhi).* The contributors included the religious philosophers Nikolai Berdyayev, Sergei Bulgakov, and

Semyon Frank; the legal theorist Bogdan Kistyakovsky; the literary critic Mikhail Gershenzon; and the eminent economist, publicist, and liberal politician Petr Struve. All of them had grown up in the climate of populist socialism and Marxism of the last decades of the nineteenth century and had revolted against it, rejecting the whole ethos of the Russian radical intelligentsia of the 1860's which had prepared the ground for it. Berdyayev and Bulgakov were ex-Marxists, and Struve had indeed drafted the manifesto of the Russian Social Democratic Party at its foundation congress in 1898. (By a nice irony it is his grandson, Nikita Struve, who now publishes Solzhenitsyn's work in Russian in Paris.)

The contributors to *Landmarks* took a searching look at Russian society, its lack of tolerance and sense of law, and in particular at the intelligentsia, which they held responsible for Russia's failure to find proper means of confronting her multifarious social and other problems. The main attack was against the narrowness of outlook and sectarianism that had led the majority of Russian intellectuals to seek solutions in an uncritical adoption or adaptation of the West European enlightenment in its nineteenth-century forms of positivism, atheist materialism, scientific socialism, etc. The authors called for a return to traditional spiritual values—which meant those enshrined in Russian Orthodox Christianity—as a necessary condition for a regeneration of the country's intellectual, cultural, and social life. All of them were united—as Gershenzon wrote in his preface to the volume—by their "recognition of the primacy both in theory and in practice of the spiritual life over the outward forms of society, in the sense that the inner life of the individual . . . and not the self-sufficing elements of some political order is the only solid basis for every social structure."[1]

---

[1]As quoted in Leonard Schapiro's article on *Landmarks:* "The *Vekhi* Group and the Mystique of Revolution," in the *Slavonic and East European Review,* December 1955. An excellent introduction to the wider context of the Russian nineteenth-century intellectual tradition, in which it is important to view both *Landmarks* and *From under the Rubble,* is the same author's *Rationalism and Nationalism in Russian Nineteenth Century Political Thought* (New Haven: Yale University Press, 1967).

Landmarks caused a furor at the time of its publication, provoking outrage in the ranks of the left-wing intelligentsia: Lenin, for example, denounced it as "an encyclopedia of liberal apostasy." Although the Bolshevik seizure of power in October 1917 was soon to overwhelm the authors of *Landmarks* and everything they represented, the volume remained influential; though it was under a strict ban in Soviet Russia, constant official attacks on it in the Stalin era—particularly during the cultural purges of 1947–48—served to keep its memory alive among Soviet intellectuals and even, through highly selective quotation, to give some idea of its contents. It seems likely that Solzhenitsyn read the full text only in quite recent years, when copies of an edition reprinted abroad began to circulate inside Russia. It must have struck him very forcibly at the time when he was writing *August 1914*, the first volume in his epic investigation into the roots of the catastrophe of 1917. So much we can judge by a passage in which he describes the effect of first reading it on a young man, Isaaki Lazhenitsyn, who is clearly intended to be a portrait of his own father at the beginning of the First World War: "And when he came to read *Landmarks*, he began to tremble—it was the complete opposite of all he had ever read before, yet it was true, piercingly true!"

Before they were dispersed in emigration, the *Landmarks* authors, now joined by several others, managed to have printed in the Bolshevik-controlled Moscow of 1918 a second volume of essays under the title *De Profundis*. In this they spoke of the year-old October Revolution as the fulfillment of their forebodings in *Landmarks* about the inevitable consequences of the intelligentsia's thirst for revolution. As Berdyayev put it in his contribution, Russia had now been seized by evil spirits like those in Gogol's nightmarish tales, or by the "possessed" of Dostoyevsky's prophetic imagination. It was not simply a change of regime but a spiritual disaster, a self-willed descent into the abyss. *De Profundis* was confiscated and banned almost immediately. Only two copies survived in the West and it was virtually unknown and unobtainable until it was reprinted in Paris in 1967. This sequel to *Landmarks* must also have made a profound impression on Solzhenitsyn, and the Russian title of *From under the Rubble (Iz-pod glyb)*[2] is a phonetic echo of the Russian words for *De Profundis—Iz glubiny.*

By modeling their collection of essays on *Landmarks,* Solzhenitsyn and his associates demonstrate their conviction that, in order to talk meaningfully about present-day Russia, it is essential to cross back over the intellectual void of the last sixty years and resume a tradition in Russian thought which is antithetical to the predominant one of the old revolutionary intelligentsia, particularly as it developed in the second half of the nineteenth century. The *Landmarks* authors had reverted to a strand in Russian thought which may be said to have begun with one of the most original and provocative thinkers of the nineteenth century, Petr Chaadayev (1793–1856), who believed that Russia's unhappy state stemmed from the fact that she had been isolated by the circumstances of her history from the mainstream of Christianity, and had thus escaped the civilizing influence of Renaissance religious humanism. When he proposed that the solution was for Russia to write off her past and join up with the Roman Catholic West, he was officially declared insane in a notorious precedent for the way in which some of Russia's dissidents are treated at the present day.

The essence of Chaadayev's belief—that history is the working out of divine reason, and that a country's culture and destiny are hence inseparable from its religion—was also shared by the so-called Slavophiles who in the 1840's fiercely debated Russia's future path with the first generation of the radical intelligentsia, commonly known as the Westernizers. The Slavophiles opposed the Westernizers, because they felt that Russia's problems could not be solved merely by borrowing the latest Western formula for the creation of a better world. Indeed they were convinced that most of Russia's peculiar difficulties had originated in Peter the Great's abrupt and undiscriminating introduction of Western

---

[2] It is hard to give a precise rendering of the title in English. The implication is of people speaking from beneath huge blocks of stone that have buried them alive.

ways and technology (but without the Renaissance spirit of free enquiry which had made it possible). This, they believed, produced a state of shock in Russian society from which it had never recovered, and led to many chronic social ills, not least to that split between the educated classes and the ordinary people which was in large measure responsible for the collective neurosis of the intelligentsia.

The Slavophiles believed that Russia could avoid the afflictions of the West—particularly those flowing from capitalism, selfish individualism, etc.—because she possessed spiritual and religious values which would enable her to say "a new word" (as Dostoyevsky was later to put it) of universal significance. A nation only justified its separate existence if it could make some unique contribution to the world at large. The Slavophiles were not reactionary nationalists or chauvinists, as is sometimes thought, but they did not accept the notion that the abandonment of what they held to be best in the native tradition automatically brought about progress. They were for the most part liberal and cultivated men, some of whom suffered from police persecution in the 1840's no less than did the Westernizing radical intelligentsia.[3]

This early liberal Slavophilism was later developed by Dostoyevsky in his publicist writings (*The Diary of a Writer*, 1873–81) into a strident anti-Western form of religious nationalism and messianism quite contrary to its spirit. Neither the *Landmarks* authors, nor Solzhenitsyn and his fellow contributors to *From under the Rubble*, have any sympathy with this brand of Slavophilism which, needless to say, subsequently degenerated even further, becoming the stock-in-trade of a primitive nationalism

[3]The actual differences between the Slavophiles and the Westernizers were not perhaps as great as they themselves thought, particularly in the later, more acrimonious stage of their debate. Both were concerned with social reform—especially the abolition of serfdom —and the Westernizers were neither as antinational nor the Slavophiles as anti-European (indeed these were in some respects, and rather ironically, the belated Russian progeny of German romantic philosophy) as their contemporaries may have been led to believe. What, at bottom, most divided them was that the Slavophiles were Russian Orthodox Christians whereas the Westernizers were atheists.

that is still very much alive today in the Soviet Union, where it evidently receives very much the same kind of covert support from the KGB as it did before the Revolution from the Okhrana. It was something quite different in Dostoyevsky that appealed to the *Landmarks* authors, as it does now to Solzhenitsyn: namely, the somber insights in his great novels into the ultimately suicidal consequences of license (or "self-will," as he called it), especially when it was allied with the militantly atheist revolutionary doctrines—the debased by-products of secular humanism—which entered into the intelligentsia after the reforms of the early 1860's like a demoniac possession.[4]

The true heir to what may be called the Chaadayev tradition in Russian thought was the remarkable poet, philosopher, and lay theologian Vladimir Soloviev (1853–1900), who did more than anyone to express and precipitate the rejection, by some part of the thinking public in Russia at the end of the last century, of the materialism and utilitarian approach to literature and ideas of the intelligentsia. The symbolist movement in poetry (in particular as represented by the greatest Russian poet of this century, Alexander Blok), and the return to idealist philosophy of such ex-Marxists as Berdyayev, Bulgakov, and Struve, owe much to him. In *Landmarks* Soloviev's influence is all-pervasive. Like Chaadayev and the Slavophiles, he saw religion as the essential element of history, culture, and society, but he was more universalist in his attitude, having no special preference for East or West, and even proposing a synthesis between Roman Catholicism and Russian Orthodoxy. He resembled Dostoyevsky in taking an apocalyptic view of the future, and his skepticism about the very idea of boundless material progress[5] is no doubt one of the several fea-

---

[4]In a brilliant discussion of Dostoyevsky in Chapter 29 of the second volume of her memoirs, *Hope Abandoned*, Nadezhda Mandelstam has noted the vast difference between Dostoyevsky the writer and Dostoyevsky the journalist. It is Dostoyevsky the writer whom Solzhenitsyn acknowledges as a kindred spirit in his Nobel Lecture of 1972 and elsewhere.
[5]Displayed particularly in *Three Conversations*, published in the year of his death and, not least because of its magnificent literary form, the most accessible of Soloviev's writings. After listening to a glowing account of progress in the nineteenth century and of the splendid prospects before us in the twentieth, a character representing the author remarks:

tures that accounts for the great revival of interest in him among contemporary Soviet intellectuals.

In sharing this interest, as in turning toward religious faith, Solzhenitsyn and his friends are by no means an isolated, eccentric group among the post-Stalin intelligentsia. They are simply the most articulate, determined, and courageous representatives of what is a conspicuous trend, as will be plain to anyone who has talked to recent émigrés from the Soviet Union. It should perhaps not be a cause of surprise that this has come about after—if not as the result of—sixty years of raucous antireligious propaganda and of assurances, repeated *ad nauseam,* concerning the unlimited material possibilities of the communist future. (Mikhail Agursky's article in *From under the Rubble* shows that there is no disposition among the contributors to feel that the West is any less self-deluded in respect to economic growth and progress.)

Such then, in roughest outline, is the Russian tradition with which Solzhenitsyn and the other participants in this volume have chosen consciously to identify themselves, and in relation to which their basic ideas must be seen. Inevitably, although there is no warrant for it in any of his writings, Solzhenitsyn will certainly be described *tout court* as a Slavophile, sometimes by persons who may think it a somewhat opprobrious term implying that he is a mystical nationalist of the kind Dostoyevsky became in the 1870's. This would be doubly misleading, both because it would be to pick out only one phase of the intellectual tradition with which Solzhenitsyn finds he has so much in common, and also to confuse the original Slavophiles, such as the wise and learned Alexei Khomyakov (1804–60) with the chauvinist Panslavists of a later period. In fact, Solzhenitsyn and his fellow contributors show their affinity to even the early Slavophiles only in a very general sense, mainly by virtue of continuing to have faith in Russia because of what they conceive to be the abiding values still preserved, despite all the odds, in her church, and by

---

"But progress is a symptom of the end." Today's newspaper readers will find this a less startling comment than did those of 1900.

their belief that a revival of these values on a broad scale is the only way to overcome the evil of the past.

It is similarly misleading to label as Westernizers, or at least to do so without considerable qualifications, those, such as Andrei Sakharov and Roy Medvedev, whose ideas about the future have been criticized by Solzhenitsyn in the course of the grand debate already going on among Russia's leading dissidents. The temptation to see here a repetition of the Slavophile-Westernizer controversy of the 1840's is overwhelming, but it should be resisted. It is the kind of seductive analogy which rapidly founders as soon as it is pursued. For one thing, there can scarcely be anyone in the Soviet Union of the 1970's who might look to the West for new revolutionary doctrines, as people did in the Russia of the 1840's. The West now has little to offer in this respect but various degraded (or forbiddingly scholastic) forms of Marxism which neither appeal, nor seem particularly relevant to people who have seen how such things work out in practice. The Russian intellectuals who are today sometimes referred to as Westernizers think in pragmatic terms of a gradual evolution of their country's political institutions. Some of them, notably Medvedev, the historian, continue to use conventional Marxist idiom in expressing their hopes for the eventual transformation of the present system into a genuine socialist democracy through the emergence of liberal forces within the ruling party—in other words, "socialism with a human face."[6] Others, such as Sakharov, the eminent atomic physicist and human rights advocate, are disillusioned with Marxism and consider that Russia's best course is toward political convergence with the Western democracies, i.e., the adoption of some form of parliamentary government.

But apart from this fundamental dissimilarity between the Westernizers of the last century and their supposed successors of today, the analogy between the 1970's and the 1840's breaks down even more decisively because of two very important features

---

[6]Medvedev argues his case in detail in *On Socialist Democracy* (London: Macmillan, 1975; New York: Knopf, 1975).

which provide common ground between Solzhenitsyn and his opponents in the present debate, and at the same time sharply distinguish them from both Slavophiles and Westerners. These are: belief in the overriding importance of law for any society, however constituted; and a total disinclination to indulge in utopian fantasy about the "best" way to arrange human affairs. If the Westernizers were given to what has been called "rationalist utopianism," that is, the dream of the perfect secular society, the Slavophiles were no less visionary by temperament, even though their ideal society was theocratic, or the realization of the Kingdom of God on earth. Both Westernizers and Slavophiles—like the whole of the intelligentsia that came after them—were notably neglectful, not to say disdainful, of the very idea of law. This lack of a sense of law (the subject of an outstanding contribution to *Landmarks* by Kistyakovsky) was part of the price Russia had to pay for her centuries of isolation, under the Tatar yoke, from the rest of Christendom.

Unfortunately, there was a tendency to make a virtue out of indifference to law. It became an entrenched part of the Russians' image of themselves as people of a "broad nature" who had no patience with the pettifogging niceties of legal formality; Dostoyevsky railed against the cold, heartless impersonality of Western legal process as one of the worst aspects of the bourgeois West. Right up to the Revolution, the radical intelligentsia gave little thought to law, and evidently felt it had no place in the ideal society, or at least that there was no need for it. Those Russian intellectuals from the old regime who survived to see the installation of Andrei Vyshinsky as Prosecutor-General of the U.S.S.R. will certainly have had second thoughts. At any event, there can be little doubt that if any good at all has come out of the reign of institutionalized lawlessness begun in 1917, it has been to produce a striking change in the attitude of Russian intellectuals toward law. In the third volume of *The Gulag Archipelago*, Solzhenitsyn's chronicle of what sixty years of arbitrary rule meant in practice, he expresses his passionate belief in the need, above all, for law. It is a belief shared by all his opponents, such as Sakharov and Medvedev in the current debate. There is also no question of utopianism, of blueprints for the future, on either side. For all of them, utopia smells of corpses.

The disagreement, therefore, between Solzhenitsyn, Shafarevich and the other contributors to *From under the Rubble* on the one hand, and Sakharov and Medvedev on the other, is not over the question of *what* is to be done (in the classic phrase that haunted the old intelligentsia, and was immortalized by two of its leading representatives: Nikolai Chernyshevsky and Lenin), but rather over the question of *how* change may come about. Or to put it in another way: where should one look first for signs of hope that Russia may gradually rise up from the abyss into which she was cast by the Revolution?

To a large extent, the reply to this question depends on a person's temperament and experience of life. Medvedev and Sakharov, as former members of the Soviet establishment, still believe that change may come through institutions, or the working of anonymous social forces. (Their opponents might say that this view is rooted in a Marxist conditioning which is so profound as to be second nature.) Nonetheless, sympathetic outside observers will, or at least should, continue to pay serious attention to what they have to say. Like the *Landmarks* authors before them, Solzhenitsyn and the other participants in *From under the Rubble* insist on the "primacy . . . of spiritual life over the outward forms of society," and are hence convinced that change can only begin in the soul of each individual member of society; they put no credence in the reality of abstract historical laws, and consider that new social formations (other than those imposed by brute force) can only arise through many people, simultaneously and by a conscious effort, adopting new values and absolute moral standards, in opposition to those instilled by the dominant system of education and indoctrination. As Solzhenitsyn puts it in one of the essays: "*We* are history."

It should be said that, in the case of Solzhenitsyn himself, this view was not arrived at by reading or cogitation. It is quite simply his *lagernaya pravda:* a truth taught by the hard school of Stalin's camps. It is possible to trace, in his novels, how he came to believe —long before he can have read *Landmarks*—that the essential ingredient of any human society worthy of the name is mysteriously present only in the soul or character of the individual members of it. (As Nerzhin says in *The First Circle:* "It was only character that mattered, and this was something everybody had to forge for himself, by constant effort over the years.") All else —History, the People (a particular favorite of the old Russian intelligentsia), the class to which a man belongs—is illusory or of no account.[7]

In the opening article of *From under the Rubble*, Solzhenitsyn sets the framework for the whole discussion by taking issue, respectfully but firmly, with the premises of Sakharov's essay "Progress, Coexistence, and Intellectual Freedom." Solzhenitsyn cannot agree with Sakharov that the present system is capable of developing into some form of democracy, if only it could rid itself of the legacy of Stalinism. Solzhenitsyn is insistent that Stalinism was simply a logical product of Leninism and Marxism, and he does not share the optimistic view that it can generate any democratic component; nor does he consider that socialism in general has in the long run ever provided any but the crassest material criteria for the betterment of the human lot.[8] All doctrines based on the concept of material progress are doomed to failure and lead to catastrophe.

Sakharov, on the other hand, hopes that intellectual freedom or freedom in a broader sense can be achieved through changes in institutions. Solzhenitsyn believes that a man can achieve inner freedom under any system if he so wishes—this is an important theme in his novels, particularly in *The First Circle*. At the same

---

[7] An illuminating study of Solzhenitsyn's views, as they are unfolded in his works of fiction, is the article by Georges Nivat, "Soljénitsyne et l'idéologie," in *Soljénitsyne: Colloque de Cerisy* (Paris, 1974).

[8] Socialism is the subject of a special study by Shafarevich in *From under the Rubble*. It should be borne in mind by Western readers that the very word "socialism" has undergone something of a semantic sea change in the Soviet Union: it has none of the cozy associations that it has for many people in the West. When Shafarevich traces the concept back to the slave states of antiquity, he speaks of a historical (and personal) experience of something which is quite remote from what has gone under the name of "socialism" in Scandinavia and Britain.

time, it is possible to be a slave to material incentives even under the freest of conditions. He dwells a good deal on the self-destructive urges in Western society, pointing out the fragility of systems in which freedom is guaranteed only by forms of government that have evolved in comparatively recent times. He does not deny that freedom of *any* kind would be very welcome, but he wonders whether parliamentary democracy, even if it were suddenly granted to Russia, would necessarily be the panacea that Sakharov and others think. Unless Russia can recover the spiritual values all but destroyed since the Revolution, such gains would be empty and result in an amalgam of the worst aspects of both Soviet and Western democracy.

In practical terms, Solzhenitsyn foresees that Russia is likely to evolve toward some kind of modified authoritarian rule. He defines "authoritarian" as "based on authority," as to some extent Russian society was before Peter the Great. The Orthodox Church and other traditional Russian institutions then provided some guarantees against arbitrary human tyranny, because their sanctions derived from God, not man. (It is in this part of his argument that Solzhenitsyn comes closest to the Slavophiles.) In later centuries there was no such restraining factor.

Solzhenitsyn points out that Russia did have total freedom for eight months in 1917—even Lenin then said that Russia was the freest land in the world—but this boundless freedom speedily led to the most boundless slavery the world has ever known. It is for this reason that he questions the assumption that freedom *by itself* would necessarily open the way to a glorious future. What is important in Russia, he feels, is that there should be a state of affairs in which, although citizens may still be compelled to render unto Caesar what is Caesar's, they do not—as now—also have to render unto Caesar what is God's.

The other essays in *From under the Rubble* deal in equally challenging fashion with various aspects of Russia's predicament. Shafarevich writes of the thorny question of the national minorities (which, taken together, form a majority over the Russians) in the Soviet Union; the new intelligentsia is compared, in the longest of Solzhenitsyn's three contributions, to that of prerevolutionary times; the relationship of the intelligentsia to the church, and the problem of the church's isolation—to some extent self-imposed—from society, are discussed by the art historian Yevgeni Barabanov and the historian Vadim Borisov. Two other articles have been kept anonymous, to protect their authors. There is no need to attempt a summary here since each of them speaks clearly enough for itself, sometimes with striking freshness of language and vision.

The publication of this joint profession of faith by a great Russian writer now living in enforced exile, and a group of intellectuals still inside the country—including one of its leading mathematicians—is an eloquent response to the recent tactics of the Soviet government in its efforts to stifle dissent. The indiscriminate use of prison and the madhouse, which is still by no means in abeyance, has been supplemented by the ostensibly more subtle policy of selective banishment abroad. The hope is evidently, by removing from the scene some of the most powerful voices that speak "from under the rubble," to demoralize and so more easily silence those remaining behind. Even in the days of Nicholas I this was not an entirely successful strategy. Nowadays, with modern means of communication, it is self-evidently doomed to failure.

Although, as I have suggested, it is surely misleading to see the present debate among the Russian dissidents as a repetition of the Westernizer-Slavophile debate of the 1840's, one cannot help observing how little has changed in the attitude of the country's rulers between then and now. That private persons should express differing opinions about the national destiny is still regarded at the best as impertinence. This remains the official attitude even when the dissenters, far from advocating drastic political reform, are dubious of the very possibility of a change of regime, and think only in terms of a shift of consciousness that may come about in the fullness of time. By the standards of any other society, Solzhenitsyn and his fellow writers in *From under the Rubble* are moderate, not to say conservative, men who abhor violence. They are undogmatic about the means and direction of social change, and propose no new ideology. They do not cry for blood, but call only for repentance. They do not put their hopes in a fresh cataclysm, or long for Russia's humiliation by her rivals on the world scene. A government that tries by all possible means to deny them a hearing in their own country can hardly be considered to have advanced much beyond its predecessor of nearly a century and a half ago—not, at least, in its attitude to intellectual dissent.

After the publication of the first of his *Lettres Philosophiques* (1836), in which he was held to have cast aspersions on Russian history, Chaadayev was sternly rebutted by Count Alexander Benckendorff, the Chief of the Third Section (secret police) under Nicholas I, in the following words: "The past of Russia is admirable, her present state is more than magnificent; and as for her future, it will surpass even the boldest of dreams." But in some ways there has been a decline. Chaadayev was placed under "medical-police supervision" in his own house, but he was not forcibly abducted to a lunatic asylum and given mind-destroying drugs. Nor was he snatched from his home and spirited away to a foreign country without even being told where he was going— as happened to Solzhenitsyn on February 14, 1974.

Select Bibliography of Max Hayward's Work

Critical Writings in Books

Preface: Vladimir Dudintsev, *A New Year's Tale*. Trans. by Max Hayward. London: Hutchinson, 1960, 48 pp.; Toronto: Clarke, Irwin (pa.), 1960.

Introduction: *Dissonant Voices in Soviet Literature*. Ed. by Patricia Blake and Max Hayward. New York: Pantheon Books, 1962, xliii, 308 pp.; London: George Allen & Unwin, and New York: Harper & Row, Harper Colophon Books (pa.), 1964, xlii, 308 pp.; Westport, Ct.: Greenwood Press, 1975 (reprint of 1962 ed.).

"The Struggle Goes On" (pp. 375–89) in *Russia Under Khrushchev* (an anthology from *Problems of Communism*). Ed. by Abraham Brumberg. London: Methuen, 1962, xi, 660 pp.; New York: Praeger (hardback and pa.), 1962, 660 pp.

Introduction and chapter entitled "Conflict and Change in Soviet Literature," in *Literature and Revolution in Soviet Russia, 1917–62: a symposium* [held at St. Antony's College, Oxford, July 1962]. Ed. by Max Hayward and Leopold Labedz. London / New York: Oxford University Press, 1963, xx, 235 pp.; Westport, Ct.: Greenwood Press, 1976 (reprint of 1963 ed.). Chapter "Conflict and Change" originally published as article in *Survey* (London) 46 (January 1963): 9–22.

Introduction (with Leopold Labedz): Alexander Solzhenitsyn, *One Day in the Life of Ivan Denisovich*. Trans. by Max Hayward and Ronald Hingley. New York: Praeger ("Books that Matter") (hardback and pa.), 1963, xxiv, 210 pp.; Bantam Books (pa.), 1963, 203 pp.

Epilogue: *Soviet Literature in the Sixties.* An international symposium, ed. by Max Hayward and Edward L. Crowley. (Papers given at a symposium held under auspices of Institute for the Study of the USSR in Bad Wiessee, September 1963.) New York: Praeger (hardback and pa.), 1964, and London: Methuen, 1965, 221 pp.

Introduction: *On Trial: The Soviet State versus "Abram Tertz" and "Nikolai Arzhak."* Trans. and ed. by Max Hayward. New York: Harper & Row 1966, vi, 183 pp.; revised and enlarged ed., 1967, vi, 310 pp.

Introduction (with Patricia Blake): Andrei Voznesensky, *Antiworlds: Poems* [*Poetry,* in U.S. ed.]. [Translations of some poems only.] New York: Basic Books, 1966, and London: Oxford University Press, Oxford Paperbacks, 1967, xxii, 120 pp.

Introduction: *On Trial: The Case of Sinyavsky (Tertz) and Daniel (Arzhak). Documents.* Ed. by Leopold Labedz and Max Hayward. London: Collins and Harvill Press, 1967, 384 pp.

Introduction (with Patricia Blake): Andrei Voznesensky, *Antiworlds, and the Fifth Ace: Poems* [*Poetry,* in U.S. eds.]. Bilingual eds. Trans. by W. H. Auden *et al.* New York: Doubleday, Anchor Books (pa.), 1967, Basic Books, revised ed., 1967, London: Oxford University Press, 1968, and New York: Schocken Books, Schocken Paperbacks, 1973, xxiii, 296 pp.

Preface ["Foreword," in U.S. ed.]: Ladislav Mňačko, *The Taste of Power.* Trans. from the Slovak by Paul Stevenson. London: Weidenfeld & Nicolson, New York: Praeger, and Don Mills, Ont.: Burns & MacEachern, 1967, 235 pp.

"Themes and Variations in Soviet Literature" (pp. 262–83) in *Fifty Years of Communism in Russia.* Ed. by Milorad M. Drachkovitch. (Paper read at an international conference at Stanford University sponsored by the Hoover Institution, 9–13 October 1967, to mark 50th anniversary of the Bolshevik *coup d'état.*) University Park & London: Pennsylvania State University Press, 1968, ix, 316 pp.

Introduction: Yuli Daniel ["Nikolai Arzhak"], *This Is Moscow Speaking and Other Stories.* Trans. by Stuart Hood, Harold Shukman, and John Richardson. London: Collins and Harvill Press, 1968, and New York: E. P. Dutton, 1969, 159 pp.; New York: Collier Books (pa.), 1970, 160 pp.

Foreword: Boris Pasternak, *The Blind Beauty.* Trans. by Max Hayward and Manya Harari. London: Collins and Harvill Press, and New

York: Harcourt, Brace & World ("A Helen and Kurt Wolff Book"), 1969, xii, 128 pp.

Introduction (with William C. Fletcher): *Religion and the Soviet State: A Dilemma of Power.* Ed. by Max Hayward and William C. Fletcher. Published for the Centre de Recherches et d'étude des institutions religieuses. London: Pall Mall Press, and New York: Praeger, 1969, x, 200 pp.

Introduction: Anatoli Marchenko, *My Testimony.* Trans. by Michael Scammell. London, Pall Mall Press, and Toronto: Clarke, Irwin, 1969, xxiii, 415 pp.; New York: E. P. Dutton, 1969; Delta Books (pa.), 1971, xxi, 415 pp.; Harmondsworth: Penguin Books, new ed. (pa.), 1971, 430 pp.

Introduction: Andrei Amalrik, *Involuntary Journey to Siberia.* Trans. by Manya Harari and Max Hayward. London: Collins and Harvill Press (abridged translation), 1970, xii, 282 pp.; New York: Harcourt Brace Jovanovich ("A Helen and Kurt Wolff Book"), 1970, xv, 297 pp.; Harvest Books (pa.), 1971, 297 pp. This introduction was originally published as an article in *Survey* (London) 74–75 (Winter-Spring 1970): 83–87.

Foreword: *Russia's Other Writers* [: *Selections from Samizdat Literature*, in U.S. ed.]. Sel. and ed. by Michael Scammell. London: Longman, 1970, and New York: Praeger, 1971, viii, 216 pp. Translations from *Grani.*

Foreword: *Ferment in the Ukraine.* Documents by V. Chornovil, I. Kandyba, L. Lukyanenko, V. Moroz *et al.* Ed. by Michael Browne. London: Macmillan, 1971, xx, 267 pp.; New York: Praeger, 1971, xviii, 267 pp.

Foreword: Marina Tsvetayeva, *Selected Poems.* Trans. by Elaine Feinstein. London / New York: Oxford University Press, 1971, xix, 103 pp.; Harmondsworth and Baltimore: Penguin, Penguin Modern European Poets (pa.), 1974, 136 pp.

Foreword: Vladimir Tendryakov, *Three, Seven, Ace.* Trans. by David Alger, Olive Stevens and Paul Falla. London: Harvill Press, and New York: Harper & Row, 1973, 252 pp.

Introduction: Anna Akhmatova, *Poems of Akhmatova.* Trans. by Stanley Kunitz with Max Hayward. Bilingual ed. Boston: Little, Brown ("An Atlantic Monthly Press Book") (hardback and pa.), 1973, xii, 173 pp.; London: Collins and Harvill Press, 1974, 173 pp.

Foreword: Nadezhda Mandelstam, *Hope Abandoned* [: *A Memoir*, in English ed.] Trans. by Max Hayward. London: Collins and Harvill

Press, 1974, xii, 689 pp.; New York: Atheneum, 1974, xii, 687 pp.; Harmondsworth: Penguin Books (pa.), 1976, 767 pp.

Introduction: Alexander Solzhenitsyn, with Mikhail Agursky, A. B., Evgeny Barabanov, Vadim Borisov, F. Korsakov, and Igor Shafarevich, *From Under the Rubble*. Trans. by A. M. Brock, Milada Haigh, Marita Sapiets, Hilary Sternberg, and Harry Willetts under the direction of Michael Scammell. London: Collins and Harvill Press, 1975, x, 308 pp.; Boston: Little, Brown, 1975, 308 pp.; London: Collins, Fontana (pa., new ed.), 1976, xii, 308 pp.; New York: Bantam Books (pa.), 1976, 306 pp.

Introduction: Abram Tertz [Andrei Sinyavsky], *A Voice from the Chorus*. Trans. by Kyril Fitzlyon and Max Hayward. London: Collins and Harvill Press, and New York: Farrar, Straus & Giroux, 1976, xxiii, 328 pp.; London: Collins, Fontana (pa.), 1977, xxii, 328 pp.

Introduction: Alexander Gladkov, *Meetings with Pasternak*. Trans. by Max Hayward. London: Collins and Harvill Press, and New York: Harcourt Brace Jovanovich ("A Helen and Kurt Wolff Book"), 1977, 223 pp.

"Literature in the Soviet Period 1917–1975" (pp. 185–230) in *An Introduction to Russian Language and Literature. Companion to Russian Studies*, vol. 2 (of 3-vol. series). Ed. by Robert Auty and Dimitri Obolensky. Cambridge: Cambridge University Press (hardback), 1977, xiv, 300 pp.; (pa.) 1980, xiv, 300 pp.

Preface and Introduction: Olga Ivinskaya, *A Captive of Time: My Years with Pasternak*. Trans. by Max Hayward. London: Collins and Harvill Press, 1978, xl, 488 pp.; New York: Doubleday, 1978, xl, 462 pp.; London: Collins, Fontana (pa.), 1979, xl, 488 pp.; New York: Warner Books (pa.), 1979, xl, 488 pp.

Introduction: Chloe Obolensky, *The Russian Empire: A Portrait in Photographs*. New York: Random House, 1979, and London: Jonathan Cape, 1980, xx, 345 pp.

Critical Writings in Periodicals

"The Eternal Triangle in Soviet Literature," *Twentieth Century* (London) CLIII, 193 (March 1953): 219–25.

"The Curriculum in Russian Studies," in "Russian Studies in the University" (a symposium, including G. H. Bolsover, "Russian and East European Studies" and H. Seton-Watson, "Russian History and Society"), *Universities Quarterly* (London) VII, 3 (May 1953): 240–46.

"The Russian and His Régime," *The Gryphon* (issue entitled *Double Gryphon*), Leeds University, Summer 1953, pp. 3–11.

"Russia Revisited" (two articles), *Daily Telegraph* (London), 20 and 21 July 1956.

"Controls in Literature 1946–1954," *Soviet Survey* [later *Survey*] (London) 21–22 (1957): 26–32.

"Dr. Zhivago and the Soviet Intelligentsia: Looking Back on an Epoch," *Soviet Survey* (London) 24 (April–June 1958): 65–69.

" 'Zhivago"s Suppression: A New Theory," *Library Journal* (New York) LXXXIV, 10 (15 May 1959): 1562–563.

"Soviet Literature in the Doldrums," *Problems of Communism* (Washington, D.C.) VIII, 4 (July–August 1959): 11–16; reprinted in *Partisan Review* (New York) 27, 1 (Winter 1960): 98–110.

"The Thaw and the Writers," *Daedalus* (Cambridge, Mass.) LXXIX, 3 (Summer 1960) [special issue on *The Russian Intelligentsia*]: 551–61.

"Pilnyak and Zamyatin: Two Tragedies of the Twenties," *Survey* (London) XXXVI (April-June 1961): 85–91.

"Introduction: Soviet Literature 1917–1961," in special Russian issue entitled "Dissonant Voices in Soviet Literature," *Partisan Review* (New York) 28, 3–4 (May–July 1961): 333–62.

"In Reply: To Soviet Comment on Partisan Review's Russian Issue" [answer to A. Dementiev, "Truth and Falsehood about Soviet Literature," *Partisan Review* (New York) 29, 2 (Spring 1962): 303–08], *ibid.*, pp. 308–10.

"Conflict and Change in Soviet Literature 1959–62," *Survey* (London) 46 (January 1963): 9–22.

"The Literary Purge in Retrospect," *Survey* (London) 49 (October 1963): 54–62.

"Solzhenitsyn's Place in Contemporary Soviet Literature," *Slavic Review* (USA) XXIII, 3 (September 1964): 432–36. (A reply to Victor Erlich, "Post-Stalin Trends in Russian Literature," *ibid.*, pp. 405–31.)

"Writers and the Police" (with Leopold Labedz), *Encounter* (London) XXVI, 1 (January 1966): 84–88. [Reprinted under title "Writers in Prison," in *Problems of Communism* (Washington, D.C.), March–April 1966, pp. 65–70.]

"Awkward Voices in Russia" (lead article on Sinyavsky-Daniel trial), *The Times* (London), 1 February 1966.

"The Case of Tertz-Sinyavski," *Dissent* (New York), January–February 1966, pp. 88–91.

"The Trial in Moscow" (with Leopold Labedz), *Encounter* (London) XXVI, 4 (April 1966): 82–91.

"Religion and the Changing Intellectual Outlook in the USSR: Summary," *Studies on the Soviet Union* (Munich) V, 4 (1966) [special issue on religion]: 57–61.

"The Moscow Trial," *Partisan Review* (New York) 33, 2 (Spring 1966): 227–39.

"A Note on Recent Developments in the Soviet Theatre," *Cahiers du Monde Russe et Soviétique* (Paris) VII, 3 (juillet–septembre 1966): 408–13. *("Hommage à François de Liencourt.")*

"Russian Anti-Semitism," *Commentary* (New York) XLIII (March 1967): 91. (Review of Elie Wiesel, *The Jews of Silence: A Personal Report on Soviet Jewry.*)

"Soviet Russian Prose" and "Afterword" (contributions to a discussion entitled "Soviet Literature: A Reappraisal" in special issue), *Studies on the Soviet Union* (Munich) VIII, 3 (1969): 108–09.

"Some Observations on Jews in Post-Stalin Literature," *Bulletin of Soviet and East European Jewish Affairs* [later *Soviet Jewish Affairs*] (London) 4 (December 1969): 15–19.

"Jewish Writers in the Soviet Union," *Jewish Heritage* (Washington, D.C.) 12, 4 (Summer–Fall 1970): 20–26.

"Journey to Siberia" (on Andrei Amalrik), *Survey* (London) 74–75 (Winter–Spring 1970): 83–87.

"How the Soviet Censors Go to Work" (review of Anatoli Kuznetsov, *Babi Yar*), *Daily Telegraph* (London), 1 December 1970, p. 9.

Contribution to a discussion with Arkadi Belinkov and others in special issue on "The Soviet Censorship," *Studies on the Soviet Union* (Munich) XI, 2 (1971).

"The Decline of Socialist Realism," *Survey* (London) 18, 1 (Winter 1972): 73–97.

"Pushkin, Gogol and the Devil" (review of Abram Tertz [Andrei Sinyavsky], *Progulki s Pushkinym* and *V teni Gogolya*), *Times Literary Supplement* (London), 28 May 1976, pp. 630–32.

"Andrey Sinyavsky's Voice," *Encounter* (London) XLVIII, 2 (August 1976): 30–37. Reprinted as Introduction to Abram Tertz [Andrei

Sinyavsky], *A Voice from the Chorus.* See section on Critical Writings in Books.

"What Is to Be Done?" (review of Boris Shragin, *The Challenge of the Spirit*), *New York Times Book Review,* 7 May 1978.

"The Vocabulary of Moscow" (review of Bernard Comrie and Gerald Stone, *The Russian Language since the Revolution*), *Times Literary Supplement* (London), 17 November 1978, p. 1339.

Special Papers and Monographs

"The Ideological Consequences of October 1956." Oxford: St. Antony's College, 1957. (St. Antony's Papers on Soviet Affairs. Roneoed typescript.)

"Potentialities for Freedom: The Restlessness of the Writers." (Paper given at a conference on "Changes in Soviet Society" held at St. Antony's College, Oxford, 24–29 June 1957. Roneoed typescript.)

Joint Editorship

Dissonant Voices in Soviet Literature (with Patricia Blake). Introd. by Max Hayward. New York: Pantheon Books, 1962; Harper & Row, Harper Colophon Books (pa.) 1964; London: George Allen & Unwin, 1964; Westport, Ct.: Greenwood Press, 1975 (reprint of 1962 ed.). Some of the material in the book originally published in *Partisan Review* (New York) 28, 3–4 (1961).

Literature and Revolution in Soviet Russia (with Leopold Labedz). Introd. and one chapter by Max Hayward. London / New York: Oxford University Press, 1963; Westport, Ct.: Greenwood Press, 1976 (reprint of 1963 ed.).

Soviet Literature in the Sixties (with Edward L. Crowley). New York: Praeger (hardback and pa.), 1964; London: Methuen, 1965.

Halfway to the Moon: New Writing from Russia (with Patricia Blake). Introd. by Patricia Blake. London: Weidenfeld & Nicolson, Encounter Books, and New York: Holt, Rinehart & Winston, 1964, 276 pp.;Toronto: Ryerson Press, 1964; New York: Doubleday, Anchor Books (pa.), 1965, xxxix, 235 pp. Most of the material in the book originally published in *Encounter* (London) XX, 4 (April 1963) under the title "New Voices in Russian Writing."

Andrei Voznesensky, *Antiworlds: Poems* [: *Poetry*, in U.S. ed.] (with Patricia Blake). Trans. by W. H. Auden, Jean Garrigue, Max Hayward, Stanley Kunitz, Stanley Moss, William Jay Smith, and Richard Wilbur. Foreword by W. H. Auden. [Translations only.] New York: Basic Books, 1966; London: Oxford University Press (pa.), 1967.

Andrei Voznesensky, *Antiworlds, and the Fifth Ace: Poems* [*Poetry*, in U.S. eds.] (with Patricia Blake). Bilingual eds. Trans. by W. H. Auden *et al.* Foreword by W. H. Auden. New York: Doubleday, Anchor Books (pa.), 1967; Basic Books, revised ed., 1967; London: Oxford University Press, 1968; New York: Schocken Books (pa.), 1973.

On Trial: The Case of Sinyavsky (Tertz) and Daniel (Arzhak). Documents (with Leopold Labedz). Introd. by Max Hayward. London: Collins and Harvill Press, 1967.

Religion and the Soviet State (with William C. Fletcher). London: Pall Mall Press, and New York: Praeger, 1969.

Anna Akhmatova, *Poems of Akhmatova* (with Stanley Kunitz). Bilingual ed. Boston: Little, Brown ("An Atlantic Monthly Press Book"), 1973; London: Collins and Harvill Press, 1974.

Andrei Voznesensky, *Nostalgia for the Present* (with Vera Dunham). Forewords by Edward M. Kennedy and Arthur Miller [U.S. ed. only]. Poems trans. by Robert Bly, Guy Daniels, Vera Dunham, Lawrence Ferlinghetti, Allen Ginsberg, Max Hayward, Stanley Kunitz, Louis Simpson, William Jay Smith, H. W. Tjalsma, Richard Wilbur *et al.* New York: Doubleday, 1978, xvii, 268 pp.; Oxford: Oxford University Press (pa.), 1980, 160 pp.

Selected Translations

Abram Tertz [Andrei Sinyavsky], *The Trial Begins.* A novel. London: Collins and Harvill Press, 1960, 127 pp.; New York: Pantheon Books, 1960, 128 pp.; London: Collins, Fontana (pa.), 1977, 95 pp. Max Hayward's translation is reprinted in Abram Tertz [Andrei Sinyavsky], *The Trial Begins* and *On Socialist Realism* ["On Socialist Realism" trans. by George Dennis]. Introd. by Czeslaw Milosz. New York: Random House, Vintage Books, Vintage Rus-

sian Library (pa.), 1965, 219 pp.; Berkeley: University of California
Press (pa.), 1982, 220 pp.

Vladimir Dudintsev, *A New Year's Tale.* London: Hutchinson, 1960, 48
pp.; Toronto: Clarke, Irwin (pa.), 1960. This translation originally
published in *Encounter* (London) XIV (June 1960): 6–19, under
title "A New Year's Fable."

Vladimir Mayakovsky, "The Bedbug" and "Conversation with a Tax
Inspector about Poetry," in *The Bedbug and Selected Poetry.* Ed.
and introd. by Patricia Blake. Poetry trans. by George Reavey.
Cleveland and New York: Meridian Books (hardback and pa.),
1960; London: Weidenfeld & Nicolson, 1961; Cleveland and New
York: World Publishing, 1970, 317 pp.; Bloomington: Indiana
University Press, Midland Books (hardback and pa.), 1975 (reprint
of 1960 ed.). All with Russian text of poems. Max Hayward's
translation of "The Bedbug" is reprinted in *Three Soviet Plays.* Ed.
by Michael Glenny. Harmondsworth & Baltimore: Penguin Books
Ltd. Plays (pa.), 1966, 218 pp.; London: Davis-Poynter ("A Davis-
Poynter Playscript"), 1974, 51 pp.

Abram Tertz [Andrei Sinyavsky], "You and I" and "The Icicle," in *The
Icicle, and Other Stories.* London: Collins and Harvill, 1963, 191
pp.; and in *Fantastic Stories,* New York: Pantheon Books, 1963,
214 pp. Other stories trans. by Ronald Hingley. Translation of
"The Icicle" originally published in *Encounter* (London) XVIII,
2 (February 1962): 44–72. Translation of "You and I" appeared in
Survey (London), April 1962.

Isaac Babel, "Kolyvushka" and other stories, in *The Lonely Years 1925–
1939: Unpublished Stories and Private Correspondence.* Ed. and
with introd. by Nathalie Babel. Other material trans. by Andrew
R. MacAndrew. New York: Farrar, Straus, 1964, xxviii, 402 pp.;
Toronto: Ambassador Books, 1964.

On Trial: The Soviet State versus "Abram Tertz" and "Nikolai Arzhak."
Trial before the Supreme Court of the R.S.F.S.R. held in Moscow
Oblast court in February 1966. Ed. and with introd. by Max Hayward. New York: Harper & Row, 1966, vi, 183 pp.; revised and
enlarged ed., 1967, vi, 310 pp.; Westport, Ct.: Greenwood Press,
1980 (reprint of 1967 ed.). For English edition of *On Trial,* see
section on Joint Translations.

Svetlana Alliluyeva, " 'To Boris Leonidovich Pasternak': Reflections on
Dr. Zhivago,"Atlantic Monthly (Boston) 219, 6 (June 1967): 133–
40.

Isaac Babel, *You Must Know Everything: Stories, 1915–1937.* Ed. and
with notes by Nathalie Babel. New York: Farrar, Straus & Giroux,
1969, and London: Jonathan Cape, 1970, xv, 283 pp; New York:
Dell Publishing, Delta Books (pa.), 1970, 283 pp.

Nadezhda Mandelstam, *Hope against Hope: A Memoir.* Trans. of *Vos-
pominaniya.* Introd. by Clarence Brown. New York: Atheneum,
1970, xvi, 431 pp.; 1973; 1976 (pa., College ed.); London: Collins
and Harvill Press, 1971, xvi, 432 pp.; Harmondsworth: Penguin
Books (pa.), 1975, 1979, xvii, 525 pp.

Nadezhda Mandelstam, *Hope Abandoned* [*A Memoir:* English ed.
only]. Trans. of *Vtoraya kniga.* Foreword by Max Hayward. London: Collins and Harvill Press, 1974, xii, 689 pp.; New York:
Atheneum, 1974, xii, 687 pp.; (pa.) 1981; Harmondsworth: Penguin Books (pa.), 1976, 767 pp.

Alexander Gladkov, *Meetings with Pasternak.* Ed., notes and introd. by
Max Hayward. London: Collins and Harvill Press, and New York:
Harcourt Brace Jovanovich ("A Helen and Kurt Wolff Book"),
1977, 223 pp.

Olga Ivinskaya, *A Captive of Time: My Years with Pasternak.* Trans. of
U vremeni v plenu. London: Collins and Harvill Press, 1978, xl, 488
pp.; New York: Doubleday, 1978, xl, 462 pp.; London: Collins,
Fontana (new ed., pa.), 1979, xl, 488 pp.; New York: Warner Books
(pa.), 1979, 639 pp.; Beekman Publishers (hardback), 488 pp.

Joint Translations

Boris Pasternak, *Doctor Zhivago* (with Manya Harari). London: Collins
and Harvill Press, 1958, 510 pp.; 3rd ed., 1966, 511 pp.; Collins
Gift Classics, 1978, 608 pp.; Fontana (pa.), 1961, 542 pp.; 1965
(re-issue); 1969 (new imprint); New York: Pantheon Books, 1958,
558 pp., 559 pp., poems of Yurii Zhivago trans. by Bernard Guil-
bert Gurney; illus. by A. Alexeieff, 1960, 780 pp.; Random House,
Modern Library, 1960, 558 pp.; New American Library, Signet
(pa.), 1960, 1961, 1962, 1974; Philadelphia: Franklin Center, illus.
by Francis Golden, 1978, 568 pp.; Don Mills, Ont.: Collins, 1958,
1960 (2nd imprint); Toronto: New American Library of Canada,
1963, 456 pp.; 1966.

Alexander Solzhenitsyn, *One Day in the Life of Ivan Denisovich* (with
Ronald Hingley). Introd. by Max Hayward and Leopold Labedz.

New York: Praeger ("Books that Matter") (hardback and pa.), 1963, xxiv, 210 pp.; Bantam Books (pa.), 1963, 203 pp. This translation was originally published in the *Saturday Evening Post* (Philadelphia), 9 February 1963.

Alexander Solzhenitsyn, *For the Good of the Cause* (with David Floyd). Introd. by David Floyd. London: Pall Mall Press, New York: Praeger, and Don Mills, Ont.: Burns & MacEachern, 1964, xvii, 134 pp.; London: Sphere Books (pa.), 1971, 1973, 1974, 142 pp.; White Lion Publishers, 1974, xvii, 134 pp.; New York: Praeger (2nd printing, hardback & pa.), 1970.

Yevgeny Schwartz, "The Dragon" (with Harold Shukman), in *Three Soviet Plays*. Ed. by Michael Glenny. Harmondsworth & Baltimore: Penguin Books Ltd. Plays (pa.), 1966, 128 pp. This edition also contains Max Hayward's translation of Mayakovsky, "The Bedbug."

Valentin Katayev, *The Holy Well* (with Harold Shukman). London: Harvill Press, and New York: Walker, 1967, 160 pp.; New York: Warner Books (pa.), 1979.

Eugenia Ginzburg, *Journey Into the Whirlwind* (with Paul Stevenson). Trans. from *Krutoi marshrut*. New York: Harcourt, Brace & World ("A Helen and Kurt Wolff Book"), 1967, 418 pp.; Harcourt Brace Jovanovich, Harvest Book (pa.), 1975, 418 pp. The English edition, entitled *Into the Whirlwind*, London: Collins, 1967, was translated by Paul Stevenson and Manya Harari.

On Trial: The Case of Sinyavsky (Tertz) and Daniel (Arzhak). Documents (with Manya Harari). French texts trans. by Marjorie Villiers. Ed. by Leopold Labedz and Max Hayward. London: Collins and Harvill Press, 1967, 384 pp.

Boris Pasternak, *The Blind Beauty* (an unfinished play) (with Manya Harari). Foreword by Max Hayward. London: Collins and Harvill Press, and New York: Harcourt, Brace & World ("A Helen and Kurt Wolff Book"), 1969, xxii, 128 pp.

Andrei Amalrik, *Involuntary Journey to Siberia* (with Manya Harari). Introd. by Max Hayward. London: Collins and Harvill Press (abridged translation), 1970, 282 pp.; New York: Harcourt Brace Jovanovich ("A Helen and Kurt Wolff Book"), 1970, xiii, 297 pp.; Harvest Books (pa.), 1971.

Suzanne Massie, ed., *Five Young Poets from Leningrad* (with George L. Kline; poetic versions by Paul Roche, John Statathos). Parallel

Russian text and English translation. London: Victor Gollancz, and New York: Doubleday, 1972, 344 pp.; (pa.), 1973.

Anna Akhmatova, *Poems of Akhmatova* (with Stanley Kunitz). Introd. by Stanley Kunitz and Max Hayward. Bilingual ed. Boston: Little, Brown ("An Atlantic Monthly Press Book") (hardback and pa.), 1973; London: Collins and Harvill Press, 1974.

Abram Tertz [Andrei Sinyavsky], *A Voice from the Chorus* (with Kyril Fitzlyon). Introd. by Max Hayward. London: Collins and Harvill Press, and New York: Farrar, Straus & Giroux, 1976, xxii, 328 pp.; London: Collins, Fontana (pa.), 1977, xxiii, 328 pp.

Kornei Chukovsky, *The Telephone* (with William Jay Smith). Illus. poem. New York: Delacorte Press / Seymour Lawrence, 1977, 48 pp.

INDEX